£7.50

!E

HAILE SELASSIE'S
WAR

ANTHONY MOCKLER

HAILE SELASSIE'S WAR

OXFORD UNIVERSITY PRESS
1984

Oxford University Press, Walton Street, Oxford OX2 6DP

London New York Toronto
Delhi Bombay Calcutta Madras Karachi
Kuala Lumpur Singapore Hong Kong Tokyo
Nairobi Dar es Salaam Cape Town
Melbourne Auckland
and associated companies in
Beirut Berlin Ibadan Mexico City Nicosia

Oxford is a trade mark of Oxford University Press

British Library Cataloguing in Publication Date
Mockler, Anthony
Haile Selassie's war.
1. Italo-Ethiopian War, 1935–36
I. Title
963'.056 DT387.8
ISBN 0–19–215867–8

Set by Wyvern Typesetting Ltd
Printed in Great Britain by
St Edmundsbury Press, Bury St Edmunds, Suffolk

CONTENTS

PART III
THE MILLS OF GOD

To Christianne

PREFACE

I AM writing this preface in a summer when the long if intermittent years of work during which this history has been designed, shaped, and altered are at last drawing to a close. Now that the book is ended it is clear that it is the Ethiopians who hold the centre of the stage. When I was writing it I considered (and planned) that it should be in equal proportions about the Italians, the British, and the Ethiopians—and probably in statistical number of pages or paragraphs this is an aim achieved. But though I hope this 'tale of blood and war' is objective and unslanted, that it is what it purports to be, a true and accurate narrative drawn from many different sources, yet it is its epic side that moves me now. Like all genuine epics it has no particular hero and no particular villain. Yet, as in any epic in which 'extremes of fortune are displayed', one side must win: and I dare say that is why I almost instinctively chose the format followed— leading from one great Ethiopian triumph over the Italians via total disaster and slow recovery to a satisfying final victory.

There is, as there ought to be, another and more rational explanation for the way this book is laid out. It seemed to me when I began my researches that far too many writers, both English and Italian, treated the central episode of this period, the Italo-Ethiopian War, as basically a European concern, a sort of dramatized diplomatic history in which the Ethiopians played the part merely of colourful extras against a picturesque backcloth. This was obviously unfair. After all it was the Ethiopians' land that was being fought over and the Ethiopians who had done most of the fighting and the dying. My original purpose then was simply to see the story of that notorious invasion from the point of view of the ignored underdog. But this purpose led me both backwards and forwards: backwards because it was impossible to understand the Ethiopian resistance (or in some cases their lack of resistance) without delving into the complicated internal history and politics of Ethiopia; and forwards because the story was clearly only half told if the eventual comeback of the Ethiopians and the restoration of the Emperor with British help were ignored.

The result is that this is now, as far as I know, the only book that covers fully and from sources on all sides both the Italian invasion of Ethiopia and the British counter-invasion five years later, subjects by so many historians and writers treated separately. It covers too the intriguing but little-known period of Italian colonial rule and Ethiopian resistance, though at considerably less length than I intended. For this book has had a curious publishing history. The original manuscript was over three times the present length. An Italian translation, published by Rizzoli under the title *Il Mito dell'Impero*, though already much shortened from the original, is perhaps twice as long as this, and its existence ought therefore to be mentioned if only for the benefit of serious students of the period who read Italian. But this version has been trimmed again and again; in particular the descriptions of Ethiopia's pre-invasion politics and of the five-year-long resistance have been reduced to less than a quarter of their original length.

As for the Battle of Adowa, this, the first chapter, though also drastically cut, could not be abandoned. For Adowa is the essential prologue to the whole story. It is impossible to understand the fiercely emotional entanglement of the two antagonists without understanding Adowa—where, as I hope will become very plain, more was lost by Italy than men and more was won by Ethiopia than a battle.

A surprising number of people encountered have been very hazy about the difference between Ethiopia and Abyssinia. It seems as well to clear up this rather crucial point at the outset. There is no difference between Ethiopia and Abyssinia. Abyssinia and Ethiopia are one and the same country. What has caused this confusion is that from the Middle Ages right up to at least the end of the Second World War, the country now called Ethiopia was generally known as Abyssinia.

This posed rather a dilemma with the book's title. Should the title refer to Abyssinia as it then was or to Ethiopia as it now is? I avoided the forked horn, as readers will have noticed, by side-stepping. The war of course was not Haile Selassie's personal possession any more than it was Mussolini's or a myriad other Ethiopians' or Italians'. But Haile Selassie's is the face—a memorable face—most often associated with the events described; and his personality is perhaps the most fascinating of all those, of whatever nationality, involved. I find it hard, even now, to analyse my own opinion of the late Emperor. Meeting him, as I did in Addis Ababa, was of great interest but very little direct help. Questions had to be submitted in writing via the British Embassy to the Ministry of Information. From there, twice tactfully weeded, they were passed to the Ministry of the Imperial Court which did the final censoring of anything indiscreet. What remained was answered briefly, courteously, banally, and in Amharic at the formal audience by His Imperial Majesty, Haile Selassie I, Emperor of Ethiopia, King of Kings, and Conquering Lion of Judah. The translation was even briefer. Supplementaries were not encouraged. Indirectly, however, the interview was extraordinarily useful in that, once news of it spread abroad, doors opened that had previously been held only politely ajar. For the Ethiopians are a secretive, reserved, and cautious race, and do not part with information easily. At the time Haile Selassie seemed frail but his still almost sphinx-like dignity gave him an air of immortality. Now he is dead. Many of my informants are also dead and an age–old system has disappeared. It had its faults but it was certainly unique and I am glad that I was in Ethiopia in time to see it in action.

'A long book,' wrote Winston Churchill in his introduction to *The River War*, 'does not justify a long preface.' Although this is now a short book, compared at least to its original length and to Churchill's twin volumes (which treat in full military detail of very similar subject-matter in much the same part of the world), enough is enough and my readers' patience is probably not inexhaustible. So let me end by recommending most strongly, as Churchill did in that case, continual reference to the maps without which the military operations cannot possibly be followed. On these maps are marked the vast majority of the two hundred and fifty-odd place-names mentioned in the text, which, though probably confusing at first, will become more and more familiar as the book progresses. As for the personal names, the 'Biographical Notes' that have been designed to help with these have been placed, perhaps illogically, at the back of the book. The object was to avoid a rebarbative accumulation of non-essential reading matter before battle—in this case the great battle of Adowa—commences.

Milton Manor   A.M.
Summer 1983

NOTE ON THE GEOGRAPHY, PROVINCES, AND HISTORY OF ETHIOPIA

ETHIOPIA is a vast and mountainous country. To the east the highlands fall away into the Danakil and Somali deserts, to the west into the jungles of the Upper Nile drainage basin, and to the south into the arid wastelands of northern Kenya. But the heartland of Ethiopia is an immense mountainous plateau, riven with gorges, defiles, escarpments, and peaks, a titanic land.

By the early years of this century the Empire was divided into a bewildering kaleidoscope of provinces, districts, and governorates. Five major provinces formed the historic kernel of the Ethiopian Empire. These five are referred to again and again in the pages that follow, and the reader would be well advised to fix the names and the relative position of the five in his mind's eye. (See in particular the *General Map of Ethiopia* and surrounding countries, on page 4. Though the names of the provinces are not marked on it, each province's principal town or city, as listed below, is.)

Tigre, the northernmost province, bordered the Italian colony of Eritrea; *Axum*, its original capital, was the religious and cultural centre of the Empire, and the legendary birthplace of Ethiopia's first Emperor, Menelik I, son of King Solomon and the Queen of Sheba.

Beghemder, the traditional heartland of the Amhara race, was ruled from *Gondar*, Ethiopia's late medieval capital and most famous city.

Gojjam, lying to the south of Beghemder in the bend of the Blue Nile, was almost an independent principality, its major town—like so many towns in Ethiopia at the turn of the century, little more than a village—being *Debra Markos*.

Wollo, the buffer state between Tigre and Shoa, was a traditionally Muhammadan province, much of which was ranged over by the ferocious Raya and Azebo Galla. The Emperor Theodore, who razed Gondar in 1866, transferred his headquarters to the mountain fortress of Magdala in Wollo. There two years later he committed suicide when faced with an invading British expeditionary force under Lord Napier. It was not till Menelik II's time that *Dessie* was founded as *Wollo*'s capital.

Shoa, became the heart and centre of a much-expanded Empire under the first post-medieval Emperor of the Shoan ruling house, Menelik II. The Amhara of Shoa, the dominant group, stemmed from the high mountain plateau of Menz in the north of the province. Moving south, Menelik changed his capital five times. Finally he shifted it from the heights of Entotto to found, in the plain just below, his 'New Flower', *Addis Ababa*—which then became, and still remains, the capital of the whole country.

Menelik's armies swept south and east, subduing various rich Galla kingdoms in the south-west—Kaffa, Jimma and Wollega—and in the south-east the more primitive territories of Sidamo, Arussi, and Bale. (For the position of these, and other provinces, see Map 3, 'The Armies of the South', p. 88.) Most important of all, the Muhammadan Sultanate of Harar to the east of Shoa was in 1887 conquered and annexed, to be governed by Menelik's cousin Ras Makonnen. Thanks to his skilful diplomacy Ras Makonnen subsequently added to his governorate a vast portion of the Somali grazing lands, the Ogaden. Ras Makonnen's son, Tafari, the future Emperor Haile Selassie, was born in Harar five years after its conquest.

On *their* conquest the Italians rather wisely combined all the southern provinces into the single governorate of Galla-Sidamo, in area almost half the country. The most frequent names of southern provinces that the reader will come across are Wollega—split into three governorates at the time of the Italian invasion, its chief town being Lekempti—and Illubabor lying to the west of Addis Ababa over against the Sudan, with its capital at Gore.

In the north the three small but powerful Christian provinces of Wag, Lasta and Yeggiu—bounded by Tigre to the north and Wollo to the south—are frequently mentioned. [For their relative positions see Map 4, 'The Battles in the North', p. 98.]

LIST OF MAPS

NOTE ON ETHIOPIAN SPELLING, PRONUNCIATION, AND NAMES

IN his preface to *The Seven Pillars of Wisdom* T. E. Lawrence wrote: 'Arabic names won't go into English exactly. There are some "scientific systems" of transliteration, helpful to people who know enough Arabic not to need helping, but a wash-out for the world.'

Amharic names won't go into English exactly, either; their alphabet has too many consonants and vowels. Fortunately, though, most Amharic names are easier on the eye and the ear than their Arabic equivalents. I have gone for the most easy and, where possible, familiar form rather than the most accurate transliteration; referring, when in two minds, and as a handy guide-of-thumb, to the Addis Ababa telephone directory.

Amharic names will be found less confusing once it is appreciated that nearly all of them have a meaning. For instance Makonnen occurs again and again, particularly in aristocratic families. Why? Because it means noble.

A few simple guidelines may help. Each individual has basically one name and one name only. There are no family names as such. Women do not change their name on marriage. Each individual's name is followed by his or her father's name—thus Tafari Makonnen is Tafari the son of Makonnen. Many names are biblical in origin; such as, to take a very common example, Mariam.

But there are numerous names which consist of one concept expressed in two words, and in these cases the two parts are inseparable. Haile Selassie, Power of the Trinity, is an obvious case in point. Thus Haile Mariam Mammo, the Patriot leader, was Haile Mariam, Power of Mary, the son of Mammo.

Readers will notice as they read on that I have often written a two-part name as one word—as for instance in the case of Fikremariam and Gabremariam. This is merely a personal preference.

The apparently inconsistent case of Asfa Wossen here and Asfawossen there is not exactly based on T. E. Lawrence's splendid conclusion to his remarks above ('I spell my names anyhow, to show what rot systems are') but a simple and, I hope, helpful way of distinguishing the Emperor's son from his namesake and cousin, the son of Ras Kassa.

GLOSSARY

SOME common Ethiopian words and names.

Ababa	Flower
Addis	New
Amba	Flat-topped mountain
Amhara	The ruling ethnic group; Semitic origins
Amharic or Amharinya	Their language. Semitic; with its own distinctive alphabet
Awaj	Decree; official proclamation.
Balabat	Literally 'Son of a Father'. Country squire or nobleman
Chitet	The levy; also the summons for war
Egziabher	God
Enjerra	A sort of bread. With *wot*, spiced meat, the staple Ethiopian dish
Ferengi	Foreigner
Galla	Probably the largest ethnic group; origins obscure; invaded the Amhara highlands in the sixteenth century and spread particularly over the south. More negroid in features. Originally pagan; never structurally united like the Amhara; now generally known as the Oromo
Gallinya	Their language
Gebar	A serf
Gebir	Traditional feast
Ge'ez	Liturgical language of the Coptic Church. As Latin to Italian, so Ge'ez to Amharic
Ghebbi	Often mistranslated 'palace'. A nobleman's residence, a cluster of buildings
Haile	Power of
Janhoy	Majesty. Used in addressing or referring to the Emperor
Mahel Safari	Army of the Centre; commanded by the Imperial Fitaurari
Makonnen	Noble
Maskal	Feast of the Finding of the True Cross. One of the two great feasts of the liturgical year. Celebrated at the end

of September, it marks the end of the rains and the beginning of fine weather

Negaret	War drum
Selassie	The Trinity
Shamma	The light Ethiopian toga, worn by men and women
Shifta	Bandit (traditional Robin Hood figure)
Shum	Appointed to/Appointed ruler of
Tabot	Ark of the Covenant. There is one in every Coptic church, kept in the central part of the octagon where only priests are allowed to penetrate
Tej	Mead. Fomented honeywine. National drink. Surprisingly intoxicating as the author can testify
Tejbeit	Low-class inn, drinking den
Tigrinya	Language of the people of Tigre. Close to but different from Amharinya—perhaps as Portuguese to Spanish
Tug	River/stream (also Wadi/Khor)
Tukul	Hut
Yekatit	One of the thirteen months of the Ethiopian calendar; roughly February. The Ethiopian year is six to seven years behind the Gregorian calendar
Worq	Golden. Often part of a woman's name
Zabagna	Watchman; guard. As in *Mitraya Z.*—machine-gun guard. (*Mitraya* from *mitraillette*. All Ethiopian names for guns are corruptions of European names: a Lee Mitford, for example is a *dimiphor*)

TITLES

TITLES were—until the Revolution of 1974—extraordinarily important in Ethiopian life and politics. Strictly speaking, none were hereditary—although certain titles went with certain posts and were normally granted to members of the same family or clan. The Emperor was not the only person with a right to award titles; but to be appointed Fitaurari by the Emperor was a far greater honour than to become, for instance, a Fitaurari created by a Dejaz. Titles originally described functions. By the twentieth century this was no longer entirely true, particularly with the military titles. Nevertheless I have divided the titles given below, somewhat arbitrarily, into categories.

MILITARY TITLES

Negus Negusti	King of Kings, Emperor
Negus	King
Ras	Head of an Army
Dejaz	Commander of the Threshold
Fitaurari	Commander of the Advance Guard
Kenyaz	Commander of the Right Wing
Geraz	Commander of the Left Wing
Balambaras	Commander of the Fort

The above are, in order of descending importance, the most prestigious titles in Ethiopia. Below are two semi-traditional titles used as equivalent to military ranks in Europe.

Shallaka	Commander of a Thousand; Battalion C.O.
Shambel	Commander of Two Hundred and Fifty; Company C.O.

COURT TITLES

Agefari	Superintendent of Banquets
Afanegus	Breath of the Negus, Lord Chief Justice
Azaz	Master of Ceremonies
Bajirond	Guardian of the Royal Property (traditionally two)
Bitwoded	Beloved—Chief Counsellor (traditionally two)
Blatta	Page
Blattengueta	Master of Pages, Chief Administrator of the Palace

Kantiba	Mayor
Ligaba	Court Chancellor
Lij	Prince—title given to young nobleman
Liquemaquas	King's Double (traditionally two)
Mered Azmatch	Honorific title given to the Crown Princes
Nagradas	Treasury or Customs Overseer
Tsehafe Taezaz	Minister of the Pen, Keeper of the Seal
Woizero	Lady (title given traditionally to noblewoman)

SEMI-HEREDITARY TITLES

Bahr Ghazal	Lord of the Sea (traditional title of the ruler of Eritrea before the Italian coming)
Jantirar	Ruler of Ambasel
Nevraid	Ruler of Axum; semi-religious
Shum Agame	Lord of Agame (the House of Sabadaugis)
Shum Geralta	Lord of Geralta
Shum Tembien	Lord of the Tembien
Wagshum	Lord of Wag (descendants of the Zagwe dynasty)

CHURCH TITLES

Abba	Father (used for a priest or bishop)
Abuna	Archbishop (sometimes used for bishop)
Debtera	Learned religious man, neither monk nor priest
Echege	Administrative head of the Ethiopian Church, traditionally the Abbot of Debra Libanos.

THE FIVE MAJOR ETHIOPIAN FIGURES OF
THIS HISTORY

Emperor Haile Selassie I, Negus Negusti, King of Kings
Better known before his coronation as Ras Tafari

Ras Kassa
Elder statesman of the Shoan ruling house

Ras Imru
The Emperor's cousin and right-hand man

Ras Seyum of Tigre
Grandson of the Emperor Johannes; always therefore a potential rival to Haile Selassie

Ras Hailu of Gojjam
Independent-minded potentate; throughout his life mistrustful of and mistrusted by the Emperor

Biographical notes on many of the Ethiopians who appear in this book are to be found at its back, including much fuller notes on the persons above. But these five all lived through, and played a great part in, the events about to be described; even a thumbnail phrase may help to fix their names firmly in the reader's mind.

THE BATTLE OF ADOWA, 1896

FIVE generals met on a mountain top in Tigre: General Oreste Baratieri, Governor of Eritrea, a vain man, and his four Brigade commanders, Generals Albertone, Arimondi, Dabormida, and Ellena. It was the evening of 28 February 1896.

The five met in General Baratieri's tent. Around them, on the heights of Mount Enticcio, lay encamped thousands upon thousands of Italian soldiers and Italian-officered native aux-iliaries, the strongest colonial expeditionary force that Africa had ever known. In front of them lay an ancient Empire, a Christian Kingdom. Twenty miles away at Adowa were encamped the armies not only of Ras[1] Mangasha of Tigre, their old enemy, but of his overlord the Emperor Menelik and of the other lords of the Empire, the armies of Shoa, Gojjam, Beghemder, and Wollo, and the levies of the South. In front of them, therefore, lay the chance of glory. For newly-united Italy, which by the grace of God, the weakness of Egypt, and the tolerance of England had installed herself on the borders of the Red Sea, this, if ever, was the opportunity to inflict her decisive colonial victory on the local native potentate. The five generals knew it. Victory would mean a vast new empire for Italy and glory for themselves; defeat was unthinkable for a European army of such a size. General Baratieri took his decision: to advance on Adowa and attack.

The first of March was not only a Sunday but by the Ethiopian calendar the Feast of St. George, patron saint of the Empire. In the Church of St. Gabriel, the Lords of Ethiopia had gathered before dawn to hear mass. The doors of the church were open. At the moment when the Abuna[1] Matteos elevated the Host, two rifle shots rang out—the agreed signal of alarm. Ras[1] Makonnen of Harar, the Emperor's trusted cousin, left the church; within a

---

[1] For a full list of Ethiopian military, religious, and courtly titles, see p. xviii. The most important noble titles, 'Ras' and 'Dejaz', are roughly equivalent to 'Duke' and 'Earl'.

few minutes he was back with the report of the Italians advancing. The Emperor took the news calmly enough. He went up to the Abuna, whispered a few words, and returned quietly to his seat. The Abuna lifted up the cross in his right hand and spoke weakly, sobbing as he spoke. 'My sons,' he said, 'this day the judgement of God will be fulfilled. Go and defend your faith and your King. I forgive you all your sins.'

The lords rose and kissed the cross. They then made their way to their respective camps: Ras Mangasha to the camps of the men of Tigre to the North, the Imperial Fitaurari[1] Gabreiehu to the Army of the Centre, the *Mahel Safari* on the southern slopes of Mount Shelloda, Ras Makonnen with him to the troops of Harar, Ras Mikael to his Wollo Galla cavalry behind the town, Wagshum[1] Gwangul and Hailu of Lasta and the Jantirar[1] Asfau to the levies of Wag and Lasta and Ambasel in the south, Ras Mangasha Atikim to the men of Ifrata, Ras Wule to the men of Beghemder, the Dejaz[1] Beshah, the Emperor's cousin, and the Liquemaquas[1] Abate to the Emperor's own men from Shoa. It is said that the Negus[1] Tekle Haimonot of Gojjam wished to stay and take communion; but the Emperor reminded him that his sins had already been forgiven and that delay was dangerous.

Only Menelik remained in the Church of St. Gabriel. Men said, later, that in his prayers he thanked God for having persuaded the Italians to advance. The Empress Taitu meanwhile had taken up her position on Mount Latsat behind her guns—six quick-firing Hotchkiss directed by the Commander of the Artillery, the young Galla eunuch, Bajirond[1] Balcha. With her, gathered under the black umbrella—raised instead of the Imperial Red as a sign of grief at battle against fellow-Christians—were Woizero[1] Zauditu, her step-daughter, and their maidservants. The Nevraid[1] of Axum joined the Empress with his crosses, his standards, and his long horns sounding. From the holiest sanctuary in Ethiopia, the Church of Mariam at Axum to which Menelik I, son of Solomon and Sheba had brought the Ark of the Covenant, the Nevraid had brought the statue of Mariam. The word spread among the Ethiopians: the Mother of Jesus had come to help the Empress.

From shortly after dawn till mid-afternoon battle raged among the mountain passes and valleys overlooking the five churches of Adowa. In mid-morning the Imperial Fitaurari Gabreiehu was wounded by a burst of machine-gun fire; an Italian prisoner, Lt.

Caruso of the artillery, saw him dying under an oak-tree. With the death of their leader the lion-maned chieftains of the *Mahel Safari* wavered and broke and fled. But by late morning General Albertone's battle-hardened Eritrean brigade had been isolated and in its turn broken, General Arimondi had been killed, General Ellena's brigade was disastrously split and General Baratieri and his staff were galloping off north towards Eritrea and safety, abandoning the stricken remnants of what three hours earlier had still been the finest colonial army in Africa, 16,000 men and 52 guns strong.

By mid-afternoon the Emperor sitting on his horse Dagnew watched the Gojjamis of the Negus Tekle Haimonot put in the final assault on the one intact enemy formation still in the field, General Dabormida's brigade. By five o'clock the Italians had fired their last round and were breaking up. An old woman said she saw Dabormida, 'a chief, a great chief, with the spectacles and the watch and the gold stars; he asked for water and said he was the general'. Towards evening, as the Tigrean highlands filled with thousands of dispersed fugitives fleeing from Ras Mikael's red-cloaked Galla horsemen, a Turkbash, commander of 25 men, rode Dabormida down, shot and killed him, robbing him of his arms, his wallet, and his scarf—or so at least Ras Makonnen a month later told General Albertone, his prisoner, giving him the dead General's sabre and scarf.

Dabormida was one of 262 Italian officers and nearly 4,000 Italian soldiers who died that day. It was the greatest single disaster in European colonial history. Nineteen hundred Italians, including Albertone, and about a thousand Eritrean askaris were taken prisoner. Infuriated by the death of their leader, the men of Dejaz Beshah, Menelik's cousin, killed all the prisoners upon whom they could lay hands—70 Italians and 230 askaris. For this crime Fitaurari Lemma was exiled by Menelik to an *amba*, a mountain-top. The Eritrean prisoners were held to have betrayed the Emperor and after long debate were punished with the penalty reserved for traitors. Their right hands and their left feet were cut off; many died during the night; 400 mutilated survivors were eventually released. But the Italian prisoners were well treated. The worst humiliation complained of was that of a soldier who was led before the Empress Taitu and forced to sing 'Funiculi, Funicula' and 'Dolce Napoli'.

There was no organized pursuit of the routed army. And there were no great rejoicings in the Ethiopian camp. Menelik cut short the boasting ceremonies and the war-songs in favour of 'Abba Dagnew', his horse-name. Later he told Dr. Neruzzini that he saw no cause to rejoice over the death of so many Christian men.

PART I

ETHIOPIA AND ITALY: THE BACKGROUND

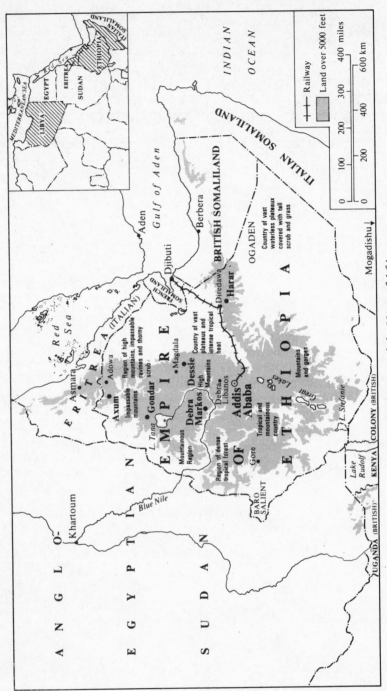

MAP I. Ethiopia and the Horn of Africa

CHAPTER I

EMPEROR OF ETHIOPIA

THE early 1920s, so crowded with events in Italy, were an unusually peaceful and settled period in Ethiopia. In 1923, Ethiopia became with Italian support a member of the League of Nations. Barely more than a quarter of a century after the battle of Adowa, relations between the two countries had mellowed to a surprising extent. In the spring of the following year, 1924, the Regent of Ethiopia, Ras Tafari Makonnen, set out on his famous European tour. With him he took Ras Seyum, Ras Hailu,[1] a score of minor nobles, and six lions. The picturesque entourage visited Jerusalem, Cairo, Alexandria, Brussels, Amsterdam, Stockholm, London, Geneva, and Athens. Rarely can a tour have inspired so many anecdotes, and in the mind of the man-in-the-street Ethiopia, symbolized by the bevy of Rases with their black cloaks and oversize hats, took on a certain significance. For the first time Ras Tafari must have realized how useful and indeed how vital a weapon publicity could be. It was a tour—and a lesson—not easily forgotten.

In Rome the visit to Italy's new ruler, the Duce, preoccupied by an internal crisis, led to few concrete results.[2] In Paris, Ras

---

[1] All three Rases were sons of heroes of Adowa. Ras Tafari's father was Menelik's cousin Ras Makonnen of Harar—hence his full name: Ras Tafari Makonnen. Ras Seyum's father was Ras Mangasha of Tigre, and Ras Hailu's the Negus Tekle Haimonot of Gojjam. For all these personages, see the Biographical Index at the back of the book.

[2] Benito Mussolini, the leader—Duce—of the *Partito Nazionale Fascista*, had formed the first Fascist government in Europe on 30 October 1922. On 30 May 1924 Matteoti, the secretary-general of the opposition Socialist Party (of which Mussolini had once been himself an ardent young leader), rose to address the Chamber of Deputies in Rome and to condemn the new regime for its violence, in what all agreed was a brilliant speech. The Duce made threatening noises. On 10 June Matteoti left the Chamber and was not seen again. Speculation as to his whereabouts was enormous and the threatening scandal immense. It was not an ideal moment for an official visit, particularly of an exotic nature. A cartoon appeared in the Italian press showing Ras Tafari whispering to the Italian Chief of Police: 'Tell me, in all confidence, did you eat him?'

Tafari presented two of his lions to President Poincaré and two more to the *Jardin Zoologique*. In London there was a heatwave, and the heavily-clothed Ethiopians in their leggings and jodhpurs and *shammas* were cheered by the sympathetic London crowds for the agonies they were believed to be suffering. Throughout the tour the Regent—tiny, black-bearded, and at thirty-two surprisingly young for a position of such apparent import-ance—preserved, as he was always to do throughout his long life, an impressive dignity.

The remaining pair of lions went to King George V. In return, the British presented Ras Tafari with an infinitely more import-ant gift: the imperial crown of the Emperor Theodore which Lord Napier had brought back to England in 1868 after Theodore's defeat and death. News of this chivalrous and diplo-matic gesture spread with surprising speed to even the remotest corners of the distant Empire. 'The act of King George V,' reported Hodson, British Consul in the isolated hill-town of Maji near the Sudanese border, 'in returning the Ethiopian crown to the Empress on the occasion of Ras Tafari's recent visit to England has created a great impression in the south-west.'

The Empress to whom the imperial crown had been thus happily returned was the Empress Zauditu, the first woman to ascend the throne of Ethiopia since the Queen of Sheba. To understand the relationship between Empress and Regent a brief excursion backwards into Ethiopian history is necessary. The Emperor Theodore had been succeeded by the Emperor Johan-nes, and the Emperor Johannes by the Emperor Menelik—in each case after a bloody civil-war. None of the three were related to either predecessor or successor. Zauditu succeeded her own father Menelik four confused, but comparatively unbloody, years after his death. She was childless, chosen as a figurehead around whom the country—or at least the Christian Amhara —could unite. But though she might reign, it was recognized that she could not rule. Therefore, when the Abuna Matteos, Archbishop of Ethiopia and the power behind the traditionalists, proclaimed Zauditu Empress in the Banqueting Hall of the Great Ghebbi at Addis Ababa on 27 September 1916, he at the same time proclaimed the progressive-minded Tafari Makonnen as heir to the throne and regent. Despite his misgivings he had done so with traditional panache. Any man who refused to accept the double proclamation would, the Abuna noted, incur the wrath of the Father, Son, and Holy Ghost, the anathema of the twelve Apostles and 318 Fathers of the Council of Nicaea, and be smitten with the curse of Arius and the reprobation of Judas. 'And with my own humble word,' added Matteos, 'I excommunicate him.'

In the Empress Zauditu's case the traditional civil war followed after rather than before her official succession. It was of fearsome intensity, though of short duration. Zauditu's rival for the throne was her sister's son, Lij Yasu, Menelik's grandson and at one stage his recognized successor—a handsome but very wild young man whom the Shoan nobles and Abuna Matteos had reluctantly decided they could never accept on the Imperial throne. Lij Yasu's father, however, Negus Mikael of Wollo, had very different ideas. As Ras Mikael of Wollo he had led the fearsome red-cloaked Galla cavalry against the Italians at Adowa; and in October 1917 he led them forth again—but this time south against Shoa. A murderous day-long battle followed on the plains of Sagalle where the forces of Wollo and Shoa clashed. It ended in a decisive victory for the Shoans. At the British Legation in Addis Ababa the Shoan capital, the Minister's young son Wilfred Thesiger watched the 'wildly exciting' victory parade. 'They came past in waves, horsemen half concealed in dust and a great press of footmen. Screaming out their deeds of valour they came right up to the steps of the throne . . . I can remember a small boy who seemed little older then myself being carried past in triumph. I can remember Negus Mikael, the King of the North, being led past in chains with a stone upon his shoulders in token of submission, an old man in a plain black burnous, with his head wrapped in a white rag.'

Among the Shoan leaders Ras Kassa was the real hero of the battle of Sagalle, a nobleman in his early forties whose fief of Salale lay in the north-west of Shoa adjoining the lands of the great monastery of Debra Libanos. Deeply religious and with a reputation for theological learning, Ras Kassa was all his life to be a byword for uprightness and honesty. By birth he had a better claim to the throne than his younger cousin Ras Tafari; but Ras Kassa was also to be one of the few Ethiopians with whom loyalty outweighed ambition. It was to his care rather than to that of the over-ambitious Regent that the Abuna Matteos and the Empress Zauditu entrusted the captured Pretender, Lij Yasu; ostensibly as a reward for the glory that he, Ras Kassa, had won at Sagalle.

To be fair, Ras Tafari never claimed to be a warrior. Where he excelled (like his father Ras Makonnen before him) was as a diplomat. On his 1924 tour he made a special point of visiting the Coptic Patriarch in Cairo, Cyrillos V. This was much more than a courtesy call and its delayed results were to help Ras Tafari towards the goal he had always had in view: supreme power in Ethiopia. In 1924 between himself and the achievement of that goal stood two major obstacles: the forces of tradition as represented by the Church, and the life of the Empress Zauditu.

Since the Council of Nicaea the Patriarch had had the right of appointing the Abuna and invariably an Egyptian Copt—that is to say, a figure over whom the Ethiopian Emperors could exercise no real control—was chosen. In 1926 death removed the Abuna Matteos, aged 83, from the Regent's path; but if another Egyptian Copt had been immediately appointed as a successor, the progressive faction of the still-youthful Regent would have been very little better-off. Instead, a long interregnum ensued during which no Abuna was appointed; Ras Tafari's visit to the Patriarch two years earlier had thus borne its fruits. Ras Tafari was always prepared to play a waiting game; but he was also skilled at acting immediately when a power vacuum became apparent. His ability as a political manœuvrer put him head and shoulders above his more emotional or slower-witted rivals. He seized this opportunity to increase the powers of the Echege in all administrative church matters. The Echege was by tradition the Ethiopian counterbalance to the foreign-born Abuna. He was always a monk, usually head of the famous monastery of Debra Libanos; and, as head of Debra Libanos, successor to the greatest of Ethiopia's holy men, St. Tekle Haimonot. He was a very important churchman indeed—and yet much more easily influenced by the executive authority of the state, personified in this instance by the Regent (though not, as the sequel was to show, totally amenable in all circumstances).

Therefore, following the death of the Abuna Matteos, a complex situation—and the Ethiopians by nature rather favour complex situations—appeared to have become almost alarmingly simplified. The precarious balance between progressives and traditionalists was broken. The Empress Zauditu appeared isolated and the Regent an important step nearer to achieving his eventual and evident aim, that of concentrating all power in his own hands. As a first step he summoned the traditional rulers and provincial governors to the capital to recognize the new situation and acknowledge his new-found pre-eminence.

They came—all except one, Dejaz Balcha. For years Dejaz Balcha had ruled the south-westerly province of Sidamo as his own personal fief, paying no taxes to the central government and very little respect. In the presence of a British visitor he had called Ras Tafari, 'half-man, half-snake', and when cautioned about this indiscretion in front of a number of his household slaves explained that it was no matter—all their tongues had been cut out.

Weeks passed. A second, more peremptory summons was sent down to Sidamo; and it is said that at the same time the Empress Zauditu sent Balcha her ring as a signal that he should come on his own terms.

Dejaz Balcha announced that he would be arriving. A month later he did arrive at Addis Ababa, but with ten thousand men. He went to his *ghebbi* three miles south of the capital, and there he and his army encamped.

The court and the populace waited to see how this unexpected bid for power would end. In his favour Balcha had his reputation as a great warrior, the loyalty of his men, his own loyalty both to Menelik and, at the time of Lij Yasu's deposition, to Shoa, and the secret support of the Empress. Against him stood the young Regent, 'the sly one', as Balcha always contemptuously called him.

The first move was made by Ras Tafari: an invitation to a banquet at the Great Ghebbi. Dejaz Balcha accepted. But might he, he asked, in order to honour his host bring his own personal bodyguard? Of course, came a message from the Regent. Incidentally, of how many men would the bodyguard consist? Of a mere six hundred, came the reply from Balcha's *ghebbi*.

The Regent's own reply was suspiciously dulcet. Still wary of treachery, Balcha warned his men that any who ate or drank too much at the *gebir*—the traditional feast—would be whipped. Mounted on his ceremonial mule and escorted by his six hundred, Balcha rode up to Menelik's Ghebbi. The banquet was splendid. Tafari was lavish with his praises of the Dejaz, of the Dejaz's men, and of the Dejaz's rule. Balcha began to believe that he had overestimated the youth. He waved at the rifles and swords which his men had brought into the hall with them and announced to Tafari that if he was not back by midnight, his army had orders to march on the capital. As the feasting and drinking grew heavier, Balcha's men began the traditional chants of the boasting ceremony in which all Ethiopian warriors indulge. They pranced up to the steps of the table at which the lords were dining, waving their weapons, praising Balcha and denigrating all the other lords of Ethiopia. Tafari's men stirred restlessly and impatiently. With sweet courtesy Ras Tafari told them to be silent—unless they had any songs to sing in praise of their guests.

Dejaz Balcha and his men left the Great Ghebbi well before midnight, well-dined, satisfied, sent on their way with a noble salute of guns. They rode back—to find the plain around Balcha's *ghebbi* a deserted wasteland. While the banquet was being held at the Great Ghebbi, Ras Kassa had paid a visit to Dejaz Balcha's encampment. With him he had brought many sacks of dollars and a number of whipping stocks. No reference was made to the whipping stocks but ten dollars was offered for every rifle handed in. Within hours Balcha's army had disintegrated; Ras Kassa herded the disarmed mob down the Sidamo road and stationed himself there to cut off Balcha should the Dejaz try to regain his province.

But Balcha knew that he was beaten—or almost. He paid off his bodyguard himself; and then with the help of the Echege took refuge in St. Raguel's Church on Mount Entotto overlooking the capital. Ras Tafari did not make the mistake of violating a sanctuary. Instead he surrounded the Echege's residence with his own troops; they drilled, they carried out rifle practice, they made their presence felt. At the same time he set up machine-guns around St. Raguel's and gave Dejaz Balcha a twenty-four-hours' ultimatum. The combination of bluff and terror worked. Dejaz Balcha surrendered. He was imprisoned for two years, and then forgiven, providing he signed a 'confession' and entered a monastery. He signed and he entered—for two years later there seemed to be no hope of overthrowing Tafari. Dejaz Birru Wolde Gabriel, who had been brought up by Menelik, was given his command.

Slowly Tafari Makonnen had been moving towards supreme power; cautiously, a step at a time, never risking a false move or one which really endangered him. From Lij he had risen to Dejaz, from Dejaz he had risen to Ras. On 27 October 1928 he moved a step further towards his ultimate aim. He was crowned Negus by the Echege, in a silken tent in the Church of the Trinity. Thus Tafari Makonnen became the only Negus in the Empire: for never in his long reign was he to give this royal title to any other. The Church was humbled; the Empress had been reduced to a figurehead; it must have seemed as if Tafari had won his long struggle. But power in Ethiopia has never easily been attained. Nor was it to be now.

In the month in which Ras Tafari was crowned Negus, the Raya Galla rose in revolt in Wollo. The revolt spread first to Lasta, then to Yeggiu, whose governor Ras Kebbede Mangasha Atikim was on a visit to Italy. Several half-hearted expeditions sent out from Wollo's capital, Dessie, failed. All Wollo was in ferment.[1] The neighbouring rulers were ordered to raise their levies and invade: Ras Seyum from Axum, Ras Gugsa Araya from Makalle, Dejaz Ayalew Birru from the Simien, and Ras Gugsa Wule from Beghemder. They moved reluctantly and slowly. At the end of the summer rains, in October, the Raya Galla ambushed and wiped out the forces of Lasta. Imru the Regent's trusted cousin was made Governor of Wollo; for the revolt looked serious.

But more serious than the revolt were the intrigues of the nobles who were meant to suppress it. Ras Kebbede was suspected of supporting the raiders; more important, it was known that Ras Gugsa Wule was intriguing with the Raya Galla leader Irissa Dangom.

Nephew of the Empress Taitu and divorced husband of the Empress Zauditu, Ras Gugsa Wule was an ambitious and personally courageous religious reactionary; but like so many of his kind slow-moving and over-cautious. For centuries Beghemder which he ruled from the ancient Imperial capital of Gondar had been the centre of the Christian Empire. Fiercely traditionalist highlanders, the men of Beghemder and their rulers inevitably resented—and occasionally challenged—the usurpers of their own traditional hegemony, whether from Tigre or Shoa. There was a common belief in Beghemder, and indeed outside it, that Ras Gugsa Wule would become Emperor. For years he had been

---

[1] And many other parts of Ethiopia were disturbed. From Maji in the south-west Consul Hodson reported 'very unsettled' political conditions; rumours that Zauditu was dead, and a desire for the return of Lij Yasu. 'If Lij Yasu is alive', the local chiefs were quoted as saying, 'we want him to be Emperor; if he is dead, show us his grave.'

distracted by the rival activities in the north of Beghemder of his young cousin Ayalew Birru: 'an adolescent', as he said indignantly, 'whom I have brought up at my court'. With Ayalew absent strenuously fighting the rebel Galla in Lasta, Ras Gugsa Wule was able to bring most of the Simien, Ayalew's territory, under his own control. Given his birth and position, he represented a far more serious challenge to the new Negus than Dejaz Balcha had done.

In particular the Ras tried to rally to his side all traditional Ethiopia by stressing that Tafari was too much under the influence of the foreigner—so much so, that secretly he had become a Roman Catholic. Clearly the quarrel with the Echege, the absence of an Abuna, the difficult negotiations that Tafari was conducting with the new Patriarch in Cairo, John XIX, all helped. But Tafari reacted quickly. A new Abuna, Cyrillos, came from Egypt; on his arrival he stressed that he had no intention of interfering in local affairs without consulting the Regent. Four Ethiopian monks were consecrated as bishops in Cairo. And finally, in January 1930, the Patriarch himself visited Addis Ababa and consecrated the Echege as bishop with the title of Abba Sauiros.

The situation was fluid. Ras Gugsa Wule was not yet in open rebellion; the Empress Zauditu was sending him message after message begging her ex-husband to come to the capital and make his submission. Both sides were raising their armies: ostensibly still to attack the Raya Galla. But in Shoa the soldiers only reluctantly obeyed the *chitet*, the summons to arms.

Elsewhere too there were half-hearted moves of support with only two or three thousand men: even less in the cases of Ras Seyum of Tigre and Ras Hailu of Gojjam, who avoided committing themselves. And there was a still more serious lacuna. Tafari had allowed the *Mahel Safari*, the Army of the Centre, to run down; in his eyes its men were too devoted to the Empress Zauditu. The new Minister of War, Dejaz Mulugueta, had only 16,000 men in all; and when he marched north to Dessie at the end of January, he had managed to concentrate only 2,000 of them. He took five cannon and seven machine-guns; and then moved on to the plains of Anchim near the Beghemder border. Meanwhile Ras Gugsa Wule was concentrating at Debra Tabor an army 35,000 strong, and utterly devoted.

Their devotion was slightly shaken by the Imperial Proclamation of Yekatit 17 (24 February) issued by the Empress and the Negus, declaring Ras Gugsa Wule a rebel. Even more important, attached to this was an anathema signed by the Abuna Cyrillos, and by the five new bishops, Sauiros, Abraham, Petros, Mikael, and Isaac and addressed to all the monasteries of Beghemder to be propagated. 'And therefore', it concluded 'you who may follow Ras Gugsa Wule, you who may attach yourself to him, be cursed and excommunicated; your life and your flesh are outcasts from Christian society.'

On 28 March the army of Beghemder crossed the border and moved south towards Shoa. It met with a novel experience. Three biplanes flew over and released on the marching army thousands of copies of the Imperial and Episcopal proclamations: the first use of psychological warfare in Ethiopia, and naturally devised by the ingenious mind of Tafari.

It was not enough to stop the men of Ras Gugsa Wule. Three days later battle was joined on the plains of Anchim. Wondossen, the eldest son of Ras Kassa, led the Shoan advance guard. Ayalew Birru commanded the right and Fitaurari Fikremariam, Commander of the Wollo troops, led the left. In the rear were the more aged generals, Dejaz Mulugueta who had been Menelik's man, and Dejaz Adafrisau who had been Makonnen's; both veterans of Adowa.

The battle began with a more dramatic appearance of the biplanes, which flew over the Beghemder army at nine o'clock lobbing small bombs and hand grenades. The armies closed, and for four hours were locked in struggle. The heroes of the day on the Shoan side were Wondossen Kassa and Ayalew Birru. The men of Gondar began to desert. Shortly after midday Ras Gugsa Wule was surrounded and called upon to surrender. He refused and died fighting. His second-in-command, Fitaurari Shumye, continued until he was captured in the late afternoon. The Raya Galla, on whose help Ras Gugsa Wule had been counting, arrived a day late. Dejaz Birru Wolde Gabriel and the army of Sidamo entered Debra Tabor unopposed. The death of the leader meant, as always in Ethiopia, the end of the campaign. The men of Beghemder resisted no longer. Ras Kassa was given all the territories of the dead Gugsa Wule; in fact the real ruler was his son Wondossen who was installed as governor at Debra Tabor. The other hero of the battle, Ayalew Birru, too closely related to the Empress Taitu's clan, now indeed its leading survivor, was

fobbed off with minor appointments and not even given the title
of Ras. His people sang:

> 'Ayalew the fool, the innocent
> Trusts men, trusts men.'

Two days after the battle on the plains of Anchim the Empress
Zauditu died suddenly in Addis Ababa. On the following day,
3 April, an *Awaj*, a proclamation, was issued in the capital: by the
common consent of the nobles and people, for the greater good
of the Empire, the Negus Tafari Makonnen was ascending the
Imperial Throne under the rank and style of His Imperial Majesty
Haile Selassie I, Negus Negusti, King of Kings.

The Coronation of the new Emperor took place after the forty-
day period of mourning for the Empress and after the rains, on
2 November 1930. It was a most splendid affair; embarrassingly
successful, for most of the guests from Europe who were invited
came. The Germans sent 800 bottles of hock, signed photographs
of General von Hindenburg, and Baron von Waldthaussen in the
flesh. The Belgians who had already sent a military mission to
train the Imperial Guard were represented by their new Plenipo-
tentiary Minister, M. Janssens; as the first delegations arrived at
the new railway station of Addis Ababa honours were rendered
by the Guard under the six Belgian officers and by the band under
its Swiss bandmaster, Nicoud. From Cairo a number of ambassadors journeyed down to represent their countries: His Excellency M. H. de Bildt, of Sweden, accompanied by Count Eric
von Rosen, a lieutenant in the Royal Horse Guards, and Count
Sten von Rosen; His Excellency Isabaro Yoshida representing
Japan; His Excellency General Muhittin Pasha of Turkey; and as
Egypt's own representative, His Excellency Mohammed Tewfik
Nessim Pasha with (reported Mr. Evelyn Waugh who voyaged
with the twenty-man Egyptian delegation to Djibuti) tin trunks
galore containing 'a handsome but unexceptional suite of bedroom furniture.'

From France came one of her two Marshals, Franchet
d'Esperey, and a Farman aeroplane. From Italy, as representative
of his cousin King Vittorio Emmanuele, came the Prince of
Udine with another aeroplane, a Breda. On his own account the
Duce added a light tank. But by far the most impressive delegation came from the British Empire, led by the Duke of Glouces-

ter. Its gifts were modest: 'a pair of elegant sceptres with an inscription composed, almost correctly, in Amharic'. With the Duke of Gloucester came—besides the Earl of Airlie and the young Wilfred Thesiger, personally invited by the Emperor out of gratitude to his father—a Marine Band under a Major Simpson, the great scene-stealer of the ten-day round of ceremonies, and a whole bevy of proconsuls: Sir John Maffey the Governor-General of the Anglo-Egyptian Sudan; Sir H. Baxter Kittermaster, Governor of British Somaliland; and Sir Stewart Symes, Governor of Aden.

The Emperor and Empress were crowned by the Abuna at a long-drawn-out Coptic ceremony in the Church of the Trinity. Of the assembled diplomats, Mr. Waugh wrote that their faces were 'set and strained. Their clothes made them funnier still. Marshal d'Esperey alone preserved his dignity, his chest thrown out, his baton raised on his knee, rigid as a war memorial, and as far as one could judge wide awake.'[1]

Addis Ababa, Ethiopia's 'modern' capital founded by Menelik, was a ramshackle city; and the screens hastily thrown up to hide the frightful slums from the gaze of the beribboned and beplumed visitors were only half a veil. The Guard was finely turned out and saluted smartly, but wore no shoes. The cars sent down to Diredawa with breakfast for the arriving guests unloaded porridge, kippers, eggs, and champagne. The unfinished hotel where the Marine Band stayed had rooms equipped with hairbrushes, clothes-hangers and brand-new enamelled spitoons.

It was a city laid out haphazardly around the *ghebbis* of Menelik and the great nobles, populated at this time by a large and mixed foreign community. At the top of the social scale came, naturally, the diplomats. By 1930 six countries had Legations in the capital: spacious legations, with *tukuls* and buildings scattered over wide

[1] Thesiger with the priggishness of a young Old Etonian did not approve of these irreverent new intruders—'During ten hectic days', he wrote, 'I took part in processions, ceremonies and state banquets, and finally I watched while the Patriarch crowned Haile Selassie King of Kings of Ethiopia . . . I looked on streets thronged with tribesmen from every part of his empire. I saw again the shields and brilliant robes which I remembered from my childhood. But the outside world had intruded and the writing was on the wall. . . . There were journalists who forced themselves forward to photograph the Emperor on his throne and the priests . . . I was thrust aside by one of them who shouted "Make room for the Eyes and Ears of the World".'

parkland on the fringes of the capital, in beautiful settings, given to the various nations by Menelik and his successors.

Sir Sidney Barton was Britain's Minister, an unabashed eccentric who for thirty-four years had been in the Consular Service in China and who, having lived through the Boxer revolt, knew what it was to have a Legation attacked. Under his authority a bevy of British consulates existed in the south and south-west of the country: at Maji where the Consul tried to control gun-running and ivory smuggling on the ill-defined and almost unadministered border where Ethiopia, Kenya, and the Sudan met; at Dangila in Gojjam where Robert Cheeseman the explorer kept an eye on the Nile waters, Britain's major imperial preoccupation; at Moyale in the remote south on the Kenya border; at Gore and Gambeila in the west and at Harar in the east: six in all.

By 1932 the Italians (whose Ministers in Addis Ababa were constantly changing) had also created six consulates: at Adowa, Gondar, Dessie, Debra Markos, capitals respectively of Tigre, Beghemder, Wollo, and Gojjam; at Magalo in the province of Arussi not far from Somalia's border; and at Harar, the great trading city of the eastern highlands, walled, white, and gated where—given the existence of a French Consul at Diredawa on the railway line below—international intrigue flourished, as indeed it had always done.

Though he was only too well aware that the British Consuls were virtually District Commissioners within his borders and the Italian Consuls spent their time intriguing with his nobles, Haile Selassie's policy, now that he was in power, was not to limit foreign influence; on the contrary if his plans to modernize Ethiopia were to succeed, he needed more and more foreign help. But he was perfectly well aware of the dangers of foreign aid and in particular of the dangers of coming to rely too heavily upon the neighbouring colonial powers, France, Italy, and Britain. Therefore he chose his advisers wherever possible from the smaller and more remote nations. That is why, for his major preoccupation, the formation of a modern army, he had turned to the Belgians.

Belgium admittedly was a colonial power in Africa; but the Belgian Congo had no frontiers with Ethiopia, and the Belgians certainly had no ambitions to expand in a territory so jealously watched over by their larger European neighbours. Moreover,

Belgian heroism in the First World War had given this little country's army a fine reputation. It was not just to train a ceremonial guard for his Coronation that the Negus Tafari had invited the Belgian Minister to send a military mission. On the contrary his aim was to form out of the Guard a small highly-equipped regular army, trained in a European style, which would enable him immediately to cow any rebellious Ras.

Unfortunately Major Polet and the five other Belgian officers had arrived in Addis Ababa just at the moment when Ras Gugsa Wule was moving into open rebellion; and after Zauditu's death, training was interrupted for a further month. Nevertheless, by 5 July 1930 Major Polet had been able to report that one infantry battalion of almost 600 men, one cavalry squadron of 125 horse, and one band of 40 men had been formed and trained. An Armenian, formerly a French NCO, Captain Gurinlian, had been recruited (for one of the difficulties the Belgians found was that of communicating with the men they were training). All had been issued with Lebel rifles, and the Negus had come regularly three times a week to watch their manœuvres, and wanted all his Guardsmen to be equipped in Belgium. By December 1933 Colonel Stevens, the British Military Attaché at Rome, out on a visit to Addis Ababa, inspected the Guard and reported to Haile Selassie that he found them 'really remarkable'.

At the same time Ethiopia had to be given a modern political façade. This meant not only the granting of a Constitution, the first in Ethiopia's history, but a whole new bevy of foreign advisers: Maître Auberson, a Swiss constitutional lawyer, Mr. de Halpert, an Englishman whose task it was to supervise the abolition of slavery, and most important of all, Mr. Colson, an American of strong character seconded from the State Department who was the real master-mind behind Ethiopia's foreign relations, and particularly in its dealings with the League of Nations.

The Foreign Minister, Blattengueta Herouy Wolde Selassie, was not, however, a puppet nor was he a negligible figure. In his early fifties, a Shoan and a writer, he was perhaps the widest-travelled of all Ethiopians. He had attended the Coronation of George V, the peace treaty negotiations at Versailles, spent time at Geneva, and accompanied Ras Tafari on his 1924 tour. 'He speaks English', said an Italian diplomatic report of 1926, 'and deserves our special attention.' His two sons Fekade Selassie and

Sirak were sent to study at Cambridge. He had been in his time President of the Special Tribunal, *Kantiba* of Addis Ababa, and editor of Tafari's progressive newspaper *Berhanena Salam*. Immediately after the Coronation he set out on a trip as Ambassador Extraordinary to Japan, officially to congratulate the Emperor Hirohito on his Coronation in 1928—a courtesy from one young Emperor to another—unofficially to see whether Haile Selassie's latest plan, of modernizing Ethiopia on Japanese lines, could be carried out. On his return he wrote a book describing and praising Japan as a model. This alarming notion was to cause a great deal of ink to flow in Western diplomatic reports; for already by 1931 Japan's invasion of Manchuria had provoked a crisis at the League; Japan was feared by the West, and the League revealed for the first time its weakness against a modernized aggressor. The Western Powers had no desire for a second Japan to rise in Africa. It did not.

The Constitution, announced in July 1931 and modelled on the Imperial Japanese Constitution of 1889, was formally signed in November. For this great occasion Haile Selassie invited all the traditional provincial rulers to come to the capital and to be installed as the first Senators of the Empire. It was yet another ruse. For, once installed, the nobles found that their new duties prevented them from returning to their provinces immediately and that when they were released, some six months later, administrators directly attached to the Emperor had been slipped in as watchdogs.

Two Rases however failed to accept the honour so graciously conferred upon them. Ras Kassa sent word that he was engaged in religious penance, and so would be unable to attend. Ras Hailu also sent word to the same effect. It was thought that Ras Hailu was aggrieved at not being named Negus by the new Emperor. This is probable; indeed it was probably Haile Selassie's greatest mistake. Menelik, after defeating in battle Ras Hailu's father the Negus Tekle Haimonot, one of his three major rivals for the Imperial succession, had personally re-crowned the then submissive King, and as a result been assured of his loyalty. Had he been named Negus like his father before him, Ras Hailu would almost certainly have been satisfied. The honour was of particular importance to him because he was an illegitimate son.

Gojjam, the rich and fertile province of which the Negus Tekle

Haimonot had been ruler, lies in the bend of the Blue Nile as it sweeps down and round from its source in Lake Tana. The steep, unbridged Nile gorge formed a natural barrier between Gojjam, Shoa to its east, and the Galla kingdoms and districts to the south. To its north, barred by almost trackless mountains, lay Beghemder, to its west the mountain escarpment that fell suddenly away to the deserts of the Sudan. Isolated by their geographical position, the Gojjamis were always semi-independent though never separatists—the bonds of religion were too strong. In all Ethiopia there was no region so devoted to its priests and, to the point of austerity, to its religious practices as Gojjam.

From 1908 onwards Ras Hailu ruled all Gojjam with increasing splendour and magnificence. European visitors, of whom there were many, given Ras Hailu's reputation for generosity and Gojjam's proximity to the Sudan and to the ever-fascinating Nile, have left account after account of his lavish hospitality, his magnificent house ablaze with that rarity in Ethiopia, electricity, his magnificent banquets where guests of the opposite sex to the horror of the traditionalists danced together, the royal welcomes, the fanfares of warriors, and his own stately courtesy and innumerable concubines. After the 1924 tour in Europe he imported Gojjam's first motor car, a Rolls Royce, in pieces, and had a street specially built in Debra Markos along which to drive it; he enquired of a visitor whether American tractors and ploughs would be the right thing for Ethiopia. In Addis Ababa he invested in hotels, cinemas, a car-hire service, and the first night-club. Like all Ethiopian nobles he was particularly pleased to be presented with fine rifles and shot-guns. In order to support so magnificent a court he taxed his people cruelly and cynically, but there appeared to be little resentment. Enthusiastic for the arts but above all for the crafts of progress, respecting in form the religious usages, he was Ethiopia's equivalent of a Renaissance Prince.

Politically Ras Hailu had always played a very careful game; rarely leaving his province except to assure the new rulers in the capital, whoever they might be, of his firm allegiance—once they themselves were firmly installed; promising his aid for military expeditions but always on one pretext or another avoiding campaigns. In 1910 his daughter Sable Wongel had been 'married' to Lij Yasu; but Lij Yasu disliked his prospective father-in-law's greed and ambition, and was more attracted by less refined

Muhammadan maidens. Twenty years later Ras Hailu had been suspected of aiding Ras Gugsa Wule; letters, it was said, were even found incriminating him. Though he was acquitted by the new Emperor, an uneasy relationship grew up.

It was therefore with joy that Ras Hailu received, instead of a more peremptory order to appear at the capital, a messenger from Haile Selassie proposing a marriage between the Emperor's son and heir Asfa Wossen, now aged sixteen, and his own second daughter Dinchinese.

In order to conduct the negotiations Ras Hailu came to the capital. He reached his *ghebbi* in Addis Ababa late in 1931 only to find that he had been outmanœuvred. Though the marriage proposals appear to have been perfectly genuine, they dragged on. It was easier, Ras Hailu discovered, to reach Addis Ababa than to leave it. Even his tardy installation as Senator did not console him: he refused to sign the new Constitution on the grounds that, contrary to Solomonic tradition, the successor to the Throne could only be chosen from the direct descendants of Haile Selassie. This was a clause to which even the loyal Ras Kassa had objected. The great nobles were prepared to accept the son of Ras Makonnen as Emperor but saw no reason why their own sons should not benefit from an equal opportunity eventually, little suspecting that almost all their own sons would, like themselves, be dead and gone long before the end of Haile Selassie's reign.

'En 1932', wrote Henri De Monfreid, 'le Negus . . . avait près du lui un mysterieux conseiller; une figure digne d'Edgar Allen Poe, le Dejaz Yigezu, un lepreux fanatique et zenophobe.' More moderately described a few years later as 'a heavy Menelikish figure . . . a man of immense standing except in the physical sense, for his legs were old and bandy', he had married Ras Hailu's eldest daughter Woizero Sable Wongel—who had first been 'married' to Lij Yasu.

At the end of May 1932, Dejaz Yigezu was taking a cure at the hot springs of Ambo when a Galla broke into the baths with the news that Lij Yasu had escaped from Ras Kassa's stronghold of Fikke and was nearing Ambo, out both for his wife and for Yigezu's blood. Yigezu stopped only to cover his nakedness with a muslin *shamma* and fled by car to Addis Ababa. It was typical of the reactions of panic that followed the news of Lij Yasu's escape.

For ten years he had been out of sight, though never forgotten, still the rightful Emperor in the hearts of many, and it now looked as if the turmoil of civil war might once again embroil the Empire and shake the new Emperor from his recent throne. A state of national emergency was proclaimed, the frontiers were closed, the phones and cables cut off, the passengers on the Djibuti train held incommunicado.

The *Mahel Safari* was dispatched to scour the frontier districts of Tigre and the Danakil country; Maillet and Corriger, the Emperor's French pilots, flew out to try and track down the fugitive from the air; and a trusted nobleman, Ras Desta Damtew, who had married the Emperor's eldest daughter Tenagne Worq, was sent off with a party of horsemen to watch the Gojjam frontier.

Four days after his escape Lij Yasu, sighted by Maillet, was arrested on the borders of Gojjam by Fitaurari Gessesse Belew, Ras Hailu's nephew. As Ras Desta was riding to take the prisoner over, he came across one of Ras Hailu's chiefs, Fitaurari Gindo, riding in the same direction. 'Why so many horses?', he asked Desta. 'For Lij Yasu', Gindo ingenuously replied.

The peril, if peril there had been, was over. Lij Yasu, laden, it was reported with golden chains, was removed to his final prison, a high-walled stone house in the mountain village of Grawa in the Garamalata range in Haile Selassie's own province of Harar, where he was watched over by the priest Abba Hanna.

As for Ras Hailu, he was tried and on 30 June condemned to a fine of 300,000 dollars and life imprisonment. On 11 July he was entrained in a *wagon-salon* bound for Diredawa, thence to be transferred to the remote province of Arussi. The engagement of the Crown Prince and his daughter was broken off.

From Debra Markos, the Italian Consul Medici had already reported to the Governor of Eritrea that authority had broken down and brigandage become rife since the virtual detention of Ras Hailu in the capital. He now added that, though the Gojjamis were happy at paying less taxes, the influx of Shoan officials to inventory Ras Hailu's goods and chattels before sending them to Addis Ababa was most unpopular. When in August Imru was promoted to Ras and nominated as the new governor of Gojjam, protests redoubled. Some of the local chiefs planned a deputation to Addis Ababa to ask the Emperor to leave Gojjam to the Gojjamis, others ('capi che hanno certa confidenza con noi'—'leaders, with whom we have a close relationship') came to the consulate to demand Italian support. An eighteen-year-old son of Ras Hailu, Alem Saguet, rebelled; Bishop Abraham of Gojjam persuaded him to accept the Emperor's pardon. He came to Addis Ababa, was publicly pardoned, stayed in Ras Desta's house, was arrested during the night and taken chained to the prison in Ankober where Ras Mangasha, Seyum's father, had died. Even more dissatisfied, though wisely he failed to show it, was the captor of Lij Yasu, Gessesse Belew. He had expected as a member of the ruling house to be rewarded with all Gojjam. Instead he was merely promoted to Dejaz and made governor of a small district.

After this there were no more plots of any consequence against the new Emperor. No doubt potential plotters reviewed with dismay the long list of their predecessors whose plots had been foiled; whether they were ex-Heirs or ruling Empresses, ancient warriors or young nobles, provincial warlords or court officials, all opponents had been outwitted or outmanœuvred by the son of Ras Makonnen; and the graves and prisons of Ethiopia were the resting-places of their bones and bodies.

Very quickly two royal marriages were celebrated, though not as planned earlier. Asfa Wossen was married to Walata Israel, Ras Seyum's daughter, and at the end of the year sent to Dessie to govern in person his own province of Wollo, under the guidance of his tutor Wodajo Ali. At the same time Haile Selassie's second and favourite daughter, Zenabe Worq, was married at the age of fourteen to a young nobleman by the name of Haile Selassie Gugsa, son and heir of Ras Gugsa Araya of eastern Tigre. By this double alliance the Emperor hoped to assure the loyalty of the two rulers of Tigre.

With the faithful Ras Imru in Gojjam, the equally loyal Ras Kassa in Beghemder, his own eldest son in Wollo, and himself in Shoa, he could at last feel a certain security. For not only was his own personal position in the capital assured but the five great provinces that formed the historic Empire were at last under control. Haile Selassie, could, in so far as any absolute ruler may, afford to relax—at least temporarily.

CHAPTER 2

FASCIST ITALY AND ITS COLONIES

In Italy too there were royal or semi-royal weddings. Amedeo son of the Duke of Aosta, an extremely handsome and extremely tall artillery officer, chose, like his father, a bride from France. On 5 November 1927 he married Princess Anne of France, daughter of the *Duc* de Guise.

Three years later, the King's only son and heir, Umberto Prince of Piedmont, married Princess Marie José, daughter of the King of the Belgians. The King was much relieved. Vittorio Emmanuele III, a man of nearly sixty, had always detested the pretensions of the House of Aosta. Cautious by temperament, he was no one's image of an impressive monarch. His legs were slightly deformed, he was very short. As a young man he had courted the ambitious and domineering Princess Helène d'Orléans, daughter of the exiled Louis Philippe. She had preferred to marry his first cousin and heir-apparent Emmanuele Filiberto Duke of Aosta, a fine figure and at least a potential warrior king. They were married at Kingston on Thames in 1895 and three years later at the Palazzo della Cisterna in Turin a son was born: Amedeo Umberto Isabella Luigi Filippo Maria Guiseppe Giovanni. 'Mon petit roi' his mother called him affectionately; and her fury was barely concealed when six years later the new king, whom his cousin referred to jovially as 'half a man', managed to produce a son and heir.

Mussolini owed a great deal to the support of Emmanuele Filiberto and the Princess Helène. Indeed, at the time of the so-called March on Rome in October 1922, it was largely the King's fear that he might be forced to abdicate in favour of the immensely popular Emmanuele Filiberto that led him against all his instincts to appoint Mussolini Prime Minister.

The young Amedeo played no part in all these manœuvrings —though Mussolini was not to forget in later years the debt he owed to the House of Aosta. In the late nineteen twenties, both before and after his marriage, Amedeo was commanding the Meharists of the Sahara, the Italian Camel Corps, in Italian North Africa.

Italy had seized the two provinces of Tripolitania and Cyrenaica in 1911, fifteen years after the disastrous attempt to conquer Ethiopia. This time there had been no resistance—barely a shot fired. But though the Turks were easily ousted, the tribesmen of the interior, the Senussi, soon turned against the infidels who had come as liberators. For years a small but fierce colonial war was waged, never dangerous for Italy—the Senussi were far too few in number to inflict anything approaching another Adowa on the invaders—but with the inevitable victories and defeats a fine training ground for the Italian Army, for the making and breaking of reputations.

General Graziani, Amedeo of Aosta's commander, had as a young infantry officer come out to North Africa in 1911 with a battalion of Eritrean askaris. Unfortunately for him he was bitten by a snake, fell very ill, developed malaria, and was invalided back to Rome. His troubles continued. He was gassed in the Great War—and very nearly lynched in the post-war troubles by the revolutionary committee of Parma who, like Shakespeare's Roman mob with Cinna, took him for an elderly and hated namesake. It was not till 1921 that he was summoned by the Minister of War from unhappy and enforced retirement and sent back to Cyrenaica. There he was to stay for the next thirteen years, gradually building up a reputation as Italy's finest colonial soldier. Like many contentious soldiers and politicians, he had begun his career as a student for the priesthood, but finding he had no vocation had left for other and more combative fields. The law and the police had seen him briefly, but by his very physical appearance he seemed cut out for a military career. His heavy sculpted features were again and again compared by admiring compatriots to those of a Roman emperor or Renaissance *condottiere*. Because he looked the part and because, unlike so many other Italian generals, he fought in Africa while they intrigued in Rome, he was forgiven much by the Italians—and there was to be much to forgive.

From 1926 to 1929 a white-bearded general almost in his seventies governed the two provinces of Italian North Africa. Emilio de Bono, a devout Catholic and a traditionalist, was already retired when, long before the March on Rome, he joined the Fascists—apparently in the hope of supplementing too meagre a pension. He had lent Mussolini's gangs of thugs, the *squadristi*, an aura that the Duce valued highly—the aura of respectability. De Bono had in a sense been the ambassador of the Army to the Fascists and of the Fascists to the Army; he had preserved the semi-benevolent neutrality of the military in the days of the March on Rome which would—as Mussolini well knew—have collapsed entirely at the first whiff of serious grapeshot; and Mussolini was accordingly grateful. Besides, De Bono was no potential threat to his own position.

The three years for which De Bono governed the two North African provinces were a period of renewed guerrilla fighting during which Graziani's star rose still higher. His commanding officer, General Malladra, referred to 'la sua figura di condottiere che tanta luce de gloria illumina'.[1] De Bono more moderately called him 'a precious element of politico-military efficiency'. In 1929, thanks largely to Amedeo of Aosta's Meharists, he defeated the Auled Suleiman at the Wells of Tagrift.

Later that year there was a general post; what in Ethiopia is known as a *shum-shir*, a switching round of appointments. De Bono went back to Rome to take over as Minister of the Colonies, and General Pietro Gazzera, a nonentity, replaced the reforming Cavallero at the Ministry of War. The two provinces of Italian North Africa were united into the one colony of Libya, and Marshal Badoglio was appointed Governor-General with—against his wishes—General Graziani as Vice-Governor for Cyrenaica.

Few men had a more curiously successful career than Badoglio. He had no great reputation as a military leader; on the contrary he was generally blamed for the disaster at Caporetto.[2] He was not and never pretended to be a Fascist; on the contrary it was he who had been ready to disperse the Fascist mobs with a whiff of grapeshot. He had been Chief of Staff of the Army, resigned and been temporarily exiled by the Fascists to the Italian

---

[1] Difficult to translate into reasonable English, like so much Fascist prose. Literally 'his appearance of *condottiere* that so much light of glory illuminates'.

[2] On 24 October 1917 the Austrians attacked in the North of Italy inflicting a vast military defeat on the Italian Army. General Badoglio commanding one of the Second Army's two Corps was absent, his 700 cannon were never fired. Only Emmanuele Filiberto Duke of Aosta commanding the Third Army came out of this defeat with both his army and his reputation intact.

Embassy in Brazil. He was not a particularly strong or impressive character. He could not even boast a profile like Graziani, or a beard like De Bono. Yet somehow, right up to the end, he was always there: the political general *par excellence*, hovering in the background, always ready to be called upon, and in the end always called upon.

In any case Badoglio's period as Governor-General was for him a mere interlude across the seas, often broken by visits to Rome. The kudos of the campaigns went to Graziani who occupied the oasis of Kufra, was promoted, thanks to Badoglio, and finally succeeded in capturing the hero of the Cyrenaican tribes, Omar el Muktar.

Graziani's achievements were undeniable. He was the hero of every Italian schoolboy, and Badoglio seems to have tolerated the whims, egoism, and suspicious pride of his subordinate with a far greater courtesy then Graziani showed to his nominal commander, whom he considered—by contrast to De Bono—to be a jealous personal enemy. But Graziani's methods were unpleasant: he relied on terror, severity, and overwhelming force. He sank concrete into the wells his nomad enemies used, and all down the desert frontier between Cyrenaica and Egypt ran cordons of barbed wire—achievements much vaunted in the Fascist press. Omar el Muktar was, on capture, shot out of hand as a rebel: a precedent that was to be remembered. Indeed the whole Libyan war was an unwitting rehearsal for a greater enterprise, a training ground where politicians, generals, and soldiers tested out the methods they were later to apply mistakenly on a far larger scale.

Amedeo of Aosta was there when the oasis of Kufra was captured. But on the death of his father in July 1931 and his succession to the title he went back to Italy: and there abandoned his career as an army officer to join the new and romantic arm now arousing such enthusiasm among young Italians, the *Regia Aeronautica*, Italy's air force.

It was Balbo, Mussolini's right-hand man and potential rival, who had caught the imagination of all Italy, and indeed of the world, by guiding a squadron of twelve flying-boats across the Atlantic to a triumphal reception in both North and South America, where the Italian communities greeted with pride and enthusiasm this outward sign of Italy's resurgence—the Duce had no partisans more devoted than those Italians who lived outside the reach of his laws. Balbo had trained himself as a pilot and in the general reshuffle of autumn 1929 became Minister of Aviation. Few Ministers lead their own pilots across an ocean never before flown over by a massed formation. Balbo did it again, this time with twenty-two naval bombers, and was rewarded with the title of Air Marshal, Italy's first.

So, like many other ambitious young men, the new Duke of Aosta transferred. He left the army as an artillery major and joined the air force as a colonel. For the next five years he was stationed in the north of Italy, at Gorizia. He lived with his wife and two young daughters in the Castello di Miramare, popular with all, joined by former *squadristi* such as Ettore Muti of Ravenna who had served in his father's army, gradually rising in rank to become commander of the air division 'Aquila', unaware of his third destiny, of the glory awaiting him in Ethiopia and his strange, almost tragic end.

Like most Italians of his class, Amedeo of Aosta took little interest in the internal politics of Italy at this period, largely because there were none. There were no elections, no strikes, no political crises, and very little violence. Or rather the violence was becoming institutionalized. There was one brief year when the fanatical Farinacci was appointed secretary-general of the Party, in effect number two of the regime, and the *squadristi* with their castor oil and their crowbars were once again loosed on the few of their opponents who dared appear in the streets. But this was a mere interlude in a period of more organized repression. Political opponents began to go into exile. The Communists were imprisoned. A new form of internal banishment, the *confine*, an Italian version of the Ethiopian system of confining dangerous nobles to mountain tops, was instituted—though in Italy islands replaced *ambas*.

In Italy the great task was the institutionalization of a Fascist State. Rules and regulations multiplied from 1931 onwards when the ascetic Achille Starace became Party Secretary; a man who it was said even wore the insignia of his office on his pyjamas. The 'Fascist style' was imposed on daily life: the Fascist salute, for instance, was not to be given sitting down, but on the other hand need not necessarily be accompanied by the raising of the hat. Teachers and civil servants and the rest were put into the ubiquitous black shirts (strictly buttoned at the neck) and Party officials forced to begin the day with military-style gymnastic exercises.

The framework of the whole system was the *Milizia*, an alternative armed force, directly at the service of the Duce, indirectly of the State. Originally set up to absorb the ill disciplined *squadristi*—De Bono had been the *Milizia*'s first Commandante Generale—its tentacles had spread and spread.

It was a curious structure; half Imperial Roman in terminology, half technocratic, with a dash of the Boy Scout and even a touch of the Wolf Cub.

To be a member it was necessary to be a tried and proven member of the Fascist Party: at the outbreak of the Second World War there were approximately 400,000 members of the *Milizia* for one million members of the Party. At first, anyone between the ages of 17 and 50 was eligible—of 'proved Fascist faith' of course. Later the structure became more baroque. *Avanguardisti* were enrolled at the age of 19; and on 21 April at the 'Solemn Ceremony of the Fascist Levy—an important annual jamboree —were presented with a symbolic musket. Later still the *Fasci Giovanili* were created: 20 to 22-year-olds who followed obligatory pre-military courses before passing into the *Fasci di Combattimenti*: and the full glory of parading in black shirt, baggy grey-green trousers, and (for the officers) a tasselled fez-style hat, carrying heavy sticks or guns behind their *gagliardetti* to the jaunty music of the Fascist bands. 'Believe, Obey, Fight', such was the motto of the *Gioventu Fascista*, the Fascist Youth.

The structure of the *Milizia* was hierarchic. Its commander-in-chief was, naturally, 'the Head of the Government and Duce of Fascismo'. Its acting head was a *Commandante Generale*: under him came 4 Lieutenant-Generals. Under the Lieutenant-Generals came 33 Consul-Generals who commanded the various *gruppi*. But the real base unit were the Legions—120 Legions each divided into 3 cohorts, each cohort divided into three centuries. The commanders of the Legions were known as Consuls—the equivalent of colonels. The other officers in descending scale of rank were the *Seniore*, the *Centurione*, and the *Capo manipolo* or captain. The *capi squadri* were the NCOs. Generally speaking the officers came from the army; and one of the sources of friction between the *Milizia* and the Army was that an officer transferring to the *Milizia* would automatically be promoted one grade. The officers who did transfer were usually, besides being Party members, those who for one reason or another found their promotion or careers blocked. The quality of the officers was, therefore, generally poor.

The militiamen themselves, the Blackshirts, were of course part-time soldiers—until a levy was decreed and they were called up for full-time service. But by 1929 most of the employees of the State—railwaymen, postmen, and the rest—had been trans-figured. There was the *Milizia Ferroviaria*—14 Legions of rail-waymen; the *Milizia Forestale*—9 Legions of foresters; the *Milizia Stradale*—the road navvies; the *Milizia Postelegrafonica*—the post office workers; the *Milizia Confinaria*—ordinary Legionaries in the frontier districts; and the *Milizia Universitaria*—6 Legions of 67,000 students. The *Instituto Fascista di Cultura* was set up; and if the intellectual of the Roman Fascists, Giuseppe Bottai, kept up some pretence of a loyal opposition with his review *Critica Fascista*, more and more the seventh commandment of the militiamen became symbolic of the general atmosphere—'Il Duce ha sempre ragione'—'The Duce is always right.'

Such was Italy in the decade that ran from January 1925 to December 1934; secure, fairly prosperous, fairly contented, and above all stable after the upheavals of the previous thirty years. The Fascist regime was generally admired, though with a strain of mockery, by public opinion in the rest of western Europe. Mussolini himself was admired without mockery. Above all, and most surprisingly, it was a peaceful regime: the warlike bluster of the early days appeared to be mere rhetoric, for Mussolini had made no sustained attempt at expansion outside Italy's recognized spheres of influence. Europe was at peace and public opinion at rest. Yet as early as 1932 the plans were germinating in Mussolini's mind of what was to be the prelude to events of considerable inconvenience and anguish, both for all Europeans and for himself: the conquest of Ethiopia.

In 1932 King Vittorio Emmanuele and his Minister of Colonies, the veteran General De Bono, visited Eritrea. They found a peaceful, loyal, and contented Colony. Ever since the peace settlement after Adowa the successive Italian governors had concentrated on building up a stable, model community, on avoiding trouble, and on entering into friendly relationships with the Tigrean rulers across the river frontier to their south.

They had succeeded in all these aims. This was all the more extraordinary because neighbouring Tigre was always a confused, bloody, violent, and agitated province. Admittedly it could hardly be otherwise with its proud and warlike mountaineers conscious of speaking a language—Tigrinya—which was close to the Amharic of the ruling Amhara of Shoa, yet distinctive enough to set them apart; conscious too of possessing in Axum the holiest city in Ethiopia, the cradle of an ancient Empire when Shoa was not even named. Ras Seyum's grandfather, the Emperor Johannes, had been the most warlike and renowned of all Ethiopia's recent rulers; Ras Seyum's father Ras Mangasha had, despite fighting side by side with the Shoan Emperor at Adowa, ended his days as a prisoner in chains in the Shoan fortress of Ankober; Ras Seyum himself had been deprived of eastern Tigre, ruled from Makalle by his rival, the elderly Ras Gugsa Araya. The lords of Tigre, with the Italians on their northern frontier in Eritrea, and the British on their western frontier in the Sudan, with the untamed and savage Danakil on their eastern marches, were subject to greater pressures and more liable to be influenced by foreign intrigue than the governors of any other Ethiopian province.

Nevertheless relations with the Italians were good. This was largely because the heartland of Eritrea, the highlands, was populated, like Tigre itself, by Christian Tigrinya-speakers. In their centre lay the Colony's capital of Asmara, a newly built, well-laid-out, small Italian city. The western gates of the highlands were guarded by the little town of Keren, up to which the single-track railway from the Red Sea port of Massawa ran.

But the lowlands were Muslim. To the west bordering the Sudan lived the powerful Beni Amer, followers of the Khatmia sect, founded by Sayed Mohammed Othman el Mirghani. To the east, stretching down to the isolated port of Assab, lay the salt flats of the Danakil desert, the hottest place on earth. Like the Tigrinya-speakers the Danakil nomads were split by a frontier: some 33,000 lived in Eritrea, but twice as many lived in Ethiopia. Unlike the Tigrinya-speakers, they were all Muslims of a sort; a confederation of loose clans owing allegiance to their Sultan at Aussa inside Ethiopian territory, probably the fiercest and most primitive of all the peoples on the borders of Ethiopia. Their teeth were filed, their reputation xenophobic, and they had accounted for more explorers than any other tribe in north-east Africa.

Out of this heterogeneous collection of different peoples, numbering perhaps a million and a half in all, the Italians had built almost a nation: to be an Eritrean and to be an Italian subject was a matter of pride, as later events were to prove. The Eritreans were surprisingly, though not invariably, loyal to their colonial rulers. In Libya the Eritrean battalions—which were mainly but not wholly recruited from the Muslim half of the population —fought well against their co-religionists. The Christian Tigrinya-speakers were a touch less trusted; yet many of their Fitauraris became NCOs in the battalions or led under Italian command the irregular armed auxiliaries, the bande[1] which each district ever since Adowa had provided. In any case the loyalty of the Tigreans was, if not to the Italians, certainly not to the Amharic-speakers and the Amhara Emperor; it was to the great lords descended from the Emperor Johannes. For years these great lords had had closer personal contacts with the Governor of Eritrea, Gasperini, than with the Shoan court. They hired Italian technicians and doctors as a matter of course; and if Ras Gugsa Araya or Ras Seyum had to visit Addis Ababa, almost invariably they found it easier and quicker—and safer—to go north by mule to Massawa, then by sea to French Djibuti, and from there by the *chemin de fer Franco-Ethiopien* via Diredawa to the capital.

Like many Tigrean nobles, Ras Gugsa Araya used to go to Eritrea for medical treatment from Italian doctors. And when his daughter-in-law Princess Zenabe Worq fell ill in the seventh month of her pregnancy, he suggested that she should go to his doctor. But the priests refused (for liturgical reasons) and her young husband Haile Selassie Gugsa (who was rumoured to maltreat her) also refused. So the Ras sent a message to the capital. Two days later Haile Selassie's personal physician and trusted confidant, Dr Zervos, flew in. It was too late. The day before, on 24 March 1933 the young Princess had died. She was aged sixteen, the Emperor's favourite daughter and the first of his six children to predecease him. Dr. Zervos flew back to Addis Ababa with the dead girl's body—an insult to her widowed husband which Haile Selassie Gugsa felt very keenly.

Only a month later, on 28 April, Ras Gugsa Araya himself died. Drink, violence, and debauchery had ruined his health, and

---

[1] These irregulars were often referred to by British officials as *banda* even when strictly speaking they should have been called *bande*. The author will follow the example of his compatriots.

the Emperor had authorized him to go via Eritrea to Switzerland. If he had set out by stretcher all would probably have been well. But tradition dictated that a Ras should travel only on his war-mule. He set out and averaged one hour a day. At Adagamus the doctor insisted that he should stop, but the priests accompanying him wished to celebrate Easter at Adigrat. Legend has it that a corpse rode into Adigrat, upright upon a war-mule. His son Haile Selassie Gugsa moved into the Italian-built Palace at Makalle.

To the north-east of the Ethiopian highlands, sweeping along the top of the Red Sea Coast to the south of the straits of Bab-el-Mandeb, and down in the east along the Benadir Coast to the northern districts of Kenya, lay in the horn of Africa the vast territories of the Somali, carved up after the opening of the Suez Canal by three colonial powers; or, if Ethiopia is counted, by four.

The Somalis must be the finest-looking race in Africa. Tall, thin, with long noses and thin lips, clad in a sort of full-length kilt, the *tobe*, they strode over the vast undulating plateaux in which they lived leading their camel herds from well to well. Courageous, avaricious, vain, and highly excitable, they were united by their language, by their nomadic way of life, by their religion, and by very little else. There was never any sort of centralized authority among the Somalis, and in their independent and egalitarian society very little authority at all. Each of the four major groupings, the Dir, the Isaak, the Hawiya, and the Darod, were divided up into a number of clans and sub-clans, and it was by his clan that the Somali nomad felt himself to be defined. He was first and foremost a Habr Yunis, or a Rer Ali, or an Issa, or a Mijurtin—one of a hundred clans—and only afterwards a Darod or a Dir, and only then conscious of being a Somali. Somali women, almost as independent as their menfolk, were—and still are—famous for their beauty.

In the year after Adowa the various foreign missions to Menelik's court agreed on the carving-up of the Somali lands. Rennell Rodd and Ras Makonnen signed the Anglo-Ethiopian boundary agreement theoretically defining the southern boundary of British Somaliland, the north-eastern boundary of the Empire. Léonce Lagarde the French Envoy defined the boundaries of the Côte Française des Somalis on that difficult territory which the Danakil and the Somali clan of the Issa shared and fought over. Italy's peace negotiator Dr. Neruzzini agreed with the Ethiopians that the future frontier between Italian Somali and Ethiopia should run at 180 miles from the coast. Meanwhile far in the south the British of British East Africa pushed their northern frontier up to the Juba river which debouched in the little Sultanate of Kismayu.

With the Fascist regime came, in the Somali territories under Italian control, a new policy and a new governor. In October 1923 one year after the March on Rome, De Vecchi a bald and heavy regular officer and, like De Bono, an early Fascist member, came out to Mogadishu. He immediately set about reorganizing, or rather organizing, the rather messy pre-Fascist system whereby Italian Somalia had been divided into two protectorates and one semi-colony. De Vecchi must have had more brains and ability than he was generally credited with, for by the end of his period as Governor he had achieved all his aims. With 12,000 troops (including many Eritreans) he moved against Yusuf Ali the Sultan of Obbia and declared the protectorate a province. In the north the ageing Bogor Isman, Sultan of the Mijurtin, held out for two years longer till he too was deposed, exiled to Mogadishu the capital of the colony, and his sultanate abolished.

With Jubaland (ceded by the British under the Treaty of London) incorporated, the Colony of Somalia consisted of seven provinces divided into 33 districts or 'Residences'. Its population was (in 1939) estimated at 1,200,000 natives and 8,000 Europeans, mostly at Mogadishu. When De Vecchi departed to become Italy's first Ambassador to the Holy See, he left behind him a well-administered colony. He had been especially successful in reorganizing the Colony's armed forces, both regular and irregular. The regular forces, the Royal Corps, numbered 134 Italian officers and 6,700 men divided into six Arabo-Somali battalions ('Arabo' because many of the men were recruited in the Yemen). The irregular forces consisted of a number of armed frontier bands—*Bande Armate di Confine*—which rose from nine in 1925 to 40 ten years later; small groups of clansmen led by Italian officers and popularly known as *Dubats* (*Dub* in Somali means turban, *At* means white). This was a success. The only fly in the ointment was the rebellion at El Bur near Obbia of a Mijurtin clansman, Omar Samanthar, who had murdered a

Residente and by evading his pursuers for over a year gained a certain reputation.

By 1930 the Italians, the British, and the Ethiopians under their new Emperor were beginning to feel that it was important to get the boundaries of their possessions exactly defined. The first Boundary Commission went to work in September, to mark out the borders in the north between British Somaliland and Italian Somalia. Colonel Clifford represented the British, Enrico Cerulli, the ethnographer and explorer, the Italians. There was no difficulty, and the boundary was ratified by an Anglo-Italian agreement signed the following year.

Colonel Clifford was also a member of the Anglo-Ethiopian Boundary Commission which two years later began the longer, more exhausting task of defining Ethiopia's frontier with British Somaliland. His opposite number was Lorenzo Taezaz, one of Haile Selassie's bright young men, an Eritrean and a protégé of Dejaz Nasibu Emmanuel, used to dealing with foreigners. And if the work was slower and more exhausting, given Ethiopian delays and absences, the atmosphere was equally friendly. The local Italian officials over whose territory the Commission had to pass were equally helpful, offering the free use of their wells —none more helpful than a certain Captain Cimmaruta. It was only the clans who were obstreperous and resisted; one of the members of the commission was killed, and thereafter the Ethiopians provided a large escort.

But it was the third part of the settlement that proved thorny; the definition of the Italo-Ethiopian frontier. The reason was probably that the new Italian governor Guido Corni wanted to be no less successful than his predecessor, and that meant the gaining of territory, a 'forward policy'. His most powerful ally was Olol Dinke, leader of the Ajuran and related to the Mozaffar dynasty which had once ruled Mogadishu. The Ajuran controlled the vital stretch of the Webbi Shebelli River that ran from Ferfer (which was definitely inside Italian territory) to Callafo (which was definitely Ethiopian). The Governor named Olol Dinke Sultan of the Sciavelli and paid him to raid Ethiopian tax-gathering expeditions—a pursuit to which he was all the more attracted by his hatred for the Ethiopians who had imprisoned his father. The Ethiopians reacted by arming Omar Samanthar. As tension grew, the anger of the Governor of Harar, Dejaz

Gabremariam, in whose province the Ogaden lay, gave way to exasperation. He led his army down the Webbi Shebelli, cleared the Italians out of the fort at Mustahil in the heart of Olol Dinke's territory, and threatened the Italian *Residenza* right down the river at Belethuen. This was in September 1931. Hastily the Italians mustered reinforcements; but an open clash was avoided and eventually Dejaz Gabremariam withdrew. Probably neither he nor the Italian Governor had come so close to open conflict on the express orders of either of their governments; it was a local, rather than a national feud, as its peaceful ending showed. It could, if Mussolini had so wished, been the pretext for war. But that was before 1932, before the Duce had seriously begun to consider the conquest of Ethiopia.

PART II

THE WAR OF THE NEGUS

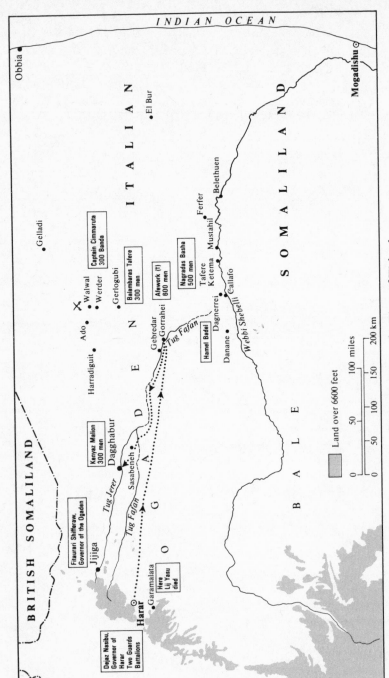

INDIAN OCEAN

Obbia

Mogadishu

BRITISH SOMALILAND

ITALIAN SOMALILAND

Gelladi

El Bur

Walwal
Ado
Werder
Gerlogubi

Captain Cimmaruta 300 Banda

Harradiguit

Balambaras Tafere 300 men

Afework (†) 600 men

Ferfer
Belethuen
Mustahil

Nagradas Basha 500 men

Tafere Ketema

Callafo

Gebredar
Gorrahei

Tug Fafan

Dagnerrei

Hamel Badel

Danane

Webbi Shebelli

O G A D E N

Kanyaz Mafion 300 men

Dagghabur

Sasabeneh

Tug Jerer

Tug Fafan

Fitaurari Shifferaw, Governor of the Ogaden

Jijiga

Here Lij Yasu died

Garamalata

Harar

Dejaz Nasibu, Governor of Harar Two Guards Battalions

BALE

Land over 6600 feet

0   50   100   150   200 km
0   50   100 miles

MAP 2. The Ogaden at the Time of Walwal

CHAPTER 3

THE 'INCIDENT' AT WALWAL

COLONEL CLIFFORD and the Anglo-Ethiopian Commissioners moved into the Ogaden in late October 1934, to study the grazing rights of certain clans that overlapped all borders. Besides the Colonel himself the British delegation consisted of two other British Army officers, a corporal and one civilian, a colonial official named Mr. Alex Curle. As the commissioners and their retinues moved down towards Walwal, Fitaurari Shifferaw, who, under, Dejaz Gabremariam, governed the Ogaden from the little town of Jijiga at the foot of the Harar hills, arrived to take personal command of the escort.

At Walwal there were over a thousand wells, the biggest concentration in the Ogaden. In Somalia a well was not just a hole in the ground with water at the bottom; it was—and is—an important piece of property. Each well was owned by a group of families, each group of wells by a clan. Wells that never ran dry were more valuable than wells that sometimes did; and if a well did run dry, the families using it would have to go and barter with their more fortunate neighbours for the jealously–guarded right to draw water. The thousand wells spread over a wide flat area; and by each well a group of nomads were camped, with their camel-skin tents, their camels, and their herds. They belonged to the Rer Ibrahim and the Mijurtin clans: the Rer Ibrahim came from Ethiopian or British-controlled territory, the Mijurtin from the former Sultanate annexed by Italy.

On the morning of 23 November the Commissioners and their escort arrived at Walwal. They found the wells already half-occupied by about 200 *bande* under a native Somali officer. Fitaurari Shifferaw pitched his camp to the north and stationed his men across a line that ran roughly through the middle of the wells facing the *bande*. Colonel Clifford and the Ethiopian Commissioners pitched their tents a few hundred yards away, side by side; and Colonel Clifford raised the Union Jack.

That day a Somali under-officer of Fitaurari Shifferaw's crossed the lines and deserted. The Fitaurari sent a threatening letter across the lines; Lieutenant Mousti, the *bande* leader, replied saying that the deserter would be sent back. But his own men refused: 'This man has taken refuge under the Italian flag', they claimed. 'Even if we die, he shall not die. He must not return to the Ethiopians.' Perplexed, Mousti sent back for instructions to his base, the little town of Werder some five miles away; and that night the Italian Frontier Officer, Captain Cimmaruta, arrived to take over the situation personally, supported by three or four hundred more irregulars.

At dawn Cimmaruta sent a note across to Clifford asking for an interview. While waiting for the reply he told his men that they, the Somalis, were lions. The interview took place at the end of the morning. Negotiations about the deserter stuck. Clifford asked Cimmaruta to pull back his men till the Commissioners' job was done. Cimmaruta refused; he suggested that in order to avoid clashes the two sides should mark out a provisional boundary line by scoring trees with knives. The Ethiopians, fearing that this would be tantamount to admitting that the Italians had a right to be so far inland, refused—and pointed out that Cimmaruta was well over 180 miles from the Somali coast. The interview ended stormily, with threats by Cimmaruta to call up 'several hundred more of my men'. In fact he went back to Werder with almost all, leaving only 100 *bande* to watch the Ethiopians.

That afternoon two Italian military planes flew low over the Commissioners' tents, and Clifford and the British officers saw one of the Italian gunners training a machine-gun on them. They sent another letter of protest to Cimmaruta saying that in view of the Italian attitude they were unable to fulfil their mission and would retire to Ado, five miles behind. In the night the comedy continued; Cimmaruta sent to inform Clifford that the British and the British alone would be allowed free circulation. Clifford naturally refused, and next day, 25 November, the two Commissions, British and Ethiopian, retired to Ado. It seemed as if an unpleasant incident had been avoided.

But the two lines stayed in position facing one another; and the comedy of communication turned to tragic farce. Cimmaruta's letters to Fitaurari Shifferaw had to be taken back to Ado to be translated into Amharic by the Commissioners, and vice versa.

In one Cimmaruta referred to the Fitaurari as 'your chief *Shifta*',[1] causing great offence. In the following days sixteen Mijurtin *bande* deserted the Italians to join Omar Samanthar, who was nearby. But it was not until 5 December that it suddenly all flared up. The actual occasion was a trivial thing: the tossing of a bone from the campfire by an Ethiopian at a Somali. But, sooner or later, with two groups of armed and hostile men camping day by day and night by night face to face, something was bound to happen. It was three-thirty in the afternoon. A bone, an insult, a gesture, a rifle raised—according to the Italians it was Fitaurari Shifferaw who called out 'Down and fire.'

But the Italians seem to have been the better prepared. Within ten minutes of the fusillade breaking out, three planes and two light tanks had appeared. An Ethiopian Fitaurari, Alemayu Goshu, was killed, and at nightfall when Fitaurari Shifferaw and his men withdrew to Ado, 107 Ethiopians had been killed and 40 wounded. It was not till a day later that Ali Nur, an ex-King's African Rifles soldier and commander of the rearguard, cut off by the armoured cars, managed to get through to Ado. From Ado the Commissioners pulled hurriedly back to Harradiguit; and when two days later Ali Nur and Lt. Collingwood followed with the baggage, they were bombed, though harmlessly, as they left the village.

That was the famous Walwal crisis, that was to set—as they say, or said—the chancelleries of Europe alight.

On 9 December Blattengueta Herouy, Ethiopia's Foreign Minister, cabled the League of Nations to protest and to demand that the arbitration clause of the 1928 Treaty of Friendship should be put into effect. On the 11th the Italian Chargé d'Affaires presented Italy's counterdemands. These were (1) that Dejaz Gabremariam should come to Walwal in person, and formally present his apologies to the representative of the Italian government while the Ethiopian detachment saluted the Italian flag, (2) that those responsible for the attack should be arrested, demoted, should also salute the Italian flag, and be punished, (3) that the Ethiopian Government should hand over 'the Somali outlaw and Italian subject Omar Samanthar already guilty of the crime of murder, the murder of the Italian Captain Carolei'. On the 14th

---

[1] *Shifta* is the Amharic word for bandit. See glossary p. xvi for this and other Amharic terms.

Italy rejected the demand for arbitration. On the 15th Lorenzo Taezaz came back from Jijiga with Fitaurari Shifferaw's written report, and Ali Nur was promoted to the rank of Balambaras. On the 21st an Italian plane reconnoitred the wells of Gerlogubi where Ethiopian reinforcements were gathering under a leader named Afework.

And on the 28th as the Italians attacked Gerlogubi with tanks and planes and the Ethiopians pulled back, M. Gérard reported to Brussels from the Belgian Legation that troops and munitions were being sent to the Ogaden, and translated a wall-inscription in Amharic, typical according to him of many, and symptomatic of Ethiopian public opinion. It read: 'When you want to eat macaroni, don't delay: chew it while it's still hot.'

By appealing to the League the Ethiopian government created a European crisis: an appeal meant debates at Geneva, open diplomatic warfare, and above all, publicity. The actual issue of Walwal, of the interpretation of the grazing rights of the Mijurtin under the 1908 agreement, the question of whether the frontier of Somalia was 180 nautical miles or 180 statute miles from the sea, of the fulfilment or not of the 1928 Treaty, and of the responsibility for the deaths on 5 December were debated endlessly and fruitlessly. Innumerable commissions sat, innumerable articles were written, and innumerable speeches were made. And the benefits of Haile Selassie's visit to Europe appeared. People remembered the dignified little man with his famous cape and collection of hats. Public opinion all over Europe stood on guard and the political leaders of Europe were dragged along—or on occasions abruptly dismissed if they could not follow where public opinion led.

But was the appeal to the League a mistake? It meant an open crisis in which Italy inevitably appeared as the bullying aggressor. It meant therefore that Mussolini's prestige was at stake. Not only for Mussolini but for all Italians it became a question of face. Politically, it was a wise move by Haile Selassie; psychologically it was disastrous. A dictator can rarely admit to his fellow-rulers when accused by foreign opinion that he has been wrong; he must threaten and bluster and justify his actions, and in the end he may be carried along by the tidal wave he has himself aroused. From the incident at Walwal events moved slowly though not inexorably to war. There were the two absolute rulers, Haile

Selassie in Addis Ababa and Mussolini in Rome, making diplomatic move and countermove, strengthening their forces hastily
but both apparently ready to negotiate, listening to suggestions
for compromise, hesitating, almost accepting this or that plan,
neither really convinced that an armed conflict could not be
avoided. Did they study each other's psychology? They must
have done; they must have been watching each other very
closely, trying to anticipate the other's intentions and foresee his
next action. But each misjudged the other badly. From Walwal to
the outbreak of war and even afterwards it was a poker game
played at a distance by two men who had only seen each other
once—and were never to meet again. Perhaps each judged the
other by what he had seemed to be in 1924. Then Haile Selassie
had observed a rattled political leader whose power was tottering
in the wake of the Matteoti crisis, and Mussolini had seen a
young, quiet, physically tiny Ethiopian, not even the ruler of his
country, a sort of Ambassador Extraordinary, surrounded by a
cohort of his peers just as impressive in personality and style. Did
either of them realize how much the other's position had changed
in the intervening eleven years, and how important it was for the
other not to lose face in the eyes of his own countrymen?

By appealing to the League of Nations, the Ethiopian Government gambled. Walwal was only a frontier incident. It was
admittedly a serious frontier incident but there had been other
serious frontier incidents—for instance the killing only a month
earlier of a French officer Captain Bertrand and his guard on the
Djibuti frontier—and they had been settled quietly and without
much fuss. Admittedly if the gamble had succeded and Italy had
backed down, Ethiopia would have gained an important asset:
the definition of all her frontiers. But if the gamble went wrong,
as it did go wrong, the risks were very great. In fact the gamble
was only justified if the Ethiopians were convinced at the time
that Mussolini meant war. If he did, they had nothing to lose and
possibly everything to gain by creating a crisis in Europe.

But did Mussolini at the time of Walwal intend to invade and
conquer Ethiopia? The answer must be a qualified no. Admittedly he had made plans for war with Ethiopia; as early as 1932,
De Bono tells us, Mussolini had mentioned in strict confidence
these plans, and De Bono's two visits to Eritrea in 1932 were
more of a military reconnaissance than a simple tour of inspection
by the Minister for the Colonies. According to De Bono, 1933

was 'the year in which we began to think in concrete terms of the measures to be taken in the case of conflict with Ethiopia'. The Duce had talked to no one else of the operation. 'Only he and I were *au courant*.' The Duce had asked De Bono what he would need. 'Money, chief', De Bono had replied, 'lots of money.' 'Money will not be lacking,' Mussolini said.

But although all the evidence goes to show that Mussolini was making plans for war with Ethiopia as early as 1932–3, it does not show that he had definitely decided on it. In a sense every Italian political leader since Adowa had made plans for war. The conquest of Ethiopia, or at any rate its transformation into an Italian protectorate, was always at the back of Italian minds, and at certain periods—in 1906 and 1926 for instance—it came to the forefront. But the drawing up of plans for war does not prove the intention to wage war. Even the fact that Mussolini circulated on 30 December his 'Directive and plan of action to resolve the Ethiopian question' does not prove that from Walwal onwards he was set on it. A close study of his diplomatic moves in the months that followed indicates how very undecided he was.

Still, the main question remains: why did the war break out at this time? Italy could have chosen many a better moment: for instance during Ras Gugsa Wule's revolt in 1930, or even when Gojjam was so unsettled two years later. As it was, Italy invaded Ethiopia at one of the rare moments when there was no internal crisis, and furthermore chose to wait till Ethiopia's army was if not modernized at least beginning to be retrained and re-equipped. Technically Mussolini could hardly have chosen a worse moment.

On 30 January 1933 Hitler became Germany's Chancellor and the framework of Europe began to crack. For Mussolini the situation was a challenge, a danger, and an opportunity. It was dangerous because a false move outside Italy might endanger his own position—as he found when the scandal following the murder of King Alexander of Yugoslavia and the French Foreign Minister Barthou by *ustachis* trained in Italy caused him to draw in his horns. It was an opportunity in the sense that the rise of a German threat meant that for France and England Mussolini's alliance was most important. Hence in order to preserve the status quo in Europe they were the more likely to give him a free hand in Africa. It was above all a challenge: let Europe see that Fascist Italy under the Duce was untamed and more dangerous than any upstart to the north. As A. J. P. Taylor says: 'Probably he was merely intoxicated out of his senses by the militaristic blustering which he had started and in which Hitler was now outbidding him.'

It would be ridiculous to explain a war merely on the grounds of a dictator's psychology. The causes of the Italo–Ethiopian war lay in history; the pretext was a minor frontier incident; but the timing can only be explained by the working of Mussolini's imagination.

CHAPTER 4

PREPARATIONS FOR WAR

FOR almost ten months after the incident at Walwal, two questions agitated opinion in Europe: was Mussolini going to invade Ethiopia and, if he did, how should the League of Nations react? Implied in the second question was a third: would there be war in Europe? It was this possibility that really kept the tension so high, not concern over Ethiopia. In terms of *realpolitik* the League was the instrument by which England and France preserved the peace, the balance of power in Europe, and their own colonial empires abroad. A challenge to the League was therefore a challenge to its two most powerful backers, and if Italy defied the League, England and France would necessarily try to bring Italy to heel—either by persuasion or by force. In January 1935 there was therefore hope of a negotiated compromise between Italy and Ethiopia, danger of a war in Africa if the compromise failed, and a barely concealed expectation felt by many in both England and France that a war in Africa would lead to a war in Europe. In a European war Italy would almost certainly be defeated and Italy's Fascist regime overthrown; the prospect of war, though dangerous, was not therefore entirely displeasing. The Ethiopian crisis came totally to dominate the political scene. The statesmen and diplomats who favoured a compromise were themselves caught up by the swell of moral indignation that swept over northern, central, and western Europe, isolating Italy and her little group of client states. But though public opinion among the Swedes, the Belgians, and even the Germans was strongly against Italy, the feelings that counted were the feelings of the British and the French.

The French were preoccupied by the rising German threat. In the first week in January, while the Crown Prince of Sweden was paying Europe's first state visit to Addis Ababa, France's Foreign Minister Laval went to Rome. The results were two: a Franco-Italian alliance the published terms of which were enough to infuriate the Ethiopians; and, far more important, a private understanding that in return for Italian support against Germany France would allow Italy a free hand in Ethiopia. If any single event reinforced Mussolini's determination to put his plans for an invasion into action it was this. Public opinion in France was evenly divided on the rights of the situation.

In England there was minority support for Mussolini on the extreme right wing and among a group of vociferous Catholic journalists and MPs. But public opinion was almost entirely against Fascist Italy. Among its most formidable leaders was Sylvia Pankhurst; behind her lay that fine Victorian tradition of public-spirited agitation by ladies of the upper middle class that from Florence Nightingale onwards had made them the bane of British officialdom. Like Stalin's Pope, she could not muster many divisions but when moral fervour moved her she was England's greatest agitator, as her mother had been before her. For the anti-Fascists in England the Ethiopian crisis was a godsend: for Sylvia Pankhurst it replaced her earlier fervours for the 'flapper vote', women's sexual liberation, and even the poems of Eminescu. Aided and advised by her great friend Silvio Corio, a left-wing journalist and refugee who remembered seeing the soldiers return from Adowa, she bombarded the newspapers—particularly the pro-Mussolini press, the *Daily Mail*, the *Morning Post*, and the *Observer*—and public figures, civil servants, and politicians with volleys of letters. She formed committees, organized rallies, was a moving spirit behind the Peace Ballot, and generally a thorn in the flesh of the diplomats.

The diplomats on the other hand were only too friendly to the Fascist regime. In Rome the British government had refused, despite Mussolini's special request, to prolong the stay of Sir Ronald Graham. But Mussolini must have been even more content with Graham's successor, Sir Eric Drummond, later Earl of Perth, of whom Ciano was to write: 'almost one of us in his love for Fascism'—another example of the power of the Fascist ideology to fascinate certain strata of the British upper classes. Furthermore Drummond had the convenient foible of trusting his domestic servants: what the valet-spy 'Cicero' got from Knatchbull-Hugessen in Turkey was as nothing compared to the dispatches purloined by the Italians from Drummond. The Comte de Chambrun, Laval's son-in-law, was France's Ambassador. With the interests of the Powers guaranteed by two such antagonists the Italian Foreign Ministry hardly had need of allies.

History, unkindly, has not drawn a veil over the months of diplomatic manœuvring designed to prevent Italy from invading Ethiopia or to punish her when she had done so. Never has so much human energy been expended in such futile attempts; or if it has, never has it been so well documented. Yet, for all it achieved, the League might as well never have met, passed no resolutions, set up no committees, heard no speeches, decided on no sanctions. It is a depressing story; and in the end marginal to the story of the Italo-Ethiopian conflict.

The little powers had no desire at all to be dragged into a European conflict. The Belgians, for instance, were on the side of the League, of France, and England. They were pleased with their important new position as advisers in Ethiopia. But on the other hand the daughter of their King had married Italy's Crown Prince. It was all most awkward. While there was a fence they wanted to go on sitting on it. But for how long would there be a fence available? Nervously in January 1935 Belgium's ambassadors took soundings throughout Europe. From Rome Prince Albert de Ligne reported that the Italians, at least for the moment, did not want a real colonial war. On the other hand they had never forgotten Adowa. 'C'est là', wrote the Prince, 'un mot que l'étranger doit bannir de son vocabulaire en Italie, à peu près au même titre que Caporetto.' But it was a name that was echoing all round Europe. In Berlin a high official told the Baron Kerchove de Dantighem that 'Mussolini n'a jamais oublié Adowa'. In Berlin's opinion Mussolini was preparing a blitzkrieg without a declaration of war—which would, however, be foiled by a British intervention from Egypt. In Stockholm, according to the Baron Villefagne de Sorinnes, the feeling was that though the Italians did not want war, France had given them scope.

On 12 February, Italy announced the mobilization of two divisions, the *Gavinana* in Tuscany, and the *Peloritana* in Sicily. The news 'exploded like a bomb' in Stockholm. But the Swedes still considered war unlikely: the difficulties of a campaign and of the terrain were too great, and Ethiopia could mobilize two million men. The Germans on the other hand thought Ethiopia could be conquered but that it would need two years. In Italy itself public opinion was, reported the Prince de Ligne, still against war. From Addis Ababa, M. Janssens, solitary *roturier*, who had reported earlier that there had been talk of 'throwing the Italians in Somalia back into the sea', informed his government that 'les milieux abyssiniens sont très pessimistes. On est convaincu qu'une guerre ne peut être évitée.'

On 22 February Graziani embarked at Naples with the *Peloritana* for Somalia. That same week the *Gavinana* division sailed for Eritrea. De Bono was interviewed by Henri de Monfried in Eritrea. On the one hand he mentioned the ten million 'poor underfed brutes' of the Ethiopian Empire whom Italy must be prepared to liberate from the Amhara; on the other he expressed the hope that they would not see the catastrophe of war. It looked as if the dispute might be settled. But Mussolini made a warlike speech to the Chamber on Walwal; the deputies rose to their feet and sang the Fascist anthem 'Giovinezza'. Haile Selassie made an equally warlike speech to Ethiopia's parliament. Count Vinci, the Italian Minister in Addis Ababa, objecting to such phrases as 'criminal intention' and 'cowardly aggression', did not attend the Emperor's forty-second birthday party. Eden, the Lord Privy Seal, visited Rome and suggested Ethiopia should surrender part of the Ogaden. When Mussolini declined the offer, Britain stopped the export of arms—not only to Italy but to Ethiopia as well. The League of Nations passed resolutions, there were tripartite talks in Paris, four arbiters reported, five arbiters were appointed, Haile Selassie demanded the immediate convocation of the League. The League met and adjourned; and all the time in Ethiopia, in Eritrea, and Somalia there were increasing preparations for war.

Haile Selassie had wisely spent much of the previous year improving his army. On 15 March 1934, nine months before Walwal, a military parade had been held at Addis Ababa, on Janhoy Meda, the base of Ethiopia's fledgling air force which —with the acquisition of six more planes—numbered twelve planes in all at the outbreak of war. Haile Selassie escorted by Ras Kassa of Salale and Beghemder and Ras Mulugueta of Illubabor presented a flag to the Imperial Fitaurari Birru Wolde Gabriel for the *Mahel Safari*: it portrayed St. George slaying the dragon. He then presented a second flag to the Commander of the Guard, Balambaras Mokria depicting the Lion of Judah. Three thousand Guards paraded, with their Belgian officers. There were three battalions, three machine-gun companies, two batteries, and a squadron mounted on big horses just imported from Australia. The Belgian officers were proud of their work. The under-officers were being taught to read and write. The soldiers were fine material, well-disciplined, and within limits well-turned-out (the Emperor himself had forbidden the wearing of boots and shoes in order not to weaken their native marching powers); characterized, according to a report of the time, by the desire for instruction, a lively but quickly exhausted curiosity, an extra-ordinary ability to imitate, and an ebullient offensive spirit.

It was Haile Selassie's aim, now that he had three battalions of what amounted to a regular army in the capital, to extend the system to the provinces. On 12 September 1934 a third batch of Belgian officers arrived, led by a strong-minded major named Dothée. Dothée and two of his officers, Captain Listray and a cavalry lieutenant with the imposing name of le Chevalier de Dieudonné de Corbeek Overloo, set up a new centre at Harar. Dothée's task was to form two infantry battalions, plus extras: 1 cavalry squadron, 1 camel squadron, and 1 armoured car squadron.

Captain Motte was sent to organize a battalion for the Crown Prince at Dessie; Lt. Cambier to do the same for Ras Desta at Yirgalem in Sidamo, and three other lieutenants were reallocated to the capital of the province of Bale, Goba.

At Bale Haile Selassie had been trying a new administrative experiment, this time on the French model. Powers were split between the civil governor Dejaz Nasibu and a military gov-ernor. An even greater innovation was that the governor and his officials no longer had to live off the taxes they could collect: they were paid a salary. Only with a man as loyal as Dejaz Nasibu could Haile Selassie dare to risk such an experiment. But before the 'model province' could really become a model the crisis intervened. In Harar, after Walwal, the Emperor needed a cool head and a trusted friend. He recalled the too-warlike Dejaz Gabremariam—the province's governor—to become Minister of the Interior and replaced him with the loyal and progressive Dejaz Nasibu. To Bale he appointed Dejaz Beiene Merid, the son of an *agafari* of Menelik's, who in his turn was replaced in his remote southern province by Ras Desta's brother Dejaz Abebe Damtew. Thus the situation on the southern and eastern frontiers in 1935 was this: the Kenya frontier was held by the two sons of

Fitaurari Damtew, Abebe and Desta; Abebe governed the smaller and remoter provinces, Desta the adjoining and extended areas of Sidamo and Borana from the little capital he himself had founded, Yirgalem. Desta was married to the eldest of the Emperor's daughters by Menen, Tenagne Worq. The next province, equally large, bounded by two rivers, the Ganale Doria and the Webbi Shebelli, was ruled from Goba by another of the Emperor's sons-in-law, Beiene Merid. Thus a ring of loyal governors, generally in their forties, and clearly attached to the Court, was set up in the South. In the south too the Emperor was concentrating his military strength.

But Haile Selassie did not intend to rely on the Belgians alone. In January 1934 a Swedish military adviser had arrived to replace Dr. Kolmodin, the previous political adviser, dead of a stroke the year before. General Virgin, a discreet man, joined Colson and Maître Auberson at the Foreign Ministry. One of his first tasks was to design livery and uniforms for all the palace staff, including huntsmen. Another was to prepare for the visit of the Crown Prince and Crown Princess of Sweden in January 1935.[1] More seriously, he and the other two members of the triumvirate drew up the dossiers to present to the League, negotiated with Sir Sidney Barton on Eden's proposals, and eventually drafted plans for the deployment of forces and for guerrilla warfare.

In the summer of 1934 General Virgin and the Emperor agreed on a project for an officers' cadet school to be opened at Oletta at one of the Emperor's summer residences, about 25 miles outside the capital. Just before Christmas a military mission consisting of five Swedish officers arrived to run it. Their leader Captain Viking Tamm of the crack 6th Regiment, Svea Life Guards, had simply answered an advertisement in a Swedish newspaper: 'The Emperor of Ethiopia . . . has applied for Swedish officers as chief instructors.' As a Stockholm official explained to the worried Belgian Ambassador in February, the officers were not, unlike

[1] A visit to which Haile Selassie attached the greatest importance. He reconstructed his father's *ghebbi* to house the royal visitors, entirely remodelling it on the lines of Lord Noel-Buxton's house in Norfolk which he had visited on his 1924 tour. The furniture was imported from Waring and Gillow, and all the Guard in Addis Ababa were put to work on the building. Only days before Sweden's Crown Prince arrived was the new palace—known as the Prince's Pleasure or the Little Ghebbi—ready. When the Crown Prince Gustav Adolf left, the Emperor moved into it from Menelik's Great Ghebbi.

the Belgians, seconded officially. Therefore the Swedish government were taking no measures to protect them, or to avoid incidents involving them. He did not mention that the Swedish government were paying half their salary. In the strict sense they were less mercenaries than the Belgian officers, who were entirely on the Ethiopian payroll.

In any event the Oletta school was set up in January 1935 and solemnly inaugurated by the Emperor in mid-April. There were 120 cadets only, chosen from French-speaking pupils of the Tafari Makonnen and Menelik schools, aged 16–20. 'On average', wrote Tamm, 'more intelligent than Swedish boys of the same age', physically weak—no gym or sport at school and too much syphilis—impulsive, not shy, not gifted mechanics, unable to stand criticism, neither truthful nor puritanical nor tidy, 'very dramatic', and sometimes inclined to overestimate themselves. One of the boys was already a balambaras, and more than half were the sons of nobles. Many brought their servants with them to Oletta. 'Not the most intelligent nor the strongest but a born leader' was Kifle Nasibu, the son of Dejaz Nasibu Emmanuel, aged twenty-one. Educated in France and Egypt, he was, in Tamm's opinion, mature, relaxed, serious, an organizer—in fact an ideal head boy.

It seems difficult in retrospect to take the Cadet School seriously as an instrument for war, but the Swedish officers did, the cadets did, and later the Italians had to. There were 45 infantry cadets, plus 25 each for the engineers, the cavalry and the artillery. The course was planned for sixteen months. History interrupted the programme, no cadet passed out, and as the real officers' training only began in the second half of the course, the cadets had very little. But the very institution of a cadet school for teenagers indicates that Haile Selassie was hoping for a long period of peace. These cadets were designed eventually to replace the officers of the Guard. The Guard had been taken over as it was and polished by the Belgians. The Emperor however must have known that its officers, already long installed, would abandon only superficially their traditional ideas of warfare and of the tactics of battle. And so it was to prove. The Guard battalions, particularly the three Addis Ababa battalions, were longer trained and therefore better disciplined than the traditional Ethiopian levies; but basically they were still the Guard of Menelik's day. Had the cadets finished their course, graduated and taken over, Ethiopia would have had a small but modern army with which to confront the Italians.

As it was, Haile Selassie was forced to seek help wherever he could hire it. As the crisis grew in the early months of 1935, every train from Djibuti disgorged its quota of adventurers, journalists, frauds, and mercenaries. Despite embargoes and difficulties arms and munitions poured in. In March the German Embassy in London denied 'categorically' having offered Haile Selassie army and air force instructors, plus 300 armoured cars on credit. A Junker monoplane with a German pilot, Ludwig Weber, did arrive, though—on standby as the Emperor's personal transport.

Among the new arrivals who were to play a role was an electrical expert, a Russian officer who had served in Turkey and Egypt, Theodore Konovaloff. He seems quickly to have gained the Emperor's confidence. In July he was sent up to Tigre to inspect Ras Seyum's forces, and remained in Tigre as Ras Seyum's European adviser—and watcher.

Also from Istanbul came three Turkish officers. They were sent down to Harar to replace Dothée, the Belgian officer (who was recalled to Addis Ababa), as advisers to Dejaz Nasibu. George Steer, *The Times* correspondent, was later to describe the trio vividly: Wehib Pasha, the chief adviser, 'an elderly stout short man in off-white trousers and gym shoes . . . a romantic'; Farouk Bey, 'a tall thin man, facially a martinet', in charge of administration; and Tarik Bey, 'a black man with a short moustache . . . a pure Sudanese . . . well over fifty'. From Harar they studied the moves that had already been made in the Ogaden.

In the six weeks following the by-now world-famous 'incident' fighting had flared up at the various waterholes around Walwal. But on 1 March a local ceasefire was successfully agreed: proof, if proof were needed, of the unimportance of the Walwal affair. Both sides seem tacitly to have abandoned Walwal itself. The Italians had pulled back to Werder, the Ethiopians to Gerlogubi.

In August the Ethiopian commander Afework moved back still further from the wells of Gerlogubi to the wells of Gorrahei, a little oasis with a stone fort. Gorrahei, at the southern end of the Tug Fafan, one of those dry desert river-beds that in the Ogaden's rainy season suddenly became torrential, was the Ethiopians' main advance post manned by a garrison of 600 men.

Jijiga where the base headquarters and government of the
Ogaden were installed, lay far away, on the edge of the Ethiopian
highlands below Harar, at the other end of a tributary of the Tug
Fafan, the Tug Jerrer. In the walled city of Harar, Steer found
Dejaz Nasibu 'tall and well-built with a hard handsome face',
already planning—for lack of machine-guns—a defensive campaign. At dusty Jijiga was Fitaurari Shifferaw, 'a nice old boy'.
Between Jijiga and Gorrahei, on the Tug Jerrer and the Tug
Fafan, were two posts. The first, Dagghabur, a white-washed
town right in the middle of the Ogaden, was held by Kenyaz
Malion with 300 men—'a fine-looking tall man with a Words-
worthian stride but a more pleasant smile'. The next, the village
of Gebredar, was also held by 300 men. Finally, Steer visited the
oasis of Gorrahei where he no sooner arrived than he was put
under arrest—'with great courtesy I must admit'—by its commander, Afework.

Afework, though xenophobic, impressed all the foreigners
who met him. He was technically subordinate to Fitaurari Shifferaw, but in effect the real commander of the Ogaden, a man of
weight and force of character, of African features, energetic,
suspicious, much loved by his men, known throughout the
Ogaden since his capture of some Italians in the recent skirmishes, and, a rarer quality in Ethiopia, an administrator of talent.

The Italians, only too aware of the threat posed by Afework,
had offered Hussein Ali of the Rer Naib, leader of an irregular
banda also six hundred strong, machine-guns and 'perhaps a tank'
if he would occupy the oasis of Gorrahei and the Mullah's fort.
But neither Hussein Ali nor the Italians had in fact appeared.
There was, technically, peace in the Ogaden. Afework, though,
was digging his 600 men in, and had set up his Oerlikon anti-
aircraft gun and his two machine-guns by the Mullah's stone fort,
the *Garesa*, at the centre of his position.

Released, Steer moved on to the two 'frontier' posts. At Tafere
Ketema on the Webbi Shebelli 500 Ethiopians under the Nagradas
Basha, 'a stout man who was always in need of advice', were
facing the Italian fort of Mustahil held by 700 *Dubats* and two
white officers, with a 15-pounder cannon and a wireless. Gerlogubi itself was held by Balambaras Tafere plus 300 men left by
Afework. A few miles away at Werder were 3,000 *Dubats* and
fifty Italian officers. In between the scattered Ethiopian posts the
Somali clans, nominally loyal, wandered.

This was the position in the Ogaden a few weeks before war broke out. It was a shifting situation where war was to be largely a matter of manœuvre, fought as if on a chequer board, by moves from square to square, from waterhole to river to well, and where numbers were, because of the difficulties of food and water, often more of a hindrance than a help.

As Steer returned to Harar, he passed reinforcements moving down to Gorrahei: one of the two Guards Battalions at Harar, with its Commander, Fitaurari Simu. In Harar itself a thousand men of the Dejaz Hapte Mikael from a remote southern province were passing through to Jijiga. The Empire, slowly and rather ponderously, was beginning to mobilize.

On the Italian side an enormous camp was being built around Mogadishu where Graziani installed himself with the Governor, Maurizio Rava. Graziani's feelings were mixed. On the one hand he was happy to have an active command again; he had been dismissed from Libya by Balbo and had spent two inactive years on garrison duties in northern Italy. On the other hand, as Italy's best-known colonial general he was aggrieved at being put in charge of the second and minor front, with strict orders to stay on the defensive and hold Somalia at all costs. To a man of his vanity it seemed, inevitably, a plot to ruin his reputation. If he were to obey orders when war broke out, he would be blamed by Italian public opinion for inactivity. If he were to advance, he would be blamed by higher authority for disobeying orders. He himself blamed not De Bono, towards whom he had always had 'the feelings almost of a son', but the Italian General Staff—by implication Badoglio, his second Governor in Libya.

On his own initiative, therefore, using money from the Colonial Ministry, and without informing the Ministry of War, he began buying lorries and 'caterpillar' diesels directly from the United States, and importing petrol from South Africa, India, even Japan, in preparation for a possible offensive. He was soon reinforced by another division formed in Libya and commanded by General Nasi: 870 Italian officers and NCOs plus 8,000 askaris, mostly Eritreans with a sprinkling of Yemenis and Libyans. These, unlike the young Sicilians of the *Peloritana*, were experienced fighting troops.

Two divisions, then, were in position on Italy's southern front—plus of course the roving frontier and irregular *bande*, and plus also the regular troops of Somalia, the six Arab-Somali battalions commanded by Colonel Frusci. It was reckoned to be enough at any rate to hold the Ethiopians if, as Italian reports said, the Ethiopian plan was to pin the Italians down in the north and invade Somalia. The Italian Consul at Harar, Giardini, was much more optimistic: within two weeks of war being declared, he was boasting openly, the Italian armies would be in that city.

It was in the north that the Italians were assembling what was to be the largest expeditionary force ever brought together for a colonial campaign. In the spring and summer of 1935 tens of thousands of officers and men sailed from Italy through the Suez Canal to Massawa. All over the Mediterranean there was feverish buying of supplies. Italian officers crossed over via Kassala into the Sudan and amazed the British District Commissioners by their camel-buying methods: if the camels' withers touched a yardstick, then the camels were bought. In Aden, Egypt, and Kenya Italian agents were buying up mule fodder and placing orders for khaki-drill uniforms.

In Eritrea itself the native battalions were raised to their full strength and formed into two highly efficient divisions—the 1st and 2nd Eritreans—under the overall command of General Pirzio-Biroli. The *bande* were assembled—the *Banda* Scimenzana, the *Banda* Seraie, the *Banda* Altopiano and the rest. Balbo was ordered to send down one Libyan battalion and a group of Libyan volunteers. But the great mass of the troops were Italians: young men of the 1911 class called up for two years in the regular army, and Blackshirt 'volunteers'.

General Villa Santa's *Gavinana* division was followed in February by the '1st *Gruppo* Blackshirt Battalions of Eritrea' (motto: 'The Life of Heroes Begins after Death') commanded by Consul General Filippo Diamanti, with Chaplain the Centurion Father Reginaldo Giuliani in attendance. But it was not till the autumn that the Blackshirt Legions really started pouring in. Five Divisions of Blackshirts were formed, each named after a famous date in Fascist history: the '23rd March'—also known as the 'Implacable'—the '28th October', the '21st April', the '3rd January', and the '1st February'.

The regular army balanced, division for division, the Blackshirts. After the *Gavinana* came General Somma's *Sabauda* Division, and then the *Gran Sasso*, the *Sila*, the *Assietta*, and the

Cosseria. Independent battalions were sent to represent the *Alpini*, the Savoy Grenadiers, and the Frontier guard. A little later two more Divisions arrived. The crack *Valpusteria Alpini* of the regular army sailed into Eritrea, while the *Tevere* Blackshirt Division was sent down to join Graziani's forces in Somalia. The *Tevere* was probably Europe's strangest military unit. It comprised one Legion of veterans from the pre-1900 years of Italy's first colonial adventures, one Legion of 'war-wounded' from the Great War, D'Annunzio's Fiume adventure, or 'in the Fascist cause' (this last category included 179 ex-*squadristi* who had taken part in the March on Rome), and one Legion of Italians living abroad—recruits came from places as far apart as South America and Australia. It also included a juvenile battalion of university students known as *I Goliardi*, fifteen hundred strong, members of the university militia. It was not so much an expeditionary force as a representative parade of Fascist Italy in uniform.

There was scarcely a well-known Fascist leader who did not appear in Eritrea. The older came on tours of inspection, the younger joined one or other of the services. The aviation was the most popular; two sons of Mussolini, Bruno and Vittorio, and Galeazzo Ciano, Mussolini's son-in-law, flew Caproni bombers in a squadron named *La Disperata*. Marinetti, the Futurist poet, joined the air force too; and so did Farinacci and Muti, 'Gin of the Green Eyes', a former and a future secretary-general of the Party. The current secretary-general, Achille Starace, was given command of a special motorized column. The '1st February' Blackshirt Division was commanded, not as was normal by a regular army officer with a Blackshirt Consul-General as second-in-command, but by the actual Commandant of the *Milizia*, the Minister Attilio Teruzzi, with a regular army officer as second-in-command. The House of Savoy was represented by two younger brothers of the Prince of Udine, who had attended Haile Selassie's Coronation, both regular cavalry officers: Filiberto Ludovico, Duke of Pistoia, commanding the Blackshirts of the '23rd March' Division and Adalberto Duke of Bergamo, second-in-command of the regular Division 'Gran Sasso'.[1]

---

[1] Filiberto di Savoia, fanatically pro-Mussolini, used to have sweets embossed with his family crest distributed every day. Despite a reputation for effeminacy he led his troops from the front, almost in Ethiopian style.

Two hundred special correspondents from Italy and forty from abroad ensured publicity for this great gathering. Henri de Monfreid, whose immensely popular novels had made the Red Sea so famous in France, represented *Le Petit Soir*; and Raoul Salan, under a false name, *Le Temps* and the *Deuxième Bureau*. Captain Von Strunk, a German Staff Officer, was sent by the *Völkischer Beobachter*; General Fuller represented the *Morning Post*, and Herbert Matthews the *New York Times*.

All this needed a monstrous effort of organization. The docks at Massawa had to be rebuilt, camps constructed, supply dumps and bases built up, and above all roads constructed. The Black-shirt legionaries were allotted most of these tasks; it was hardly the glory which they had come out for, but morale was high. They were in any case better paid and better fed than the regular troops, though even the regulars were paid in a day as much as an Italian peasant could expect to earn in a week.

A million silver Maria Theresa dollars were minted in Italy (on the original press which after 1896 the Italian government had bought from the Imperial mint) and sent out to Eritrea. They were intended to be used by the Expeditionary Force to pay the peasants of the lands through which they marched. But many were handed over to the Political Office set up by De Bono under Colonel Ruggero of the *Bersaglieri*.

The purpose of the Political Office was to prepare the political terrain; or, more crudely, by a combination of bribes, promises, and threats, to win over as many Ethiopian potentates as possible to the Italian cause. The difficulty was that the alliance of one would almost automatically mean the enmity of the others, so bitterly did the lords of Tigre, where naturally the Italians concentrated their efforts, pursue their traditional rivalry.

In March the Political Office weighed the pros and cons of trying to win over Ras Seyum, only to reject the idea. Firstly 'he had never been a warrior'; secondly he was on suspiciously good terms with the British at Kassala and Khartoum; thirdly 'his will never be a true, real absolute dedication but a constant veering between treachery and trickiness, as was the case with his father Ras Mangasha.' It was decided that if Ras Seyum should approach the Italians, the policy would be 'to play him, not to reject him'. Instead, some of his sub-chiefs could be corrupted with promises of money and possessions, though with others, in particular with the Wagshum Kebbede of Wag and the Nevraid Aregai of Axum, it would be necessary to move very carefully.

The Italians were not approached by Ras Seyum. But they were approached in May, by Haile Selassie Gugsa of Makalle. After the death of his young wife, Princess Zenabe Worq, Haile Selassie Gugsa had become increasingly discontented. Even when on 11 May his territories were increased by Imperial decree, he ruled an area less extensive than that previously governed by his father Ras Gugsa Araya. While still in Addis Ababa, he paid a friendly visit to the Italian Minister, Count Vinci. Back in Tigre he visited Asmara where on 28 May he assured the Governor of Eritrea, Gasperini, of his desire for an alliance with Italy. It needed little brains, he said, to understand the tyrant Haile Selassie's plans for Tigre, his aim being to stir up a quarrel between himself, Ras Seyum and the Shum Agame, Dejaz Kassa Sebhat, in order to have a pretext to impose a Shoan ruler.

Three days later Haile Selassie Gugsa put forward a precise plan. The Italians should invade now while Ras Seyum was absent in the capital, and move down to Quoram on the borders of his own territory, which 'can be defended with stones alone'. This would be 'the spark that would set all Ethiopia aflame'. The Emperor's only way of escaping death would be to flee by aeroplane, 'and enjoy in Europe the wealth which he has dishonestly accumulated and deposited in European banks'. At Quoram the Italians would be defended by a double screen: the malaria of the surrounding lowlands, and 'my Azebo Galla'. If operations had to be delayed till October, he would himself attack Adowa and kill Ras Seyum. Italy should meanwhile move troops forward to face Ayalew Birru and Wondossen Kassa in Beghemder.

Haile Selassie Gugsa added his estimate of the balance of power in the North. He himself could raise 30,000 men, half with rifles, plus one cannon and 14 machine-guns. Ras Seyum only had 5,000 real followers. Ayalew Birru (whose son was married to Haile Selassie Gugsa's sister) might support a revolt against the Emperor out of both personal ambition and disgust at not having been created a Ras. Wondossen Kassa in northern Beghemder had only his 'soft and unwarlike Amhara' to pit against the 'fierce and bellicose warriors of Tigre'. The same was true of Ras Imru of Gojjam.

The Italians found this enthusiasm almost embarrassing. Haile Selassie Gugsa was only twenty-seven years old; and although cunning, seemed already to be following in his father's footsteps as far as drink and debauchery were concerned. De Bono was later to put him down as 'of much less intelligence and influence than his father'—but that was after the event.

As it was, Gasperini sent him away with a million lire, a plea for discretion, and the promise of two Eritrean 'deserters' to teach him Italian and of an Italian engineer to survey Quoram. He would be called upon when the moment came. He was, the Italians felt, 'loyal' to Italy. Like his father he coveted Ras Seyum's territory. What was to be done with him eventually? Possibly he should be made Negus of Tigre?

The Emperor, inevitably, learnt of this treachery. Wodajo Ali, the Crown Prince's tutor and adviser at Dessie, visited the Ethiopian Consulate in Asmara and flew to the capital in mid-September with copies of bank receipts of the money paid to Haile Selassie Gugsa by the Italians. But the Emperor refused to take it seriously. 'Most of my chiefs', he is reported to have said, 'take money from the Italians. It is bribery without corruption. They pocket Italian money and remain steadfast to Ethiopia.' It was one of Haile Selassie's few errors as a judge of men.

By mid-September, however, the Emperor had other, more serious preoccupations. Events were rapidly moving to a head. Meanwhile, however, the formalities were preserved. On 3 September a memorial service for Queen Astrid of the Belgians was held in Addis Ababa. For the last time the diplomatic corps assembled in full strength. Ras Mulugueta and Count Vinci exchanged greetings. Janssens reported that the Emperor's rifle-bearer was now always by his side.

On 4 September the League reconvened to study 'the threat of war'; a committee of five was appointed. On 6 September Janssens told Blattengueta Herouy that the Belgian Military Mission would be withdrawn in case of war; five officers might however remain to organize a police force (this was Sir Sidney Barton's idea) provided France, Britain and Italy agreed. On 9 September Haile Selassie sent a note to the League offering concessions to Italy and the adjustment of frontiers. On 11 September, Sir Samuel Hoare, Britain's Foreign Secretary, made a strong speech in Geneva warning that aggression would be met with force; Laval, more moderately, supported him. Sylvia Pankhurst cabled her congratulations. On 13 September the Home Fleet was mobilized and sent to the Mediterranean. The Italian Fleet moved out to the Dodecanese and up to La Spezia. Europe trembled on the brink of war. On 15 September ten Belgian ex-officers recruited directly by the Ethiopian Minister in Paris arrived at the railway station in Addis Ababa to be greeted by Tasfai Tagagne, director-general of the Foreign Ministry, and by hordes of excited journalists.[1] On 18 September the committee of five reported to the League suggesting rectifications of frontiers and a virtual economic protectorate of Ethiopia. On 21 September Rome declared the committee's report 'unacceptable'. On 25 September Haile Selassie asked that neutral observers should be stationed on Ethiopia's frontiers, and the Foreign Office instructed Sir Sidney Barton to tergiversate. On 26 September the League set up a committee of fifteen. On 27 September the great feast of Maskal that marks the end of the rains was celebrated all over Ethiopia. At Adowa Ras Seyum's troops, armed with new Mausers and machine-guns, paraded. At Addis Ababa the King's Maskal was celebrated with the traditional Dance of the Priests and boasting ceremonies of the warriors.

Ras Mulugueta, now Minister of War in place of the disgraced Fitaurari Birru Wolde Gabriel, dressed in the finery and lion's mane of the traditional warrior lord, used the traditional licence of the day to give the Emperor some frank and open advice. 'Janhoy', he proclaimed, 'you take too much notice of foreigners and their worries. This is foolish and against tradition. Rely on your own countrymen!'

On 28 September Haile Selassie gave a farewell audience to General Virgin, who had been suffering like his predecessor from altitude sickness. Next day the Emperor showed himself to

---

[1] They wore khaki and decorations but no Belgian army flashes, Janssens noted. Van Zeeland, the Belgian Foreign Minister, outwitted by Haile Selassie in this unexpected way, reacted furiously: they were at once to be sent back to Belgium, he demanded, and to leave from Djibuti not later than 30 September. His demands were, naturally, ignored.

These mercenaries, led by a fifty-three-year-old Colonel, called themselves the Unofficial Belgian Mission. Major Dothée complained that their members did not salute him. Colonel Reul retorted that he himself had not been saluted at the station by Dothée's officers. 'Les annales militaires de la camaraderie ne comportent aucun exemple de ce genre.'

wildly enthusiastic Shoan levies, but still delayed issuing the order for mobilization. On 30 September Ras Seyum gave a dinner in his *ghebbi* at Adowa; his own 'adviser', the White Russian Theodore Konovaloff attended, also Dr. Franca, the Italian Consul at Adowa, and the old Dejaz Gabremedhin, the Shum Tembien.

On 1 October *banda* from Eritrea occupied Moussa Ali, a mountain in Danakil territory just inside Ethiopian territory. Sultan Mohammed Yayo of Aussa had no way of informing Addis Ababa, but a French plane from Djibuti spotted the incursion, and M. Bodard, the French Minister at Addis Ababa, took the news to the palace. Dr. Franca left his Consulate at Adowa early that morning, burning his papers, but was arrested near the frontier by Kenyaz Abbai Kassa. In the evening, Haile Selassie sent orders for his release and promoted Abbai Kassa to Fitaurari. On 2 October the Emperor spent much of the day in prayer at the Church of Mariam on Mount Entotto. At eleven the courtyard of the Ghebbi was thronged with soldiers. Four servants carried in the *Negaret* of the Negus Negusti; two jet-black flag-bearers stood on either side as a fifth servant struck it repeatedly with a wooden staff. And when the Ligaba Tassa had finished reading out the Imperial *Awaj* proclaiming mobilization, thousands of waving swords flashed above the heads of thousands of yelling swordsmen. That night at 9 p.m. the church bells were rung all through Italian Eritrea: the gaily sinister sounds of Christian nations at war.

CHAPTER 5

INVASION

In the early hours of 3 October a hundred thousand Italian troops crossed the frontier. Yet the first stage of this particular invasion was surprisingly peaceful, almost idyllic. Under the mild aegis of De Bono it was a most traditional affair. Irregular skirmishers on horse and foot cleared the way as long columns of infantry and mules trailed behind. Behind them in their turn followed the road-builders and the lorries. A hundred thousand men did not goose-step across the frontier like a single man. They wended their way slowly forward in three columns.

On the right General Maravigna's Second Corps headed directly for Adowa. On the left General Santini's First Corps followed the so-called 'Imperial Road', the track that led south across the frontier to Makalle, Dessie, and eventually Addis Ababa. Their immediate objective was Adigrat. In the centre General Pirzio-Biroli's Eritrean Corps advanced towards Entic-cio, the mountain base where Baratieri's troops had camped for weeks before moving down upon Adowa. 'We have been patient for forty years,' announced Mussolini to the vast excited crowds that filled Piazza Venezia. 'Now we too want our place in the sun.'

Four days later Adowa, Enticcio, and Adigrat had been occupied by three columns—without battle and almost without incident. As the invading forces crossed the Mareb, the nine planes of *La Disperata* had taken off and dropped their bombs and leaflets on Ras Seyum's capital. Fourteen people and many cows were killed. Ras Seyum, Abba Isaac, the Bishop of Tigre, and the Ras's men moved out to caves in the mountains near by. Next day a few hundred men under Dejaz Sahle skirmished with the vanguard of Second Corps. Proudly the Dejaz brought back to Ras Seyum the uniform of Lt. Morgantini of the *Banda Serae*, the first Italian officer to be killed in the war and the only Italian officer to die in the actual invasion. No other fighting occurred.

As General Villa Santa, commander of the *Gavinana* Division, rode into the hovels of Adowa on 6 October, Ras Seyum dispatched his war-leaders east and west, and decided himself to fall back on the Tembien mountain range one week's march away.

The Italian troops advancing into 'hostile' territory, fraternizing with the Tigreans, singing gaily and interminably their favourite song 'Faccetta Nera', were pleasantly surprised by the lack of resistance. De Bono and the Italian commanders were less surprised. As early as July they had learnt from their informers that Ras Seyum had planned to abandon Adowa and then encircle them. They knew too that Haile Selassie had issued strict orders to the lords of Tigre not to resist the Italian advance: his purpose was to show the world who was the aggressor. It was more amazing that his orders had been so nearly followed.

So Adowa fell, and General Santini rehoisted the flag that he had seen hauled down as a lieutenant. Even though the Italian press could hardly boast a great military victory, the stain of the great disaster suffered forty years before was to some extent erased, honour vindicated, and defeat avenged. The priors of the six convents of Adowa submitted a few days later. The Cathedral Chapter of Axum, less the Nevraid, came to offer their respects, and on 15 October De Bono entered on horseback amid polite ululations the holy city of Axum, seat of the Queen of Sheba and the descendants of Solomon. On the western flank it was a happy and triumphant time.

On the far eastern flank, though, there had been an unexpected hold-up. The Italian armoured column which on 2 October had taken Mt. Moussa Ali set out boldly across the low-lying Danakil desert towards Sardò and the Awash valley. On the first day, only twenty-two miles out, the little Fiat-Ansaldo tanks hotted up to 120 degrees. On the following day the tanks and their crews collapsed completely.'

It was, however, on the eastern prong of the main advance that a really worrying delay occurred. The First Corps had admittedly occupied Adigrat without resistance. But this was just a stage in the first bound that was to lead them to Makalle, the capital of eastern Tigre and to Haile Selassie Gugsa.

If all had gone according to plan, there would have been at Adigrat a message from Haile Selassie Gugsa to announce that he had declared for Italy and that the road to Makalle lay open. Instead, on 8 October, came a frantic appeal from the young Ras for Italian help to fend off Dejaz Haile Kebbede of Wag and seven thousand of his men. There was no second messenger. Three days later Haile Selassie Gugsa himself appeared at Adigrat with only 1,200 men instead of the tens of thousands he had promised. Santini found him 'uncertain and fearful' and though Rome received the news well, swelling his troops in press reports to ten times their number, something had clearly gone very awry. Santini should have been with Haile Selassie Gugsa forward in Makalle. Instead Haile Selassie Gugsa was with Santini back in Adigrat. The spark that was to have set the Empire aflame with revolt had damply fizzled out. A half-furious, half-alarmed Mussolini immediately decided to send Badoglio and his under-secretary at the Colonial Ministry, Lessona, out on a 'tour of inspection'.

Back in the safety of Asmara, Haile Selassie Gugsa was given a smart uniform with red-striped trousers and high-laced boots and appointed Governor of all Tigre, which De Bono had rather prematurely annexed. Though the Italians in their disappointment were to treat the princeling-traitor with barely concealed contempt, his defection was a serious blow for the Ethiopian cause. As news of it spread, the Ethiopian peasants wondered and the Ethiopian lords looked with suspicion at their fellow peers, calculating who would be the next to change sides. At the time of Adowa the Italian invasion had caused the only Italian-supported rebels, Ras Sebhat and his men, to rally, patriotically, to the Emperor. This time the opposite had occurred.

Yet, as it happened, this was the first and last open defection to the Italians of an important noble and his men. There were in the following months to be revolts and plots, but never, till defeat, an open changing of sides. The Italians, deceived by the known rivalries, had under-estimated the inner cohesion of Ethiopia's ruling class when threatened by outsiders.

Badoglio and Lessona arrived at Massawa on 17 October, exactly a fortnight after the invasion had been launched, to find the Italian armies still halted on the Adowa–Enticcio–Adigrat line. Technically the object of their ten-day tour was 'to study the possibilities of operations towards the Sudan'. Relations with England were tense, sanctions were about to be imposed, and there was fear that the British would, illegally, close the Suez Canal, thereby cutting off Italy's expeditionary force and almost inevitably precipitating at least a local colonial war between the European powers.

But there were undertones to the tour which posed a more immediate threat to De Bono. The usual bitter and unsavoury personal intrigues which lay concealed under the apparently smooth surface of the Fascist hierarchy, and which were years later to break out and destroy the whole edifice, smouldered viciously away.

De Bono knew of course that his appointment had been controversial. He was already verging on seventy, more a figure of fun than respect to his soldiers and young officers, whom he would address as *Figlioli*, and hardly the dynamic conqueror of a new Empire. His plans were to advance by slow and easy stages, building roads and supply-bases before each new bound, winning territory by threats and promises where possible, treating the native population well, fighting only when fighting was unavoidable. 'Go out to Ethiopia', Mussolini had said ten months earlier, 'with an olive branch in your cap'. De Bono was almost the ideal leader for the slow and peaceful conquest of an Empire. But unfortunately for De Bono, and perhaps for Ethiopia too, Italy did not have time of the sort De Bono had mentioned—two or three years. Where Badoglio and Lessona toured the front, they were greeted with cries of 'Long live the General! We want to make war!'

When Badoglio returned to Italy, he submitted a long written report to Mussolini. Santini's First Corps he found most satisfactory, and its commanders full of decision. Maravigna was, in his opinion, too keen on winning medals; and Second Corps's mules were in bad shape. As for the Eritrean Corps, it was the best of the lot. Pirzio Biroli was 'extraordinarily popular with everyone, very active and a master of tactics'—'a hell of a swell egg' in the more informal expression of Mortimer Durand, an American journalist attached to the Expeditionary Corps.

Only at the end of his report did Badoglio turn to the vital question, the question of the commander. He judged De Bono to be suffering from a bad case of what he tactfully called 'Eritrean psychology'—any open reference to Adowa was still, it seems, anathema in all circumstances—and to be avoiding battle. He contrasted De Bono, 'a tired, almost totally exhausted man' with the 'energetic, highly active' Baldissera, the Governor who replaced Baratieri after Adowa and under whom Badoglio had served forty years before.

As the armies paused, cables flew between Asmara and Rome. On 20 October Mussolini cabled 'We will have no complications in Europe till the British elections in mid-November.[1] But by that date all Tigre up to and beyond Makalle must be in our hands . . . with the ending of the arms embargo time is working against us.'

On 2 November, under pressure to advance, De Bono moved his headquarters forward to Adigrat. On 3 November Pirzio-Biroli's Eritreans and Santini's First Corps advanced to meet a few miles north of Makalle. On the 8th the Italians were in sight of the town. Haile Selassie Gugsa's men raised the cry 'Makalle, Makalle'. There was no resistance. It seems that Dejaz Haile Kebbede had sacked the town—the *Ghebbi* constructed by the Italian Negretti for the Emperor Johannes was in ruins—and then the Army of Wag had fallen back into the interior. Santini and Haile Selassie Gugsa entered the town together.

There were headlines in the Italian press, and articles recalling 'the desperate resistance of Galliano' at the time of the Adowa campaign. Whereas the press remembered Galliano, Mussolini, his imagination always a bound ahead, remembered Toselli.[2] On 11 November he cabled De Bono 'to continue the march to Amba Alagi without delay'. De Bono cabled back the same day: 'Apart sorrowful historical memory which in my opinion needs no vengeance, position of Amba Alagi has no strategic importance and is tactically useless since can be turned on all sides.' It was De Bono's last cable as commander of the Italian Expeditionary Force.

Meanwhile the first serious fighting was about to occur on the left flank of the main Italian thrust. Two native battalions and the Libyan battalion sent by Balbo had been detached to form the 'Eastern Lowlands Column'. With three *bande* this formed a column 2,500 strong that moved forward on 3 November

---

[1] Mussolini feared that the Labour Party, more belligerent and anti-Italian than Baldwin's National Government, might sweep into power and, at the very least, close the Suez Canal [see below p. 67].

[2] Just before the Adowa campaign Captain Toselli and a handful of Italians had been overrun by the hordes of the Imperial Fitaurari at Amba Alagi after a heroic last stand. Major Galliano had subsequently escaped, much less heroically, from Makalle—only to be killed at Adowa.

through the Danakil desert to protect the flank of Santini's corps as it advanced from Adigrat to Makalle.

The column was commanded by General Oreste Marriotti. One of the thirty-odd Italian officers with him was a young lieutenant-colonel, Raimondo Lorenzini, who would later become Italian Ethiopia's most famous soldier. Thirty camels carried four mountain pack-guns, four chests containing 10,000 Maria Theresa dollars, and 10,000 rifles to be distributed to a group of Danakil whom the Political Office expected to join the column before they reached the wells of Elefan.

For three-and-a-half days they marched across the salt plains, trying to trace the route from their inaccurate maps, setting up the pack-guns and mounting sentinels at night. It was only after they reached Elefan that any Danakil appeared and then a mere 200. They trekked slowly forward to Damalle and Au; at Au the local chiefs coming in to submit informed them that the Shum Agame, Dejaz Kassa Sebhat, with 400 trained men and 100 regulars was preparing to attack them. Marriotti dispatched a letter to Dejaz Kassa, reminding him of the long friendship between the Italians and his father Ras Sebhat. There was no reply.

At dawn on 12 November, Marriotti's column, already behind-hand (for Makalle—as they knew by wireless—had been occupied four days earlier) left Au. Four hours later they reached a small gorge half a mile long, the dry bed of the Enda river.

For three long hours more they toiled up through the gorge in the great heat. Their flank guards, the *Banda Massawa*, were only thirty yards up the mountainside on either side of the winding column. On the left flank there were clear bird-calls, two notes, insistently repeated. The column straggled. The advance guard, of 200 Danakils under Colonel Belly, was almost at the far end of the gorge, and the supply column and rearguard still had not entered it. Marriotti in the centre, suddenly unquiet, sent a runner forward to halt the van and a runner back to order up the guns.

As the camels came forward and the battery was being unloaded and set up to cover the ridge in front, the Ethiopian ambush was sprung. Firing broke out from three sides. The artillery officer fell with a bullet in his ankle, twenty-three of the camels were killed, and an entire gun crew was wiped out. Colonel Belly, a sixty-two-year-old veteran, wounded in the hand and knee, led a charge up the ridge in front. But five machine-guns were playing on the column, and the charge was halted. For a few minutes it looked as if even the Eritrean askaris would break and run. They were rallied by their lion-skin-clad NCOs.

Firing continued spasmodically all day. But even worse than the firing were the mocking notes of the Ethiopian trumpeters. On a distant hill-top Dejaz Kassa Sebhat with his staff and his field-glasses could be seen directing the battle. Twice a recce plane flew over but saw nothing. The 26th Colonial Battalion tried a flank attack from the rear but was pinned down.

As night fell, the situation seemed almost hopeless. The Italian troops slept where they had gone to ground—no fires, no smoking, no shots. Radio contact with base had been lost. Just before dawn Marriotti sent a small band of scouts up the hillside in single file in a desperate attempt to gain the heights before another day brought destruction. They found, to their joyful amazement, that the Ethiopians had vanished in the night; and the chance, the near certainty, of annihilating an Italian column had vanished with them. Four days later the starving column limped into Makalle—having watched during those four days aeroplanes dropping supplies half a day's march behind them.

Meanwhile, on 14 November, the British General Election had been held, and by 17 November Mussolini had had time to digest the result and the reports from his various embassies in Europe. In a sense the result were a relief. The Labour Party, which was ready to close the Suez Canal and go to war, had won only 184 seats, and the National Government under Baldwin was returned to power with 430 seats. But it was only the lesser of two evils. Baldwin had campaigned on the slogan of 'All sanctions short of war', and on 18 November sanctions, which had been voted a month earlier by the League of Nations, were imposed. The 19th of November was proclaimed a Black Day in Italy. The Italian people, embittered by their sudden status as Europe's outcasts, which they neither understood nor felt they deserved, united in sullen resentment and wounded pride around their leader. Their leader, embittered by the failure of French promises—Laval had told Chambrun that he would be forced to support the British at Geneva—needed, and needed urgently, a quick advance and if possible a quick victory.

This was all the more urgent because oil sanctions had not yet been imposed. Mussolini had made it clear that oil sanctions, the only sanctions that could literally bring his invasion grinding to a halt, would be viewed by Italy as a *casus belli*. The powers had hesitated, unwilling to call what might not be a bluff. But from all sides pressure was mounting on the politicians. Oil sanctions were due to be debated at Geneva on 12 December, and it seemed likely that Britain's favourite young politician, Anthony Eden, now Minister of League Affairs, would press for their imposition. If oil sanctions were voted and imposed, Italy would probably have to accept a peace based on the ceasefire line—wherever that might then be.

It was therefore in Mussolini's eyes vital to gain as much territory as possible by 12 December. De Bono would not, even when prodded, advance, and De Bono therefore had to be replaced. Of the generals available the Chief of the General Staff was the obvious choice. He had visited the ground, studied the troops, had his hands on the reins of the organization, and above all knew Mussolini's mind. Badoglio sailed out from Italy again barely a fortnight after he had sailed back from Massawa.

De Bono had returned from Makalle on the 17th to find *Telegrama di Stato* 13181 awaiting him. It announced that with the fall of Makalle his 'Mission' had been completed and that Mussolini greeted him with unchanged cordiality. 'I replied at once,' he wrote. 'Among other things I said in my telegram that my recall was in any event a pleasant surprise. But that was a huge lie.' Next day he learnt that he had been named a Marshal of Italy. On 26 November he went to meet Badoglio on his arrival at Massawa, and passed out of the history of Ethiopia, and indeed almost out of the history of Italy till his fatal vote against Mussolini at the Grand Council of Fascism on the night of 8 September, nine years later.

On the southern front, there had been no solid advance but a series of skirmishes and one major event: the death of Afework. Two days after war was declared the Italians attacked Gerlogubi near Walwal and the Ethiopian post of Dolo down by the Kenyan border. At Gerlogubi, a desert crossroads used by the Rer Ibrahim, the Mijurtin, and four other clans, the Italians lost ten men, and Balambaras Tefere twice as many before he fell back on Gorrahei. At Dolo where the two garrisons lived side by side,

Italian emissaries crossed to warn the local commander Mukria to evacuate before hostilities began. 'I am Fitaurari', he replied, 'that is: Chief of the Advance Guard. I shall do my duty. Every square metre and every *tukul* will be defended to the last drop of our blood.' He was buried where he fell. The Italians raised a cross, and saved his wife and children.

Ten days later, they attacked the third frontier post, that of Tafere Ketemma on the Webbi Shebelli. Olol Dinke meanwhile raided north and captured Dagnerrei, where his own cousin Hamil Badel had been appointed district governor by the Emperor. Hamil Badel was taken prisoner, and offered a sumptuous tent, a fine dinner, and women. That night he was strangled on Olol Dinke's order by his own brother.

More seriously, the Italians prepared to move against Gorrahei where Afework's forces had now been joined by the second Guards battalion from Harar. There were three thousand men, with mortars and machine-guns, led by Afework, Ali Nur, Omar Samanthar, Fitaurari Baade, and by the two Guards battalion commanders, Fitauraris Simu and Kebbede.

Colonel Frusci prepared an operation on a large scale, using all his six Arabo-Somali battalions, 150 lorries, 9 tanks, and 20 armoured cars. They were not to be needed. On 2 November twenty Italian planes bombed the Mullah's stone fort. Afework was badly wounded in the hand and the leg. Two days later he lapsed into a coma. Before he died he told his men to bury him on the spot. 'Do not take me back,' he said. 'Even my body should fight the Italians.' But his men disobeyed him, for it was unthinkable that they should not give their leader Christian burial. With one of the few motor-trucks that supplied them they took his body back to the nearest burial ground, the Church of St. George at Dagghabur.

When the Italian columns setting out from Gerlogubi and Ferfer reached Gorrahei on 7 November, they found a deserted camp, huts burnt, and 500 rifles abandoned. Afework's death and the continued bombings had demoralized the whole force. Even the Guards battalions had fled, and the efforts of Fitaurari Baade to rally a few men further back were barely successful. The Italians motored forward to the village beyond Gorrahei, Gebredar, and having captured the enemy rearguard pushed on fast eighty-one miles to the north, to the junction of the Tug Fafan, now in flood, and its tributary the Tug Jerrer. There they were halted by a large and well-armed Ethiopian force; whereupon they retreated to their new bases at Gorrahei and Gebredar. The chiefs of the Rer Dalal and of the Abdallahi came in to submit—and also Abdel Krim ibn Mohammed, the only surviving son of the Mullah, with 1,000 rifles.

With a touch more dash and daring Frusci could have pushed on to Dagghabur, Jijiga, and even Harar. The Ethiopians were demoralized and disorganized, and the Somali clans were ready to take part in what was from their point of view another round, Italian-officered, of the centuries-old struggle against the Christians of Ethiopia.

Two events steadied the shaky Ethiopian position. On 11 November Colonel Maletti's column fell into an ambush. Three of his little Fiat-Ansaldo tanks were trapped and dismantled. The victor Fitaurari Gongol was himself badly wounded and taken back to Harar. It was only a half-victory—both sides ran back for thirty miles after the encounter—but nevertheless it was encouraging.

The second event was a sudden and unexpected visit by the Emperor in person. On 11 November he flew down to Jijiga and drove out at dawn to the picturesque town of Dagghabur, a town of a few thousand inhabitants that lies flat in the heart of the desert on the Tug Jerrer, dominated by its white mosque, the most important in the Ogaden. There he distributed rewards and punishments: medals for those who had captured the tanks, which were exhibited to him complete with their twin machine-guns; a wreath for the tomb of Afework, promoted posthumously to the title of Dejaz of the Ogaden; thirty lashes and two stabs of the bayonet to Fitaurari Simu, condemned to death by Nasibu for cowardice; and a flogging to the other Guards Battalion commander, Fitaurari Kebbede. Thus, having in his own fashion steadied the morale of his troops in the Ogaden, Haile Selassie flew back to his capital to consider his next move.

In the six weeks that had passed since the war had begun the Emperor had divided his attention between military and diplomatic matters. For hours on end he would preside over the *gebirs*, the traditional feasts in the banqueting hall of the Great Ghebbi where his warriors expected to be entertained as they passed through on their way north or east or south. There they would feast on raw meat, get drunk on *tej* and entertain their Emperor and their lion-maned chiefs with their dances and boasting songs. From such feasts Europeans were excluded. In order to avoid the incidents that might arise when the wilder of these levies mistook any white-skinned *ferengis* for the Italian enemy, the warriors were confined, except for their one visit to the Ghebbi, to camps on the outskirts of the city.

For much of the rest of the time the Emperor was closeted with his foreign advisers and the various diplomats, planning Ethiopia's tactics at Geneva, and resolving the thousand-and-one problems that the vast influx of foreigners had created. There were scores of impatient journalists crowding the bars complaining at the censorship imposed by a barely literate Belgian officer of the Reul group, kept in check—just—with never-fulfilled promises of visits to the front by Lorenzo Taezaz, head of the Press bureau, and fed with wildly optimistic and inaccurate accounts of Ethiopian victories in the North. There were the problems posed by Count Vinci and the Italian military attaché, Colonel Calderini, who refused to leave the Embassy for Djibuti until their last consular agent was safely in from Arussi. There were the problems of the two Belgian military missions and the policing of the city which Sir Sidney Barton, mistrusting the capabilities of the young police chief Balambaras Abebe Aregai, was continually harping upon. There were the difficulties of dealing with adventurers such as the 'Black Eagle of Harlem', Colonel Hubert Fauntleroy Julian, a would-be pilot who succeeded in crashing almost immediately one of the Ethiopians' few planes. And then there were the pleasanter tasks of apportioning the assistance that had begun to flow in. Some of the assistance was military and needed no apportioning. Sir Sidney Barton, always wary of the natives, had had his Embassy guard strengthened by two companies of the 5/14th Punjabis from Aden. Lady Barton meanwhile organized the Ethiopian ladies as bandage-makers for her medical unit. 'They, though this is *not* the custom of the country, responded splendidly', an observer noted. And the French were, as Mr. Evelyn Waugh, back again, reported, 'firmly entrenched at Diredawa; half the town was a French fort'—100 *Tirailleurs Sénégalais* had been imported from Djibuti. But most aid was medical. As the Ethiopian army had only a rudimentary medical service of its own, the various volunteer units of the Red Cross coming from Europe stepped in to fill the gap.

The volunteers were a heterogeneous lot: missionaries; a local Greek doctor, Dassios; a pair of Irish adventurers, Brophil and Hickey; a sixty-two-year-old Englishman, a Master of Fox-hounds, Major Gerald Burgoyne (who gave his age as 52); and a young Swedish stunt pilot, the black sheep of his family, Count Carl von Rosen, who flew out a two-seater plane, the first plane ever marked and recognized by the Red Cross. With such volunteers as these, Sweden, Britain, Holland, Egypt, and Finland organized their own Red Cross Units, while the Swiss doctor in overall charge tried to control the rest and appease the wounded pride of the Ethiopian Medical Corps.

It was chaotic, and the organization of mules and supplies and escorts and contacts was chaotic, but in the end the different units did set off for the different fronts. It was just another example of the difficulties and delay that struck all Europeans so strongly but which in Ethiopian eyes were normal. The Pothez fighter for instance, had no bullets, and the smaller monoplanes no spare parts. Still the Emperor had never really intended to launch Mischa Babitchev and his twelve planes against the 400 Italian bombers. They were used for carrying messages and personages from place to place, and though there were various accidents, not one of them was shot down in the air by the enemy. Communications were always shaky. There were not enough wireless sets or telephone lines, and this problem was to grow more and more serious.

Then there were the politico-administrative difficulties. What, for instance, to do with the restless young cadets of Oletta? Send them as military advisers to the Rases, as the Emperor suggested? Teenagers to advise greybeards: fortunately the scheme fell through. On 15 November Tamm suggested that a special brigade officered by the cadets should be organized. The Emperor accepted the plan, and left Tamm to work out the details with Makonnen Haptewold. It was not a satisfactory arrangement, for Tamm found the Director of Commerce 'inefficient and lazy' and guilty of 'what in Europe would be called sabotage'. Nevertheless it kept the four remaining Swedish officers and the cadets, 'Tamm's boys', busy.

Meanwhile the armies had mobilized. On 17 October Ras Mulugueta and the *Mahel Safari*, seventy-thousand strong, had jogged for four hours past the Emperor before moving out by foot along the 'Imperial Highway', the only road in the central

Empire fit for motor-traffic, that went from Addis Ababa to Dessie. From Dessie Ras Mulugueta moved slowly north, halting to burn and raze the villages and flog the chiefs of the recalcitrant Azebo and Raya Galla. In Gondar Ras Kassa had called the *chitet* and raised 160,000 men. With a third of this number he too moved north.

On the left, Ras Imru was moving up from Debra Markos, the capital of Gojjam, with 25,000 men. Dejaz Ayalew Birru had raised 10,000 mountaineers in the Wolkait and Simien and was threatening the Eritrean frontier.

Great events were impending in the North. A week after his return from the Ogaden the Emperor left for Dessie by motor-car accompanied by Colonel Reul—'très en faveur à ce moment' reported Janssens—and Captain Viseur, his secretary Wolde Giorgis, the former Minister of War, Fitaurari Birru, and followed by the three battalions of the Guard. Before leaving he appointed Dejaz Yigezu 'Deputy for overall home affairs', almost Regent, and under him Blatta Takele Wolde Hawariat, a young and extremely bright favourite of the Emperor, as Director-General of the city of Addis Ababa.

CHAPTER 6

THE ETHIOPIAN COUNTER-ATTACK

ALMOST simultaneously then, at the end of November 1935, the two rival war-leaders reached their new headquarters in the North, Dessie for Haile Selassie and Makalle for Badoglio.

Badoglio was not particularly happy with the situation he found. South at Makalle, Santini's First Corps was out on a limb. North-east at Adowa, Maravigna's Second Corps was equally isolated. Between the two, as the crow flies, lay the almost trackless mountains of the Tembien behind which Pirzio Biroli's Eritreans were loosely linking the two ends of the Italian front. It was too reminiscent of Adowa on a large scale: divisions this time, not brigades, strung out in a long line with sketchy communications between them and the Ethiopians massing in front, ready to pounce on first one and then another isolated group. For Badoglio had no doubt that the Ethiopians were massing. All the air-reconnaissance reports brought news of approaching armies. It seemed hardly the moment for the great push forward from Makalle, which would only lengthen his lines of communication and leave an even greater gap in the Italian centre through which the Ethiopians might drive. Badoglio hesitated, went on a tour of inspection, had the Tigreans of Haile Selassie Gugsa disarmed, confined all journalists to Asmara, and ordered his air force to bomb Dessie.

Dessie was bombed for the first time on 6 December. The Emperor who had installed himself in the only modern building, the Italian Consulate, was photographed personally machine-gunning the raiders, and great indignation was aroused in Europe by the bombs the Italians dropped on the American Hospital where Dr. Dassios's Red Cross units were housed. The Italian bombs could hardly have fallen at a better time or on a better place from the Ethiopian point of view. This incident and the photographs of Ethiopia's fighting Emperor help to explain the immense tide of indignation that swept Europe when only three days later the Hoare–Laval proposals were leaked by a Paris newspaper *L'Echo*.

It was not only Mussolini who was worried about the decisive oil sanctions debate due to be held on 12 December. The British and the French were equally nervous, and disinclined even to risk war with Italy. Since the Tripartite talks in Paris in August, Maurice Peterson, the Foreign Office East Africa expert, had been in touch with Comte Alexis de St. Quentin of the Quai d'Orsay. Between them they had drawn up a plan which was approved by the French and needed only the approval of the British government. At Laval's urgent request Sir Samuel Hoare, on holiday in Switzerland, came secretly to Paris. The plan was approved. Secret copies of it were sent simultaneously to Rome and Addis Ababa—the only mishap being that the following day the secrets were published in the French press and almost immediately reproduced all over the world.

Under the Hoare–Laval proposals, Ethiopia was to cede two belts of territory to Italy. These were more or less the two belts which the invading Italians then controlled: basically the Ogaden on a line east of Dagghabur, and most of Tigre apart from the holy city of Axum. But, furthermore, Italy was to have 'economic rights'—a virtual protectorate—over most of the south of the Empire excluding Illubabor and the Baro Salient. In return Ethiopia was to be allowed an outlet to the sea at Assab, and a corridor through the Danakil desert leading to it—a 'corridor for camels', as *The Times* put it.

The plan was not all that different from the numerous compromise proposals already put forward, such as those made by Eden on his June visit to Rome. But the situation, and feelings, had changed so dramatically that, when the Emperor rejected it as 'a prize offered to the aggressors', he exactly echoed what Europe was thinking. The British public were particularly indignant because it was Hoare who only a few weeks earlier had made a thumpingly warlike speech warning Italy off at Geneva. 'Rumours were rife', wrote Duff Cooper, then a backbencher, 'of the terrible strength of the Italian navy and of the "mad-dog act" to which further irritation might drive the Duce. But before the Duce had time to declare himself [i.e. on the plan] there arose a howl of indignation from the people of Britain. During my experience of politics I have never witnessed so devastating a wave of public opinion. That outburst swept Sir Samuel Hoare from office.' Amidst a flurry of cabinet meetings, leading articles, public meetings, and debates in the House of Commons, the plan was rejected and Hoare forced to resign. Laval and his Ministry fell a week or two later. Unfortunately, amidst the flurry the oil sanctions debate passed almost unnoticed. No firm decisions were taken, and it became obvious that oil sanctions would not be imposed. The Duce breathed a sigh of relief, made a rousing speech on the 'war of the poor, of the disinherited, of the proletariat'—and returned to his office to consider whom he could find to replace the dilatory Badoglio. For Badoglio was proving as slow if not slower than De Bono, covering his hesitations with cables on the great virtues, indeed necessity, of a 'strategic defensive battle'. On the other hand with the threat of oil sanctions removed, the urgent need for an advance had, from Mussolini's point of view, vanished. In any case a 'strategic defensive battle' did seem to be about to occur.

THE NORTHERN FRONT

The first of the armies to reach the north had been the army of Beghemder. In early November, Ras Kassa and his two sons Wondossen and Aberra Kassa, accompanied by Bajirond Latibelu Gabre, had swarmed up into the mountain stronghold of Amba Alagi. On 17 November marching across from the Tembien with 15,000 men Ras Seyum reached Ras Kassa's camp. He prostrated himself and kissed Ras Kassa's feet. Ras Kassa raised him, and kissed him on the cheeks.

The two leaders stayed by the great pass of Amba Alagi, the gates of central Ethiopia, and planned their strategy. The levies of Beghemder and Tigre were joined by the armies of the three small but warlike provinces that lay north of Wollo and just behind them; the forces of Wag under Dejaz Haile Kebbede, of Lasta under Fitaurari Andarge, and of Yeggiu under Dejaz Admassu Birru, Ayalew's brother.

But though the Emperor was by now in Dessie, it was not till the second week in December that the army of Ras Mulugueta at last arrived. The *Mahel Safari* camped on the right side of the mountain on Gerak Sadek, the feature that the British were later to name the Triangle. Thus the vast Ethiopian forces under the three Rases on and around the stronghold of Amba Alagi faced the sixty battalions and 350 guns which Badoglio was concentrating at Makalle some thirty miles to the north.

But it was not here that the armies were to clash. For over at the other end of the Italian front, as Ras Mulugeta's armies were moving on to the mountain, the Ethiopians struck their first blow.

Ras Imru had marched north from Gojjam with 25,000 men, a long and difficult march of over six hundred miles. By early December his column, his own Shoan troops in front and the Gojjam levies behind, were north of Gondar approaching Dabat. There on 4 December they were bombed for the first time. When the panic was over Ras Imru found that his army had been almost halved in strength. Dejaz Gessesse Belew, Lij Yasu's captor and Ras Hailu's nephew, had deserted and was heading back to Debra Markos with most of the Gojjam levies.

By now Ras Imru was in the territory of Dejaz Ayalew Birru and in touch with this chief. Ayalew Birru had been ordered to harass and if possible to invade the western Eritrean lowlands, which were guarded on the Italian side only by two native battalions and irregular *bande*. His men had been raiding up to Om Ager but Maravigna had sent his *bande* down from Adowa and Axum, and thereafter the fords of the Takazze were closely guarded. Ayalew Birru fell ill, and, in the words of a Swedish doctor flown up to look at him, 'underwent a cure, abiding his time'.

Though indeed he was no longer young and active, but a stout almost corpulent man in his fifties, Ayalew's illness verged on the diplomatic. After the fall of Makalle his son had sent a message offering to come over to the Italians. De Bono had sent a personal letter back in reply addressed not only to the son but also to the father—a letter which he considered so important that he had mentioned it *only* to the Duce. For Ayalew Birru was no callow and untried princeling. Unlike Haile Selassie Gugsa, he was a war-leader of great reputation. If he had gone over to the Italians it would have been a major triumph.

He did not go over. But he was careful not to press his attacks too hard and to restrain as far as possible his more warlike Fitauraris. Ras Imru and his leaders may not have had proof; but they suspected that they could hardly count on the 10,000 men of Ayalew Birru. It was a difficult situation for the Ras—in the territory of a doubtful ally, nearing the frontier of a superior enemy, half his army gone, his men shaken by a bombing raid, and with Dejaz Gessesse Belew hurrying back to Gojjam presumably to try and seize power there in his absence.

At this stage a Pothez flew in to Dabat, with orders from the Emperor at Dessie. Ayalew was to halt his attacks along the Setit, join his forces with those of Imru, and the two together were to march on the Takazze. Imru immediately sent off a column in broad daylight in the opposite direction, to the north-west. The ruse worked, the column was spotted and bombed by the Italians, and its direction reported. Thereupon Ayalew Birru and Imru moved north-east by night.

The valley of the Takazze marked the boundary between western Tigre, now held by the Italians, and Beghemder—a swift-flowing river in a deep gorge. At this time of year in the middle of the dry season the river was low. Just before dawn on 15 December the Ethiopians after an all-night march forded the Takazze at two places. Imru's advance guard, 2,000 strong, found their ford unguarded. Nine miles upstream, the ford at Mai Timchet, on the main Gondar–Adowa mule-track, was protected by a small stone fort. Fitaurari Shifferaw, the commander of Ayalew Birru's advance guard, crossed the river, wiped out the post in the darkness, and pressed rapidly up the mountain trail that led to the main Italian position on the pass of Dembeguina above. Shortly after dawn they met an Italian patrol riding out: the leading Ethiopians fired too early, the horsemen fled, the Ethiopians charged wildly, but Fitaurari Shifferaw, himself mounted, stopped them.

Major Criniti, commander of the *Gruppo Bande Altopiani* garrisoning the pass, called up Axum for air support and was reinforced on the ground by a squadron of light tanks. One tank was sent out to reconnoitre below the pass. The men of Fitaurari Shifferaw clamoured to be allowed to shoot it through the heart and, despite his orders to let it pass, opened fire. The tank's twin machine-guns fired back, and most of Shifferaw's men turned and ran. But Balambaras Tashemma crept round behind the tank, jumped onto it, and started hammering on the turret shouting 'Open'. The stupefied Italian gunners opened as the driver tried to reverse. With sweeping sword the Balambaras beheaded them.

Criniti's men, horrified, had watched the scene from their post above. They attempted to break out, led by nine tanks and Major Criniti on horseback. They nearly succeeded. Two thousand of Shifferaw's men immediately turned tail. 'Are you women?', yelled the Fitaurari. 'Can't you see that I am here?' He blew his war-horn. The fugitives rallied. Major Criniti was wounded and two Italian officers killed. The column retreated back into the shelter of the pass.

Now totally encircled, the Italians drove their baggage train out in a wily attempt to distract their enemy with hopes of plunder. There was a short sharp furious fight as this plan failed, and the Ethiopians pursued the confused mules back into the Italian camp, killing the wounded, looting and slaying. The Italian troops rallied on a hill, but most of their officers had been killed and they decided to surrender. They raised their hands—a gesture the Ethiopians did not understand, finding in it an unusually favourable opportunity to kill all they could.

Realizing their mistake, by now desperate, the Italians rushed downhill rallying round the almost static tanks. Fitaurari Shifferaw was killed; his eighty-year-old father Fitaurari Negash stood over his body crying 'My son!'; Shifferaw's confessor, who had followed him into the fight, called over to the father: 'I will take care of your son but you will be damned if you don't avenge his death.' The old man wiped his tears away, drew his sword, and rallied the Ethiopians who were hesitating, falling back, letting the Italians through. 'Youngsters,' he shouted, 'Shifferaw is not dead. He orders you: do not let the enemy escape. Follow me.' The Italians were overrun by their raging enemies. The lorries into which they were piling were overturned and burnt. One tank swivelled round. The Ethiopians leapt on it and killed the crew inside. Two more were overturned and burnt. Another was abandoned by its crew as they tried to cross a small river; as they leapt out, they were shot. Two more were captured, another turned over and destroyed. 'Cristos, Cristos' called the crew of one tank as they came out. They were almost the only prisoners to be taken that day. The *bande* were hiding behind overturned tanks and trees: 'Don't let these dogs escape,' cried Negash.

It was 4 o'clock in the afternoon when Imru's men, led by Fitaurari Teshegger, appeared in a cloud of dust from the west, chanting their war-songs. The two remaining tanks were captured and their crews killed. The disorganized fugitives were chased by the two columns almost at spear's length up the road that led to the town of Enda Selassie five miles away. Enda Selassie was cleared at the point of the sword, and there the Ethiopians, exhausted and victorious, halted their pursuit.

At Enda Selassie the Ethiopians were only thirty miles from Axum. As they advanced a lorried Blackshirt column and ten more tanks were sent out to counter-attack. They were ambushed two or three miles down the road. Big stones were rolled across their path. The driver of the leading tank was killed and the others jammed behind. The whole column was a sitting target. Two tanks slipped sideways and stuck. Another two had lighted torches hurled under them by Ras Imru's men and burst into flames. Two more prisoners were taken. The Italian column retreated as best it could; and next day the Ethiopians pressed on till they were only twelve miles from Axum. There on the ridge of the Shire range they took up their positions. Behind their victorious advance guards Ras Imru and Ayalew Birru's men moved massively across the Takazze into Tigre.

It had not been a very bloody battle—even the Ethiopians claimed only to have killed 500 of the enemy. But it had shown the Ethiopians that in open fight they with their swords and rifles were a match for Italian-trained troops. Italian officers had been killed. The little Italian tanks with their fifteen-degree traverse had been proved almost useless. In hand-to-hand fighting the air force could not intervene, and morale was enormously high. Only Dejaz Ayalew Birru, who had given Fitaurari Shifferaw strict orders not to advance beyond the fords, was discontented. Ras Imru was happy both with the capture of fifty machine-guns —alone of all the armies, his had had none—and of the large town of Enda Selassie which controlled the Takazze fords. He moved forward to the Shire ridge and considered a direct attack on the Axum-Adowa area. But there were thirty Italian battalions there, and 193 guns; it was too powerful a force to attack directly.

Instead, Ras Imru decided on a long, bold thrust. He sent out raiding parties, left his advance guard on the Shire ridge, with the mass of his men in the Takazze valley behind, and set out across the waterless rock desert of Adi Abo with only a few thousand men, heading for the almost-undefended supply depot of Maravigna's Second Corps at Adi Quala, in Eritrea, on the other side of the Mareb. The Mareb was no obstacle, even lower than the Takazze, a mere trickle. Badoglio, far more worried than his prosaic later account might seem to imply, gave orders for two counter-measures.

The first was conventional: an attack by 12,000 men on the Af Gaga pass that led through the Shire ridge. It was put in on 25 December. The Ethiopian vanguard numbered some 8,000. There was bitter fighting for a day and a night, both sides pulled back, and the Italian column eventually rejoined Second Corps having lost under two hundred men. If the attack had been intended as a show of strength and a diversionary thrust it was successful. But if Maravigna had hoped—as seems probable—to break through the Ethiopians on Shire and drive them back to the Takazze, it was a failure.

The other counter-measure was drastic and decisive. Ras Imru had to be halted at all costs before he invaded Eritrea, destroyed the supply depot, and cut Second Corps' lines of communication.

It was the morning of 23 December. Italian planes flew over Ras Imru's column which scattered and took cover, used by now to daily bombings. But that day strange cylinders fell from the sky, which broke as soon as they hit the ground, and gave off a colourless liquid that spread all around. When the colourless liquid touched the exposed limbs of the Ethiopians, it burnt. Several hundreds had their hands, their feet, and their faces scalded. Some were blinded. 'It was a terrifying sight,' said Ras Imru. 'I myself fled as if death was on my heels.' The effect on morale was even more terrible. The Italian pilots flew on to drop the rest of their cylinders on the Ethiopians in the Takazze valley, and Imru's damaged and demoralized troops fell back to the Shire. The first and best-led Ethiopian offensive was over, halted by the use of gas—mustard gas.

On 15 December, as Ras Imru and Ayalew Birru's men crossed the Takazze, the army of Wag attacked in the Tembien. The little town of Abbi Addi, the centre round which the battles in the Tembien were to rage, lay about half-way between Makalle and Adowa, half-way along the 150-mile-long Italian front. For most of those 150 miles the wild mountain gorges are impassable; only at the centre did the mule tracks heading north from Socota, the capital of Wag, wind through Abbi Addi and over the Warieu Pass towards the centre of Tigre.

When Ras Seyum shifted his men to Amba Alagi, the advance guard of the Eritrean Corps, Consul-General Diamanti's 1st

Blackshirt *Gruppo*, had moved forward and occupied Abbi Addi, setting up its headquarters on the precipitous heights of Worq Amba, the 'Golden Mountain' that flanked the pass to the north.

On the 15th, Dejaz Haile Kebbede led his army, now 10,000 strong, across the Gheva to recapture Abbi Addi. Their morale was high, though only one man in six had a rifle and the whole force had only two or three machine-guns. Haile Kebbede, who had been brought up at his uncle Wagshum Gwangul's court and taught, like all the nobles, to ride, to swim, and above all to shoot, told his men that as the Wagshum Gwangul had fought and won for Menelik at Adowa, so he and they would fight and win or fight and die for Haile Selassie. On the 18th the men of Wag attacked fiercely, but they were confronted with guns and tanks and on the following day with four Eritrean battalions of the I Brigade hastily pushed up by a worried Pirzio Biroli. Their attack was held. At dawn on the 22nd the Eritreans counter-attacked and captured Amba Tsellere, the mountain that over-looked the town, driving the enemy on to the plain. But then unexpectedly and inexplicably, Diamanti retreated.[1]

The army of Wag reoccupied Amba Tsellere and, moving down into the little town, prepared despite their heavy casualties (they had lost one man in ten and had no means of caring for the wounded) to attack the Pass. This was the crucial moment. Had they moved forward and captured the Pass, the whole of Tigre would have been opened up to a swarm of Ethiopian invaders. But orders reached them by runner from Ras Kassa on Amba Alagi halting them where they were. And while they halted, Badoglio reversed the movement of the Eritrean Corps which he had been concentrating at Makalle and sent battalions back to reinforce the ten already in the Tembien.

From Dessie the Emperor had been watching the development of the situation. His planning had been hampered by his lack of contact with Ras Imru and Ayalew Birru—it took four days for their runners to reach the telephones at Dabat—and with the Tembien. But he now sent orders up to the three Rases which

---

[1] 'In spite of the success of the action', wrote Badoglio, 'the commander judged it necessary to withdraw his victorious troops from Mt. Tsellere to Abbi Addi. This decision, founded on an entirely personal appreciation of the local situation did not enable us to attain from the engagement the result which the heroic conduct of the units concerned should have given us.' It was of course a Blackshirt, not a regular army, unit.

changed the whole shape of the battles to come. The armies had been concentrating on one stronghold, Amba Alagi—the prelude, it seemed, to a single enormous battle with the Italians at Makalle. But now they were spread out sideways and in depth. Ras Mulugueta and his 70,000 men were sent forward to hold the vast mountain plateau of Amba Aradam, thirty miles to the north of Amba Alagi, while Ras Kebbede with the Shoan levies of Ifrata marched up from Dessie to take over Amba Alagi. Ras Kassa, Ras Seyum with the armies of Beghemder and Tigre, plus those of Lasta and Yeggiu were ordered down into the Tembien to reinforce the decimated army of Wag.

Thus a vast encirclement threatened the Italians. On their right Adowa and Axum were threatened by Ras Imru and Dejaz Ayalew Birru. On their left Ras Mulugueta on Amba Aradam blocked any possibility of an advance south and menaced the entrenched camp at Makalle. In the centre, the most vulnerable point, Ras Kassa and Ras Seyum had by 9 January reached Abbi Addi and were building up their forces ready to thrust through and split the Italian line. If Badoglio weakened Makalle to reinforce the Tembien, Ras Mulugueta might move forward; if he pushed Maravigna forward on his right, Ras Imru would again circle round to attack his lines of communication.

Badoglio concentrated his guns, over 300 of them, back at Makalle, reinforced the Tembien with some of the troops gathered at Makalle, formed a Fourth Corps out of the newly-arrived *Cosseria* division and the '3rd February' to protect his lines of communication north of Adowa from another excursion of Ras Imru, loosed his bombers against Ras Mulugueta on Amba Aradam—and cabled Mussolini on 11 January informing him that he would have to hold up the long-promised offensive in order to face an Ethiopian attack.

In fact it was the Italians who attacked first in the Tembien, perhaps unaware that there was now not just the little army of Wag but over 100,000 Ethiopians opposing them. Pirzio Biroli's Eritreans sallied out from the Warieu Pass on the morning of 20 January, outflanking the main Ethiopian position, only to be halted by Wondossen Kassa. Next day the Eritreans attacked again, and the Blackshirts—Diamanti's four battalions reinforced by the three legions of the '28th October'—poured down from the Pass to assault the mountain slopes. To Konovaloff, who had withdrawn with Ras Seyum to watch the attack from a hill-top it seemed that the Italian tactics had barely altered since Adowa: foot-soldiers in line and in column, their officers on mules commanding the attack, pack-batteries and machine-guns supporting. There was stiff fighting in the east as there had been the day before. In the centre Diamanti's battalions managed to reach the west slopes of Debra Amba by the early afternoon. But as they fell back they were heavily attacked, and half the officers of the 2nd and 4th Blackshirt battalions were killed. The chaplain, Centurion Father Giuliani, was speared as he was giving the last sacrament. The '28th October' led the chaotic withdrawal to the Warieu Pass: yet another Blackshirt débâcle.

All next day the battle raged even more fiercely below the Warieu Pass, where the Blackshirts of General Somma's 'October 28th' wavered under the attacks of Dejaz Admassu Birru. When dusk fell, the attacks were continuing and the Blackshirts near to breaking. To Badoglio, anxiously awaiting the next radio messages at Makalle it looked as if the Pass would fall.[1] If the Pass fell and the Ethiopian armies poured through, the whole Italian front would be split wide open, Eritrea exposed, Makalle open to attack from the rear, Maravigna's Corps cut off.

That night was for the Italians the worst of the campaign. At Badoglio's staff headquarters in Makalle no one slept. Orders went out—to the Intendant General, to remove or if necessary to destroy all supply depots north of Adowa and of Makalle; to General Aimone Cat, of the air force, to bombard the Tembien with mustard gas; and to his own staff, to draw up immediate plans for evacuating Makalle, for the retreat of 70,000 men and 14,000 animals. Those who saw the General said that they had never seen a man so obviously worried and so close to almost irrational panic as Badoglio that night.

By dawn, much to Badoglio's relief, the radio brought better news. The Blackshirts had held through the night, and a relief column of real soldiers, Vaccarisi's 2nd Eritrean Division, was arriving. All day Ras Kassa pressed his attacks but by the evening of the 23rd the Ethiopians were withdrawing to their original positions. Next day they spent mourning their thousand dead and tending the wounded, twice that number. On the Ethiopian side the expectations of a second Adowa were beginning to fade.

---

[1] Lessona in his memoirs surpassed himself in the art of understatement. 'A division of Blackshirts, commanded by General Somma, passed a moment of crisis when faced by enemy attacks.'

These Italians, unlike their fathers, were brave men, *gobos*, their artillery was powerful, and their planes piloted by 'Mussolini Lijj' flew low and boldly. The second Ethiopian offensive was over.

Badoglio cancelled his orders, and remained at Makalle, weighing up the lessons of the battle. He concluded that though the Ethiopian army had been modernized, the progress made had been 'superficial rather than profound'. The leadership was still in the hands of the Rases, of 'churchmen' like Ras Kassa and 'irresolute leaders' like Ras Seyum. The tactics were the traditional Ethiopian mass attack, not the more dangerous guerrilla warfare for which Ras Imru alone had shown the slightest aptitude. The staff organization was of the most elementary kind, with 'only a very few wireless sets which, most obligingly, were of more use to me with my admirably working interception and decoding service'. Badoglio concluded that the 'vast and well-conceived plans' of the enemy had been foiled and that Ras Imru would not 'water his mules at the sea'.

At Dessie Haile Selassie reflected bitterly on the way his orders were disobeyed. Time and again he had ordered the Rases not to mass their men, but to use guerrilla tactics and to harass rather than confront the Italians. It had been hopelessly unrealistic. By all their traditions and training the Ethiopians, men and leaders alike, were opposed to the idea of guerrilla warfare. 'A descendant of the Negus Negusti Johannes', Ras Seyum had declared, 'makes war but cannot carry on guerrilla warfare like a *shifta* chief.' The Emperor would have agreed with Badoglio's comments on his staff organization, particularly on his inability to contact Ras Imru. On the other hand even if the Italian line had not been broken, the Ethiopian line had been held—and there were good points. Firstly, though the Italian officers were brave, their men were poor. The enemy had had to rely on their native troops to rescue them from a sticky position, and there was already a slow trickle of Eritrean deserters, indignant at being given the hardest and most dangerous tasks. Secondly, mechanized warfare was less decisive than had been feared. The small Italian tanks were of little use in mountainous country, and the Ethiopians had quickly adapted themselves to bombing raids, which now caused few casualties. The gas was a problem, but more frightening than dangerous; it tended to settle in the valleys and the Ethiopians soon got into the habit of taking to the heights when it was dropped. Even when it touched them, burns could be stopped. 'You men must always be washing,' Ras Imru told his troops. Thirdly, the feared desertions had not occurred. There was even news that Haile Selassie Gugsa's men were deserting him, peeved at being disarmed on Badoglio's orders.

Admittedly the Wollo army was of doubtful loyalty—Ras Mulugueta had used it mainly to escort the vast herds of cattle needed to feed his men—and Gojjam was in revolt. But the Emperor himself was at Dessie to keep Wollo under control, and he had sent the Nevraid Aregai with a thousand men over from Wollo and Dejaz Hapte Mariam Gabre Egziabher up from Lekempti with another thousand to relieve the small Shoan garrison at Debra Markos, now being besieged by Dejaz Gessesse Belew. Meanwhile he had liberated almost all his political prisoners including Fitaurari Birru and the veteran Dejaz Balcha, and had even brought Ras Hailu from his remote prison to the Little Ghebbi, where he was later interviewed by a number of journalists to scotch rumours of his death.

For their part, faced with a common enemy, the nobles, even those who had stood in the way of Tafari Makonnen's rise to power, seemed to be forgetting their feuds and rallying around the Lion of Judah. There was one old enemy who was, fortunately for the Emperor, no longer there to rally round. Lij Yasu had died in 1935 in the village where he had lived for three years in the Garamalata mountains. What exactly was the cause of his death and at what point in the year it occurred is uncertain. Possibly as late as November, that is well after the invasion had been launched. There were the inevitable rumours of murder.

It was not on either side a chivalrous war. The Italian frightfulness in the air was equalled by the Ethiopian frightfulness on the ground. Lt. Minnetti of the air force was beheaded publicly in Dagghabur which he had bombed and strafed. It was to avenge his death that the Italians first used mustard gas. From then on atrocity followed atrocity, inevitably exaggerated by the side that suffered it, denied by the side that inflicted it. On 15 December Major Burgoyne wrote from Dessie:

Four planes did a lot of damage here unfortunately all around and through the Swedish Hospital and among the Press. Of course 6000 ft. up it was impossible for the planes to see the Red Cross on the roof and anyway no doubt their firing is erratic, however no excuses taken and before the planes had disappeared the Emperor had sent a protest to Geneva and then all wires were cleared for the Press and Europe was inundated with descriptions of the damage to the hospital.

But only three weeks later at Waldia he was bombed again.

'Your tent's gone' said the vet. It had too. A real good shot. The Eytie seeing the red roof put six big bombs carefully around it . . . fortunately beyond covering everything with earth and breaking my medical chest it did not do me any harm. The Eytie dropped three or four big bombs on the town but mostly let them have incendiary bombs—little things which did small harm beyond burning down the houses and chucking splinters about. But it was too evident that he deliberately bombed my tent. He never dropped one of any sort near my men's tents forty yards away. Can't understand the idea.

and a few days later after tending the wounded of Waldia bombed heavily the day before:

'Most of my patients were women and girls wounded in back, stomach, thighs, breasts, arms and ankles. It's tragic that we can't raise a couple of fighting planes against this "walk-over" the Italians are having, *one* fighter might set them back! I wonder they aren't sickened at just dropping death on the population, they are supposed to be *soldiers* but this is like taking the cat's milk.'

'I fight sitting,' Galeazzo Ciano had joked. Vittorio Mussolini in his book *Flights over the Amba* wrote lyrically of the beauty of the red flower of blood spreading beneath him. This was the path that led first to Guernica, and then to Rotterdam, London, Dresden, and Cologne.

Neither side took many prisoners. Menelik had taken nearly two thousand at Adowa but in the whole campaign the Ethiopians took only five—four of them at Dembeguina. They were well enough treated, sent to Dessie where the Emperor used them as gardeners. But five was an unbelievably small total. There were this time no half-regrets on either side at shedding the blood of fellow-Christians.

THE SOUTHERN FRONT

Badoglio subsequently claimed to have held and broken a great Ethiopian offensive in the north—a dubious claim. For what little evidence there is goes to show that the Emperor's original plan had been simply to contain the Italian invasion in the north with

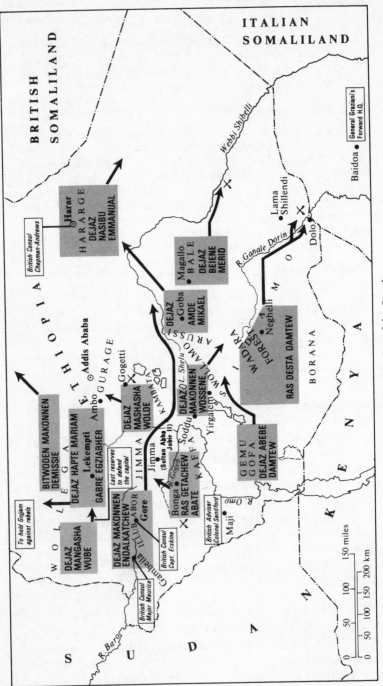

MAP 3. The Armies of the South

the traditional forces of the Northern Provinces bolstered by Ras Mulugueta. Meanwhile his own more modern troops would invade Somalia in the south where the Italians were so much weaker, and sweep them into the sea.

It was this rather than the evenly-balanced situation in the north that was on the Emperor's mind in the third week of January. For much had been happening in the south.

In the Ogaden, after the death of Afework, the Italians had halted while the Ethiopians were rapidly building up their strength. The levies of Arussi, 3,000 strong, were established at the base headquarters, Jijiga. The Dejaz Abebe Damtew had led his army, 3,000 more, over from his remote southern provinces of Gemu and Gofa on the Kenya border to Dagghabur. There he had been joined by the far stronger army of Illubabor, 12,000 men led right across the Empire from Gore by the giant Dejaz Makonnen Endalkachew.

Steer went down to tour the Ogaden again and brought back his usual vivid impressions of these three leaders and their troops. The Dejaz Amde Mikael of Arussi was a 'nice elderly man' . . . seen 'in a supreme moment of drunkenness'; Abebe Damtew 'a typical good Amhara officer . . . but his province was wretchedly poor with scarcely a modern rifle'; Dejaz Makonnen Endalkachew was 'much more wooden, less soldierly and less spirited than Abebe'. What most impressed Steer was the fantastic ochre and pink head-dresses of Abebe's levies plus the two Adowa cannon and the three young lions he had brought with him. He did not appreciate—he probably did not know—the importance of Dejaz Amde Mikael's position as head of the Moja, the second of the two aristocratic clans of Menz. With Dejaz Makonnen Endalkachew, head of the Addisge there too, in Ethiopian eyes the finest and most prestigious fighting lords of Shoa had taken the field in the south.

Meanwhile the Turks and the Belgians were organizing a strong defensive position in the low mountains south of Dagghabur where the Tug Jerrer joined the Tug Fafan: Ethiopia's 'Maginot Line' as Wehib Pasha baptized it. Not that there was much co-operation between the three Turks and the three Belgians of Reul's mission; 'parmi ces types-là', said Farouk Bey, 'il y avait des avocats, il y avait des commerçants, il y avait des comédiens d'ailleurs.'

But militarily the Ogaden was quiet. While Dejaz Nasibu

dispersed his troops to right and left, and prepared to move his own headquarters down to Dagghabur, there were only skirmishes here and there—a successful night raid, the first of its kind carried out by the Ethiopians when 150 men captured the wells of Harradiguit—but no major operations.

It was in the southern half of his sector that Graziani realized that he would have to meet a threat. The forces of Bale led by Dejaz Beiene Merid were moving down the Webbi Shebelli. More dangerous still, the forces of Ras Desta were assembling in Sidamo to move down the Juba and turn Graziani's left flank.

Ras Desta Damtew, then forty-three years old, was something of an eccentric among Ethiopian nobles, with a curiously mixed reputation (for one who in his twenties had run away to become a monk at Debra Libanos) as an entrepreneur and an *enfant terrible*. His family was of the old Shoan nobility—he would hardly have been permitted to marry the Emperor's eldest daughter if it had been otherwise—but he had as little taste as the young progressives of inferior birth for the traditional amusements of the Amhara aristocracy, the feasting, the horsemanship, the boasting, and the drunkenness. In consequence he was less popular than his brother Abebe, particularly among the Amharo-Galla nobles and soldiers, the *barud-lets* and *melkegnas* who had settled in Sidamo with Dejaz Balcha and who had lived an independent and almost tax-free life, their land worked by the native serfs of the Sidancho tribes under the *gebar* system. They looked back nostalgically to the severity of their old governor, who had instituted hanging even for minor offences, and with suspicion on their new one. Had not his father Fitaurari Damtew visited Russia? Was he himself not founding towns, Yirgalem and Wondo, a strange and un-Ethiopian habit, centres of administration and bureaucracy, where Dejaz Balcha had been content with the old traditional nomadic camp? Was he not another *ferengi*-lover like Tafari Makonnen? Had he not arrived in the province with a *ferengi* officer, who was presuming to reorganize their tried military habits?

The *ferengi* officer in question was a young Belgian, Lt. Cambier, born by a mere coincidence in Odessa, and a member of the official Belgian Military Mission. Three weeks after the declaration of war when Ras Desta was already calling the *chitet* at Yirgalem, and Major Dothée had already summoned his scattered officers back to Addis Ababa, news came to the capital that Cambier was dead. A plane left Addis Ababa next day, his body was flown back and he was buried with military honours in the European cemetery at Addis Ababa. 'Pleurisy', said one official report; 'acute infectious poliomyelitis', said another. But there were suspicions of suicide—and of murder by a Sidamo chief. In any event Cambier died, and one of Reul's mercenaries, Lt. Frère, was sent to replace him.

By November the Sidamo army, at least 20,000 strong, had reached Magallo, north of Neghelli. It was a well-armed and well-equipped force, so well-armed indeed that the Italians were convinced that Ras Desta had been receiving rifles from the British in Kenya. The troops were led by two Fitauraris, Ademe Anbassu and Tademme Zelleka, and the half-trained Guards battalion was commanded by Kenyaz Bezibeh Sileshi. They were in touch, via Ras Desta's precious wireless, with the Emperor at Dessie and protected from the air by Oerlikon anti-aircraft guns. They were moreover working in close co-operation with the forces of Bale, the adjoining province to the north. It looked to Graziani like a well co-ordinated movement, particularly difficult to counter because Ras Desta's right flank was protected by the Kenya border. It would become particularly threatening if it was combined with an offensive in the Ogaden. It was in any case particularly dangerous because only fractions of the *Tevere* Blackshirts and of General Nasi's Libyan Division had arrived, and Graziani had therefore only General Pavone's *Peloritana* Division and the native troops of Somalia to count on. On 13 November Graziani moved his headquarters forward to Baidoa and personally assumed command of the Juba sector.

Fortunately for Graziani's peace of mind Ras Desta's advance through the almost trackless forests and mountains of Southern Sidamo was slow. This meant that it was Dejaz Beiene Merid of Bale, 200 miles further forward on the Webbi Shebelli, who was first into battle. The action that ensued was decisive: not because of its importance—Dejaz Beiene's men attacked a raiding party of 1,000 *Dubats* sent forward under Olol Dinke—but because Dejaz Beiene was badly wounded. With their leader out of action, the Ethiopians' morale cracked: a presage of what was invariably to happen in this war. Both sides fell back.

At the same time Graziani intercepted a panicky wireless message from Dejaz Nasibu to the Emperor predicting that Olol

Dinke's force was Graziani's advance guard and putting it at 5,000 strong. So, Graziani could calculate, the Ogaden was no threat after all—on the contrary he now knew that the Ogaden's commander was all nerves. Indeed it would be hard to exaggerate the importance of these wireless interceptions. Thanks to these both Graziani and Badoglio knew exactly what was going on in the minds of their rival commanders. They knew not only how the Ethiopians were judging their own plans but also how they were planning to react. There was not a major move or a major attack made, therefore, by any of the Ethiopian commanders who possessed a wireless that was not known in advance by the Italian generals. If there was one single factor that more than any other helped the Italians to win the war it was this.

Graziani was now confident that the centre of the Ethiopian prong, the advance down the Webbi Shebelli, was broken, and that therefore the whole Ethiopian offensive had gone badly wrong. He ordered Olol Dinke to move north of the Webbi Shebelli up into Ogaden; there he would be in a position to hold off any sudden move southwards by Dejaz Nasibu—in the unlikely event that such a move should occur. On 4 January Graziani cabled Mussolini, 'On the Juba front I consider grand strategic offensive Ras Desta Damtew paralysed and broken up.'

By 6 January Ras Desta's forces, hammered continually by the Italian bombers as they advanced down the palm-shaded valley of the Juba, were in a semicircle about sixty miles from Dolo. Their left flank rested on Lama Shillendi which was still held by the two Ethiopian guards battalions of Bale. The whole force was over 250 miles from its base.

On 9 January Graziani's wireless interceptors tuned in on Ras Desta's wavelength and started transmitting their own messages and orders, causing for three days immense confusion.

On 10 January Graziani seized the initiative. He moved his troops up to the Dolo area and prepared to attack on both sides of the Juba which was in flood. On 12 January his troops were in position and next day they moved forward in three columns. The central column, with tanks, armoured cars, and the motorized machine-gun detachments of the Aosta Lancers, commanded by General Bergonzoli, drove up the right bank of the Juba.

Ras Desta's men were not, it seems, expecting the attack. Their morale had been very high but the continued daily air raids, culminating on the day before the attack by a massive bombing raid of 50 Capronis, had sapped their spirit. The main Italian column fell on the Sidamo advance guard commanded by Fitauraris Ademe Anbassu and Tademme Zelleka. It broke through and confused fighting spread for twenty miles around, lasting all day. But in the flat plains by the river the Italian tanks and the armoured cars and the motorized lorries were able to manœuvre with an ease impossible in the rocky mountainous defiles of the North. By the following morning when the Italians advanced again, the army of Sidamo was an almost disorganized rabble, fleeing back along the tracks down which they had so confidently advanced, bombed and machine-gunned as they fled. Only the rearguard on the left of the river held up a flanking column for another day and a half. Lt. Frère sent a cable back to Reul's headquarters. 'Situation désespérée. Télégraphier femme tout va bien.' The advancing Italians found a copy of the cable with Frère's papers at Ras Desta's hastily abandoned head-quarters where they captured the Ras's luggage, his *negarit*, and his flag—as well as an enormous quantity of cattle, stores, and material. By the 19th the Aosta Lancers, Bergonzoli's advance guard, were in Neghelli. On the 23rd columns were sent out north of Neghelli into the thick forest of the Wadara where Ras Desta's men were rallying, and south towards the Kenyan frontier. The reports were that 3,000 of Ras Desta's men had been killed, and the Ras himself and Lt. Frère were fleeing back to Yirgalem. The Digolia Somali of the lowlands came in to submit at Dolo and the Galla Borana of the highlands at Neghelli. Graziani issued a proclamation abolishing the *gebar* system, and received the congratulations of a Mussolini happy both that supplies from Kenya into Ethiopia had been cut off, and that the Italian armies had penetrated as 'liberators' into 'the territory of the Gallas'.

It had been a highly successful operation, the first real defeat that the Italians had inflicted on the enemy. Not everything had gone entirely smoothly, however. For one thing the Italian advance was halted in the Wadara forests. The column sent out from Neghelli met stiff resistance, and the Aosta Lancers had 47 casualties. That was not too serious in itself. For of all the ways of invading Ethiopia the southern route was the slowest and most arduous; and Graziani had never had any real intention, still less any orders, to push up through the wilds of Sidamo towards the central Lakes and then on to Addis Ababa.

But there had been a much more serious incident about which not a murmur was allowed to escape: a mutiny of the Eritrean troops. Some of the Eritreans of the Libyan Division had been fighting for over twenty years round Tripoli and Benghazi. When the division was formed, they were told that they would be going home to Massawa. Instead, the steamers carrying them touched at Massawa and sailed on round the Horn to Mogadishu, to another land of deserts and more fighting.

The 4th *Gruppo* of General Nasi's Libyan Division, commanded by Colonel Maramarcio, was moved up into the Dolo section ready for the attack on Ras Desta. Before the attack twelve men under Geraz Gebrai deserted; and then at night several hundred more under Fitaurari Tegai Negussie, all from the four battalions of the 4th *Gruppo*. They took with them forty machine-guns.

What followed was very confused. The deserters planned to join Ras Desta but only two or three hundred of them in fact managed to do so. The rest wandered around lost, attacked by the Borana Somalis, and pursued by armoured cars and bombers. At one point a large group walked through General Agostini's lines on the Dawa at midnight, as tense as the troops that woke up all round and stood to arms, but by one of those curious spontaneous truces that occur in all wars, not attacking and not attacked. It was extremely awkward for General Nasi who could threaten and pursue but could hardly shoot, for fear that the mutiny might spread to his other three regiments. In the end nearly 600 of the deserters were picked up in Kenya by a strong KAR force under a disagreeable British officer, who disarmed them and threatened to take them back to General Graziani's headquarters in Baidoa.

It was almost as embarrassing for the Kenya government as it had been for Graziani. In fact the Eritreans were interned at 'No 1 Eritrean Deserters Camp' at Isiolo just north of Mt. Kenya. General Nasi sent the 4th *Gruppo* back to Mogadishu and there disbanded it, scattering the askaris he considered trustworthy among his other battalions. It had been a serious incident, but it was to have no immediate consequences; the deserters' example was not contagious.

The news of Ras Desta's defeat caused near despair at Dessie. The Emperor had been counting on his better-armed and better-trained forces in the south and in particular on his son-in-law. Although the Italian advance had been held and a line was being fortified at Wadara, there were grave reports of dissension among the Sidamo leaders. There were the usual rumours of treachery, and the mutual accusations that are flung about in a defeated army. Fitaurari Ademe Anbassu was flogged for having lost fifty machine-guns; there was talk that he had revealed Ras Desta's plans to the Italians. With desertions and dismissals the total strength of the army was down to under 10,000 men, and many of the Sidamo leaders were requesting a stronger leader. The Emperor saw that he would have to intervene. He sent two of his aeroplanes flying over central Sidamo, dropping leaflets requesting the army to obey Ras Desta until Dejaz Balcha and Dejaz Gabremariam should arrive. There was probably never any real intention of allowing Dejaz Balcha back into his feudal territories; even at his age he could still be dangerous once Ethiopia had won the war. But Gabremariam had been Balcha's Fitaurari before he became governor of Harar, and everyone remembered his 1931 expedition when he had chased the Italians down the Webbi Shebelli.

So the Emperor sent Dejaz Gabremariam down from Dessie with orders to reconcile the quarrelling leaders and restore morale in Sidamo. It was a victory for the old Ethiopia of Menelik over the new Ethiopia of Haile Selassie.

At the same time the Emperor ordered Dejaz Makonnen Wossene, Governor of the heavily populated central southern province of Wollamo across the Lakes, to reinforce Ras Desta. Dejaz Mangasha Wolde, Governor of the other heavily populated province of Kambata, just to the north of Wollamo, had already moved up to Amba Alagi with tens of thousands of his levies. By now all the levies of the south-east and the central southern provinces had joined or were moving towards one of the fronts. The only reserves of the Empire lay at Dessie in Wollo and in the south-west.

CHAPTER 7

THE BATTLES IN THE NORTH

IN the North Badoglio now had eleven complete divisions—two Eritrean and nine Italian, organized into four Army Corps and reserves. Seven of these eleven divisions were concentrated at Makalle; an imposing force. On 4 February Badoglio issued operation orders to their commanders. The same day Ras Mulugueta reported to the Emperor at Dessie that 'an attack in force is imminent'.

Dessie, the capital of Wollo, had been the Emperor's headquarters for over two months. His sons, the Crown Prince Asfa Wossen and the child Duke of Harar, were with him. So were the battalions of the Guard from Addis Ababa—protection, if need be, against the half-trusted levies of Wollo. Thousands of roadbuilders were busy widening and improving the track that ran north through the highlands of Wollo for eighty miles to the little town of Waldia.

There the track went down into a low and dusty plain that to the east melted into the Danakil desert. This was the no man's land that stretched for fifty miles between the highlands of Wollo and the highlands of Tigre, *shifta* country. In its centre lay Cobbo, a market for the Azebo Galla and a village of evil repute. Only large and heavily-armed parties could safely traverse this plain.

From the foot of the Tigre highlands a mule-track with seventeen hairpin bends led up to Quoram on the plateau, where the British Field Hospital under Dr. Melly was established. Mule and foot were the only form of transport in the Tigre highlands; but by a near-miracle Dr. Melly had managed to get his 18 lorries up the escarpment. There on 4 February at Quoram he was joined by Major Burgoyne and the 200 mules of Burgoyne's Red Cross unit. All around them were encamped the 12,000 well-armed men of the Bitwoded Makonnen Demissie, the army of Wollega-Ardjo.[1]

---

[1] This was one of the three armies of Wollega. The Bitwoded Makonnen was a

Dessie, the Imperial headquarters, lay about 280 miles by road and track from Makalle in the northern highlands of Tigre where the invaders were massing their forces. Up the roads and over the tracks army after army had gone tramping. Up and down these tracks the Italian aeroplanes ranged, bombing—almost unopposed—the columns of marching Ethiopians and the towns and villages and encampments that lay along the route. By 4 February the Ethiopian forces were strung out over 250 miles from south to north, from Dessie to the mountain plateau of Amba Aradam.

Six miles long and two to three miles wide, Amba Aradam rose high above the surrounding countryside, facing Makalle and blocking any possible move south. It was real *amba*, flat-topped, covered with crevices and canyons and caves, impregnable on the north and north-east where the Tug Gabat ran round its flanks through precipitous ravines, falling steeply away in the rear to the spur of Antalo, behind which lay the broad plain of Mahera. For five weeks Ras Mulugueta had been encamped on this mountain; with him were Dejaz Auraris the Shoan governor of Menz, Wodajo Ali the Crown Prince's tutor, and two powerful nobles of Wollo, Ras Gabre Hiwot Mikael, son of the Negus Mikael, and Dejaz Amde Ali. Half of Ras Mulugueta's 70–80,000 men were on Amba Aradam's top, half spread out around its flanks. He had 400 machine-guns, ten cannon, and a few anti-aircraft Oerlikons. Behind him the plain of Mahera was alive with the cattle gathered en route and herded up to feed his vast army. At the village of Antalo the Tigrean peasants held markets every day, pushing the prices of their honey and sweetmeats up exorbitantly. The telegraph line ran from Imperial headquarters at Dessie to the port of Buie in the Mahera plain; from there a runner had to take messages up to the Ras on the mountain.

On 5 February the Emperor ordered the Bitwoded Makonnen's 12,000 men forward from Quoram. They marched out across the wide and fertile plateau of Lake Ashangi. At the far end of the plateau lay the town of Mai Ceu, the only sizeable town between Dessie and Makalle, governed by Dejaz Aberra Tedla, a Shoan chosen for his vigour and loyalty to the Emperor, posted

highly-respected potentate, famed for his hospitality, his amours—he had eloped with the Emperor's favourite niece—and for his ability to take machine-guns to pieces and reassemble them blindfold. According to foreign observers his army, equipped with ten Oerlikons by the Emperor, was the most modern in the North.

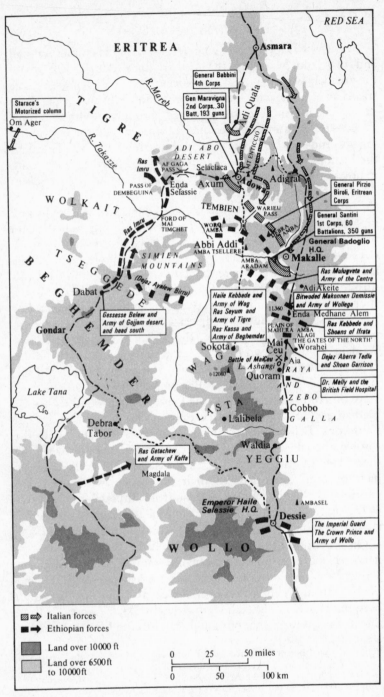

MAP 4. The Battles in the North

with a Shoan garrison in the heart of the territory of the Raya Galla.

They marched through Mai Ceu. To the north of the town the heights of the vast mountain stronghold of Amba Alagi towered above the whole of the Tigrean highlands, dominating the narrow twisting track both to the north and the south. This was both the pivot and the assembly-point of the whole Ethiopian line. Bitwoded Makonnen found the forces of Ras Kebbede encamped on the heights of Amba Alagi, on the spur to the north-east of the track. Below Amba Alagi to the north lay the little village of Enda Medhane Alem; almost thirty miles further on was the mountain plateau of Amba Aradam where Ras Mulugueta faced Badoglio and awaited the Italian attack.

On Sunday 9 February Badoglio called forward the journalists from Asmara to Makalle and held a confident, almost boastful press conference. On Monday 10 February four divisions began moving forward before dawn. Badoglio's plan was simple enough; not to attack Amba Aradam frontally, an impossible task, but to carry out a double encircling movement. Two Blackshirt divisions were to squeeze Amba Aradam in the centre, occupying Ras Mulugueta's attention, while two regular divisions were to sweep round in a wider encircling movement and pinch the mountain off at its rear, meeting at Antalo. Thus Ras Mulugueta and his whole army would be trapped.

Into the preparation of the battle Badoglio had poured all his experience as a commander in the Great War. This time no one could accuse him of failing to use his guns. For weeks his 280 cannon had shelled the *amba* from Makalle; 170 aeroplanes had bombed it again and again. The barrage and the bombing reached a climax as the attack began. Carried to their starting point by hundreds of lorries along specially prepared roads, First Corps, Santini's *Sabauda*, and the '23rd January' moved forward on the Italian left and Third Corps, the *Sila* and the '23rd March', on the right. On the 10th they crossed the Tug Gabat. The next day, under torrential rain, they advanced without meeting opposition. It was not till the third day, Wednesday 12 February, that the Blackshirts of '3rd January' were pinned down on the side of Enda Gabor. There they lost 47 men killed, not a high figure, but Badoglio mistrusted the Blackshirts after the near disaster at the Warieu Pass. He quickly pulled them out and replaced them with the best of his reserve divisions, the *Valpusteria Alpini*. On both flanks the Italian encircling movement was well under way. It was at this moment that the army of Wollega intervened.

On the Tuesday the Bitwoded Makonnen from the foot of Amba Alagi at Enda Medhane Alem had seen the bombing and the shelling that meant an Italian advance was in progress. He got through to Ras Mulugueta by cable, and was ordered to remain at Amba Alagi and prepare its defences. Ras Kebbede had even before this appealed to the Bitwoded Makonnen to draw up his army alongside his own on the heights of Amba Alagi. In Ras Kebbede's opinion Amba Aradam was doomed.

But the Bitwoded Makonnen had, as he reminded his chiefs, been specifically ordered by the Emperor to support Ras Mulugueta. 'How then shall we meet the Emperor', he asked, 'offering him only bad news when we ourselves have not even tasted the bitterness of battle?' In any case, ignoring Ras Kebbede's advice and Ras Mulugueta's orders, he led the men of Wollega forward and after a long night's march reached the plain of Mahera behind Amba Aradam next day.

For the last time he exchanged messages with Ras Mulugueta. He proposed that Ras Mulugueta should withdraw before the net had closed. Ras Mulugueta flatly rejected the idea. Adding that Amba Aradam was about to be outflanked from the east he gave strange but laconic instructions: 'Fight if you want to—where and when you like.'

That night the Bitwoded Makonnen left the bulk of his army on the Mahera plain and moved off to the east with a small picked force, to halt the encircling left claw of the *Sabauda* division. It was a ten-mile march across craggy ground swept in parts by Italian searchlights. The objective was a group of Italian machine-gun positions set up the afternoon before and sweeping the plains in front. In the half-light before dawn the Ethiopians crept down a long ravine past the deserted stone huts of the village of Adi Akeite. A dog barked. The Bitwoded Makonnen divided his men into three parties, himself to lead the centre. Fitaurari Gete, his veteran commander protested: 'Are not the professional soldiers to lead?' Makonnen lost patience and raged at him, accusing him of lack of confidence in his leadership. 'I have lived my life under your roof and served your father', replied the Fitaurari, 'and I will follow you now and you will see that I shall fall before you.'

As they slipped up through the candelabra trees the alarm was given; and the desperate assault began. By 10 a.m. the Wollegas had captured all the advanced machine-gun positions but half their force were killed or wounded, exposed on a stony ridge to the Italian guns behind and the bombers which the Italians now called up. The Bitwoded Makonnen Demissie had been hit in the first assault, machine-gunned from the side through the hips. His men got him off the ridge and carried him back mortally wounded to the cave on the plains of Mahera where his army lay. He lived for another night, and died in the cave in the morning of 14 February. His chiefs kept his death a secret. Their one aim now was to get his body back to his own part of the country and bury it there. It was a matter of honour. But at the same time his death had to be concealed.

Major Burgoyne was still with the Wollega army. That evening the chiefs called him to the cave and with one assistant he performed possibly the most macabre operation that an amateur surgeon has ever been called upon to do. The body of the Bitwoded Makonnen was carved in two and sealed in a pair of war-drums.

Friday night was a night of violent rainstorms and winds. The Wollega army, believing its chief to be wounded but alive, followed the closely-guarded *Negarits* back to the foothills of Amba Alagi. There they were met by Ras Kebbede who had heard the news of Makonnen's death and had had a grave dug for him. 'I told him so', he said gazing at the war-drums. But the chiefs of Wollega would not use his grave.

For Badoglio this had been one of 'two brief counter-attacks' which had held up the final assault he was now preparing. On Saturday, 15 February, the mists surrounding the mountain cleared by 10 a.m. and the four Italian divisions pressed forward to close their pincer. It was a day of fierce and desperate hand-to-hand struggle. But Ras Mulugeta's men were demoralized by weeks of inactivity, of being hit without being able to hit back, cooped up in caves and ravines, bombed and gassed and shelled, barely daring to move in the hours of daylight. Casualties had been increasing from day to day, the small medical unit under a Pole, Dr. Belau, had become completely swamped. But even though the Wollega army had retreated, the *Sabauda* and the *Sila* failed to join up at Antalo that day. In the twilight Ras Mulugeta, his Cuban machine-gunner Del Valle, and his staff slipped out through the gap. All around the remnants of the Army of the Centre died in caves or desperately tried to escape. The *Alpini* scaled the sheer eastern flank of the mountain; but it was the Blackshirts of the '23rd March' who were allowed the credit of being the first to hoist the Italian flag in the centre of Amba Aradam. This took place to the accompaniment of the accepted Fascist cry of their enthusiastic commander, Filiberto Duke of Pistoia: 'Per il Re, per il Duce, eja eja eja alala!'

It had been the biggest colonial battle ever fought, and it was hardly Ras Mulugueta's fault if his mountain stronghold fell so comparatively easily. It was not the sort of battle for which the Ethiopians had been prepared, and they can hardly be blamed for failing to imagine the effects of a blitz that lay totally outside their experience. If Ras Mulugueta had withdrawn he would have left the armies of the Tembien exposed. To advance with his ten guns against the massed batteries and divisions that for weeks had been fortifying the perimeter of Makalle would have been suicidal. Yet even a suicidal attack would have been more in the spirit of the Ethiopian fighters than a passive, demoralizing, defensive stance. Ras Mulugueta missed his chance of attacking three weeks earlier when the battle in the Tembien was in the balance. Even so, and all allowances made, it was a pitiful defence. Badoglio's troops advanced like Baratieri's at Adowa in four separate and disconnected columns. If Ras Mulugueta had concentrated on halting and if possible destroying one of the enemy's divisions, rather than feebly opposing all four, the Italian offensive must have been thrown into confusion and Badoglio's nerves, always taut, might have broken. But perhaps by the time the attack developed Ras Mulugueta knew in his heart of hearts that defeat was inevitable. His last orders to the Bitwoded Makonnen Demissie were orders that only a totally incompetent or an utterly despairing military leader could have given.

It is said that the Italians found 8,000 bodies on Amba Aradam. They burnt the bodies and for months afterwards the plains around smelt of charred flesh.

At 2 a.m. on the Sunday morning Ras Mulugueta and the people with him, only 50 armed men in all, reached the little village of Enda Medane Alem at the foot of Amba Alagi.

The narrow pass back over Amba Alagi, bombed and strafed, became a death-trap for the survivors of the *Mahel Safari*, raided according to Badoglio's account 546 times in the days that followed. For four days Ras Mulugueta tried vainly to halt and rally the fugitives. On the night of Wednesday the 19th he sent word to Ras Kebbede over on the north-east spur of Gerak Sadek telling him that the position was being abandoned. Yet Amba Alagi was a far stronger position than Amba Aradam and more difficult to bypass or encircle. Ras Kebbede protested: his army was still untried, and to abandon Amba Alagi was to throw the road to Dessie open. But he, unlike so many of the other commanders, obeyed orders.

It took many days for Ras Mulugueta, Ras Kebbede, and the rearguard of the army of Wollega to straggle back to Mai Ceu. All around the Raya Galla were in revolt; and when on the 24th Ras Mulugueta and his men crossed the hump of the Dubai pass, they saw in front of them a town in flames, mercilessly bombed, its inhabitants fleeing to the mountains.

The Rases camped in the plain. Next day the *shiftas* of the Raya Galla attacked Aberra Tedla's compound inside what remained of Mai Ceu and set his residence on fire. It was then that Ras Kebbede's men intervened, sending swift parties up and driving the raiders off. They had won only a brief pause, however; news came that the *shiftas* were massing on the road to Quoram to cut them off. But the news was also that the Emperor was now moving up with his army from Dessie. The last and best-trained of the Empire's armies was moving to the North.

On the morning of the 27th loose and barely organized groups left Mai Ceu retreating south across the plateau of Lake Ashangi; the wounded on muleback and litters with Major Burgoyne, the Wollega rearguard still escorting the body of the Bitwoded Makonnen. Ras Mulugueta and his red-turbanned drummers and his son Shallaka Tadessa Mulugueta followed, a little ahead of the scattered army of Ras Kebbede. In the first bombing raids one of the two mules carrying the Wollega *negarits* was hit directly, and the war-drum shattered. The Wollegas buried the remnants hastily by the side of the road under an acacia tree, and dragged the surviving mule up to the nearby church of St. George. There the second *negarit* was buried by the priests with Christian funeral rites, to the roll of Ras Mulugueta's war-drums.

It was past ten o'clock in the morning. Ras Mulugueta hurried on with the vanguard through the continual crackle of *shifta* rifle fire. Three Capronis came over as Tadessa Mulugueta and Major Burgoyne reached the ford of Ahayo. A bomb fell between them.

It killed them both instantly. As the planes circled and returned, machine-gunning the bodies, a servant ran to tell Ras Mulugueta of his son's death. He hurried back through the *shiftas'* fire. Hordes of Raya Galla seized their chance of revenge on the hated Shoans, poured out of the woods, and in the confusion engaged Ras Kebbede's army. Probably they never realized, when an old lion-maned warrior fell straddling his son's body, that they had just succeeded in killing Ras Mulugueta, Minister of War, Imperial Fitaurari and Commander of the Army of the Centre.

On the morning Ras Mulugueta died, Badoglio launched his second attack—in the Tembien. Rumours of the great battle at Amba Aradam had already spread, and were confirmed, first by Dejaz Aberra Kassa (who had headed for the Tembien on abandoning Mai Ceu) and then by Italian leaflets dropped from the air. The Bitwoded Makonnen's death was more of a blow to the morale of the Ethiopians than the defeat of Ras Mulugueta, unpopular with all for his severity. It was a demoralized and much reduced army that the Italians had to attack. There were 50,000 armed men or less facing the Italians instead of the 150,000 that had attacked them a month before. It was always difficult to keep any large Ethiopian army in the field. After a month or two the levies, badly fed and inactive, would start to trickle back to their homes; and though a smaller army was certainly more manageable and more easily supplied, the sight of their comrades leaving was bound to demoralize those who remained behind.

Ras Kassa knew that an Italian attack was imminent and that a large force of Italians was moving down the Gheva valley to cut him off from the rear.[1] But his was a strong defensive position; the mountains were almost impregnable. Ras Kassa ordered his men to prepare torches to use against the enemy's tanks as Ras Imru had done, and waited almost with confidence for the Italians to break themselves on the lower slopes of the mountains, as they had done before. What Ras Kassa had failed to allow for was Italian mountaineering skill. To climb the sheer cliffs of the Golden Mountain, Worq Amba, would have been an exploit even by daylight. To climb it by night and when it was occupied by the enemy was a heroic feat.

---

[1] This was the Third Corps, the *Sila* and the '23rd March', which Badoglio had swung round from Amba Alagi. Pirzio Biroli's Eritrean Corps in full strength was to put in the main attack from the Warieu Pass.

At 1 a.m. on 27 February sixty men reached the northern foot of the mountain. Each carried besides his climbing kit and two days' supplies a musket, 120 cartridges, and 5 hand grenades; the group also had three light-machine-guns. Over half were Blackshirts of the 114th Legion; twenty-five were askaris of the 12th native battalion; all volunteers. Their commander was a twenty-six-year-old *Alpini* lieutenant, Tito Polo. For an hour and a half their climb was held up as they filed, one by one and silently, past an advanced enemy outpost. The sentries were asleep and slept on, undisturbed. It was not till 5 o'clock, dangerously near first light, that the climbers were under the peak. Twelve men were sent to the right, twelve to the left. An hour later, just before dawn, they crept out on to the top of the mountain guarded by thirty sleeping Ethiopians. Stealthily, two machine-guns with their crews were roped up, then another group of eight with their grenades ready. No watcher gave the alarm, no sleeper stirred. An order, shots, grenades—it was all over in a few minutes. The Italians held the top of the mountain.

Or rather they held the northern peak. Another group that tried to scale the southern peak were pinned down half-way. At dawn Pirzio-Biroli's battalions advanced from the Warieu Pass to encircle Worq Amba, and to attack Debra Hansa on the other side of the Pass. Fighting raged all day in the north. Fourteen times the Ethiopians counter-attacked up the steep slopes against the little band of Italians and Eritreans on the peak. But the machine-guns beat them back time and again. 'Come, come', shouted the Eritreans ironically. 'We too are the slaves of Menelik!' In the late afternoon Dejaz Beiene Abba Seqsib leading the last attack was killed. From Debra Hansa, Dejaz Mangasha Yilma led an attack against the Pass. His army, at first successful, was cut in two, and Mangasha Yilma only escaped by playing dead.

When night fell, Fitaurari Zaudi Abba Korra still held the southern peak of Debra Amba; while at Debra Hansa the men of Kambata under Dejaz Mashasha Wolde had driven back the Eritreans and were convinced that victory would be theirs on the morrow. But by noon the next day the Italian guns were hammering the southern peak, the Italian bombers were out, and six battalions were encircling Aberra Kassa on Debra Amba from the west. Dejaz Mashasha Wolde had appealed for help to Aberra Kassa, and when no help came, he indignantly retreated. There was general confusion, and to add to it reports of the Italians closing in from the south. Ras Seyum was sent back to stop them in the Gheva valley; Ras Kassa reinforced his son on Debra Amba. At dusk there was firing in Abbi Addi itself, and the Europeans with Ras Kassa were told to leave for Quoram. By the early afternoon of the 28th another Italian victory was in the air, and resistance only sporadic. Once again, however, the Italians failed to close the trap. Ras Kassa and his two sons, with Ras Seyum, and an advance guard under Dejaz Mashasha Wolde and Fitaurari Zaudi Abba Korra crossed the Gheva. Mangasha Yilma went a different way. What was left of the armies of Wag, Lasta, and Yeggiu had made their own escape already.

Dejaz Haile Kebbede had led their breakthrough. There was a running night battle, during which the men of Wag suffered the worst casualties they had known against the advance guard of the Third Corps in the valley of the Gheva. Flares dropped by Italian planes lit up the whole area. For the Ethiopians it was as if the night had turned to day.

Bombed all the way, the relics of the armies reassembled at Socota, where the aged Wagshum Kebbede supplied them all with food and reinforced them with fresh troops. They had thought Ras Mulugueta would hold Amba Alagi, but the rumour was that Amba Alagi too had been abandoned. They waited to learn where the Emperor was and what were his plans and his commands. And while they were there Dejaz Mashasha Wolde of Kambata died of his wounds.

On the evening of the fortieth anniversary of the battle of Adowa, 1 March, the Emperor reached Quoram by mule, having left his car at the foot of the Tigrean highlands. There he met Ras Kebbede and Captain del Valle and heard of the deaths of Ras Mulugueta, of Mulugueta's son, and of Major Burgoyne. In Addis Ababa the Abuna Cyrillos ordered a fast of eight days, a strict fast, bread and water, no meat, no eggs, no *tej*, to be observed by men and women alike. And on the Italian side Badoglio had shifted his headquarters to a tent at Adi Quala from which he was directing against Ras Imru the third phase of his 'battle of annihilation.'

Ras Imru had known very little of what was going on at the main battlefields to his west. Messages and orders via the cable office at Gondar, or the telephone post at Dabat, took five to eleven days to reach him; and when they did, they were often out of date. In early February a message from Dessie had arrived announcing a planned Italian advance on Gondar—'at that time quite premature', as Badoglio put it—and ordering Ras Imru to remain on the defensive. Ras Imru had a marked tendency to obey orders and so he confined himself to sending out raiding parties behind the Italian lines and building up his defences around Amba Coletza on the Shire range.

Badoglio was confident of success not only because some reports put Ras Imru's total strength at only 25,000 men, 'in a poor moral and material state', but also because of the 'attitude of Dejaz Ayalew Birru who had shown in various ways that he was not averse to submitting to our rule.' Nevertheless Ras Imru had been Italy's most dangerous opponent, the only Ethiopian commander who had attempted to manœuvre, to cut communications, to threaten a counter-invasion, and to raise revolts in the Italian rear. Badoglio was taking no risks. Three reinforced divisions of Maravigna's Second Corps were to move west from their Adowa-Axum base. At the same time two divisions of Babbini's Fourth Corps would cross the Mareb from the north and cut off the Ethiopians in the rear.

Second Corps was only sixteen miles from Ras Imru's position by road and track. Fourth Corps was fifty miles away and had a waterless and trackless desert to cross. So Babbini's two divisions from the North did not arrive until the day the battle was over. But even without their help the three divisions of Second Corps outnumbered and outgunned Ras Imru, already confused by long and contradictory orders arriving from the Emperor. What was surprising was not that the Italians won, it was that they met with any opposition at all.

On 29 February Maravigna's Corps advanced in an enormously long column that moved forward on both sides of the motor road: first the 'April 21st', then the *Gavinana*, the *Gran Sasso*, plus the Eritrean Brigade and the camel corps. It was more of a procession than a military advance. No scouts were thrown out and no special precautions taken. At a fork in the road the Blackshirt division branched off towards its objective, the heights of Acab Saat, and the *Gavinana* marched straight on towards Selaclaca.

The advance guard of the *Gavinana*—two battalions and an artillery group—was ambushed and almost surrounded by 6,000 of Ras Imru's men who had crept up over broken ground. Most of the rest of the Division was sent up to the rescue, and Maravigna, in great alarm, halted the whole advance and stood on the defensive all that night and the following day, much to Badoglio's disgust.

By 2 March Maravigna had rearranged his line in a more military fashion. His three divisions advanced in parallel columns, the 'April 21st' on the left, the *Gavinana* in the centre, and the *Gran Sasso* on the right. The guns and bombers had given the Ethiopian positions a pounding in the morning. But, instead of sitting under the enemy fire, Ras Imru, reinforced on the right by 4,000 of Dejaz Ayalew's men led by Fitaurari Teshagger and his own son Fitaurari Zaudi, ordered his men out to the attack. The fiercest fighting took place in the early afternoon, as both sides moved forward. Often the Italian guns had to fire at point-blank range. On their right the *Gran Sasso* was in difficulties, and had to be rallied by the Duke of Bergamo.

As Badoglio put it: 'the Corps again failed to reach its assigned objectives and in the evening after slow progress it consolidated its position on the heights . . . retaining its original formation.'

In fact this was the bitterest day's fighting the Italians ever had to face in the North. In the morning in ferocious hand-to-hand fighting the Ethiopians had driven the Italians back several hundred yards. But in the afternoon Fitaurari Zaudi Ayalew was caught by machine-gun fire as he led half his father's forces across to help the wavering troops of Ras Imru and lost 1,000 men. Ras Imru's personal guard fought desperately. But by dusk over half had been killed and the cave from which Ayalew and Imru were together directing the afternoon's battle had been spotted and bombed. By evening the Ethiopians, except for the remnants of Ras Imru's personal guard, had only 20 rounds left per man. Their casualties had been heavy, and their fierce counter-attacks had failed. Maravigna's Corps had fired 10 million cartridges and 50,000 shells—'as much', noted Steer, 'as the whole Ethiopian northern line possessed at the beginning of the war.'

Next morning when the three Italian divisions advanced again, they found an 'absolute void' in front of them. The Ethiopians had disengaged during the night, and were retreating to the Takazze—a manœuvre that might have succeeded, as it deserved to succeed, had it not been for the Italian command of the skies. In Badoglio's words 'under the constant onslaught of our aircraft it very quickly turned into a disorderly riot'. The fords of the Takazze were difficult, steep, and—what should normally have given Ras Imru's men shelter and cover—thickly wooded. But 'in addition to the usual effective bombing and machine-gun fire small incendiary bombs had been used to set on fire the whole region about the fords, rendering utterly tragic the plight of the fleeing enemy.'

Badoglio immediately set about exploiting his success. Within days he had two columns organized and heading for the ancient capital of the Empire, the city of Gondar. The III Brigade of Eritreans moved straight down across the Takazze fords to mop up what was left of Ras Imru's forces. In fact these had virtually disintegrated. Ras Imru himself had barely managed to hold together a few thousand men in his hasty retreat, and south of the Takazze the whole countryside was full of demoralized fugitives from Ras Kassa's armies in the Tembien.

As the Eritrean Brigade followed the main caravan route into Beghemder, a motorized column was sent out from Asmara way over to their right along the safer, because emptier, edges of the frontier with the Sudan. Its commander Achille Starace, Secretary-General of the Fascist Party, was not a man to miss an occasion for bombast. When the column of 433 lorries and 3,400 men reached Om Ager, just before crossing from Italian territory and 'invading' Ethiopia, their commander halted and harangued his men. 'We are a poor nation,' cried Starace. 'That is good, for it keeps our muscles firm and our shapes trim.' It was Starace's pet theme—a fitness fanatic himself, he had Party Secretaries in all Italian towns cycling to work and beginning the day with press-ups. He proceeded to elaborate. 'Rich nations eat too much, get fat and their digestions become upset. That is what's the matter with most Englishmen. Moreover upset digestive systems addle the brains. This is the only way we can explain their attitude to us. They thought Mussolini would take off his hat and humbly bow submission. How wrong they were!'

As the column drove cautiously down through Beghemder, there were rumours of British troops massing at Gallabat on the Sudanese frontier, ready to march to the protection of Gondar. No doubt inspired by their leader, Starace's men declared themselves 'ugly and pugnacious' and talked of shooting on sight any British or Sudanese who might dare cross their path. None did.

Indeed they met with no opposition at all. Nor did the Eritrean column. By mid-March Ras Imru had been deserted by all but his own personal bodyguard of 300 men. He managed to telegraph a message through from Dabat north of Gondar to Dessie just before the Eritrean column arrived and cut the line. It read:

The greater part of the Gojjam troops have deserted and refused to fight except in their own province. The few who remain have been corrupting even our own personal following. We have not been able to carry out our projects. The local clans have not only deserted but have shown little respect for their overlord Dejaz Ayalew Birru, replying to him with rifle fire.

This last rather poignant sentence may have been Ras Imru's tactful way of excusing Ayalew Birru. Ras Imru had put forward a plan to organize guerrilla warfare in Ayalew's own mountainous territory of the Simien but the Dejaz would not hear of it, and the plan was dropped. Far to the Ras's rear, south of Beghemder, Italian planes were dropping leaflets and ammunition to the rebels in Gojjam, the province of which he was still theoretically governor. The outlook for Imru and his isolated band of followers appeared at this juncture to be poor indeed.

CHAPTER 8

MAI CEU

THUS by mid-March the north of Ethiopia was in Italian hands, the enemy's armies were disintegrating, dissidence and open revolt were spreading, and Italian columns were moving out in all directions.

In the centre Santini's First Corps occupied Amba Alagi without resistance, nine days after Ras Mulugueta had abandoned it. From the 'Gates of Alagi'—Alagi Ber (which was renamed 'Passo Toselli' almost immediately)—the Italians could look down at Mai Ceu and across the plain of Lake Ashangi towards the heights of Quoram where the Emperor was assembling his forces. All around and behind Quoram, down in the hot plains below, the countryside was in open revolt. Bands of Galla, hundreds sometimes thousands strong,[1] were snapping at the flanks of the Imperial armies, roaming like wolf-packs, dangerous, scenting blood, loot, and ruin, barely kept at bay.

Parallel with the main Italian advance Bastico's Third Corps had turned south from the Gheva valley and was moving through the northern highlands of Wag towards Socota, more slowly because their advance was held up by the aged Shum Tembien, Gabremedhin.

Over in the East, on the Italian left, a column had at long last crossed the Danakil desert. On 11 March its vanguard of irregulars after sixteen days marching across the salt-pans of this sunken sea, supplied by twenty-five aircraft en route, reached the fertile oasis of Sardo, capital of the Sultan Mohammed Yayo and the only place of importance in the whole Danakil desert. Sardo was only 120 miles from Dessie—technically Mohammed Yayo owed allegiance to the Crown Prince—and only 150 miles from the railway at Diredawa. An airfield was organized, and within

[1] The Political Office had distributed over six thousand rifles to the Azebo and the Raya bands.

two weeks 12 Italian aeroplanes were at Sardo, a threat to the Dessie–Addis Ababa road and more important still, a threat to the railway and a first step to the linking of Badoglio's and Graziani's forces.

The Emperor meanwhile remained at Quoram, with his court officials and his Guards, Ras Kebbede's army from Amba Alagi, and very little else. Italian propaganda was having its effect. A series of communiqués had to be issued from Dessie and Addis Ababa. The first denied that the Emperor was ill or had been wounded. The next denied that a villa was being prepared at Djibuti and that the Emperor was getting ready to leave his Empire, 'which is more devoted to him than ever'. The third denied categorically that Ras Kassa had been in contact with the enemy. More communiqués followed, denying once again that Haile Selassie was planning to leave, denying that direct negotiations had been opened with the Italians, denying that Ras Desta was in disgrace, even claiming that 5,000 Azebo Galla, though bribed to revolt, had rallied to the Imperial cause. A penultimate communiqué denied that the Crown Prince Asfa Wossen had been wounded and taken to the capital. A final communiqué denied the most serious report of all, that of a revolt in Wollo.

The Crown Prince had not been wounded. But there had been if not a revolt at least a serious plot at Dessie. The ringleader appears to have been the sixty-seven-year-old Ras Gabre Hiwot Mikael, Governor of the district where his mother Woizero Zennabish, widow of the Negus Mikael, still lived. Also involved were a cousin of the Empress Menen, Dejaz Amde Ali of Lagagora; and, curiously, one of the most respected Shoan nobles, Dejaz Auraris, the Governor of Menz. All three had been with Ras Mulugeta on Amba Aradam. These were all leaders of the older generation. In the eyes of many Wollo people Ras Gabre Hiwot was their rightful ruler, and outside the town of Dessie his word carried more weight than that of Wollo's official governor, the Crown Prince. Nothing is known of the details or aims of this plot. It seems unlikely, though, that it was pro-Italian. More probably, there were the beginnings of a conspiracy to depose the Crown Prince and possibly the Emperor, or in any event to put the direction of the war, now that Ras Mulugeta was dead, in more soldierly hands—that is to say, in the hands of the traditional warlike nobles. As it turned out Ras Gabre Hiwot, Dejaz

Amde Ali, Dejaz Auraris, and another Shoan noble were arrested and sent in chains to Addis Ababa. Almost at the same time as Ras Imru was cabling his pessimistic message from Dabat, the Emperor sent an equally despairing letter by runner to Ras Imru.[1] 'Our army', wrote Haile Selassie,

famous throughout Europe for its valour has lost it name, brought to ruin by a few traitors, to this pass it is reduced.

You will certainly have heard of the brave deaths of Dejaz Mashasha Wolde, of the Dejaz Beiene and of the Bitwoded Makonnen. Since death is an inevitable thing, it is well to be able to die after performing such deeds as theirs.

Those who were the first to betray us and those who afterwards followed their example, namely the chiefs of the forces of Wollo such as Ras Gabre Hiwot, Dejaz Amde Ali, and others also of the army of Shoa, namely Dejaz Auraris . . . have all been arrested.

. . . For yourself if you think that with your troops and with such of the local inhabitants as you can collect together you can do anything where you are, do it. If on the other hand, your position is difficult and you are convinced of the impossibility of fighting, having lost all hope in your front, and if you think it better to come here and die with us, let us know of your decision by telephone from Dabat.

From the League we have so far derived no hope or benefit.

Yet Haile Selassie's situation was not entirely hopeless. He under-estimated the effect his own presence would have. From Socota the capital of Wag, Haile Kebbede at first sent only his Fitaurari, Tafere, to join the Emperor. But when Haile Selassie summoned him and his army as well, they went willingly, confident because *Janhoy* himself was there. An entirely fresh army came up from the south-west: the levies of the rich province of Kaffa, commanded by Ras Getachew Abate. The other leaders who had fought at Amba Aradam and the Tembien came in—except for Admassu Birru who had retreated south-west towards the borders of Beghemder with his men from Yeggiu.

The greatest of the surviving potentates, Ras Kassa and Ras Seyum, reached Quoram from Socota at midday on 19 March. The Emperor had seen neither of them since the war had begun, and their arrival, with their troops, understandably boosted his morale. Next day he moved up to the position of Aia on the

---

[1] Which Ras Imru never read. The runner was intercepted by the Italians and it was Badoglio who received the letter.

forward slopes overlooking the plain of Lake Ashangi and in a cavern hollowed out of the rock set up his advance headquarters, facing the enemy's positions at Mai Ceu. On the 21st he sent a radio message, very different in tone from his despairing letter to Ras Imru, to the Empress Menen:

Since our trust is in our Creator and in the hope of His help and as we have decided to advance and enter the fortifications and since God is our only help, confide this decision of ours in secret to the Abuna, to the ministers and to the dignitaries and offer unto God your fervent prayers.

The Emperor of Ethiopia had decided to follow the millenial tradition of his predecessors and lead his own troops into battle. Badoglio's wireless messengers intercepted the message. He immediately cancelled the orders for his proposed advance, and disposed his forces to await the Imperial attack.

It was fitting that the great battle of the war should be fought not between subordinates but between the Commander-in-Chief of the Italian armies and the Emperor in person. The two protagonists of the armed conflict were now facing each other in the central highlands half-way between Magdala which had seen the death and defeat of one Emperor and Adowa which had seen the glorious victory of another. The subordinate commanders had made their moves, won or lost, and been swept aside. The stage was cleared. Both the Emperor and the Marshal must have realized that the impending battle would decide the fate of an Empire, and neither of them, in his heart of hearts, could have wished it otherwise.

For this decisive action Badoglio had called up his best troops; soldiers from the northern valleys at the foot of the Alps, the levies of Savoy loyal to the dynasty and proud of the historic traditions of the army of Piedmont, three divisions of regular infantry from the North of Italy, three Legions of Blackshirts, and almost the whole of the Eritrean army, Christians and Mohammedans mixed, ready to fight as they had for fifty years past for the flag of Italy against the central Empire. With the Marshal were two senior generals, Pirzio-Biroli of the Eritrean Corps and Santini of the First; six divisional commanders; and under them many more generals commanding brigade after brigade of Italian troops, and battery after battery of Italian guns, many times the strength of the army that had perished under Baratieri at Adowa.

On the Ethiopian side could be found most of the greatest names of the Empire. Their fathers—Ras Makonnen, father of the Emperor himself, Ras Mangasha father of Ras Seyum, Ras Mangasha Atikim father of Ras Kebbede, the Liquemaquas Abate, father of Ras Getachew—had led their armies to victory at Adowa. As for Ras Kassa, he had himself fought at Adowa as a boy of fifteen beside his father while his grandfather defended the western marches of Shoa against the rebel Galla. Ethiopia's history since Adowa had been shaped by these men and their families. In the eyes of their followers they stood as symbols of the Christian Empire and its independence.

With the four Rases and the Emperor and Dejaz Haile Kebbede, the heir to the Zagwe Dynasty and nephew of the Wagshum Gwangul, were nobles of the court and war-leaders of the provinces. The Emperor had brought with him his former Minister of War, the Imperial Fitaurari Birru Wolde Giorgis. There were courtiers of the old type, veterans who had themselves like Ras Kassa fought as youngsters at Adowa, and officers of the new army—notably Shallaka Mesfin Sileshi, himself one day to be the most powerful man in Ethiopia after the Emperor. There were priests and bishops and even women fighters. There were British-trained officers, ex-King's African Rifles, French-trained officers from St. Cyr, and Belgian-trained officers. But apart from the Russian Konavoloff there were very few foreigners still with the Emperor. It was an almost purely Ethiopian army, though the best-equipped of all, with 400 machine-guns, a battery or two of 75 pounders, six mortars and enough Oerlikons to make the Italian pilots wary.

Above all morale was high in the Ethiopian camp because the Emperor was with them and because they were going in to the attack.

On the afternoon of 24 March the Emperor held a great feast, the traditional *gebir* with raw meat and *tej* in the cavern at Aia, sitting on an improvised throne flanked by Ras Seyum and Ras Kassa. Konavoloff had been sent off the day before disguised as a Coptic deacon to spy out the enemy lines, and the Emperor had spent the morning studying the Italian camp through his binoculars. After the feast there was an improvised council of war, confused and long-lasting. The Emperor wanted to attack that night. Some of his chiefs on the other hand were for retreating to Waldia or even to Dessie. The debate went on for hours. Sarcasms were hurled at those who suggested a retreat but the attack was postponed—as Badoglio learnt from a wireless message—till Saturday the 28th or Monday the 30th. It was unthinkable for the Ethiopians to attack on a Sunday.

Hour after hour over the next few days the Azebo Galla trooped into the cave at Aia, receiving—often from the Emperor's own hands—ten or fifteen dollars, long striped silk shirts, or black satin capes. The hope of winning them over had been one of the main reasons for delaying the attack. They promised their support and were told to harry the Italian flanks.

Tuesday 31 March was, finally, the day decided on for battle —it was St. George's Day. Many of the Ethiopian troops, half believing that St. George their patron saint had fought with them at the battle of Adowa, thought it a day of great hope and good omen.

Badoglio knew that the enemy would attack as ferociously as they had done at Adowa. He planned his defence accordingly. His three best divisions manned his front line, where the passes that led back to Mai Ceu debouched on to the plain of Lake Ashangi. On the Italian right he placed the crack *Valpusteria Alpini*; in the centre the 2nd Eritrean Division; and on the left the 1st Eritreans. Then in the second line lay three more, the *Sabauda*, the Blackshirts of the '23rd January' and, drawn far back to the north to prevent an enveloping movement on the Italian left, the *Assietta*.

The Italians, knowing in advance of the attack, had had time to fortify their positions, put up thorn *zeriba* hedges, site their guns, and bring up by pack mules all the supplies they needed from their motor-transport base twenty hours away by mule. They knew not only that an attack was imminent but almost certainly when it was coming. The radio messages of the enemy were being intercepted, and many of the Azebo Galla had come in to obtain more dollars and better weapons from the Italians and to warn them that the attack was planned for the Monday. Finally on Monday evening an officer of the Guard deserted and warned the Italians to keep their eyes well open that night.

At 3 a.m. on St. George's Day the Italian front line was woken and askaris were sent out to patrol no man's land. At 5.45 two Mauser shots broke the silence and two red Verey lights flared up into the sky, as the alarm was given simultaneously on the front of the *Alpini* and the 2nd Eritreans. From the slopes of Quoram the Ethiopian guns and mortars opened fire, playing upon the front line of the *Alpini*, held by the Piedmontese of the *Intra* battalion, the Ligurians of the *Feltre*, and the Veronese of the *Pieve di Teco*. The rattle of machine-guns joined in. Many Italians were killed. A battery of Schneider 75s directed by an ex-St. Cyr cadet, Kenyaz Chifli, was particularly effective, and the Ethiopian mortars wiped out all the officers of the opposing 8th Battery. As the first Ethiopian assault went in, their artillery fire switched towards the slopes of the eastern Mecan pass in front of which lay the 2nd Eritrean Division. Though surprise had been lost, the battle was, for the Ethiopians, beginning well.

It was a simple enough battle as battles go; almost a textbook affair. Again and again that morning the Ethiopians hurled themselves forward with ferocious courage against the static lines of the three Italian Divisions. Again and again the Italian guns and riflemen, well-situated and beautifully protected by the thorn *zeribas* to their front, cut swathes through the advancing ranks of the Ethiopians and drove them back. Only once did they have to use the bayonet. The discipline of the defenders was such that they never rashly ventured out in pursuit of the retreating enemy. What pursuit there was was done, as always, by the Italian planes. And all through that long long morning the rival commanders nervously eyed the hordes of Azebo Galla gathering at Warahei on the eastern flank of the battlefield, aware of their treacherous instincts and their conflicting promises.

In the half-light before the sun rose the first wave of Ethiopians had broken itself on the *zeribas* and had been driven back. The second column, 15,000 strong, under Ras Kassa's command, plunged furiously for the weakest point in the Italian line. Driving through the 3rd *Gruppo* of Eritreans, they nearly opened up a fatal gap between the *Alpini* division on the right and the 2nd Eritreans in the centre. By 8 a.m. however the air overhead was filled with the sound the Ethiopians had come to dread: sixty planes machine-gunned and bombed the rear of Ras Kassa's column (and of Ras Seyum's diversionary attack on the far right too) before flying on to strafe the Emperor's headquarters.

After a brief pause Haile Selassie launched his third and what he hoped would be his decisive assault. The Imperial Guard under Ras Getachew moved forward against the already wobbly Italian centre. This time the battle lasted a wearying three hours; passing through the crumbling 2nd Eritreans, the Guard turned on the comparatively fresh 1st Eritreans, was met with withering fire, halted, was attacked by the bayonet, and then by the combined artillery of both divisions. Finally, sullenly, they gave ground. By midday the great assault had been beaten off, and the Guard in their turn fell back to lick their wounds.

A long lull ensued. It was still anybody's victory. For the Ethiopians, though beaten back, had not been pursued, still less routed. All three divisions in the Italian front line had been badly mauled and were running low on ammunition.

By early afternoon the sky was overcast and intermittent rain was falling. The attacks of the Italian planes were slackening. Haile Selassie reinforced his columns and ordered a general assault all along the front in a last attempt to break the Italian lines before nightfall. This time his lion-maned chieftains and uniformed captains moved forward together. Hand to hand fighting raged all along the line, particularly fierce at the junction between the two Eritrean divisions and on the far edge of the Italian right, held by the *Alpini*, where the Ethiopians were desperately trying to turn the flank.

It was at this moment that the horsemen of the Azebo Galla at last intervened. It must have been with despair that in the confusion of the battlefield Haile Selassie watched them moving forward from over on his right, not—as he was surely hoping until the very last moment—to roll up the 1st Eritreans and sweep the whole Italian line away in confusion, but instead to fall upon the rear of his own embattled warriors. Pursued by the Galla, machine-gunned by the enemy, bombed from the air, the Ethiopians fell grimly back once again to the slopes of Quoram.

With dusk the danger of another major assault that day had disappeared. But all that night the Italians worked feverishly to repair their fortifications and collect munitions, fully expecting a further attack the next day. The 1st Eritreans who had taken least part in the battle, had only 15 cartridges per rifle, and 2 magazines per machine-gun. The mules bringing up munitions and supplies did not arrive till the following evening.

Haile Selassie, as the Italians suspected, was indeed planning to attack again the next day. Had he done so, it might have been as decisive a victory as Adowa. Behind the three frontline divisions of the Italians were three more, but they were not so good and above all not nearly so experienced. If the Italian front had cracked, their second line might not have held in the face of fleeing troops of their own side. The *élan* of the Ethiopian onrush that had carried them through to victory at Adowa could have carried them through to a second and greater victory at Mai Ceu. Furthermore the Eritreans, their traditional opponents, had suffered severely, losing almost a thousand killed that day, roughly decimation of the line—casualties severe enough to demoralize any army.

But the Ethiopian leaders met in council and rejected the Emperor's plans. Despite their courage all their assaults, even the assault of the Guard, had failed. The Azebo Galla had betrayed them once more and therefore the route back to the safety of Shoa promised to be difficult and dangerous. There were many dead and more wounded. Heavy rains were beginning to fall. Faint counsels prevailed.

The rains fell all next day. The Ethiopians collected their dead and, amidst the wailing of their women and the chanting of their priests, buried them on the plain of Lake Ashangi. Among the dead were two Fitauraris and three Dejaz: Dejaz Wanderat, who had been wounded at Adowa; the Emperor's own nephew, Dejaz Mangasha Yilma, son of Ras Makonnen's eldest son; and Dejaz Aberra Tedla, the governor of Mai Ceu.

But it was not till the following night that the Emperor finally agreed to order a retreat.

CHAPTER 9

APRIL 1936

APRIL was for the Ethiopians a month of almost unrelieved disaster and for the Italians of almost uninterrupted success. It could hardly have been otherwise in the North. One after the other the Ethiopian armies had been defeated and, with the Imperial army itself battered and withdrawing, it seemed to the Ethiopians that only God who had so often before saved their Empire from the invaders could save it again. Divine intervention apart, the Ethiopians could count on only two assets: the person of the Emperor, miraculously unharmed, and the Army of the South.

On 1 April, the day after Mai Ceu, Gondar, the historic capital of Beghemder and, until Theodore's reign, the Imperial capital as well, had fallen without resistance. Starace raised the Italian flag at 10 a.m.; two hours later General Kubeddu, who had been tactfully camping outside Gondar for almost a week, led his Eritreans into the city. There the two columns halted. There were rumours of Ras Imru in the east, of 40,000 men gathering at Ifag to the south, of 8,000 with Ras Kassa at Debra Tabor, all concentrating to advance—with British help—and recapture Gondar.

In fact there were no concentrations, no plan, and no British help. Ras Imru had nearly been cut off in Gondar by the Italian advance. He had made his get-away through *shifta*-infested country and was heading for Gojjam and Debra Markos. The Italians met no resistance at all in Beghemder—all the more extraordinary because this was the heart of the Amhara highlands, the traditional last bastion of the Empire, and it was only to be expected that their advance would be contested step by step by the local chiefs and peasants alike. There had been in Beghemder no open revolt against the Emperor, as had happened in Gojjam, but there was no resistance to the Italians either, and this can only be explained by the events of 1930. Then the chiefs and people of Beghemder led by Ras Gugsa Wule had been defeated and bombed by Haile Selassie and his Shoans; five years later Haile Selassie and the Shoans were themselves being defeated and bombed by the Italians. The Amhara of Beghemder had followed their imposed rulers, Ras Kassa and his son Wondossen, to the north. They had done their duty, dispersed or been dispersed, seen Ras Kassa and Wondossen defeated, and themselves returned to their homes and farms. They did not fight for the Italians, but they would no longer fight against them.

On the night of 2 April Ethiopian GHQ issued what was to be its final war communiqué—announcing a great victory at Mai Ceu—and the Emperor finally ordered a retreat. The retreating columns set off before dawn the next day; the Emperor in uniform with a pith helmet was riding a white horse. It was a fine morning, and the retreat was, if not orderly, at least as unchaotic as could be expected in the circumstances. The circumstances however changed in the early morning, as the two latent threats materialized. The Azebo Galla began harassing the army's flanks and the Italian planes appeared. From then on it was carnage and confusion. Flight after flight of Capronis dropped bombs and mustard gas on the retreating Ethiopians: 150 planes flew out, of which only one was shot down, though 28 were damaged. All that day and the following day the pounding from the air continued as the armies attempted to cross the Golgola plain. The rivers were full of corpses. The rearguard commanded by Ras Getachew was savagely attacked by the Azebo Galla. In those two nightmarish days the Imperial army lost more men than had died at the battle of Mai Ceu itself. By the evening of the 4th the Emperor had decided in near desperation that it was impossible to continue the retreat. The columns turned wearily and clambered back up to Quoram. There in the comparative safety of the highlands they dispersed, heading west across country, moving only by night, all semblance of order or organization lost.

Men made for their own lands. Haile Kebbede, badly wounded by a bullet in the neck at Mai Ceu, was taken back towards Wag; not however to Socota which had been occupied a week earlier by Bastico's Third Corps. Wondossen Kassa headed not to his governorate at Debra Tabor in Beghemder but to Lasta, south of Wag, his grandfather's country, where the inhabitants were both warlike and loyal to the Shoan Emperor. Aberra Kassa his brother made for the Kassa fief of Salale in northern Shoa. Ras Seyum, now aged nearly 50, was ordered by the Emperor to go north and wage guerrilla warfare in Tigre; Ras Kebbede went back to Ifrata probably with similar orders— orders Haile Selassie must have known were almost impossible to carry out. Inconsistent, too—for the Emperor, despite his early insistence on the merits of guerrilla warfare for others, had himself in the end fought the traditional large-scale battle for which all Ethiopians were physically and above all mentally trained. Ras Kassa and Ras Getachew with the remnants of their forces and of the Guard accompanied Haile Selassie as he moved off, away from the snarling Azebo Galla of the plains into the friendly highlands of Wag and Lasta.

Three days later a decree for general mobilization was issued in the capital. All able-bodied men were to rally, with or without arms, all citizens were immediately to report suspicious activities to the authorities, and so forth—the last pathetic symptoms of imminent collapse in any regime. More to the point, the very last army was summoned from the south-west, the levies of Wol-lega-Saio led by the governor of that province Dejaz Mangasha Wube, to defend the capital. Captain Tamm and his two remain-ing co-officers started planning to use the cadets and their 'brigade'; and Blatta Takele Wolde Hawariat to collect arms.

On the 9th the Eritrean Corps moved from the battlefield at Mai Ceu, at first encountering 'slight remnants of resistance' but soon 'amidst displays of jubilation and homage on the part of the local inhabitants'—in fact, though Badoglio neglects to mention it, the Azebo Galla. But even past the dusty plains and into the Wollo highlands there was no resistance. As cavalry patrols of the advance guard of Pirzio-Biroli's corps entered Dessie, the Crown Prince and his entourage, Wodajo Ali, his tutor and the real governor of Wollo, Fikremariam the commander of the Guard and of the Shoan garrison, left without a fight. 'On great strips of cloth stretched across the decorated streets of the town', noted Badoglio, 'the population had written in the local language "The Hawk has flown".'

Where was the Emperor meanwhile? The answer strikes the outsider strangely. The Emperor had not been reorganizing his army or falling back hastily to the capital or contacting the Powers in a last, desperate, appeal for aid. The Emperor had been at Lalibela praying. He had lost a battle and almost lost an Empire, so he made a pilgrimage. The record of those three days belonged to him and his thoughts alone; Badoglio intercepted no messages, earthly or celestial. He may not even have known at the time where his opponent was; and when, a year or two later, he published his own account he made no comment either as a general or as a Christian upon Haile Selassie's 'lost days'. And yet it would be interesting to know if the Italians were impressed by a gesture that they must in their bones have understood, though one which they would no longer have imitated.

The famous rock churches of Lalibela had themselves been constructed by the Zagwe kings as a fortress. It must have crossed Haile Selassie's mind that it would be fitting for an Emperor to die there. If it did, it was a passing thought. He, his Rases, and his escort after three days of prayer headed south-east towards Dessie, only to find as they neared the town that it, together with the province of Wollo, had been abandoned. Shoa now lay open to the invaders.

Rumours of the fall of Dessie had reached Addis Ababa on 16 April. The Emperor's whereabouts were unknown except to a few, and there was an atmosphere of impending catastrophe. From Dessie a road of sorts—the 'Imperial Highway'—led to Addis Ababa, and between Dessie and Addis Ababa there were no organized defences, virtually no troops, no real reason in fact why the Italians should not drive straight down the road into the capital.

Blatta Takele Wolde Hawariat, the governor of Addis Ababa, did his best. He hired 70 men to spread contradictory and optimistic rumours in the bars and *tej beits*, and a young Canadian to set up a training camp on his own land at Sabata west of Addis Ababa where a few Shoans were instructed in the elements of guerrilla warfare. He formed a Patriotic Association and gathered 800 volunteers in St. George's Cathedral to swear that they would never betray their country. He assured the foreign embassies that they would be defended. But the diplomats, aware both of his patriotic xenophobia and of the difficulties of ensuring that such a promise be kept, strengthened the defences of their enclaves and started warning their nationals to be ready to leave their homes and move bag and baggage into the safety of the embassy compounds.

The Belgian officers insisted upon leaving for Djibuti. They were mercenaries, unprotected by their government, and it is possible that the Italians might have been hard, indeed savage, with any who fell into their hands. The three remaining Swedish officers, however, were still officers in their country's regular armed forces, and felt no such fears for their own personal safety if captured. Captain Tamm's immediate reaction therefore was to gather his cadets together and attempt to defend the capital. The cadets responded enthusiastically. So it came about that the last Ethiopian 'army' to move out to the north to stem the rolling Italian advance was a group of half-trained teenagers advised and encouraged by three barely more experienced Swedish officers.

How and where was the enemy advance to be stemmed? 116 cadets were not by themselves a force sufficient for the defence of more than the school in which they were being trained, and in any case Addis Ababa, lying at the foot of the mountains of Entotto, was not a city that could ever be defended in itself. But as the road snaked between Dessie and Addis Ababa, it rose at one point to a pass even higher than that of Amba Alagi. It was here at the Pass of Ad Termaber that Tamm decided to stage his Thermopylae.

By this time Tamm did not merely have his cadets to count on. Months before, with the Emperor's approval, he had set about forming a brigade, and by mid-March the Brigade was ready to move. It consisted of 870 NCOs, 4,100 men, 117 riding mules, and 1,298 pack mules. The numbers were impressive, but the troops were of poor quality, the last of the levies, old men of sixty who had been at Adowa and boys of fifteen, enthusiastic but already deserting through disappointment at not having been immediately sent to the front.

Over this ragged half-armed and half-trained band the young cadets reigned with intoxicating titles: Kifle Nasibu, Colonel and Brigade Commander, Negga Haile Selassie, Chief of Staff and Second in Command, and as Battalion commanders two cadets later to become famous, Essayas Gabre Selassie and Mulugueta Bulli, one of the few Galla officers (and therefore invaluable, as a third of the troops were Gallinya-speaking peasants with whom the cadets, their officers, could communicate only by gesture). The two machine-gun companies—which had only 30 machine-guns—were commanded by Abebe Tafari and Assefa Araya.

There were six cannon, without shells, and rifles for only 2,000 men.

On 17 April Tamm went to the Great Ghebbi and berated the assembled Ministers for having refused to listen to his continual pleas for proper equipment for his brigade. 'It was with a feeling of bitter satisfaction that I told them what I thought.' Now—at once—they needed mules, ammunition, uniforms, and money —no more promises from Makonnen Haptewold, but immediate proof of goodwill. Tamm was told that the Tsehafe Taezaz (Minister of the Pen) Haile was already at the Pass with 300 men, and the veteran Dejaz Metafaria covering a track to the west with another 1,000. He left the Great Ghebbi with written confirmation of the promises made. At the Oletta school when Tamm reported the good news, the soldiers and cadets danced with joy.

At dusk on 19 April the Brigade Staff, Kifle Nasibu, Negga Haile Selassie, one rifle company, and Assefa's machine-gun company were ready to depart. Twenty lorries, machine guns, and money had been promised. By 1 a.m. sixteen lorries and the machine-guns had arrived; as the journey could only be made by night for fear of Italian planes it was late. Tamm took his convoy into the capital, routed out Makonnen Haptewold and demanded the money within an hour. Within an hour, and for once he had it[1]—a sign that even the Ministers in the capital realized how dangerous the situation was. The 30,000 dollars weighed 840 kilos. When Tamm got back to his convoy, he was met by a very upset young Chief of Staff. 'Two lorries have escaped,' said Negga. 'Which direction?' 'To the Front.'

For another day Tamm waited vainly for more lorries. Next evening the convoy at last set out, in the middle of the night passing the Crown Prince and his escort as they entered the outskirts of Addis Ababa. At Debra Brehan 80 miles north they stopped for petrol and met heading in the other direction Lij Legesse Gabremariam, son of the Dejaz, with the five Italian prisoners from Dessie and some cannon which he refused point-blank to hand over.

They were forced to stay at Debra Brehan that day. The lorry drivers, Hindis and therefore British subjects, went on strike: so far and no further. None of Tamm's cadets or their men knew

---

[1] 'Les Ethiopiens sont des très braves gens', Major Dotheé had often commented, 'mais il est malheureux qu'ils soient si difficiles à se separer de leur argent.'

how to drive. It was a depressing day in every way. (It was an equally depressing day in the capital. 21 April was the 2,690th anniversary of the Founding of Rome, and an occasion for panicking as the rumour spread that Mussolini would choose this day to occupy Addis Ababa.) A group of journalists driving back from Dessie told the cadets the Wollo army was retreating. Tamm, Kifle, and Negga decided to halt the army and rally it. But when during the day the fugitives drifted in, without food, begging for bread, leaderless and refusing to return, the cadets realized it was useless; it was no longer an army but a rabble. Their first contact with war was the depressing vision of a defeated army.

That night they finally found drivers and reached Ad Termaber. The following morning Tamm and Kifle visited Tsehafe Taezaz Haile: red-eyed, a beard, a coat, a raincoat, and black shoes with holes cut for the small toes, a detail which confirmed the Swede in his judgement—a bureaucrat. The position was not as strong as Tamm had foreseen; the slopes were steep but not impassable. The Tsehafe Taezaz had dug the road up but, ignorant of the most elementary military rules, was unable to cover the 'obstacle' he had created with fire. Below, the local village chief, a Geraz, had refused to allow the road to be blown, alleging that this would cause a local revolt. There was no news of Dejaz Metaferia and his thousand men meant to be covering the caravan track from Worra Ilu. Sending out patrols Tamm discovered five more tracks that came up from below and could be used to outflank his position. He cabled back to the Crown Prince and Makonnen Haptewold informing them that instead of barring a narrow mountain pass he would have to cover a front of 25 miles.

Badoglio had arrived with his staff at Dessie, apparently unaware that 75 miles to the south a Swedish officer and two companies were preparing to bar the advance of his two Army Corps into Addis Ababa. He was preoccupied not with opposition but with triumph and the correct way to exploit it. For weeks he had been planning the final triumphal march. A spendid mechanized column would sweep down from Dessie upon Addis Ababa and occupy the capital, impressing the natives, cowing any opposition, strong enough to occupy the capital, the suburbs and the railway. It would be more a question of engineering than of military art—repairing the 250-mile Imperial Highway which

Badoglio scathingly called 'a bad cart-track'. The lorried columns, escorted by a squadron of tanks, and three groups of mechanized artillery, were already moving across the plain of Mai Ceu towards Dessie. The *colonna de ferrea volonta*—the 'column of iron will'—Badoglio christened the column; a brilliantly chosen phrase for the Italian press to fasten on, as indeed it did.

But Badoglio at the same time took, though he did not publicize, his precautions. The flanks of the 'iron-will column' were to be protected by two parallel columns advancing on foot: the I (Eritrean) Brigade on one side and the detached Group of Eritrean Battalions which had fought at Mai Ceu on the other.

As these columns gathered at Dessie and as Tamm feverishly tried to organize the defences of Ad Termaber, Kubeddu's III (Eritrean) Brigade occupied the town of Bahr Dar on the southern side of Lake Tana. They had crossed the Blue Nile and were now in Gojjam. They met no opposition.

Meanwhile the war in the Ogaden had after a long lull flared up again. Prodded both by Mussolini and Badoglio, Graziani at last resumed, or prepared to resume, his advance on Harar. Dagghabur had been bombed, Harar had been bombed, Jijiga, the base of Nasibu's operations had been honoured with a personal and flying visit from General Ranza, the air force commander on the southern front, and 'reduced to a mass of ruins'.

On the ground, in the desert interspersed with wells and fortified posts, the two masters had been moving their knights and their pawns forward. In the centre of the chequer board Colonel Frusci and his mechanized Arabo-Somali battalions were based at Gorrahei, now the Italian forward airbase. There they faced the main Ethiopian defensive position in the hills of Sasabeneh, in front of the town of Dagghabur, Nasibu's headquarters. In the upper Ogaden General Agostini, with a mixed group of Blackshirts of the Forest Militia, *Carabinieri* and other elements was concentrating forward of Walwal at Gerlogubi. In the lower Ogaden, between the Webbi Shebelli and the Tug Fafan, were Graziani's most experienced troops, the Libyan Division of General Nasi. They were concentrating around Danane which Olol Dinke had in January occupied without opposition.

The two Italian Divisions, the *Peloritana* and the *Tevere* Blackshirts were, significantly, held back in reserve by Graziani. Less preoccupied by politics than Badoglio, or possibly less experienced and less astute, he had failed to realize the importance of allowing both units at least a symbolic presence in the front line. A general of colonial experience, he was fighting a colonial war with the colonial troops he knew and trusted.

The Italian plan was clear; a three-pronged attack with, as the biggest thrust, a lightning attack on the left designed to cut off the fortifications at Sasabeneh rather than to assault them frontally. But the Ethiopians did not wait to be surprised and attacked. For the last time in the war by attacking first they attempted to disrupt a proposed offensive, to break up a concentration and to pursue a beaten army.

In the lower Ogaden Abebe Damtew with his 3,000–4,000 levies from the south, reinforced by Makonnen Endalkatchew and his Wollegas, led the attack. With them came the wife of Dejaz Hapte Mikael, the first arrival at Harar, governor of a small southern province; her husband was sick back in Jijiga and she was commanding his troops. The total Ethiopian strength was about 10,000. They had a tank, plenty of ammunition brought by mule, and their morale was high. Dejaz Abebe had always had a better reputation as a war-leader and fighter than his brother Ras Desta, and his men were keen to show that they could succeed where the Sidamo army had failed.

Dejaz Abebe and Dejaz Makonnen advanced against General Nasi on 14 April. Nasi advanced at the same time, and for three days fighting spread over the whole area between Birkat and Danane. This was the major battle of the Ogaden, the only large-scale fighting that took place there, confused as it must be when the ground is such that it is impossible to talk of a front, only of a series of separate combats, and when the climate is such that fighting has to halt while both sides seek water and rest.

In the end Nasi's Eritreans and Olol Dinke's Ajurans and Hussein Ali's Rer Naib beat the men of Wollega, and of Gemu-Gofa, and of Kulu who had travelled so far to fight. Where men on foot fought with men on foot, the battle swayed homerically first to one side, then to another. But Nasi had formed two mechanized columns on the right, and as these columns encircled their rear Dejaz Abebe and Dejaz Makonnen pulled back. The gamble had failed.

By the 23rd the Italians were advancing on all fronts in the

South, and Graziani could congratulate himself that, despite an unexpected incident in the lower Ogaden, his moves were being made according to plan.

In the centre of the Ethiopian defences at Sasabeneh opposite Frusci and his mechanized battalions the three Turks inspected their half-prepared trenches and gun-sites, considered anxiously the morale of the two Guards battalions that had fled from Gorrahei six months before, thanked the stars or their Gods that the Belgians had gone and that they could count on some stout defenders such as Omar Samanthar and Fitaurari Baade, and hoped for a second Dardanelles.

Graziani launched his attack on the following day, 24 April. There was little hand-to-hand fighting in this 'Battle of Manœuvre' that followed in the next four days. The very concept of a fortified position isolated in the desert and easily outflanked was a bluff, as the Turks must have known and the Ethiopians soon realized. The clans south of Dagghabur led by the Ugaz Mohammed Othman of the Ogaden Malinga came in to submit, and when the Italians put in their textbook attack on Sasabeneh itself on 28 April, there was only sporadic resistance. Dejaz Nasibu and the other leaders were back in Harar, their levies disintegrating, as had happened in the North, thinking only of returning to their own lands while the leaders debated. Only Fitaurari Malion and his 2,500 men, more or less intact, were in position at Jijiga covering the mountain gates, the Marda Pass, that led up from the Ogaden desert into the highlands at Harar. Thus on 30 April, six days after the final action had been started, Graziani's advanced columns entered the town of Dagghabur, 'capital' of the Ogaden. At Dagghabur it was reported that a platoon of Italian soldiers rendered military honours at the grave of Afework, an opponent whom even they had respected. The route to Harar lay almost open.

Far over on the other side of the Empire Debra Tabor had been occupied. On the day that the Italians put in the final attack on Sasabeneh two battalions from Starace's column, the 'Mussolini' Blackshirt Battalion and the 11th Native, put in a surprise attack that met with no resistance at all. Ras Kassa and Dejaz Ayalew Birru had been reported there, but Ras Kassa was many miles away and Dejaz Ayalew Birru had left as the Italians approached. Over in the centre however there was a leader, unfitted for

guerrilla warfare, who was already negotiating. Ras Seyum had
sent a letter to General Bastico at Socota, the substance of which
was: 'I have done my duty. What are your terms?' Both
diplomatically and on the ground, it had been a week of movement for the Italians on the now vastly extended northern and
southern fronts.

For the last Ethiopian defenders of the capital, Tamm's cadets, it
had on the other hand been a static time in a confined position. In
those six days the situation had, if anything, deteriorated on Ad
Termaber. Italian planes had flown over but had not shown much
interest. That was encouraging. But then 45 men and all the
sentinels had deserted during the night, and the Tsehafe Taezaz
Haile had left to 'inspect' Ankober in the rear. When would the
rest of the Brigade come? Two battalions under Lt. Bouveng had
been due to set out on foot the same night as Tamm and his
advance guard left by lorry. The rest of the Brigade had been
ordered to follow a week later under the third remaining Swedish
officer Thornburn. But there was no news. Bouveng and the two
vital battalions had not arrived, and the only way of contacting
Addis Ababa was by the telephone office at Debra Brehan, 45
miles back, the line to which functioned only intermittently.

On 28 April there were reports of two enemy columns only 40
miles away. At noon after a morning of heated but unrewarded
effort Tamm and Kifle had to admit that the line to Debra Brehan
was totally useless. In the evening there was shooting in the
foothills below. Negga Haile Selassie from his advanced post in
the valley reported that Italians in 100 lorries were making a
bridge over the little river, and away in the Awasa desert the
enemy's camp-fires were burning.

Next morning the Italians had bridged the stream, and the
Geraz in the village down below, whom Tamm suspected of
treachery, had locked himself in his house. Clearly an assault on
Ad Termaber was only a matter of hours away. To hold the Pass
there were only a handful of cadets, two companies badly
reduced both in numbers and morale by desertion, and two or
three hundred peasants commanded by Tsehafe Taezaz Haile's
son, Lij Ayele. Tamm was faced with a dilemma: to stay, hoping
that Bouveng would arrive like Blücher at Waterloo, and to
direct the defence; or to go and find out what was happening and
where and why. Both decisions were dubious. He took the more

dubious of the two, he went. Abandoned by their two seniors, the young Ethiopians, Lij Ayele and Kifle Nasibu, prepared to face the attack.

Half-way to Debra Brehan, Tamm met the lorries of Dr. Melly's British Ambulance Unit and advised them to turn back. They did so. At Debra Brehan the phone was out of order, so that night Tamm drove 25 miles further back still. As Bouveng later related, his sentinels had seen his car pass at 3 a.m.—in other words Bouveng's two battalions were still over 80 miles from Ad Termaber. They had left Addis Ababa four days earlier and had therefore covered a highly creditable forty miles a day. But they had left three days too late.

On the night of 29 April Tamm finally got through on the phone to the Crown Prince and asked him to send out a plane to find Bouveng's battalions and drop orders urging them to push forward. The plane was sent out, but the pilot dropped his orders from 5,000 feet up, and not surprisingly Bouveng never received them.

Even if he had, it would have been too late. Badoglio's mechanized column had halted at the foot of Ad Termaber, the 10,000 foot-high pass. Gallina and his veteran askaris of the III Brigade were ordered to put in the attack. The inhabitants of the village down below guided them up the different mule tracks. It was quickly over; no Thermopylae, for the lorries were there ready for the retreat, and the handful of cadets were at their first battle, not their last. One cadet and fifty men were lost, and so the Italians occupied, almost without resistance, the second of the great mountain passes that stood between Asmara and Addis Ababa. If the first, Amba Alagi, had been seriously defended or even if Bouveng's mere two battalions had arrived in time at the second, the results of the invasion might perhaps have been different; for in war a tiny event can lead to the most unexpected results, and a won skirmish be of more importance than a lost battle.

As they drove back toward Debra Brehan, the cadets met Bouveng and his men marching northwards. It seems that there were no further thoughts of resistance, that they took Bouveng and their fellow cadets and what arms they could on the lorries and drove back towards the capital. What became of their troops is unknown. Presumably they were ordered to disperse or dispersed of their own accord, abandoned by their young offi-

cers. At Debra Brehan a white flag was already flying, and the
inhabitants were hostile.

It was the afternoon of the last day of April. Tamm was already
back in the capital. After telephoning the Crown Prince, he had
decided only too humanly to drive on back. At the outskirts of
the city he met Thornburn: the main body of the brigade, with no
lorries and few mules, had not even departed. When he reached
the Ghebbi he learnt from Makonnen Haptewold that Kifle
Nasibu had phoned through from Debra Brehan: the Pass had
been given up, and there was nothing between the Italians and the
capital except 175-odd miles of undefended tracks. He was asked
to help defend Addis Ababa and refused immediately. He saw the
Crown Prince and said that he and his fellow Swedish officers
would have to resign forthwith.

On the way into Addis Ababa, before seeing Thornburn,
Tamm had passed another returning cortège: the cortège of the
Emperor.

CHAPTER 10

NINE DAYS IN MAY

FINDING Dessie occupied, Haile Selassie and his escort had veered off far from the path of the invading armies to the town of Fikke in Salale, the Kassa stronghold. The Emperor finally reached Addis Ababa, a month exactly after the battle of Mai Ceu, to find a city near to panic and expecting the arrival of Italian columns from one moment to the next. A council was held at the Ghebbi on that, the Thursday afternoon. The Emperor, Ras Kassa, and Ras Getachew who were still with him, and the other survivors of Mai Ceu, were depressed and hesitant. But those who had stayed in the capital were not prepared to abandon the struggle. One man spoke out firmly, Blatta Takele Wolde Hawariat, the young Director-General of the City. His plan was that the government should move to the south-west, to Gore in Illubabor. The rains were already beginning and the Italians would not be able to cross the Blue Nile or to move down the tracks to the west that led through Wollega-Lekempti, governed by the loyal Dejaz Hapte Mariam Gabre Egziabher. Addis Ababa would fall, but Ras Imru would wage guerrilla warfare in Gojjam, Ras Seyum in Tigre, and Wondossen Kassa and Haile Kebbede in Wag and the provinces north of Wollo. At Gore, moreover, the government would have a supply route open from the neighbouring Sudan via Gambeila. Without much enthusiasm the plan was accepted. That evening a few lorry-loads of papers and files left the capital for the West.

Friday 1 May was a confused day. Even at this last minute Haile Selassie had been hoping for a miraculous solution in Europe. There is evidence that he had sent a message from Fikke to Sir Sidney Barton asking whether Britain would propose extensive sanctions. As the day wore on, the decision to go and fight in the remote south-west, cut off from Europe and all diplomatic contacts except that of a minor British consul, came to appear more and more hopeless. The only way to stop the Italians was to bring pressure upon them in Europe. The idea of a direct and dramatic appeal by the Emperor to the League of Nations germinated.

But Haile Selassie wavered. There was a fighting spirit abroad that morning. The *Negarit* was beaten at the Great Ghebbi, and an Imperial Decree, an *Awaj*, was issued ordering that the capital itself should be defended. The plan was for 5,000 men to march north and meet the Italians: the men of Dejaz Mangasha Wube, freshly arrived from Wollega-Saio, the last unused army, and the men of Ras Getachew who had escorted the Emperor and their commander back from Mai Ceu. Probably it was Blatta Takele who inspired the Emperor to issue this decree. It was certainly Blatta Takele who assembled his 800 sworn volunteers, armed with new rifles which he had deliberately held back from the northern front, on Janhoy Meda. 'They are prepared to die for you', said Blatta Takele. 'They shout like this', replied Haile Selassie, 'with your machine-guns behind them but none would fight for us. The masses would betray us.' By this time it must have been apparent that neither Mangasha Wube's nor Getachew's men were going to obey the *Awaj*. The stage had been reached when orders, even Imperial orders, were only half-obeyed if at all.

Another council was held that afternoon at the Little Ghebbi, a disjointed affair that went on for hours as arguments swayed backwards and forwards. At one point Ras Kassa took the Emperor aside; when that happened the rest of his council knew that the Ras would monopolize the Emperor for hours. The Empress followed Ras Kassa, lecturing her husband on his duty to go to Europe, while Ras Getachew and the Crown Prince stayed joking in the room next door. At another point, Blatta Takele marched dramatically into the Green Salon with a pistol barrel in his mouth. '*Janhoy*', he said, 'are you not the son of Theodore?'[1]

Later Lorenzo Taezaz told Tamm of the arguments that were put forward at that council. There was no point in continuing the armed struggle. In any case it was too dangerous to go to the west, for the inhabitants of Jimma were hostile. The League of Nations was the only hope. His Majesty must go himself and the sooner the better. For at any moment the Italians might cut the

---

[1] Implying that suicide was better than flight or capture. The Emperor Theodore had shot himself at Magdala rather than fall into the hands of the British. A gesture that Blatta Takele must have remembered when the day of his own death came.

railway and as the journey took the best part of two days, every minute lost was dangerous.

It seems that there was a vote, and that the council voted 21:3 in favour of the Emperor leaving the country. The three who voted against: Blatta Takele, Dejaz Yigezu, and—rather surprisingly—the Foreign Minister Blattengueta Herouy had all spent the war in the capital.

That night was wet and windy. Tamm passed the evening at Dr. Hanner's house and, much to his relief, Bouveng finally appeared—with Kifle and the other young officers. 'This is the end of Ethiopia. This is thanks to our own chiefs. Go, God bless you. Save yourselves,' the cadets, weeping, told the embarrassed Swedish officers. Late that night as they went back to their hotel, the Swedes heard shooting. It was rumoured that the Italians had reached the railway at Awash. It was rumoured also that the Emperor told his servants to pillage 'this accursed town' but asked them to spare the Ghebbi. It does not seem very true to character, though in moments of despair it is always difficult to say how even great men will react. And at that moment Haile Selassie must have been very close to despair indeed, aware that he was about to take a decision that in the eyes of most of the Amhara race would brand him a fugitive if not a coward. No Emperor, however unfortunate, not even Lij Yasu, had fled from the Empire and his defeated followers to appeal to foreigners abroad. Even the young Crown Prince had been suggesting to his own followers—to Fikremariam, the commander of his troops, and Gurassu Duke a captain in his bodyguard—that he should abandon his father and go with them as a *shifta* to the hills.

To both these men as well as to Balambaras Abebe Aregai, the chief of police, Blatta Takele had already handed out some of the rifles that he had held back in the city. 'If the Emperor should flee,' Fikremariam was reported to have said that evening to Blatta Takele, 'our honour demands that we should ambush the train at Akaki and that he die at our hands.'

The Emperor did flee, and the fact that among his subjects were armed, violent, and determined leaders such as Dejaz Fikremariam and Blatta Takele whose emotions were as tense as their nationalism was extreme perhaps explains the method of his departure. A train was made ready that night, and the Empress and the Imperial family and the household with the household goods and many of the nobles and courtiers boarded it. But the watchers in the city would have noted that the Emperor was not on the train when it puffed out of the station an hour or two before dawn. In fact the Emperor and his immediate suite left the Little Ghebbi surreptitiously and rode out to join the train at its second halt, Akaki, ten miles down the road. Haile Selassie brought with him a 'house-guest' whom he must have judged too dangerous to leave behind in Addis Ababa: Ras Hailu. So there was no ambush at Akaki. The train chugged eastwards into the rising sun, heading towards the Awash bridge, half-way to Diredawa—which might for all the train's occupants knew already be in the hands of the Italians.

Blatta Kidane Mariam brought the news of the Emperor's departure to Blatta Takele and Fikremariam. They drove out hastily to Akaki to find the news was true, and the train had already gone. It seems that they could hardly believe that an Ethiopian Emperor had really decided to leave his people. 'My country', cried Blatta Takele, 'there is no-one to defend your cause.'

At 8 a.m. a second train left the station for Djibuti; this was the usual service—the only unusual thing about it being its sudden popularity. The three Swedish officers were on it and Lorenzo Taezaz and most of the Ministers and notables of the court. In one or other of the two trains eighty-odd nobles or personalities, sometimes with, sometimes without their families, were heading for Djibuti, and exile: Ras Kassa, Ras Getachew, and even the two who had voted against departure, Blattengueta Herouy and Dejaz Yigezu. But it was not entirely a *débandade*, though it must have seemed very like one to the crowds of wailing relatives at the station. The evening before, the Emperor had sent three radio messages out: the first to Ras Imru at Debra Markos (where Ras Imru had at long last met up with his wireless operator Gabre Maskal and the wireless unit) appointing him Regent, the second to the Bitwoded Wolde Tsaddik down in the south-west nominating him as President of the Provisional Government at Gore, and the third to the remnants of the Guard ordering them to rally to Aberra Kassa at Fikke. The triangle in the West —Debra Markos, Fikke, Gore—would hold: symbol of Ethiopia's independence while her Emperor made a last appeal in person to the assembled nations.

In the capital these finer considerations of strategy and diplomacy were lost on those who remained. Crowds began gathering in the streets, at first good-humoured, as if on a public holiday. But as the morning wore on, and more and more of the foreign residents were summoned to the safety of the embassy enclaves, the remnants of the various armies drifted into the centre swelling the mass of those already there and began to eye with increasing interest the deserted houses of the lords and the *ferengi* and the stores of the nervous Indian shopkeepers.

Pillaging was mild at first, but at some stage that day Blatta Takele, the only remaining authority, suggested that the city be fired. 'Are you mad?' asked Blatta Kidane Mariam. 'The world will say that Tafari was the only stabilising force.' Blatta Takele was not mad but he was—and was to remain until his death—a man of violent emotions. He must have seen it as a ritual purification, the burning of a city that was built by Europeans, infected by European influence, and about to fall into the hands of Europeans. He rode through the city with Balambaras Abebe Aregai, setting an example. 'From the departure of the Emperor,' the Belgian Minister reported, 'the town was systematically put to the sack and one could even note at the head of the rioters the presence of the chief of police.'

It is not easy to sack a city, particularly when the *tukuls* of the ordinary inhabitants and the churches have to be respected, the foreign embassies are guarded, and even the Indians have barricaded themselves in their stores. Mischa Babitchev flew off in the early afternoon; he landed at Awash—not in fact yet in Italian hands—where Tamm saw him and heard only that looting had begun. But by evening pillaging and burning had spread. Rifles, if possible machine-guns, were what every able-bodied Ethiopian was after. Negga, one of the Crown Prince's guards, who has left an account of those days, went into the railway station to get arms. He was fired at—probably, though he did not realize it, by a group of French railway employees who, led by the military attaché Colonel Guillon, were quickly converting the station into a fort. There was fighting all around the station. As Dr. Hanner drove his car away from it, he was fired on. So Negga went up to the Great Ghebbi and looted the palace and found Menelik's sword and saw the torn *Negarit*; and then with his band went to the market at Arada and took 10,000 dollars from the shop at Kerkos and divided them among his men and had himself photographed: he 'was about to engage in battle when those with me deserted me.'

Where Negga and his like failed, Blatta Takele was better prepared. He had been planning for guerrilla warfare and had cached machine-guns on his own land at Sabata on the western outskirts of the city. But before he led his volunteers out he had a violent quarrel with Abebe Aregai whom he knew to have contacted an official at the French Embassy. He threatened to machine-gun him unless he left immediately for Jiru in eastern Shoa where he had his own lands and people. As the refugees crowded into the embassies—the French Embassy underneath Mt. Entotto that night had 2,000 of 16 nationalities, including 300 children camped in their grounds—Abebe Aregai and his ten men left for the North-east and Blatta Takele for the West. Of the young administrators only Blatta Kidane Mariam remained in Addis Ababa, with Blatta Takele's approval, to organize a 'Youth movement' and a 'Women's movement' inside the city.

In the early hours of Sunday 3 May, the first train, that carrying the Emperor and his family, stopped at the half-way station of Diredawa. Here in a French enclave, already surrounded by French officers and Senegalese troops, the Emperor was almost in safety. There was little danger of finding the railway cut in the Danakil desert that lay ahead, and not much more of being bombed or strafed. By the time he reached Diredawa, however, the Emperor had changed his mind yet again and was determined not to leave his country. The British Consul at Harar, Chapman-Andrews, had come down with his escort of 40 British Somaliland policemen to meet him. The Emperor's latest plan was to join Ras Desta in Sidamo, presumably together with his daughter Tenagne Worq, Ras Desta's wife. 'It took me some time to dissuade him but it had to be done', said Chapman-Andrews afterwards. 'The military situation was quite hopeless.'

An event that was to prove of the greatest importance, though the details of exactly what occurred are obscure, happened during that halt at Diredawa. When the second train arrived, two hours after the Emperor's train had left, a third train passed it heading in the opposite direction back towards Addis Ababa. This train was carrying Ras Hailu.

Some say that Ras Hailu simply walked out of the carriage where he was 'guarded' and none dared stop him. It is possible that he 'escaped' in this way. It is possible that Haile Selassie released him as an act of clemency. It is possible too that he had come to a secret agreement with the Emperor to return to Addis Ababa and to act as a clandestine representative of Ethiopia with the Italians. But it is more likely that both the British and the French representatives, well aware of the importance and the position of Ras Hailu, explained firmly to the Emperor that while they were willing to accommodate the Imperial family and the Imperial household and indeed the Imperial court they could hardly accept Imperial prisoners, however eminent, as well. Thus, as the Emperor left the Ethiopian scene, Ras Hailu stepped back on to it. What his feelings were at this dramatic reversal of his fortunes after four long years in the shadows are unfortunately unknown, as are the feelings of the nobles in the second train as they saw him passing them and heading back towards the capital which they had left so hastily, and towards a fate which—if uncertain—was likely to be more dramatic and more attractive than the life of exile that faced them.

In Harar the news of the Emperor's departure hastened the final débâcle. The five Dejaz gathered there left the city—three, Nasibu, Makonnen Endalkatchew, and Amde Mikael, heading for the safety of the coast, two—Abebe Damtew and the ailing Hapte Mikael—back towards their far southern provinces. In the Ogaden, Omar Samanthar fought a final rearguard action between Dagghabur and Jijiga, in which he was badly wounded but escaped capture. It was enough to stop Graziani pressing forward as he could have done—and was being urged to do.

Meanwhile, in the capital the looters and pillagers, now armed, were beginning to attack the embassies. At midday the Turkish Legation was assaulted, then the US Legation over on the far side of the city. Sir Sidney Barton who had long foreseen and planned for this situation sent out armed lorries to rescue the Turks and to bring in the women from the US compound. He sent a note round to Janssens at the Belgian Embassy almost next door advising him to abandon it and come over. But the Belgians had 10 Europeans, 15 Congolese askaris, 20 Mausers and 2,000 cartridges. They decided to hold on.

All over the city the *ferengi* in their enclaves were being besieged. The British Consul, Mr. Hope Gill, went out to join Mohammed Ali and the Indians who had barricaded themselves in at their famous stores. Three French diplomats made a sortie down to the station four miles away where they were relieved to find Colonel Guillon well-armed. But there was almost a disaster at the French Embassy itself where the local *zabagnas*, or guards, suddenly turned their three machine-guns on the Europeans. Fortunately M. Bodard had prepared underground bunkers in the cellars and after a strategic withdrawal the French re-established order inside this perimeter. There *was* a disaster for the British. The Red Cross Unit was quartered in the Menelik School, about half a mile from the Embassy just above the crossroads of Arat Kilo. Dr. Melly went out bravely with his lorries collecting wounded in the city. He was shot and killed —the second British leader of a Red Cross Unit to die in the war.

In the minds of the excited populace, intoxicated with *tej*, looting, and freedom from any restraint, a white skin meant an Italian and an Italian meant an enemy. Ludwig Weber, the Emperor's German pilot, wearing his Richthofen cap, took three other armed Germans with him to the Junker on Janhoy Meda. 'I am the Government', he told the guards who wanted some authorization to let him and the plane go. There was one thought in the mind of all the Europeans, and of most of Western Europe as the messages from the Embassies were reported on the radio and in the press: a paradoxical but understandable thought—how soon could the invading enemy, the Italians, reach the capital?

Not that there was any real danger in the British enclave with its 150 well-armed and well-trained Punjabis, or at the Japanese and German Legations, two fortresses that supported each other. As for the French, next day Monday 4 May, the Quai d'Orsay ordered another company of Senegalese to be sent up from Djibuti by rail while in the city French lorries went out to pick up Lazarist missionaries (who refused to come in) and reported that the Little Ghebbi was being sacked and was surrounded by flames. At dusk the Belgian Embassy was attacked—by 150 *shiftas* and the Imperial Guard according to Belgian reports—but a swift appeal to Sir Sidney Barton brought a patrol of Sikhs round in the rear, and two more attacks later that night were easily repulsed.

There was shooting too at the station where Dejaz Yigezu's men opposed Ras Hailu's arrival.

As Ras Hailu arrived in Addis Ababa, the Emperor and his suite were setting sail from Djibuti. On his arrival at Djibuti, Haile Selassie had been received with military honours and before embarking on the British cruiser HMS *Enterprise* that was to take him and his suite to Haifa, had seen 'his' foreigners for a few moments. Tamm found him 'a broken man'. 'With a few words he thanked us and wished us success and happiness.' Before the *Enterprise* sailed, Nasibu and Makonnen Endalkatchew and Wehib Pasha arrived, after rocambolesque adventures involving a taxi-ride all the way from British Somaliland. 'C'est fini', was Nasibu's only and uninspiring comment. But Wehib Pasha was very proud because his men had held on till the propaganda, the news of the Emperor's defeat and rumours of his departure, had broken their spirit. There was last-minute trouble with the British authorities who refused to take all the Ethiopians on board. Forty-seven of the 80-odd were eventually embarked, though Nasibu and Makonnen Endalkatchew were allowed on only to say farewell to their Emperor and tell the story of the Ogaden front. On land the forlorn bystanders heard the cry of wailing rising from the ship, and the Imperial salute for the last time, as the *Enterprise* sailed away.

By then, in Addis Ababa the danger was almost over. The Italians were nearby. There was even an attempt by Ciano, Mussolini's son-in-law, to land his plane on Janhoy Meda: he wisely veered off again as he was fired on. In the evening the I (Eritrean) Brigade, the foot column, had reached the outskirts of the city. Lt. Toselli came to the French Embassy, presented Marshal Badoglio's compliments, thanked M. Bodard for saving the lives of the five Italian prisoners and obtained from him the keys of 'Villa Italia', the Italian Embassy. It was almost a social occasion: polite Europeans rescuing besieged Europeans from a savage horde. But both must have felt a false note in the ceremony, for the besieged Europeans had until only sixty hours before been on the side of the savage horde.

So it was with mixed feelings of relief and a certain bitterness that the refugees and the staff of the British Legation lined up at the gates and fences the following afternoon when Badoglio's column finally made its triumphant entry into the capital. The British compound, on the outskirts of the town, was the first major group of buildings on the road along which the 'column of iron-will', rather curiously preceded by a string of journalists' cars, had to drive. There were 2,000 vehicles, tanks and lorries included, and 25,000 men. The Eritreans marched by with flowers on their rifles, brandishing the swords they had captured. Some of the European refugees clapped politely as the first Italians drove by but stopped when the Blackshirts in the column began hissing and jeering at the Union Jack.

At Buckingham Palace that day, Tuesday 5 May, Baron de Cartier presented his letters of accreditation to the new monarch, Edward VIII. Eden came across to tell him that the Belgians besieged in their Legation had been rescued by Sikhs. The Italian Ambassador, close behind, explained that the delay in the arrival of the troops had been due to the roads being blown up and the deluge of rains. But at the US Embassy that evening Churchill told the Baron that 'Mr. Mussolini must be only too glad at the present spectacle. It throws a rather vivid light on the reactions of a people which is today turning on even the Powers which imposed sanctions.'

Churchill's suspicions—the the Italians had deliberately delayed their advance in order to allow the world to see the barbarity of the Ethiopians and appreciate at its real worth their own famous slogan of the 'civilizing mission'—appeared to be confirmed indirectly by Badoglio's comments: 'If any doubts had still remained', he was to write, 'as to the state of barbarism of these people, the condition in which we found Addis, destroyed and sacked by the express order of the Negus before he left, was quite enough to dispel them.'

What with the rains, the roads and an ambush,[1] it is quite possible that the Italian mechanized column could not have reached Addis Ababa before the afternoon of the 5th. But what is equally certain is that the Eritrean Brigade on foot were there before them, and perfectly capable of occupying the city centre. Probably Badoglio did not deliberately plan the spectacle of desolation, but he certainly did plan that the triumphant entry into the enemy capital should be reserved for his already famous column and that its thunder should not be stolen by the unmechanized Eritreans who had arrived more quickly and more efficiently on foot.

In Rome where the occupation had not been expected till the following day the officials and the people were caught a little off-

---

[1] The rains had been heavy, the gap in the road blown by the Tsehafe Taezaz Haile much more effective than Tamm had allowed for; and on its final stage the column had been ambushed—an entirely spontaneous effort—by a local *balabat*, Haile Mariam Mammo who had fought at Mai Ceu.

stride. But as the church bells rang and the loud speakers summoned the uncertain populace to Piazza Venezia, the Duce appeared on the balcony and announced to the 'Blackshirts of the Revolution, Men and Women of Italy', that Addis Ababa had fallen to the glorious troops of Marshal Badoglio. The news, and general enthusiasm for it, spread throughout Italy as the troops of Badoglio spread throughout Addis Ababa.

Badoglio himself and his staff, plus Lessona and Bottai out from Italy for the occasion, went straight to 'Villa Italia', the empty Embassy. They spent a quiet, calm, and sober evening, for Badoglio was always self-controlled and cool if not cold in temperament.

As for the mass of half-armed and disbanded soldiers, the looters and the *shiftas* of Addis Ababa, they—like many of the ordinary population—took to the hills as the Italians approached. Negga, more ingenious than most, disguised himself as a monk and wearing the monk's *qub* or cape 'took a cross and went down the hill. I watched the Italians marching into Addis Ababa on Tuesday'—'and', his account adds, 'began killing them on Thursday. I killed by night and in the daytime I again became a monk, calling myself Memhir Haile Mikael.' It was symptomatic. Though the capital was occupied, the war was only half-won.

On Wednesday Italian patrols occupied all the important points in the city, and started setting up control posts and disarming stragglers. Bottai was appointed Governor of the City and moved into the Little Ghebbi. The Legations were officially informed that the Italians had now assumed the Government of Ethiopia and were warned to have no dealings with any other so-called authorities. Uncertain how to proceed *vis-à-vis* Badoglio, M. Janssens cabled Brussels for advice: 'Dois-je faire visite ou simplement laisser ma carte?'

As the Italians started moving from the city outskirts towards the surrounding villages, various groups of armed Ethiopians took to the hills. Those with Blatta Takele were fortunate; they had a leader who both knew his own mind and possessed arms. Blatta Takele went to the church of Meta Abo at Sabata where his father was buried and produced 60 Czech machine-guns hidden under the altar. He sent 15 to Gurassu Duke (who had fallen back to his own lands at Wolisso, thirty miles south-west of Addis Ababa on the Jimma Road) and set off, slowly, towards the seat of the provisional government, Gore.

At Oletta the small group of remaining cadets—about 40, with 40 machine-guns, mules, and a few camp-followers—moved out into the hills as the Italians approached, uncertain what to do and where to go. Most of them, like the senior in rank, Essayas, were from Tigre or the North. There were stories of the Gallas to the west of Addis Ababa in the Mecha and Ginderabat districts rebelling, but nevertheless a small group set off to try to get to Gore. Two days later a smaller group led by Mengistu Neway returned to report that it was impossible to cross the Galla lands. Any group of the Amhara however large would risk being massacred, and the rest of their companions including Tekle Gabre Hiwot had been killed.

The state of mind of the cadets was typical of that of all the disbanded groups of ex-soldiers, large or small, moving back into the hills as the Italians approached. They were torn between a feeling that they should go back to their homes and lands, for any further struggle was useless, and the natural reluctance of the armed Ethiopian to submit to a foreign invader and, even more humiliating, hand in his weapon. Everywhere they were looking for leaders, but as their natural leaders had left, they were uncertain where to turn. More and more, and not only in the districts around the capital, they tended to group around the *balabats*, the country landowners; or the *shifta* bandit leaders, or indeed men who played both roles, like Haile Mariam Mammo who had been imprisoned for murder before he was released to fight at Mai Ceu.

Such natural leaders, however, that remained, that is to say high officials of the court or the army, or relatives of the Imperial family or the Rases, were the focus around which the uncertain groups tended almost automatically to gather. Thus the cadets were joined by Desta Tana, a nephew of Dejaz Yigezu, who advised them to join Mesfin Sileshi at Wormara. The bandsmen of the Imperial Guard, who had been left to guard the Empress when the battalions went north to Mai Ceu, sent a man to Zaudi Asfau to ask if they could join him. Zaudi Asfau Darghie was one of those imperial cousins who had been exiled or imprisoned—in his case for twelve years—until Haile Selassie declared a general amnesty before moving north. The son of Menelik's first cousin, he already had 100 men with him before he was joined by Wolde Johannes the bandmaster and his well-armed men. Another group, also in the West, formed around another released prisoner, a revenant from another age, Dejaz Balcha, whose ferocity and hate for the Italians appeared to have been dimmed neither by old age nor by his enforced monastic life. As for the individualist Negga he slept in the Church of Abbo on Entotto, and went down by day to the city in his disguise. He shot—according to his own account—two Italian soldiers plundering, then an Italian commandant at Janhoy Meda. 'I shot him, his wife came out. I shot her too', then he tried to stop the Italians bringing back the head of Fitaurari Bantyergew—'I failed in this because I could not pierce their car with my bullets', and finally attempted a major coup. 'I gave 3,000 dollars to a woman to catch Badoglio for me, but she betrayed me. Another woman was too soft for the job.' Finally, however, Negga, like the rest, went to join a chief: in his case Dejaz Fikremariam, who had already been his commander in the Crown Prince's guard, and around whom a guerrilla band was forming south-east of the capital.

From the Italian point of view the occasional act of terrorism or even assassination was irrelevant. They were so firmly in control of the capital that by Friday 8 May 50,000 refugees had come down from the hills and the life of the city was beginning to function normally.

On the same day Graziani's forces at last entered Harar. Nasi's Libyan division had come up from the south across a muletrack, and simultaneously Frusci's mechanized columns moved through the Marda Pass and the Babile gap. The pincer movement was unnecessary. There was little resistance, and none organized, though Fitaurari Malion commanding the rearguard had been in Harar only the day before. Two hundred Amhara were killed by Frusci's *dubats* in the exhilaration of reoccupying the second city of the Empire, and then order was restored. 'Graziani', Badoglio had told Lessona, 'will find a Marshal's bâton waiting for him in Harar.' Not that day. Graziani had had an accident at Jijiga. When the ruins of the little town were occupied, he visited its Coptic church, and inside the church fell into a deep concealed hole which he was convinced had been prepared for him as a sort of mantrap. From that incident it is possible to date what was to become a paranoiac hatred of and suspicion towards the Coptic clergy.[1]

[1] To be fair, the Italians had their grounds. When 'monks' like Negga were shooting down their officers or bribing potential Judiths to seduce their Holofernes,

Saturday 9 May was a great day for the Italians. They learnt to their satisfaction that Haile Selassie on his arrival at Haifa had been greeted only by the Mayor and a District Commissioner, Mr. C. Pirie Gordon, and that at Jerusalem he had been installed at the King David Hotel, not as had generally been expected as an honoured guest at the residence of the High Commissioner, General Sir Arthur Wauchope. The official British attitude was clearly cool.

In the west of Ethiopia the Gojjami rebels had come in to submit to Starace at Bahr Dar and to ask him for arms. Three columns, one 5,000 strong led by Gessesse Belew, were setting out for Debra Markos with Italian air support. It looked as if at last the population of a whole Amhara region was siding openly and in arms with the Italians, and as if Ras Imru would be trapped by the rebellious subjects of his own province, now enthused by the news of the release of their 'rightful' ruler, Ras Hailu.

In the centre Ras Seyum submitted formally to General Bastico at Socota, offering him his sword which was symbolically accepted and then returned. The oath he swore was worded as follows: 'I swear to be loyal to you, your mighty King, your just leader, and your victorious general, Marshal Badoglio. Henceforth your King is my King, your commanders are the commanders of my people.' And in the East a column of lorried Blackshirts of the Tevere Division commanded by Colonel Navarra motored down from Harar to Diredawa where the French officers of the Senegalese battalion formally handed over the public buildings—the customs house, railway station, and *ghebbi*—to them. The Italian flag was raised at 7 a.m., and just after midday the 45th Infantry Battalion arrived by rail and was received at the station by a guard of honour of Consul General Parini's 221st Legion. The armies of the North and the South had linked up, and the Blackshirts, symbolically and suitably first present, had welcomed their comrades-in-arms of the regular army.

But the climax of a great day for Italy occurred, as was fitting, in Rome. This time the Party had warning, and the enthusiasm of the Italian people, intoxicated by the joys of victory, was given a chance to express itself. Never, before or after, were Fascism and

when Czech maching-guns were cached in altars, and holes in churches were concealed like elephant-traps, it was understandable that the spirit of ecumenism should not have been widespread.

Mussolini as popular as in that period and at that hour. At 8 p.m. that spring evening, heralded by the blaze of trumpets, the Duce stepped on to the balcony of Palazzo Venezia to announce to a wildly excited crowd that stretched down the Corso and over to the Colosseum, the annexation of Ethiopia. In every Italian city, town and village, loudspeakers relayed his speech. As he proclaimed Vittorio Emmanuele III Emperor of Ethiopia and an imperial salute of 101 guns boomed out over the capital, Rome echoed to the massed chant that had last been heard centuries before in the dying days of the falling Caesars—'Imperatore! Imperatore!'

CHAPTER 11

AFRICA ORIENTALE ITALIANA

FEW statesmen in Europe had expected the outright annexation of Ethiopia. But once the policy of annexation was decided on, it was applied wholeheartedly by the Minister for the Colonies, Lessona. By the Organic Law of 1 June 1936 the whole of the Horn of Africa was reorganized as *Africa Orientale Italiana—AOI*—to be ruled by a Viceroy who was at the same time Governor General. The man appointed was, logically enough, Marshal Badoglio.

Africa Orientale Italiana was divided into five provinces, each with a military Governor. The administration was closely controlled by Rome. The five Governors, though under the general authority of the Viceroy, were to correspond directly with the Ministry of Colonies on 'the ordinary affairs of government' and could appeal over the Viceroy's head to Rome. On the other hand there was a certain military unity; the Viceroy was *ex officio* commander-in-chief of the armed forces.

Under the Governor were Commissars—equivalent to the District Commissioners in British colonies—installed in all the major towns and under the Commissars Residents and Vice-Residents. The plan was for a very tight system of control, uniform throughout the whole vast Dominion, and clearly there was no place in it for the native rulers. 'No power to the Rases' was the slogan on which Lessona based his policy of direct rule. This meant that after a brief period of hope during which Ras Hailu may have dreamt of the title of Negus of Gojjam and both Ras Seyum and Haile Selassie Gugsa of that of Negus of Tigre, they were relegated to the shadows.

In any case Gojjam and Tigre no longer existed as such. Tigre was incorporated in the province of Eritrea, and Gojjam (with Beghemder) in the province of Amhara. The province of Harar extended almost up to the outskirts of Addis Ababa, and all the

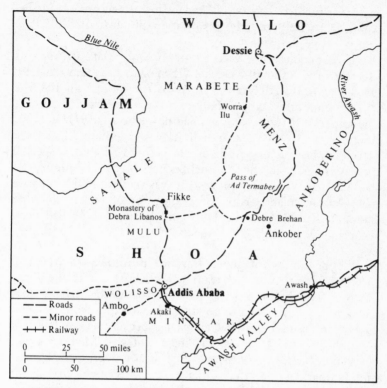

MAP 5. Shoa and Addis Ababa

provinces of the South—eastern, western, and central—were united to form the one vast province of Galla–Sidamo.[1]

These administrative divisions were, of course, applicable only on paper. On 1 June, far from being at the seat of his governorate of Galla–Sidamo in Jimma, General Geloso was forming a 'Special Lakes Division' to face Ras Desta at Yirgalem. But even the mere paper division of the country into governorates and residencies helped to convince both Italian and European public opinion that the war was won, the Empire conquered, and the Italian administration almost in place. This impression, totally

---

[1] The fifth province of *AOI* was Somalia. The capital, Addis Ababa, was the seat of the Viceroy and with its surrounding districts formed a separate entity of its own.

false, was furthered by two linked events: the return of Marshal Badoglio to Italy and the repatriation of most of the Italian troops.

The first of the three Viceroys of *Africa Orientale Italiana* was Viceroy for less than two weeks. When on 21 May Graziani, still bruised from his fall, arrived in Addis Ababa, at Villa Italia he found a euphoric Marshal Badoglio chain-smoking as always. The relations between the two had never been good. Graziani, always touchy, aware that half Italy's schoolboys had been betting on his reaching Addis Ababa before Badoglio, suspected the commander-in-chief of deliberately keeping him in the shadows, and Badoglio knew it. It was therefore with surprise that Graziani read a copy of a telegram of resignation that Badoglio had sent to the Duce and learnt that he had been recommended as Badoglio's successor.

At the beginning of June Graziani, promoted to Marshal, installed himself and his team of collaborators at the Little Ghebbi. The Emperor—the ex-Emperor as the Italians now called him—was *en route* to London. He had sailed from Haifa on 23 May in a cruiser—HMS *Capetown*—specially sent by Baldwin to carry him safely across the Italian-infested Mediterranean, reached Gibraltar on 29 May, lunched at Government House, and embarked on the Orient Line Steamer *Orford* for Southampton. On 3 June he received a tumultuous welcome at Waterloo Station in London. Among the thousands there to greet him were the Ethiopian Minister, Dr. Martin, with whom he drove to the Legation in Prince's Gate, George Steer, *The Times* correspondent who had stayed to the end and been expelled by the Italians, Von Rosen the young Swedish pilot, and a new and devoted admirer, whom he had never met until then but had often heard of—Sylvia Pankhurst. 'We have been very happy here', said Haile Selassie, much moved, 'in the way we have been received by the British people.' Quiet modesty was never to the taste of the Pankhursts. 'In those irresistible eyes', wrote Sylvia, 'burns the quenchless fire of the hero who never fails his cause.'

In the days that followed Haile Selassie was visited privately by Eden, and by the Duke of Gloucester, attended a Foyle's literary luncheon, and was joined by Blattengueta Herouy and Dejaz Makonnen Endalkatchew from Jerusalem. But though an honoured, he was very clearly in official eyes an unofficial guest. Edward VIII refused to invite him to Buckingham Palace; and when Haile Selassie lunched at the House of Commons, the Prime Minister Stanley Baldwin hid behind a table to avoid meeting him. There was intense diplomatic activity in London, Rome, and at Geneva as Haile Selassie and his advisers prepared their appeal to the conscience of the civilized world. But on 10 June the Chancellor of the Exchequer Neville Chamberlain, in a speech outside the House, called the continuation of sanctions 'the very midsummer of madness' since there was no way of restoring the Emperor short of military action.

At last on 30 June, in Geneva, the Emperor fulfilled the purpose for which he had fled abroad and arose to address the Assembly of the League of Nations. A small picturesque figure with his famous cape and beard—dignified as always, sadder than before—he could be sure of a sympathetic audience, all the more emotional because their collective conscience was pricking. To the general amazement and outrage, as he rose a group of Italian journalists hissed and barracked. 'A les portes ces sauvages,' cried Tiatulescu, the Roumanian delegate, and only their prompt expulsion saved these rash journalists from a near lynching. Haile Selassie spoke in Amharic, quietly and reasonably. If force was allowed to triumph over the Covenant, then the collective security of small states was threatened. Emotion came only at the end of the speech with the Emperor's final question: 'What reply shall I have to take back to my people?'

None. Sanctions were in fact, as Eden said, serving 'no useful purpose'—if indeed they ever had. One after another the representatives of the three Great Powers—Eden, Blum, Litvinov—called for their abandonment. Only the South African delegate was for continuing them. On 15 July they were officially lifted. By then the Emperor had returned to London and was preparing for the bitter life of an exile. He went to Worthing for a holiday, then down to Bath where he stayed with his three oldest children at the Spa Hotel and later, preparing for the arrival of the rest of his family, bought a small villa, 'Fairfield', that was to be his home for the next miserable years.

The Empress Menen and the two youngest children, Princess Tsahai and Prince Sahle, arrived on 20 September. By the end of the year the most depressing of problems that afflicts ex—monarchs was afflicting her husband: the imperial silver plate was sold off by auction—16,000 ounces, by Messrs Puthick and Simpsons. For the next year-and-a-half money and the climate were the Emperor's greatest worries. Haile Selassie was involved in a series of legal actions. The Empress fell ill as the English winter drew on and had to return to Jerusalem. The children were split, and spent much of their time travelling from England to Palestine. There the nobles of the Empire, previously so great, were concentrated in Jerusalem living miserably and poorly at or near the Ethiopian convent and church in the Street of the Abyssinians—the *Rechov Habashim*. A few had scattered; Makonnen Haptewold, for instance, had gone to Paris where he helped to run a small *pension*. The Emperor sent what money he could to the nobles. It must almost have been a relief when in October the news came that Dejaz Nasibu, who was being treated for tuberculosis in a Swiss clinic, had died in Davos. So finished the life of Haile Selassie's chief collaborator in modernizing Ethiopia, miserably and far from his country but at least with the view of mountains to console him a little at the end.

By mid-June, in what was now *Africa Orientale Italiana*, the rains had set in and movement on any scale, particularly by motorized columns, had become impossible. There was nothing to be done until *Maskal*, the celebration of the Finding of the True Cross by St. Helena, that marked the end of the rainy season. Then Graziani would have to plan for two separate military campaigns in the South, in the new province of Galla-Sidamo; one against Ras Imru who had reached Gore in the south-west and the other against Ras Desta, whose forces were being reorganized in Sidamo in the south-east by Dejaz Gabremariam. Graziani was well aware that there was no contact between the two Rases and saw no immediate or potential menace there.

In the North and around Addis Ababa there were no coherent or undefeated armies left. The Political Office was busily negotiating with all the minor and major war-leaders who had not yet formally submitted.

For submission was a very formal affair. On 24 June a ceremony was held at the Little Ghebbi to mark the submission of Ras Kebbede Mangasha Atikim and of the Muslim notable, Sultan Abba Jobir II of Jimma. Fortunately a French journalist was present and has left a vivid description of this extraordinary affair.

Sixty Ethiopian dignitaries were seated in front of the throne in the Salle d'Honneur on red leather chairs—in the front rank, Ras Hailu, with his rich embroidered cape and bare head resembling 'a figure of the wars of religion, a bird of prey, powerful and dangerous'. Behind him sat the two Wollo nobles who had been sent in chains by Haile Selassie to the capital after the failed Dessie conspiracy, Dejaz Amde Ali, balding, and Ras Gabre Hiwot, 'his face marked by his captivity'. The black gold-embroidered capes of the nobles contrasted with the blue red-lined capes of the clergy. At midday the cannon sounded. An hour later, an hour late, the Viceroy, bareheaded, wearing a grey uniform, made his entrance. All rose and raised their right arms in the Fascist salute as the Fascist hymn 'Giovinezza' was sung.

Graziani took his seat on the dias facing the two chiefs due to submit with General Magliocco, commander of the Aviation: Colonel Calderini,[1] known to many of those present, and the Federal Secretary of the Party, Guido Cortese.

'In the name of God', said Graziani ('Bismillah' interpreted an Arab-speaking Italian; 'Egziabher', added the Amharic interpeter) 'I speak in the name of the King of Italy, Emperor of Ethiopia (all rose to salute) and of the Duce of Fascism Benito Mussolini (all rose to salute again). To you, Ras Kebbede Mangasha. To you Abba Jobir of Jimma . . . here is the act of submission to the great and powerful Italian government. For our friends justice and generosity. For our enemies force and the law . . . Rome . . . Amen.'

More Fascist salutes, and all chorused Amen. Ras Kebbede mounted the dais to take the oath—a small, leathery man, with lively eyes and a black beard. It seems that he had not come back to the capital with the Emperor but had gone to his governorate of Ifrata in northern Shoa; probably Ras Hailu's friendship with his dead father had been decisive, though possibly (as was rumoured) he had been offered a gratuity of 172,000 lire payable on submission. He was followed by Abba Jobir, a fat young man 'smiling with a curious rictus', wearing 'large granny spectacles and a turban'.

Graziani rose to speak again. Where were their roads and ports? 'Where is your Negus who had denied his race, hoarded in his banks the gold which is the blood of his people, chained Hailu

---

[1] The ex-military attaché at the Italian Embassy—his absence from Addis Ababa had therefore lasted less then seven months.

and Gabre Hiwot who are of the blood of your Rases? Here is
the Duce of Fascismo. Let the past die! Attention!' All rose:
three salutes to the King 'A noi!' Three salutes to the Duce: 'A
voi!'

Graziani looked round the assembly and picked out a white-
turbaned priest. 'Wait', he said, 'the old man wants to speak. I am
ready to hear everybody.' The priest came up to the dais and
mumbled inaudibly. Only half-satisfied, Graziani wound up by
explaining: 'You must not always say yes to me. Tell me my
errors. Give me your confidence.' The Fascist hymn again, a final
bevy of extended arms and the ceremony was over.

Such was the atmosphere of the new regime: semi-farcical, and
semi-military, marked by an almost total incomprehension of the
nature of Ethiopian society by the Italian military rulers and
presumably, underneath their polite ambiguity, by an equally
total incomprehension of the nature of Fascist society by the
leading Ethiopians—with the language barrier making communication even more impossible.

What is striking is the extent to which it was not just a military-
colonial but a specifically Fascist regime. As in any Italian region
the Federal Secretary was already installed, with a position and
powers parallel to that of the civil and military authorities, and
responsible not to the Ministry of the Colonies but to the Party
Secretary in Rome. Very soon the whole apparatus of the Party
was in place. A *Casa del Fascio* and a Militia headquarters were set
up in the centre of Addis Ababa and Fascist federations and
federal secretaries in each of the five governorates. More important from the military point of view was the Blackshirt organization, though the Blackshirt battalions were, generally speaking,
used as garrison troops in the large towns and their rôle was
confined to keeping order.

The submission ceremony was also symptomatic of the
importance of Ras Hailu. 'He was the man', wrote Graziani later,
'in whom I put my confidence. He became my councillor and . . .
I authorized him to form a *banda* over a thousand strong.' Thus,
though Graziani emphasizes there was no special post or position
given to Ras Hailu and his title was purely honorific, he was in the
eyes at any rate of the Ethiopians the most important figure in the
new regime. He used his influence with varying success to
persuade the remaining nobles to submit and the Italians to treat
them humanely. He was not however allowed to set foot in his

own lands of Gojjam; in whichever direction he and his *banda* were sent out, it was not to be across the Blue Nile.

The other Rases, less trusted, were it seems kept in their *ghebbis* at Addis Ababa under a form of mild house arrest such as most of them had at one time or another known under Haile Selassie —Ras Seyum, Ras Kebbede, Ras Gabre Hiwot, and, soon, Ras Getachew who for obscure reasons came back from Palestine to submit. They and the other famous war-leaders such as Dejaz Ayalew Birru and his brother Admassu who had also submitted fade away into obscurity under the rule of the Viceroys. They had no place in the new and confident life of a Fascist capital city.

CHAPTER 12

THE ATTACK ON ADDIS ABABA

THE history of the Ethiopians in the months and years that followed Haile Selassie's departure is the history of a race that was searching desperately to apply the imperial principle in almost unprecedented circumstances: that is to say, in the presence of a foreign conqueror, and in the absence, more and more marked, as death, exile and submission made their inroads, of members of the Imperial blood. Even in a period of peace the Emperors had found it difficult to extend their authority over the whole country. In a period of occupation, it was impossible for a leader, however powerful, to command or even to co-ordinate activities outside his own zone of influence. Yet if the events of this period are to be understood, the unity of principle underlying the rivalries, violence, and confusion of the surface must be grasped: the principle is that of a continual quest for an Emperor, even if only an Emperor at a local level. The practice is that of the rise and fall of a series of what it would be accurate to call pretenders to the Imperial privileges, if not to the Imperial throne.

The outward signs of Imperial privilege were known to all the Amhara. As word spread throughout Shoa that Aberra Kassa was riding on a golden saddle under a red umbrella, men flocked to the Kassa lands near the monastery of Debra Libanos. Aberra Kassa had of course more than a colourful paraphernalia; he had, as was also known, money. His position was very strong. Appointed head of the Kassa family by his father and governor of the district of Salale, he was by far the greatest lord in Shoa, in blood, prestige, and actual power. Himself of the Imperial blood, he was married to a daughter of Ras Seyum, Woizero Kebbedech, and his younger brother Asfawossen was married to a daughter of Ras Hailu. Though young, he had won a reputation as a war-leader in the Tembien; the remnants of the Guard that had followed his father and the Emperor from Mai Ceu had been placed under his orders. Perhaps most important of all, he had the support of the Church. The Bishop of Dessie, Abba Petros, had joined him at Fikke.

The position of the Coptic Church at this time was ambivalent. The Echege had fled to his old convent at Jerusalem, but the Abuna Cyrillos had submitted in the capital. The Abuna Cyrillos had however neither the power nor the prestige of his predecessor, Matteos. He was too recent an arrival for it to be forgotten that as an Egyptian he was a foreigner. Of the four Ethiopian bishops only Abba Abraham of Gojjam had submitted; he had followed, as was inevitable, the lord to whom he was in a certain sense chaplain, Ras Hailu. But Abba Mikael of Gore was in the south-west with the provisional government of Ras Imru, and Abba Isaac of Tigre was thought to be with Wondossen Kassa near holy Lalibela. Abba Petros as Bishop of Dessie represented the Crown Prince; and so, by joining the sons of Ras Kassa at Fikke, he conferred on them a semi-imperial status as well as the support of the Church. The implication was that these were now the heirs to the throne.

With Aberra Kassa was his young cousin, Lij Abiye Abebe. Shallaka Mesfin Sileshi, another cousin, brought with him his own stepson, Lij Merid Mangasha. It was a different generation that now prepared to take up and direct the struggle that their fathers had abandoned. It was as if the board had been swept clean, leaving full scope for men in their teens and early twenties, exhilarated by their unexpected power, though still very conscious not only of their heritage but also of their relative rank. It is indicative that the Oletta cadets Essayas and Abebe Tafari gave twenty of their precious machine-guns to Aberra Kassa, and only two to Mesfin Sileshi. Machine-guns were a more effective mark of rank even than red umbrellas. Aberra and Asfawossen Kassa now conceived the boldest project of the war: a combined counter-attack on the Italians and the recapture of Addis Ababa. It was not so fantastic and aberrant a project as it might at first have seemed. If the Italians had captured Addis Ababa so easily, it was because as a city Addis Ababa, lying at the foot of the mountains, surrounded by eucalyptus forests, sprawling shapelessly over an enormous area, was almost impossible to defend, at least against an attacking army possessing artillery. The Ethiopians no longer possessed any artillery. But the other disadvantages which had made any defence impossible for them now made it just as difficult for the Italians.

Although the Italians were firmly in control of the city itself and officially of high morale, less officially their morale was low. The weather was bad, the city was by Italian standards a hovel, the natives unfriendly, the troops going home, supplies scarce, and the immediate future uncertain.

In those first weeks of the occupation following the departure of Badoglio and of most of the troops of the 'iron-will column' the Italians lived in the unreal atmosphere of the half-besieged. If they raised their eyes, they could see hills and mountains occupied by roaming bands of armed and hostile Ethiopians. If they lowered their eyes, they could find no trace of those habitual and psychologically reassuring features of every Italian town, a wall running round the town centre and a dominating fortress. Shapeless, without exits or entrances, Addis Ababa was open to infiltration everywhere. Throughout the month of May and the first weeks of June there were continual rumours of impending Ethiopian attacks. The fact that these rumours were never substantiated did nothing to reassure the nervous garrison and the still more nervous civilians. The existence of the railway seemed to be their only link with a civilized life; by the railway supplies came in and troops went out. The other lifeline, the road to Dessie and the North, was uncertain and, particularly in the rainy season, most difficult.

There was an especially bad period from mid-June to mid-July when the city was almost denuded of troops, and Graziani was anxiously waiting the arrival of the Tessitore column from Dessie, and more reinforcements from Somalia. With their safe arrival, the strength of the garrison rose to just over 10,000 men—not an enormous number for the perimeter they had to cover, which Graziani estimated at 25 miles. General Gariboldi, the Military Governor, adopted the only possible solution: he built little forts round the perimeter of the city, covering as far as possible the roads and tracks that led in and out of the *tukuls*, and concentrated the rest of his troops in various tented camps and temporary barracks in different points of the city.

By June the railway, the capital's lifeline, was under continual attack. There was, however, more letter-writing than fighting in those weeks. The hills and paths of Shoa were criss-crossed with messengers: from the Viceroy with greetings and demands for submission to the *balabats*: from the *balabats* and local leaders to each other; from Ras Hailu and Ras Seyum on the prompting of the Political Office to their sons-in-law; and from Aberra and Asfawossen Kassa, juggling with many possibilities, to the Viceroy, to their fathers-in-law, to the *balabats* and to the war-leaders now established all around the outskirts of Addis Ababa.

Early in July a council was held at Debra Libanos presided over by Abba Petros. Zaudi Asfau, Haile Mariam Mammo, Abebe Aregai and many of the local *balabats* attended. Dejaz Balcha and Dejaz Fikremariam, whose men had been raiding the railway, were unable to come in person but sent representatives. Abba Petros appears to have been the moving force in the five-day-long discussion, the man who really co-ordinated the plans and lifted the morale of the young leaders, by prophesying to them that victory was certain if they attacked the capital.

Plans were drawn up for a combined attack to be launched just before dawn on 28 July, Hamle 21 by the Ethiopian calendar. They were carefully drawn up and well-prepared; Aberra Kassa with Mesfin Sileshi, the cadets and the main force were to attack from the north, through the northern suburb of Gulele. Their objective was the market area of Arada, the heart of the city, and St. George's Cathedral, its centre. Abebe Aregai from the north-west was to move past the French Embassy and seize the Little Ghebbi. From the west Fikremariam, moving in south of the road along which Badoglio's column had entered the capital, was to pass the British Embassy and occupy the Great Ghebbi. The southern half of the city was allotted to the weaker forces of Dejaz Balcha and Zaudi Asfau. Their task would be to isolate the railway station and the new Italian airbase in the Bole area. Priests were sent with letters hidden in their turbans to Blatta Takele and Gurassu Duke in the south-west, ordering them to move up in support and cut off the Italian garrison recently installed in Ambo.

It was a bold plan, particularly for leaders who had no means of direct communication with each other except by messenger. Its success would depend on co-ordination, and timing—always difficult in the best-planned military operations, never a strong point of the Ethiopians but more likely to be achieved now that there was a sprinkling of European-trained cadets in positions of influence. As regards the opposition, the planners seem to have been well-informed. They knew that the overall strength of the Italians was not great; they had precise information about the artillery brigade on Mount Entotto and the cavalry squadron in Gulele; more important, with the rains there was less danger of attack from the air. Above all, the rewards of success were greater than the penalties of failure. The recapture of Addis Ababa, the destruction of the Italian garrison, possibly the death of the Viceroy Graziani—it would mean renewed fighting everywhere, attacks on isolated and weakened Italian garrisons or columns; with the rains the impossibility of any reinforcements for or retaliation by the Italians; the end of submissions and the return of the submitted; almost certainly confusion in Italy, rejoicing in Europe, drama at the League, and the end of the war.

Aberra Kassa, with Mesfin Sileshi and the Salale levies, spent the Sunday night encamped on Entotto and attacked as planned before dawn on the Monday morning, Hamle 21, the day of Mariam. They poured straight down the road through the market area towards St. George's Cathedral. Apparently it was a complete surprise. Italian civilians were walking in the streets, and at first there was no resistance at all as the leading Ethiopians reached the Giorgis bridge and approached the Cathedral and the city centre. The first Italians they came across and attacked were engineers working on a well. But when the alarm was given, General Gariboldi reacted quickly. Presumably the Italians had had plans ready to repulse the often-rumoured assault, and it was merely a question of putting these plans into operation. Two battalions, a Blackshirt battalion of the 221st Legion, and the 8th Native, were sent to the Little Ghebbi where Abebe Aregai's men were infiltrating and threatening Graziani in person. Regular infantry and armoured cars, soon reinforced by two more Eritrean battalions and a group of *carabinieri* all under the command of General Tessitore, moved up to St. George's Square.

On the Tuesday morning serious fighting began as the Italians attempted to cut off the northern invaders in their rear and attack them from the front. Though Gariboldi did not know it, this was the only column that had reached its objective, or very nearly done so. Abebe Aregai was being beaten back from the Little Ghebbi. Fikremariam, held up by the river Qebana, had not even attacked the Great Ghebbi. Balcha had not arrived. Zaudi Asfau, arriving but isolated, refused to attack in the south on his own. Gurassu Duke, further away still on the southern outskirts of the city and without any real hope of success, hesitated and finally withdrew when no messengers came to him.

It was Abba Petros who rallied the Ethiopians and led them in person back towards the city centre, joking with the high-spirited cadets, telling them to die and being told that they wanted to live and fight first. Aberra Kassa sent men to bring him back to safety, but Abba Petros said that he in any case had come to die. Carrying his cross, wearing his bishop's robes, he marched straight forward into St. George's Square in front of the Cathedral where the Italians and the *banda* were massed, followed with understandable hesitancy by a group of young men.

By then Graziani and Gariboldi were confident that the situation was under control. There was still fighting in the outskirts, and General Tessitore had orders to prepare an attack on Fikremariam for the following day, Wednesday. But Aberra and Asfawossen Kassa were retreating. Their men had dispersed in small groups all over the city, and the main fighting was in the eucalyptus trees all round the northern and north-eastern outskirts of the city where the *banda* were hunting and being hunted by men most of whom had been their comrades-in-arms a few weeks earlier.

By the time Dejaz Balcha with his few hundred men finally arrived and attacked the Bole airport district, Tessitore and his Eritreans were mopping up the only remaining organized group, the men of Fikremariam, in the area of Ras Getachew's *ghebbi*. The main attacking force had already retreated during the night to Mesfin Sileshi and Haile Mariam Mammo's lands near Mulu. Although two days later two columns commanded by Gallina and Tessitore set out in pursuit, it was too late. For once the Ethiopians lost fewer men in retreat than they had in battle.

Lack of co-ordination, the rains, Italian superiority in weapons, hesitancy by the leaders, indiscipline among the men, indifference among the population and particularly among the Gurage of the market-place, the dubious tactics of a mass advance down a main road—there are a dozen reasons why the attack on Addis Ababa failed. Probably however if more documents were available it would become clear that the decisive element was the attitude of Ras Hailu: both the Italians and the Ethiopians have played down his importance subsequently for similar though contrasting reasons. It was he who at that time held the balance of power in the capital; not so much via his thousand armed men—an important but not decisive element—as through the influence and prestige he possessed. A sudden attack by him on the Italians would have roused the city and shaken even their faithful Eritrean troops. Whether it was distaste for treachery, innate caution, love of Italy, fear of the long-term results of success by Ras Kassa's sons, or the genuine desire to avoid bloodshed and play a moderating role that restrained him is uncertain, and probably always will be.

On 1 August, back in Salale, Aberra Kassa wrote to Graziani announcing that 'I have stopped all fighting'. The danger of a mass assault on the city was over and Graziani settled down to issuing orders that his car should be saluted 'fasciamente—cioe alzando il braccio'—'in the Fascist manner, that is to say by raising the arm'—and planning his autumn campaigns for the end of the rains.

CHAPTER 13

THE HUNTING DOWN OF THE RASES

RAS IMRU, Regent of Ethiopia, had reached Gore in mid-June nearly six weeks after the Emperor's departure. Gore in the south-west had the advantage of having a British Consulate and therefore a means of communication with the world outside and in particular with London. It had the disadvantage of being, as the British Consul put it, 'stranded in a sea of Gallas'. Its further disadvantage was the character of the then British Consul. Captain Erskine was young, highly ambitious, prejudiced against the Amhara, and extremely pro-Galla.[1] His reports were larded with references to 'the despotic Tafari regime', condemnations of the 'never-ending intrigues of Ethiopian officials which are the breath of life to them', and the 'supineness of the self-seeking treacherous smooth-spoken and bigoted Amhara officials.' He dreamed of becoming Ethiopia's Lugard, of proclaiming a British Mandate over the south-west and creating what would be in effect a logical extension to the British East African Empire. Economically the south-west was already a British protectorate; and from the Galla point of view a British mandate would have been preferable to Shoan or Italian rule. Just before Ras Imru's arrival Galla potentates had indeed formed a 'Western Galla Confederation' and were appealing to Eden for recognition and protection. In the opinion of infuriated Sudan Civil Service officials (who rather welcomed the prospects of an Italian administration) Captain Erskine was 'impetuous to the point of irresponsibility.'

A further complication was the presence at Gore of Bitwoded Wolde Tsaddik, described by Erskine as 'a pleasant old gent of 68

[1] Deeper in the south-west, at Maji, Colonel Sandford, an older man and an adviser to the governor, was in total contrast devoted to Haile Selassie and an admirer of the Amhara. Sandford had been in the Consular Service in Addis Ababa himself but had resigned in Lij Yasu's time to try his hand at a series of enterprises which had added to his experience and knowledge of the country though not noticeably to his fortunes.

who had been sent to the south-west the year before as the Emperor's representative.' He had been appointed President of the Provisional Government at Gore by Haile Selassie just before the Emperor's departure for Djibouti. But though 'an ineffective leader' he was not entirely helpless. He had with him a fairly large body of Shoan troops. There were several other smaller Shoan garrisons scattered throughout the south-west—the largest of them, at Jimma, already under attack by the people of that city. Six hundred regulars sent out by the Bitwoded Wolde Tsaddik to relieve that siege deserted on the way and became *shiftas*. It was symptomatic of the confused and demoralizing situation in the south-west.

Ras Imru was no more optimistic of his eventual chances of holding out than was to be expected of a leader who had been bombed, harried, and pursued for over a thousand miles. On arrival in Gore he sent a cable to Haile Selassie via Erskine asking him to open negotiations for surrender with the Italians and warning that if the Emperor were to refuse he would approach Ras Kassa in Jerusalem as an intermediary. He himself was thinking of settling in Uganda and, once again via Erskine, asked the British Government for permission. Erskine was delighted with Ras Imru's plan to surrender or, better still, to leave. Unfortunately for the gallant Captain, however, at the beginning of July first the British government (though tempted) rejected the idea of a mandate; and secondly a group of warlike Oletta cadets arrived at Gore.

With their followers (who included 50 Eritrean deserters) the cadets numbered only 350-odd but the young men such as Kifle Nasibu, Belai Haileab, and the two sons of the Ethiopian Minister in London, Joseph and Benjamin Martin, were cock-a-hoop. They had just succeeded in ambushing and killing in Wollega a group of high-ranking Italian officers, including General Magliocco the Commander of the air force and Colonel Calderini, the former Military Attaché who had flown in unescorted in an attempt to win over the Galla leaders. It looked as if an efficient and modern armed force might be organized under the leadership of the high-spirited cadets.[1]

Unfortunately, there was a further complication. Ras Imru

---

[1] Who, Erskine reported to Eden in mid-July, suffered from 'socialistic ideas, one of their ideas being to shoot the Emperor'.

depended for money on the tribute of the gold-mines of Asosa, controlled by the aged but loyal Sheikh Hojali of the Beni Shangul. But in July Sheikh Hojali was attacked by traditional rivals from the Wollega Galla and forced to flee to the little post of Kurmuk on the Sudan border. This blow almost finished off the provisional government in the south-west. In mid-September, Ras Imru and the Bitwoded Wolde Tsaddik held a council: Imru stated that he would catch the steamer from Gambeila in the lowlands of the Baro Salient to Malakal in the Sudan and Wolde Tsaddik that he would submit to the Italians after the rains.

On 29 September the British Consulate at Gore was officially closed. The date of departure for the last steamer from Gambeila (where there was also a British Consulate, run by Major Maurice, a bachelor long-installed in his own little trading kingdom of the Baro Salient) had been fixed: 14 October. But when the last steamer arrived, chugging up the Baro river from the opposite direction, from the Sudan, it carried an unexpected passenger. This was George Herouy, son of Blattenguetta Herouy. He had been with his father and the Emperor at 'Fairfield' near Bath and he had persuaded the British authorities in the Sudan to allow him through for humanitarian reasons. His ostensible purpose was to collect his wife, Ras Imru's daughter, who was with her father in Gore.

George Herouy brought with him a series of letters from Haile Selassie and most encouraging, though entirely fictitious, news: the Emperor would shortly be landing at Gore escorted by fifteen British fighters; Eden in a personal interview had promised British military intervention; and much more of this sort. Erskine was taken aside personally by the Bishop of Gore, Abba Mikael, and asked if it was true that the Duke of Harar—Haile Selassie's second and favourite son, then aged twelve—was about to marry a British Princess. 'The false hopes thus raised', he later reported furiously to Eden, 'have now started a wave of resistance which up to the end of September had practically subsided, and now the return of this insignificant lying individual George Herouy has led the remnants of the Amhara to believe that powerful help from Europe is forthcoming.'

Justified or not, Haile Selassie had once more outwitted his allies and enemies, and succeeded in raising the morale of his supporters. He had made sure that an independent Ethiopia, however reduced in size and power, fought on. The last steamer sailed from Gambeila on 14 October carrying an ex-British Consul to six months' leave and subsequent obscurity, but leaving the Regent at Gore to face the inevitable Italian attack.

Ten days later on 24 October an Italian column occupied Lekempti, the capital of the Wollega lands, pre-empting an attack planned by the cadets against Ras Hailu at Ambo. This was one prong of a two-pronged Italian movement, of which the second prong was designed to open up Jimma. Abba Jobir, the Muslim Sultan of Jimma, had already set out with a thousand men armed by the Italians to recapture his ancestral territory. It is said that he offered three dollars for the head of every Amhara Christian brought to him and that the Italians had to step in and stop the killing that followed. Meanwhile, however, Blatta Takele Wolde Hawariat had moved down from Shoa and reinforced—temporarily—Jimma's Shoan garrison. As Abba Jobir and his column halted, Ras Imru and the cadets and the Shoan troops that remained loyal to him moved out of Gore. Attacked by the Wollega Galla, they headed south-east towards Jimma and Maji where the remaining Shoan garrisons lay.

It now became essential for the Italians to drive their second prong home. On 3 November Graziani sent out a mechanized column under Colonel Princivalle down the Jimma road. The Colonel's orders were to link up with Abba Jobir *en route*; that done, to move on and seize Jimma.

It took the column three days to cover thirty miles, and on the third day they were attacked by an almost forgotten enemy, Dejaz Balcha.

The old Galla had a lifetime of blood and cruelty behind him. As a boy he had lain on his first battlefield castrated by the conquering Amhara; as a young man he had fought under the Empress Taitu at Adowa and seen the Eritreans of Albertone's brigade waver and break under his guns. He had led the armies of Shoa against Lij Yasu at Harar and the armies of Sidamo against Ras Tafari in Addis Ababa. His loyalties were not to Tafari the son of Makonnen but to Menelik his master and the old Empire. Not for Balcha Abba Nefso the defeat, exile, or submission that had shamed the sons of the generation of Menelik. He must have foreseen that this would be his last battlefield, as with his miserable band of two or three hundred men he opposed the mechanized columns of his old enemies from Europe, he who had once commanded the Imperial cannon and led armies thousands strong. Perhaps he repeated to himself with ironic bitterness the phrase with which the warriors of Ethiopia often went to meet certain death: 'Come, this night is our wedding night'.

According to one version this is how Dejaz Balcha died. When the fighting and the firing were over, he sent word to the Italians that he wished to surrender. Two Italian officers and a priest whom he had known went, with an escort, to receive his surrender. They found him sitting alone. Unsuspectingly, they went forward, only to see in the last moments of their own lives the ferocious old man draw a machine-gun from the folds of his *shamma*—dying as he had lived in a hail of bullets and a welter of blood, taking to Hell or Heaven with him three of the hated *ferengi* invaders: treacherous, impressive, almost heroic.

In the last fortnight of November the Italian columns occupied Jimma and Gore, where the Bitwoded Wolde Tsaddik submitted. The Bishop of Gore, Abba Mikael, not only refused to collaborate but excommunicated those who had. He was first imprisoned, then publicly shot—the second Bishop to be executed by the Italians.

Meanwhile, Blatta Takele had at last reached Ras Imru's encampment in the forests between Gore and Jimma. He put forward plans for guerrilla warfare and for cutting down Ras Imru's army (which with its camp followers had swollen to a total of over twenty thousand: men, women, and children) to three thousand well-armed men. When his proposals were rejected, he invited the cadets to join his own forces—nearly all refused—and left blowing his war trumpet, predicting Ras Imru's capture or death within fifteen days.

November had been a month of extensive manœuvring by both sides all over the south-west of Ethiopia. The impression is of a hunt rather than a war, with the Italians as huntsmen harassing their still-dangerous enemies, driving them from covert to covert while the Ethiopians twisted and turned, changing their plans almost daily as they tried to break through the net tightening around them. In December the net closed. On the 13th, Colonel Princivalle and Abba Jobir caught Ras Imru on the banks of the River Naso. There was fierce day-long fighting between the Jimma army and the Shoans, unexpectedly surprised in a stretch of open country. By nightfall Ras Imru had broken away but his ammunition was almost exhausted. At the end he and his men were fighting with swords and knives and he had learnt that a third column under Tessitore was moving down to cut him off in the north.

Five days later, heading towards Maji, pursued by Tessitore, Princivalle, and their Galla allies, Ras Imru and his men tried to cross the river Gogeb only to find its fords held by Colonel Minniti of Malta's column and—cruellest cut of all—by the last of the local Shoan garrisons. Imru sent three of his own officers to negotiate with Colonel Minniti. The Italians demanded unconditional surrender; Ras Imru said no negotiations were possible till the people with him had been evacuated from the firing zone. It was agreed: the women, children, and the old men were led through the firing lines. Still Ras Imru procrastinated. As the day drew on, the Italians threatened to use mortars and planes and warned that they had orders from Graziani to gas the camp unless Imru surrendered within a few hours, and to kill the civilian hostages. 'That', said Ras Imru, 'will be their wedding day!' It seems that his main reason for delay was to give the fifty Eritrean deserters with him a chance to escape under cover of night. All that night the discussions, courteously conducted, went on. By dawn when the Ethiopians assembled and laid down their arms, the Eritreans had slipped through the enemy lines, avoiding the inevitable punishment of death, and were heading for the Kenya border.

Having ordered his men to destroy their weapons, himself having thrown into the stream a pistol given to him by his cousin the Emperor, Ras Imru mounted a mule and rode unarmed into the Italian camp, escorted by a Kenyaz Dejene wearing— unwisely—the uniform of a senior Italian officer with its gorgeous decorations. With Ras Imru surrendered Kifle Nasibu, Belai Haileab, and many others of the surviving cadets, also Yilma Deressa, Joseph and Benjamin the two sons of Dr. Martin, George Herouy, Ras Imru's son-in-law, and Haddis Alemayu who had been with him in the Shire—the élite of the youngest generation of arms-bearing Ethiopians. They had been promised their lives and—except for Kenyaz Dejene who even more unwisely boasted of how he had obtained his uniform—the promise was at the time kept.

So ended the Regency, the Provisional Government, and the flickering independence of the Empire of Ethiopia kept alive in the south-west for six months after the departure of the Emperor. It had been a weak flame at best, a desperate expedient designed by Haile Selassie to give him some legal and territorial basis on which to plead for the help of Britain and of the League. It seems unlikely, whatever the embittered cadets might have thought, that the Emperor's own presence in the south-west, or indeed anywhere else in Ethiopia would have changed by an iota the result.

The Italians flew Ras Imru to Addis Ababa where Graziani himself courteously welcomed him at the airport with many of the submitted lords. From Addis Ababa he was flown to Italy. Mussolini had the good taste not to parade him in Rome. Ras Imru was confined on the island of Ponza in the little house where seven years later Mussolini himself was to be imprisoned.

On 19 December, the day following Ras Imru's surrender, Ras Kassa's eldest son Wondossen Kassa was killed. He was caught in the caves near the source of the Takazze by the Wollo *banda* of Captain Farello and shot as a rebel on the orders of General Tracchia, Graziani's right-hand man. In this strange way the death of Ras Gugsa Wule six years earlier was avenged by the Wollo Galla who had then arrived on the plains of Anchim too late to save him.

Wondossen's younger brothers, Aberra and Asfawossen Kassa, were by then ready to submit. After the failure of the attack on the capital they had fallen back on Fikke and in the quiet months of the rains reopened negotiations with their fathers-in-law Ras Hailu and Ras Seyum and directly with the Italians. Towards the end of November, Aberra Kassa refused an appeal from Abebe Aregai for a hundred men and a cannon to block a predicted advance by General Tracchia from Debra Brehan. 'It is not now the time for us to fight', wrote Dejaz Aberra to Abebe Aregai, 'for at present we cannot completely defeat the Italians. For every attempted battle they will retaliate by burning our houses, crops and cattle.' The group of cadets at Fikke—twenty or thirty, now including Essayas, Abebe Tafari, Negga Haile Selassie, Mulugueta Bulli and Mengistu Neway—had been trying to persuade Aberra Kassa and his brother to join Ras Imru at Gore. As the signs of submission became more and more evident—five Italian prisoners were sent back with gifts, Abebe Aregai's war-tribute was refused, it was known that the Italians had promised Dejaz Aberra land—the cadets decided to leave Salale and join Haile Mariam Mammo on the lands around Mulu. Dejaz Aberra got wind of their plans and tried to disarm them; even when they were safely with Haile Mariam Mammo, Dejaz Aberra sent Mesfin Sileshi to beg them—unsuccessfully—to return. They were determined to stay with a leader whom they knew would fight, even if he were not a great nobleman.

In the second week of December, four Italian columns started moving in menacingly towards Fikke. The fifth column was that of Ras Hailu from Ambo. It was he who right until the last minute carried on negotiations with his son-in-law and guaranteed him life and lands. On 16 December as the five columns were closing in messengers from Ras Hailu brought to Fikke the final ultimatum: a letter from Graziani to Dejaz Aberra Kassa dated five days earlier: 'Now I tell you to surrender', wrote Graziani, 'and I assure you nothing will happen to you. Why do you want to die uselessly?'

Only his cousins had remained with Dejaz Aberra: Mesfin Sileshi and the two younger men, Lij Merid Mangasha and Lij Abiye Abebe. They suspected Italian treachery. 'If you want to be killed', said Mesfin, 'shall I kill you?' But Aberra had decided to take Ras Hailu's advice. More hesitantly, his brother Asfawossen—who had also received a letter, but from Ras Seyum writing 'as a father-in-law to a son-in-law'—agreed with him.

The exact sequence of the events that followed is difficult to disentangle. Messengers on horseback went to and fro between Fikke and the two closest columns of the enemy, General Tracchia's and Ras Hailu's. An aeroplane flew low over Fikke, word came that General Tracchia's advance guard was only a mile away to the north, and Dejaz Aberra, still undecided, took his men out of the town to the lowlands. That evening Colonel Belly, who was with Ras Hailu, came—apparently in person—to the camp, and Aberra and Asfawossen finally decided to submit. Aberra however sent his wife and baby son away with Mesfin and the two cousins, a last-minute concession to their pleas and threats.

A letter was sent up to General Tracchia who had now occupied Fikke:

'To General Tracchia
As you have assured me in your letter to me that our lives

will be spared, we shall assemble our armies and receive you by peaceful parade in a place called Bidigon.

Aberra Kassa'

Ras Hailu in person led Aberra and Asfawossen to General Tracchia's camp. While they were in the tent drinking coffee with the General, the men of their escort were disarmed, apparently without difficulty, and taken away (they were released the next morning). A group of *carabinieri* entered the tent and arrested the two brothers. It was 21 December, three days after Ras Imru had surrendered. At 7 p.m. the men in the escort heard a volley of shots in the centre of the town.

Tracchia sent a laconic cable to Graziani: 'Dejaz Aberra and brother shot dusk in piazza of Fikke'. Graziani sent a cable to Lessona repeating Tracchia's message and adding 'Situation Salale liquidated'.

The third drama was meanwhile moving more slowly to its inevitable conclusion. The figure who really inspired the resistance in the south-east was one of the Italians' oldest and fiercest enemies, Dejaz Gabremariam. Sent down from Dessie by the Emperor to reconcile Ras Desta and his Fitauraris, he had only half-succeeded in that but had wholly succeeded in restoring a fighting spirit and a coherent front against the enemy. It was Gabremariam to whom the Sidamo nobles looked for leadership; and though Ras Desta's personal courage was never doubted, it was Gabremariam who with 4,000 men had barred the Italian advance throughout the rainy season.

On 14 October General Geloso launched the by-now traditional three-column attack on the enemy who had been facing his positions only a mile or two away and keeping him from his rightful honours as Governor of the new Italian province of Galla-Sidamo. The advance Ethiopian position was outflanked and the leader who held it killed. Six days later Gabremariam's main body was attacked, the old Dejaz wounded, and his army forced back. But Geloso's advance was slow and difficult, his flanks and his supply-line (of mules) continually threatened, and by the end of October the Lakes Division had not moved forward very far or very effectively. Ras Desta and Dejaz Beiene Merid were still, though cut off almost entirely from contact with the outer world, at their respective capitals, Yirgalem and Goba, still both in control of their respective provinces, Sidamo and Bale.

A month later the situation had changed drastically. Another Italian column had at last pushed up through the Wadara Forest from Neghelli and was threatening to cut Sidamo off from Bale. Simultaneously a third, inevitable, thrust came down from Addis. A lorried column commanded by Captain Tucci and consisting mainly of Dejaz Toclu Meshesha's Tigrean *banda* left the capital on 23 November and a week later had wound down through the Lakes. *En route*, Tucci recruited and armed 5,000 of the Arussi Galla. In Sidamo the Sidanchos rose and started killing the Shoan settlers. Yirgalem was occupied without resistance on 1 December. Gabremariam, abandoned by many of his men, joined Ras Desta in the rugged mountains on the borders of Bale.

On 7 January Graziani flew down to Yirgalem to direct operations in person. But despite bombing raids and encircling movements Ras Desta and Dejaz Gabremariam escaped south. The Viceroy, frustrated, flew on to tour the provinces of Harar and Somalia while, doubling back towards the north-east, Ras Desta and Dejaz Gabremariam crossed into Bale and finally joined forces with Dejaz Beiene Merid. Beiene Merid had about 3,000 men and the reduced army of Sidamo cannot have numbered many more.

General Nasi now took overall command of operations and ordered down a fresh column of three Libyan Battalions under General Kubeddu. The combined armies of the Ethiopians once again broke out of the net encircling them and headed north, though not until the comparatively fresh troops of Bale had been defeated and dispersed. In the first week in February two more columns joined in the chase. Nasi, with the skill that was always to distinguish his manœuvres, ordered a deliberate pause to allow the Ethiopians to regroup and form a compact body. The Italians waited while the scattered bands drew together again under their leaders and moved wearily back towards Lake Shela, perhaps 2,000 strong. On 17 February Captain Tucci and his swollen *banda* made contact; on the 18th they attacked and on the next day were reinforced and moved in for the kill.

This time there were no negotiations held and little chivalry shown. The final battle of the Ethiopian war was fought, bitterly, at Gogetti. The relics of the armies of Sidamo and Bale were outnumbered even by the forces facing them, and outside the immediate area of the battle stood column after column of encircling troops ready to fall on them if necessary. It was not necessary. That day Dejaz Beiene Merid and Dejaz Gabremariam died. Old and mortally wounded, Gabremariam asked an Eritrean under-officer to give him the *coup-de-grâce* to avoid falling prisoner to the Italians. The Eritrean's was the only honourable act of that day. Beiene Merid was taken prisoner and shot. Four months later an Italian lieutenant, Cesare Alberini, was paid 10,000 dollars' reward for their deaths. By this stage the war had become no more than a meretricious man-hunt.

But Ras Desta escaped. Wounded, with one servant, he headed for his birthplace in Gurage, the village of Maskan. Tucci's *bande* pursued him; on 23 February Tucci reached Maskan only to find Ras Desta had passed through and fled further to the south-west. Even the people of his birthplace had abandoned him. The *bande* marched all that night, and at dawn in the hamlet of Egia surrounded the *tukul* in which Ras Desta had taken refuge. It was the last day of his life. The hours dragged wearily by while Tucci waited for the inevitable instructions; in the late afternoon, an hour before sunset, Dejaz Toclu Meshesha's Tigreans tied him to a tree and shot him. So died the Emperor's son-in-law, husband of his eldest child, the Princess Tenagne Worq. Colonel Natale pronounced an ungracious funeral oration: 'He was not worth more than the slave who followed him from hedgerow to hedgerow.'

The war was over; the conquest of Ethiopia was complete.

CHAPTER 14

YEKATIT 12

ON 17 February 1937 it was announced that to celebrate the birth of the Prince of Naples the Viceroy in person would distribute alms to the poor at the Little Ghebbi. The ceremony was fixed for forty-eight hours later. On the evening of 18 February there was a reception at the French Consulate-General. It went on till the early hours of the morning. Graziani had a satisfactory talk with the railway chief, M. Gerard, but noticed that both the Consul-General M. Bodard and his wife Pierrette were nervy; a nervousness he put down to 'dissapore coniugale'. He himself appears to have been in the best of humours, looking forward to good news from Ras Desta's hunters at any moment.

19 February, Yekatit 12 in the Ethiopian calendar, was a Friday. Notables and people rose early to flock to the ceremony at the Little Ghebbi: among them two young Eritreans, Abraha Deboch and Mogus Asgedom. Before they left his house Abraha Deboch laid an Italian flag on the wooden floor and pinned it there with a bayonet; to the handle of the bayonet he tied an Ethiopian flag.

'Raise all of your arm well', proclaimed the Viceroy at the Ghebbi as the ceremony began, 'extend it high towards the sky and towards the sun to salute the resplendent Majesty of King Vittorio Emmanuele III, your and our sovereign, and also in salute of the Duce of Fascimo and creator of a new Italy, Benito Mussolini.' Submissions of notables were made, planes flew past, and at eleven o'clock officials started distributing coins as alms for the priests and the people.

Among the notables who had arrived that day was Haile Selassie Gugsa. An Eritrean interpreter, Rosario Gileazgi, who for years had been working for the Italians, was introducing him to Major Pallavicino of the Political Office as Abraha Deboch and Mogus Asgedom slipped forward through the crowd towards the colourful group of clergy, nobles, and officials gathered on the steps in front of the Ghebbi.

All assassination attempts at public ceremonies follow roughly the same pattern: incredulity and half-awareness, followed by confusion, shock, and the beginnings of panic. Abraha Deboch and Mogus Asgedom managed to lob as many as ten hand-grenades that exploded on or around the steps of the Little Ghebbi before themselves escaping in the chaos that followed, leaving a group of wounded and dying men behind them.

The Abuna Cyrillos's umbrella-bearer was killed and the Abuna wounded; as were the Vice Governor-General, Armando Petretti, the Viceroy's *chef de cabinet*, and over thirty others. Graziani himself was rushed to the Italian hospital; the third grenade had exploded on his right and 365 fragments had penetrated his body. At the hospital he was operated on immediately and soon declared out of danger. The most seriously injured was General Liotta, the Commander of the Air Force, whose leg had to be amputated.

The news soon spread through the city. In the panic following what appeared to them to be the signal for a general massacre the Italian *carabinieri* had fired into the crowds of beggars and poor assembled for the distribution of alms; and it is said that the Federal Secretary, Guido Cortese, even fired his revolver into the group of Ethiopian dignitaries standing around him. 'Cars were going here and there', Rosario Gileazgi recorded, 'people running, machine-guns firing. . . it was a big disorder, Ethiopians running from Italians, Italians from Ethiopians . . . it was said before that Ras Desta would menace the city and that Ethiopian patriots would come and kill every Italian.'

Rosario Gileazgi followed his chief to the *Casa del Fascio* in the centre of the city to which all the Blackshirts were rallying. There he heard the Federal Secretary give the orders that set the city aflame. 'Comrades', proclaimed Guido Cortese, 'today is the day when we should show our devotion to our Viceroy by reacting and destroying the Ethiopians for three days. For three days I give you *carte blanche* to destroy and kill and do what you want to the Ethiopians.'

The emotions of the months of tension and actual fear in which the Italian population had lived, cut off, insecure, threatened continually with invasion or infiltration from the surrounding hills, forced to control themselves and to treat distantly with a suspicious native population who barely responded to their first natural gestures of friendliness, exploded. Protected legally and psychologically by their black shirts, the labourers and minor officials and lorry drivers and first settlers let loose all their hatred and frustration. It was back to the days of the *squadristi* in Italy but on a larger scale. Most of the burning was done with oil and petrol, most of the killing with daggers and truncheons to the crys of 'Duce! Duce!' and 'Civilta Italiana!' 'These men are barbarians', the horrified Petretti is reported to have said, 'and nothing can be done'.

The killings and the burnings spread all over the city on Friday night, and the arrests on Saturday morning. There was blood in the streams, and dead bodies over and under the bridges. It is not clear whether the regular Blackshirts of the garrison—the 'Diamanti' group—took part in the killings and burnings, but it is certain that the Italian officers of the regular army and the Eritreans took no part at all, and that the *carabinieri* tried where possible to control if not to stop the Blackshirts. On the Saturday lorries toured the streets, some picking up the bodies, others collecting prisoners. The Blackshirts were burning the smaller houses now, on 'hygienic' grounds, and writing their names on the bigger houses as a form of personal annexation. They were tripping up running Ethiopians in the streets with their truncheons and beating out their brains, going to the Bank of Italy to change the dollars they had looted during the night, raiding the houses of Armenians and Greeks and lynching their servants, raking in corpses and throwing them on lorries, even posing for photographs with the bodies of those they had killed. On Saturday evening a group armed with jerry-cans tried unsuccessfully to burn down St. George's Cathedral.

'A second night of massacre followed', wrote a Hungarian doctor, Dr. Ladislas Rava. 'I was again in my room. Since the beginning of the massacre I had kept my Ethiopian servant there with me, forbidding him even to show himself at the window, as any sight of him by an Italian might have meant his death. He had a little house beside mine which was spared on the first night but burned on the second. He sat during those terrible hours quite speechless and with his head in his hands. I dared not ask him what he thought.'

On Sunday, the 21st, there were no Ethiopians in the streets. The smell of burning and death hung over the city as groups of Blackshirts circulated in their cars and lorries. In the afternoon the authorities stepped in firmly. A plan to bomb the Cathedral from the air was halted, Graziani issued a proclamation from his hospital bed, and the Federal Secretary sent out orders from the *Casa del Fascio* to his section commanders instructing them 'to end the hostilities'.

In the three days of killing how many people had been killed? The Ethiopians later put the figure at 30,000; the Italians admitted a few hundred. Probably somewhere around 3,000 would be an accurate estimate—not a vast massacre as racial massacres go, though peculiarly horrifying because committed by a people normally so humane. But this figure would only cover the victims of the half-organized massacre in the capital; not the scores who were tried and shot there in the days that followed or the hundreds if not thousands that were killed as a result of Yekatit 12 all over Ethiopia.

In the capital a military tribunal was set up immediately after the assassination attempt; on the Friday afternoon sixty-two Ethiopians were tried and in the evening shot.

In the wake of the assassination attempt the Italian authorities decided to make a clean sweep of all Ethiopian notables, young and old. In the week immediately following Yekatit 12 many more were summarily tried and shot; particularly the young men who had surrendered with Ras Imru and who were suspected, probably justifiably, of plotting against the regime. Among those executed were Kifle Nasibu, Belai Haileab, Benjamin and Joseph Martin, and George Herouy. Then with the first reactions —whether of panic or deliberate 'frightfulness'—over, and as the investigations into the assassination attempt proceeded more calmly, the executions were stopped and the remaining prisoners packed off to different destinations: the most important to internment in Italy, another more numerous group of several hundreds to the Dahlac islands in the Red Sea, and finally several thousand across the Ogaden to a particularly unpleasant concentration camp set up at Danane.

It seems that it was at this time or shortly afterwards that even the leading Rases who had submitted were sent to confinement in Italy: Ras Seyum and Ras Gabre Hiwot certainly, the others possibly, but Ras Hailu not. The capital was thus cleared of all possible or potential conspirators against Italian rule.

Meanwhile the killings spread to the provinces; specially directed against the Amharas as an exchange of telegrams with the reluctant Governor of Harar, General Nasi, indicates.

On 1 March Graziani cabled to Nasi ordering him to shoot all Amhara notables and ex-officers 'according to the directions of the Duce repeated 1000 times yet little observed by many. . . . Give assurance with the word "shot" but let the assurance be serious.' Two days later, having received a (presumably) dilatory reply from Nasi, Graziani cabled with, if less hysteria, even more cold ferocity. 'Shoot all—I say all—rebels, notables, chiefs, followers either captured in action or giving themselves up or isolated fugitives or intriguing elements . . . and any suspected of bad faith or of being guilty of helping the rebels or only intending to and any who hide arms. Women are of course excluded except in particular cases, and children.' On 21 March he cabled to Mussolini who was visiting Balbo in Libya to say that since 19 February there had been 324 summary executions, 'of course without including in that figure the repressions of the 19 and 20 February', and that 1,100 Amhara men, women, and children had been sent to Danane. On 31 March he cabled to Lessona to give the total of summary executions carried out by 28 March all over the country: 1,469.

By the end of April the ferocity of the Viceroy appears to have been diminishing. On the 23rd Nasi reported in a long cable that 600 chiefs who had surrendered or abandoned Fitaurari Baade or had submitted had been executed in accordance with instructions; would it be permissible to offer clemency and life to Fitaurari Baade[1] if he handed over his rifles and captured weapons? Four thousand persons, including 200 chiefs with 2,000 rifles, had surrendered with Fitaurari Malion; many had relatives in the Pelizzari *Banda* and among the Amhara battalions; furthermore if they had passed into British Somaliland what trouble they would have caused! Would his Excellency the Viceroy therefore please rescind his order to shoot fifty-four chiefs, which would create panic in the Chercher area? Two days later Graziani cabled his reply repeating his general directives but adding a saving clause: 'Anyhow since in these questions it is

---

[1] In fact at the end of March Fitaurari Baade crossed into British Somaliland with 1,200 men, women and children. They were interned in a refugee camp near Hargeisha. All around the border of *Africa Orientale Italiana* the same sort of thing was happening. In July, no less than 6,000 men, women, and children (including Negga, who became a monk) crossed into Kenya. They were taken down to Isiolo where a camp was set up six miles away from the more closely guarded Eritrean Deserters' Camp.

shades of opinion that count I leave your Excellency to settle the matter as you think best. Graziani.'

The month of May, however, was to see one more bloody and atrocious massacre.

The May killings were the direct and in a sense the logical result not only of Italian policy at this time but more precisely of the Italian investigations into the assassination attempt.

The more that became known about the two escaped terrorists the more paradoxical their action appeared. Not only were they both Eritreans but the ringleader Abraha Deboch had in fact been an Italian informer. During the war he had been imprisoned by the Ethiopians and after his release by the Italians he had been employed by Major Pallavicino to work for the Political Office. Furthermore it appeared that Abraha Deboch and Mogus Asgedom had always met at the German Consulate-General where the man with whom Mogus Asgedom shared a house was employed. *A priori* it would have been hard to imagine a more unlikely pair of would-be assassins in a city pullulating with bitter and reckless ex-soldiers of the Ethiopian armies than two Eritreans of whom one was employed by the Italian Political Office and the other had links with the German diplomatic envoy.

Naturally enough, the Italians suspected that there was more to the assassination attempt than met the eye; and thinking back to the evening of 18 February Graziani was less inclined to put down the Bodards's display of nerves to marital disputes. The first logical suspect would have been Dr. Strum, the German Consul-General: a worrying line of investigation which the authorities appear quickly to have dropped. 'Character and origin European without a doubt', Mussolini commented when he had studied the details of the assassination attempt. And apparently he added 'Intelligence Service or Comintern'.

The British almost immediately became the chief suspects. As early as Saturday 20 February the parties of Italians breaking into Ethiopian houses were, Dr. Ladislas Rava mentions *en passant*, searching for British-made hand-grenades. Tafere Worq Kidane Wold, the interpreter at the British Consulate-General, was arrested and interrogated, presumably despite British protests. A certain Mr. Lee, a consular official, left Addis Ababa the day after the assassination attempt; as he was thought to be the resident

Director of the Intelligence Service, his sudden departure was taken as yet another proof of British complicity. Suspicion fell not only on the Indian trader Mohammed Ally—in whose shops all over the Empire plots were hatched, Graziani recorded, 'under the guidance of expert foreign elements'—but even on Major Pallavicino and his English wife.

The investigations of the Military Advocate Francheschino revealed, however, a new fact and oriented the inquiry in a totally new direction. Abraha Deboch had ten days before the ceremony left Addis Ababa with his wife and had taken her—and here the Ethiopian accounts confirm the results of the Italian enquiry—to the monastery of Debra Libanos.

Graziani remembered that at the ceremony the Abuna Cyrillos had appeared 'pale'. Further investigations proved that the monks of Debra Libanos had been in Addis Ababa in the first week of February, to apply to the government for financial grants. They had left on their return journey twenty-four hours before Abraha Deboch, with whom they had clearly therefore been in contact during their week in the capital. It was also discovered that on his escape from the city Abraha Deboch had gone back to Debra Libanos to collect or warn his wife, and it was suspected that he might still be there, hidden by the monks.

Francheschino's report was sent in eight weeks after the assassination attempt, in mid-May. Graziani, who was still in hospital, studied it and took his decision. On 19 May he cabled the conclusion of the report and his orders to General Maletti. After reference to 'a nest of murderers under the guise of monks' it ended with the chilling instructions: 'Therefore execute summarily all monks without distinction including the Vice-Prior.'

On 20 May the monks assembled for the feast of the greatest of the Seven Holy Men and founder of their monastery, St. Tekle Haimonot. Colonel Garelli, the local commander, attended—reluctantly, according to the post-war evidence of his interpreter, but all the same attended. After the ceremony the monks were arrested on his orders and by his men. Some were taken by lorry to Shinkurst, others to Debra Brehan. 297 were shot, plus 23 laymen, considered to be their accomplices; the young deacons attached to the monastery were kept in custody at Debra Brehan. A week later, another telegram followed: their 'complicity having also been proved' the 129 deacons at Debra Brehan were also shot. Of the whole population of Ethiopia's most famous religious centre, only 30 schoolboys being educated at the monastery and possibly the Prior, Tekle Giorgis, survived. General Maletti reproached Colonel Garelli for not having caught Abraha Deboch. And Graziani cabled to Rome: 'In this way . . . of the monastery of Debra Libanos . . . there remains not a trace.'

Graziani's increasing paranoia was alarming even the colonial officers for whom he had been a hero ever since the Libyan campaign. Orders went out to arrest and execute all soothsayers, fortune-tellers, bards, and suspicious vagabonds. The communiqué which was issued on the death of Ras Desta and circulated to all commands was couched in the language used by those who regard themselves as the chosen instruments of destiny: 'Dopo attentato ignobile del giorno di 19 la guistizia di Dio habet indicato palesemente sua condanna colpendo uno dei capi ancora rebelli . . . oggi catturato e ucciso Ras Desta da colonna Tucci. Dare massima diffusione.'[1] Rumours spread that Graziani, tortured by the pain of his scarred body—'this tunic of blood that I have been wearing for the last ten years', as he called it at his trial after the war—lay awake at night planning revenge and focusing his hatred on the nobility of Amhara and the Coptic clergy, remembering the hole in the church at Jijiga. He lay for seventy-eight days in hospital, and when he came out, more rumours spread: that ever afterwards he surrounded his sleeping quarters with barbed wire and a battalion of armed men, living in perpetual fear of another assassination attempt.

In this way was the birth of the baby prince Vittorio Emmanuele, heir to the thrones of the House of Savoy, bloodily celebrated in Italian East Africa.

In Europe, however, and particularly in England the sufferings of Ethiopia did not go unnoticed. A month after the Italian occupation Sylvia Pankhurst had published the first number of a broadsheet that was to survive for many years: the 'New Times and Ethiopia News'. Month after month her editorials attacked the pusillanimity of British governments and officialdom. Her principal reporter, an Indian named Wazir Bey who had taken refuge in Djibuti, was in close touch with the Ethiopian Consul

---

[1] 'After the ignoble assassination attempt on the day of the 19th the justice of the Lord has clearly shewn His displeasure, striking down one of the leaders still in rebellion . . . This day Ras Desta has been captured and killed by the Tucci column. Give maximum publicity.'

there, Lij Andergatchew Messai. His reports brought news of great Ethiopian victories and enormous Italian casualties to the liberal middle-classes who were curious to know what really was going on in Ethiopia. At the time of the Yekatit massacres of which only garbled rumours reached the free press of Europe, the circulation of the 'NTEN' climbed to 25,000. It published in full Haile Selassie's appeal to all Christian Churches after Yekatit 12 condemning the Italians for their crimes, an appeal which led the Archbishop of Canterbury, Cosmo Lang, one of the Emperor's most loyal defenders, to raise the topic in the House of Lords. Thanks to Sylvia Pankhurst and other devoted supporters of the Emperor—such as Sir Sidney Barton, now retired, George Steer in these years of exile a personal friend of Haile Selassie, and Colonel 'Dan' Sandford, who had found a niche as treasurer of Guildford Cathedral—Ethiopia and its fate remained, at least sporadically, in the public eye.

CHAPTER 15

THE DUKE OF AOSTA

THE previous October Mussolini had made his famous 'olives and bayonets' speech in Rome, announcing a new era of prosperity for the second Roman Empire. 'In seven months', he had said, 'we have conquered the Empire but we will need even less time to pacify and occupy it.' Seven months later, a year after Haile Selassie's flight, his forecast seemed astoundingly accurate. The new Empire appeared solidly established and its future prosperity—based on fine communications, Italian administration, and a powerful native army—in theory assured. The nobility and intelligentsia of the old Empire had been liquidated or imprisoned; the last of its war-leaders defeated. The rank and file of its troops were either disarmed or enrolling—it was the Duce's own scheme, as intelligent as it was grandiose—in the *armata nera*, which was planned to become at 300,000 strong by far the largest black army in Africa. Calm was established almost everywhere except for a few scattered rebel bands in the outlying regions of Shoa.[1]

Graziani spent the summer of 1937, the rainy season, recuperating from his wounds in the pleasant Italian-style colonial town of Asmara. Gradually however, to the amazement and alarm of Italian officials, serious though unconnected incidents began to occur in regions which had been considered not so much pacified as naturally peaceful. In the last days of August there were almost simultaneous but apparently uncoordinated attacks by *shifta* on garrisons near Debra Tabor and near Bahr Dar. By 1 September all garrisons in Gojjam

---

[1] In the spring of 1937 Abebe Aregai had only 40 men with him, and Mesfin Sileshi only 30. They and four surviving Shoan leaders attempted to set up a co-ordinated resistance movement in Shoa but failed. Mesfin Sileshi headed for the Sudanese border with Blatta Takele Wolde Hawariat and Zaudi Asfau. Abebe Aregai, Haile Mariam Mammo, and Dejaz Auraris of Menz stayed in the mountain highlands to the north of Addis Ababa, the heartland of Shoa which the Italians and the *bande* could penetrate but never control.

—Gojjam which had welcomed the Italian invaders almost as liberators—were threatened. By *Maskal* the revolt had spread north to the Wolkait and to the lowlands of Armachecho on the Sudan border. Columns *en route* to Gojjam were attacked and surrounded. In Wollo rebels sacked Quoram. In Beghemder a strong column of five battalions sent out from Gondar to rescue a besieged garrison was itself attacked and cut in two, with one battalion, the 6th Arabo-Somali, almost annihilated. There was no denying the evidence. What had at first been put down to the isolated activities of *shiftas* could no longer be minimized. By the end of the rains the former provinces of Gojjam and Beghemder, the new governate of Amhara, so easily conquered and so peacefully held, were aflame with revolt.

Bewildered, baffled, and enraged by the totally unexpected and daily worsening situation in an Empire which he and his officials had considered pacified, Graziani directed his first fury against the only rebel whose name and reputation were known, the leader of the bands who had attacked and sacked Quoram, Dejaz Haile Kebbede of Wag. The *bande* of the Wollo Galla were reinforced, rearmed, and let loose on Wag and Lasta. Their savagery was, in the words of an Italian officer, 'horrendous'. Haile Kebbede was captured and beheaded. His head was exposed on a pike in Socota. Certain of his relatives reported that his head was packed in ice and sent to Italy afterwards, though it is hard to believe Italians capable of such pointless barbarity. But his son Lij Wossene and his wife Woizero Shoanish escaped across the Takazze into Beghemder, and from that time on raids and bitter fighting never ceased in Wag.

Killings and atrocities, however, no longer acted as a deterrent, for the Amhara had been driven to desperation. The internal feuds and quarrels which had made so many of them accept, if not welcome, an alternative to their Shoan rulers were submerged in the face of a common enemy. Their leaders had been treacherously killed. Their clergy had been treacherously massacred. Like any race faced with extermination they instinctively rebelled.

The rebellion began spontaneously, in local uprisings and under local leaders whose names were almost unknown outside their immediate areas of influence. In Bircutan it was Fitaurari Mesfin Redda who with forty shepherds attacked the local *banda*. Elsewhere it was *banda* leaders themselves such as Dejaz Mangasha Jimbirre of Faguta who suddenly took to the hills with their men. In Armachecho the rebellion started at a wedding-feast. As the bridegroom and his friends sang war-songs, their fathers grew furious and asked what brave deeds they had done that entitled them to sing so boldly. One greybeard said that he had fought the dervishes with a sword alone, whereas the younger generation, even though they had rifles and ammunition, permitted their enemies to live as neighbours, peacefully. The wedding feast ended with all the guests, bridegroom in the lead, marching out to attack the local fort.

In Gojjam the killing of the clergy and of the monks of Debra Libanos, news of which travelled slowly, was at first hardly believed. Gojjam was the most orthodox, the most traditionally religious, of all Ethiopia's provinces. Horror when the news was confirmed led instinctively to rebellion. At the end of November the Italian authorities hastily summoned Church officials at Addis Ababa and had the aged half-blind Bishop of Gojjam, Abraham, elected as Abuna. But by then it was too late. The delegation from Gojjam even refused, with considerable courage, to take part in the vote. The anathemas launched against the rebels by the new Abuna had much less effect than the excommunication launched against Abraham by the Coptic Patriarch in Cairo. By then a change of policy was in the air; by then it had been officially announced that the Viceroy would be replaced.

Lessona, one of the most incessant intriguers in the Duce's entourage, can at least claim credit for having written *Memoirs* which reveal with frankness the poisonous atmosphere of the Fascist hierarchy and his own distasteful personality. He made no secret of his contempt for Graziani. It was he who in the summer of 1937 spread the rumours in Rome that Graziani was deliberately lingering in his hospital bed out of fear and, later, that Graziani had taken refuge in the safety of Asmara, where 'he slept at night barricaded in the governor's palace, surrounded by barbed-wire, machine guns, armoured cars and a battalion of guards'. He therefore seized upon reports of the outbreak of the revolt as a legitimate tool for disposing of the Viceroy.

Mussolini, who knew his man, did not take all Lessona's reports at their face value. Nevertheless it was obvious that a serious revolt had broken out and that Graziani's methods —which, the Duce did not forget, were also Lessona's methods

—had failed. Mussolini's attitude towards Ethiopia was strange. Neither he—nor for that matter the new King-Emperor—ever visited *Africa Orientale Italiana*; and once the conquest was achieved he seems to have felt a profound indifference to the Empire. His only object was that it should become prosperous in peace and self-sufficient in war. For this he was prepared to invest enormous sums of money, but clearly total pacification was the *sine qua non*. The moral question of the rights and wrongs of Graziani's policy of repression was not of the least interest to him. The policy had failed; and as it had failed both the policy and its executors would have to be changed. On 15 November the Minister for *Africa Italiana*, Lessona, was called to Palazzo Venezia with the commander of the air force division 'Aquila': Amedeo, Duke of Aosta, who left the meeting as Viceroy-designate.

What prompted Mussolini to select the Duke of Aosta can only be guessed. Thirty-nine years old, very popular with the armed forces and in Italy generally, he was nevertheless a minor figure who had had little chance of distinguishing himself in any way. Perhaps it was precisely his easy-going insignificance that appealed to Mussolini, perhaps also a sense of gratitude to Amedeo's dead father, Emmanuele Filiberto. And though the King, Vittorio Emmanuele, had objected to this putative revival of the fortunes and possibly the ambitions of the House of Aosta, his objections, which can hardly have been convincing even to himself, were overruled.

So inexperienced a Viceroy could not be expected to direct the military operations against the rebels: the question of who was to be 'troop commander' under the Duke of Aosta in *AOI* became a matter of almost farcical intrigue. Lessona had his own candidate—General Cavallero—but Cavallero's enemies in Rome included among many others the Chief of the General Staff, Badoglio; the Foreign Secretary, Ciano; and the Party Secretary, Starace.

Nevertheless when he went to see Mussolini a week after his previous interview, Lessona heard to his pleasure that his candidate Cavallero had indeed been chosen. With considerably less pleasure he saw that the Duce had a further decision to announce. Embarrassed and nervously twiddling his fingers[1] Mussolini

[1] According to Lessona's account. Probably however the Duce was enjoying himself.

informed Lessona that 'naturally' the Minister would have to be changed at the same time as the Viceroy, and that as a Prince of the royal blood was taking over as Viceroy, he himself would have to resume the office of Minister of the Colonies—or rather, as it now was, Minister for *Africa Italiana*. Exit Lessona. His had been a brief and fatal Ministry: the three corner-stones of his policy, direct rule, racial separation, frigidity towards the Church, being the basic causes of all the disasters in Italian East Africa, present and to come. Enter Teruzzi: for though Mussolini took over the nominal direction of the Ministry, Teruzzi, ex-Commandant-General of the Milizia, ex-commander of the only Blackshirt Division in the Ethiopian war never to fire a shot, was as Under-Secretary (and subsequently as Minister) the real director of colonial affairs in Africa—for as long as there remained any colonial affairs to direct.

With the final departure of Graziani[2] Italian East Africa got off to what Mr. Helm of the British Consulate-General called 'virtually a fresh start'. New personalities replaced old in all the key positions. Of the five governors of provinces, the only one who remained in place was General Nasi at Harar. With the new personalities there appeared an entirely new policy. The military tribunals which had been ordering summary executions up and down the country were suppressed, and the Duke of Aosta liberated 1,000 of the detainees at Danane. Even Teruzzi's first visit, marked by the opening of the magnificent engineering tunnel under Ad Termaber, the 'Mussolini pass', went off without a hitch. Serfdom was officially abolished and 400,000 *gebars* given their own land in Galla–Sidamo. The Duke of Aosta was 'indefatigable'. A 'better class of administrator' appeared. All in all it was the sort of regime the British could both recognize and approve. From the beginning of 1938 till the autumn crisis in Europe, relations between the Italians and the British improved dramatically—much to the dismay of the exiled Emperor and his

[2] Graziani instead of leaving at once (as dignity required) stayed on in Eritrea much to the general embarrassment, attempted to oust Cavallero in his own favour and only then, when he had failed, went back to semi-disgrace and a retirement that at the time seemed permanent. In the summer of 1939 just before the outbreak of World War II he had an audience with Mussolini in which he asked melodramatically to be allowed to return to Somalia as a simple colonist. Mussolini most graciously gave his permission and recommended the former Viceroy to grow bananas. 'Our market always needs them', said the Duce, apparently straight-faced.

little band of friends and supporters, for whom 1938 was to be a dismal year indeed.

General Cavallero, the new troop commander, took up his command on 12 January 1938. He wasted no time. On 14 January he flew up to Gondar to confer with the new Governor of Amhara, General Mezzetti; and on 29 January Italian columns started marching out against the rebels.

It was the beginning of a year of marching and counter-marching, manœuvring and fort-building over lands of almost inconceivable grandeur where mountain range after mountain range stretched away unendingly to unseen horizons. With the disappearance of that centralized authority represented by an Emperor, a vast number of leaders, small and large, emerged all over the central highlands, the traditional heartland of the Amhara race. They all tended to act independently, which meant that their internal alliances and enmities were often shifting. To some extent they all considered as their real enemies their neighbours and rivals, so that lives were as likely to be lost in skirmishes against rival Dejaz as against the Italians. And they were all in diplomatic contact with the 'enemy'. Families and clans were divided, but through the 'loyal' members contact could be kept with the Italian-officered *bande* from whom rifles and ammunition could be bought or 'stolen'.

In Beghemder most of the rebel leaders were men of the *balabat* class, the squirearchy, the gentry, who had fought the Italians half-heartedly under the leadership of Ayalew Birru. Returning to their own lands, they had at first submitted—to 'revolt' later and seize what power and authority they could. There were no dominant war-leaders or men of particularly noble birth or descent among them. This was in many ways an advantage; if one leader was eliminated or defected to the Italians, the resistance was not seriously weakened. Furthermore no strong rival blocs formed. At times, too, the Beghemder *balabats* showed themselves surprisingly capable of united action. For instance they set up a more or less systematic taxation system; the countryside was under their control; food supplies were well-organized; and in the hills their letters and messengers circulated freely. Men, as always, carried arms; and watchers on the hilltops warned of any important Italian movement.

The Italians were understandably confused by the situation in

Beghemder, which offered no precise objective at which they could strike. In neighbouring Gojjam however, the situation was both more threatening and yet in a sense easier to get to grips with. Four powerful rebel leaders had emerged, of whom three were connected with the ruling house of the Negus Tekle Haimonot. These three were Dejaz Negash Bezibeh, grandson of Ras Hailu's eldest brother; Dejaz Mangasha Jimbirre married to Ras Hailu's daughter, Woizero Sable Wongel; and Dejaz Hailu Belew, brother to Dejaz Gessesse Belew (now dead, generally believed to have been treacherously poisoned by the Italians) whose revolt against Ras Imru and aid to Starace's column had opened up all Gojjam to the invaders. The fourth rebel leader, 'Lij' Belai Zelleka, was of a very different type. Energetic, young, vain, and aggressive he was the ideal *shifta* leader, controlling the forests of south-eastern Gojjam. In moments of boasting he adopted a title or rather an honorific form of address reserved (like *Janhoy*) for Emperors alone and called himself *Atse* '*Begolbetu*'—Majesty 'By my own power'.

Around these four leaders gathered many others, the great chiefs, the *Arbenya Alekas*, the smaller chiefs, the *Gobaz Alekas*, and the young guerrilla groups of the *Kamoniche* (a word which means, rather appealingly, 'I am not less than the others'.) But between the four, though there was contact, there was no co-operation. To the west of Debra Markos, Negash Bezibeh and Mangasha Jimbirre were open rivals and often on the verge of attacking each other; in the east the respected Hailu Belew resented both the airs and the activities of the vainglorious self-styled 'Lij', Belai Zelleka.

Yet, despite these rivalries, in the short space of a few months the rebellion in Gojjam had become by far the most serious of all the rebellions in Italian East Africa. On 15 March 1938 the British Consulate General reported that Debra Markos, the capital, was surrounded by rebels and cut off; and a fortnight later added that all available troops, including cavalry with only a few weeks' training, were being sent into Gojjam; that petrol rationing had been imposed in Addis Ababa; and that General Cavallero was personally directing a veritable invasion.

On this last point the Consul-General did not exaggerate. No less than sixty thousand men, supported by aeroplanes and tanks, took part in the 'invasion' of Gojjam. While columns fanned out in all directions, Cavallero himself flew from fort to fort planning a new network of garrisons. By mid-May operations were over, and on 31 May the Viceroy's government announced in Addis Ababa that Gojjam was officially pacified.

Meanwhile, however, a new menace had appeared in the mountains to the north of the capital. News filtered out that a new Pretender had arisen, a sixteen-year-old son of Lij Yasu, Meleke Tsahai. The Tabot, the Ark of the Covenant, the Ark of St. George which had accompanied Menelik to Adowa, had been smuggled out from St. George's Cathedral in the capital after Yekatit, and it was now said that Meleke Tsahai had been crowned Emperor at the Three Ambas by Abebe Aregai, on whom he had bestowed the title of 'Ras'.

The appearance of a new Emperor, the 'Little Negus', was a threat the Italians could not ignore. Three other sons of Lij Yasu had already attracted support—Lij Girma (fortunately in the remote southern province of Gemu-Gofa), Lij Menelik (a half-Danakil whom the French were grooming as a possible pretender), and Lij Johannes in Beghemder with whom the Italians were busily negotiating. But a properly consecrated Emperor in the Shoan heartlands and under the control of the best-known of all the rebel leaders was a much more formidable affair. On 1 June, General Cavallero, back from Gojjam, moved columns hastily into position around the Ankober mountains. The object was to trap Abebe Aregai and stop him slipping across the Imperial Highway into the almost impenetrable heartland of Menz.

The only leader rash enough to attack was Haile Mariam Mammo. He attempted to break through the cordon with 500 men but was mortally wounded on 6 June, and his band dissolved into little groups. His death looked like the beginning of the end for Abebe Aregai, who attempted—for the third time—to cross the Highway on 18 June and for the third time failed. On 24 June, however, the rains began to fall. With the rains, movement in the roadless mountains became impossible, and the hunt was called off for the season.

Operations resumed smartly on 1 October, with the Italians employing rather different tactics. Three *Gruppo Bande*— Criniti's, Farello's, and Rolle's—moved into the Ankoberino. This meant fighting on roughly equal terms between opposing groups of irregulars. But by the third week in October, the disheartening news reached General Cavallero that Abebe Aregai and all his men had finally succeeded in crossing the Highway and had joined Dejaz Auraris.

Dejaz Auraris, the Nestor of the Resistance, was not only a respected Shoan noble but governor of the heartland of Shoan traditions and of the Shoan kingdom, Menz. Ten thousand feet above sea level, bounded on all sides by steep mountains, cold and invigorating, Menz covered 850 square miles of upland plateaux. Cavallero flew up on 30 October to direct operations in person, and desperate fighting followed on both sides. Rolle's *Bande* meanwhile was sent down to Shoa's 'western sector' which had suddenly become troublesome. Two rival rebel leaders were operating around Wolisso on the Jimma Road, Gurassu Duke and Olona Dinkel. Gurassu Duke was in the end the better-known—and the longer-lived—but in his day Olona Dinkel was as legendary. The Italians put a price of 50,000 lire on his head and the Viceroy by special order doubled the price already put on Gurassu Duke's head.[1]

The fighting in November was hand-to-hand and many were killed on both sides, but it was inconclusive. Indeed, despite all Cavallero's campaigns (and more large-scale attacks had been launched in Gojjam, particularly against Mangasha Jimbirre on Mount Faguta), the fact remained that the whole year's operation had been inconclusive. By December the exhausted Italian troops had been withdrawn from Menz. It was said later that there was hardly a stone village in Menz where the Eritreans or the *bande* had passed that had not been plundered and as far as possible destroyed. But 'Ras' Abebe Aregai and Dejaz Auraris were still alive. Admittedly the 'Little Negus', Meleke Tsahai Yasu, had died of illness—a happier event from the Italian viewpoint, but hardly an achievement. The four major rebel leaders in Gojjam, and the two minor rebel leaders in Wolisso were still in control of their territories. Menz was totally unconquered. The only lasting benefit of all the operations had been the killing of Haile Mariam Mammo.[2] Very little had been effected or even attempted in the

---

[1] Gurassu Duke had been a member of the Crown Prince's bodyguard under the orders of Dejaz Fikremariam (Fikremariam had disappeared, presumed dead, soon after the attack on Addis Ababa). Olona Dinkel by contrast was a Wollega Galla. The reason the Duke of Aosta doubled the price on Gurassu's head was that Gurassu had hanged an Italian emissary, the engineer Sebastiano Castagna. Graziani had already used Castagna in abortive negotiations with Ras Desta; so Gurassu's suspicions can be excused.

[2] And, though only incidentally, the dispersal of the three remaining Shoan leaders

vast areas between Debra Tabor and Gondar, or between Gondar and Armachecho, or to the north of Gondar towards Tigre.

'The Duce', noted Ciano in his diary entry for 1 January 1939, 'returned to Rome yesterday and we had a long discussion. He is very displeased with the situation in the AOI and pronounces a severe judgement on the work of the Duke of Aosta. Amhara is in fact still in full revolt and the 65 battalions that are garrisoning it are forced to live inside their forts.' The same day Mussolini sent an angry cable to Amedeo of Aosta which ended: 'We still have six months before the rainy season to liquidate Aregai, Mangasha and Gurassu, names which are already appearing in the European press as leaders of the increasingly successful resistance against Italy. MUSSOLINI.' The year 1938 had, for the Italians, ended badly.

On 4 January hard on the heels of Mussolini's telegram and Ciano's comments the Minister Teruzzi was sent out on a tour of inspection. The Italians called him a 'ouragan'. 'He has roared around upsetting everything and everyone,' reported the British Consul General. '. . . His arrogant and pompous attitude towards all with whom he came in contact has rendered him intensely unpopular. . . . The local Italian joke is "Why does Teruzzi prefer brunettes?" Answer "Because gentlemen prefer blondes?" ' 'General Teruzzi sounds a nasty man', minuted the Foreign Office, 'even for a Fascist dignitary.'

During Teruzzi's visit the Duke of Aosta sent a long and secret report to Mussolini, playing down the extent of the revolt. He reported that Abebe Aregai was ill and tired and had only one thousand armed followers, that Gurassu Duke was a fugitive, and that only Mangasha Jimbirre remained a threat. But at the same time General Cavallero was criticizing to his crony the Minister the Viceroy's 'lack of maturity' and suggesting that until the country was properly pacified the Duke of Aosta should be limited mainly to a ceremonial role. This suggestion eventually became a demand for 'full powers' for himself, Ugo Cavallero.

A month later the Duke of Aosta was recalled for 'talks'. On 10 March he flew to Rome. Ciano noted in his diary on 14 March

in the West. On 3 June Blatta Takele Wolde Hawariat and Mesfin Sileshi had crossed the border into the Sudan, with 175 Amhara, 36 Galla, 25 women and 13 machine-guns. Zaudi Asfau and the bandleader Wolde Johannes had trekked back towards Shoa, but failed to reach their goal and submitted.

that 'The Duke of Aosta speaks with notable optimism of the situation in the Empire. I must however add that of all the people coming from there he is the only optimist.' The future looked dark for Aosta. In the fortnight he spent in Rome the lights were dimming in Europe too. Hitler invaded Czechoslovakia; and the British and the French braced themselves for war.

CHAPTER 16

EDGING TOWARDS WAR

AT the beginning of 1939 the French had quadrupled their garrison and strengthened their defences around Djibuti. Five thousand highly professional soldiers under the command of the energetic General LeGentilhomme (whom a British colleague described as 'a very live wire aged 55 or 56') posed a serious threat to the Italians in case of war. In January the Duke of Aosta had cabled Rome announcing that a 'surprise operation' had been prepared against Djibuti, 'to be carried out by 15 motorized battalions plus a horde of 6,000 Azebo Galla and another horde of 6,000 Danakil who are already in position near the frontier'. The French and the Italians, in Africa as in Europe, were almost eager to be at each other's throats.

But despite the war-clouds in Europe the British and the Italians, at least in Africa, were still extremely friendly. On his way back from Rome, still to all appearances Viceroy, Amedeo of Aosta stopped off in Cairo. Britain's proconsul in Egypt, Sir Miles Lampson (who stood well over six feet and was married to an Italian wife), found the Duke 'tall, good-looking, athletic and very affable and friendly' with—even more important—'never a fault in his sense of humour'. On 28 March Mr. Bateman, a High Commission official, dined with him and was no less impressed—as much with what he spoke ('English, French, Spanish, German and possibly Amharic') as with what he said. On Europe, Aosta was hopeful: 'Thank God that idiotic Spanish venture is over. I don't see perpetual peace in the offing yet. But don't take too literally all that Mr. Brown (i.e. Mussolini) says.' On Ethiopia he was almost apologetic: 'Supposing you had shoved all the scum of London's East End into Ethiopia and let them run wild, you can imagine the sort of thing that would have happened. That's just what we did and I have to clean it up somehow.' The following day the Viceroy flew on to the Sudan

where for two nights he was the guest of the Governor-General at
the Palace in Khartoum.

In his previous role as Governor of Aden the Governor-General,
Sir Stewart Symes, had attended the Emperor's Coronation in
1930. But he does not appear to have been favourably impressed
by Ethiopia, its people, or its rulers. He was all for peace and
quiet and good relations with the neighbouring colonial power.

Under Sir Stewart's aegis the real administrator of the Sudan
was the Civil Secretary, Douglas Newbold, a very conscientious,
rather harassed, and much-loved bachelor. At the age of 19, fresh
out from Oxford and Perthshire, he had taken part in a British
expedition sent to help the Italians against the Senussi and had
been in at the capture by Graziani of Omar El Muktar. His
sympathies were basically pro-Italian. Later he had joined the
Sudan Civil Service and become District Commissioner at
Gedaref in Kassala Province, supervising the 10,000 square miles,
the territory of the principal Beja tribe, the Hadendoa, that ran
along the Ethiopian border. At the end of those seven years of
countering the cattle-raiders and the ivory-smugglers he had
written, 'No wonder Isaiah said "Woe unto the Ethiopians!" ' It
was a typical Sudan Civil Service attitude. Newbold's diaries and
letters are a running commentary on relations between the
Italians of *Africa Orientale Italiana* and the British of the Anglo-
Egyptian Sudan.

The other power in the Sudan was the commander of the
Sudan Defence Force, 'a wiry little terrier of a man', as Newbold
called him. General Sir William Platt, CBE, died only in 1977,
though for the previous thirty-eight years he had been living in
retirement. His life spans what are now almost mythical epochs
of Britain's military history. He was born eleven years before
Adowa and fought on the North-West Frontier and in the First
World War. Just before coming out to the Sudan he had spent a
year as ADC to the King. He was a martinet and a distinctly
crusty martinet. He was also, if orthodox, a very good soldier.
But in March 1939 he was just settling in to his job—he had
arrived in January—and was almost totally ignorant of Ethiopia.

The Sudan Defence Force, which he commanded, had been
formed in 1925 by General Hudleston. Later described as 'a
curious organization, unique in the annals of British arms and
typical of them', its British officers used the traditional titles of

the Egyptian Army. General Platt was the *Kaid*; the four units, grandiosely named the Western Arab Corps, the Eastern Arab Corps, the Equatorial Corps, and the Camel Corps (which included the Sudan Horse), were each commanded by a *Miralai*, Commander of a Thousand. Under them came *Bimbashis*, commander of an *Idara* of two hundred and fifty men, and a whole series of native ranks running from *Uzbashi* down via *Ombashi* to the simple private or *Nafar*. The whole force was barely 5,000 strong.

The Duke of Aosta was not the only man craftily planning surprise attacks on colonial neighbours. Captain Whalley, Dick Whalley, had been British Consul in Maji before the Italians took over. Thereafter the Sudan government had pulled him back and left him to stew at Towoth Post on the Boma Plateau, a little police post down in the deep south among the 'bog barons'. He was one of the few colonial officers positively antagonistic to his Italian opposite number who, according to Whalley, had been forbidden by the Viceroy to carry a revolver 'owing to an incurable habit of firing it in the face of any native who gets in his way'.

From the autumn of 1938, certain that war would come, Whalley had been mulling over a scheme to foment revolt in *AOI* with two of his cronies, Captain Erskine, the former British kingmaker at Gore and *El Miralai* Cave *Bey*. Cave commanded the Equatorial Corps which kept the peace in the lands of the Shilluk, the Nuer, the Dinka, and the Anuak as far as the borders of Uganda and the bad lands of the Karamoja and the Turkana. In February 1939, with the approval of both of them, Whalley presented his scheme to the new *Kaid*.

All that Whalley asked for was the thousand men of the Equatorial Corps, 4,000 rifles, and 200,000 rounds to arm the rebels who were expected to flock in, a few planes to drop leaflets, and the use of the Eritrean deserters from the Maji area, most of whom had wound up in the Kenya camps. Or rather that was not all; he also asked for a gentleman to whom in accordance with the rules of military security he referred rather coyly as 'H.S. Esq.'

This was the first time that the suggestion had been aired that the Emperor should be brought back into play. For good measure, Whalley threw in a further idea: that another friend of his, another young Assistant District Commissioner, should

'invade' Italian East Africa further north at Kassala with the
Crown Prince. This was Wilf Thesiger, ex-Danakil explorer,
whose father, as Whalley had no doubt heard, had sheltered the
young Asfa Wossen in the days of Lij Yasu.

'Utterly fantastic', commented Sir Stewart Symes before
forwarding the scheme on to the Foreign Office at the end of
February 1939, and he added some disparaging remarks about
those who saw themselves as second Lawrences. But Cave *Bey*
had taken the precaution of mentioning the scheme to *El Lewa*
Stone *Pasha* (Brigadier Stone) in Khartoum, and so the Governor-General was unable to suppress it entirely—as he would
almost certainly have liked to have done, particularly because he
was on such good terms with the Duke of Aosta.

It was understandable that Sir Stewart Symes and company, who
were charmed by the very anglophile, polo-playing Duke, found
it almost impossible to envisage him as a potential enemy, and
thought it most distasteful that their own subordinates should be
drawing up wild schemes for invading the territories which he
was trying, much in the spirit of the best British colonial
governors, to administer. There was a positive vogue for Aosta
in British circles. Lennox-Boyd and Lady William Percy came
out to Italian East Africa to pay him a 'delightful' visit. Dodds-
Parker of the Sudan Civil Service followed them, was invited to
'Villa Italia' as a personal guest of the Viceroy and felt an
inclination to resign his post and join *The Times* as a special
correspondent in Addis Ababa. The Governor of Kenya was
positively jealous of Sir Stewart and wrote to the Consulate-
General in Addis pleading for a private visit by the Duke to
Nairobi.

Inside Ethiopia too the Viceroy's star was in the ascendant. He
flew back from Khartoum to Addis Ababa on 1 April. After a
tense fortnight of waiting and wondering it became clear that in
the local struggle for power he had won what the British
Consulate-General described as 'a minor but gratifying victory'.
General Ugo Cavallero was recalled to Italy *en disponibilité*. The
Viceroy himself took over command of the armed forces, with a
comparative nonentity, General Luigi De Biase, as his Chief of
Staff.

But there was no repetition in the spring of 1939 of the vast
military operations of the previous year. The difficulty was, as

the Foreign Office pointed out to Lord Halifax, that 'the East African Empire is for the moment a bankrupt concern'. In millions of lire the cost for organization and administration of *AOI* had been 3,000 for 1936–7, 4,100 for 1937–8 and 3,500 for 1938–9. But this was nothing compared to the military operations, which had cost 17,519 for the 1936–7 season and 9,000 for the 1937–8 campaigns, vast sums of which the first had brought results but the second had not. The Italians did not suffer from the British complex that colonies must be self-supporting and were prepared to invest huge sums of money in road-building, schools, hospitals, and administration. But to spend three times this amount on futile military operations year after·year was clearly impossible. If the liquidation of Mangasha, Aregai, and Gurassu had not been achieved by major operations, it was unlikely to be achieved by minor ones. As the columns sent out became fewer, the negotiators became more numerous.

General Nasi, known to get on well with the Duke of Aosta, was moved from Harar to Addis Ababa as Vice Governor-General and *ex-officio* Governor of the reconstituted governorate of Shoa. With the arrival of a civilian governor in Harar in his place it was understood that the project of a surprise attack on Djibuti (which had inevitably leaked out) had been called off, though the 'Danakil horde' continued to keep a close watch all around the French colony's frontiers.

At the same time General Platt submitted his report on Whalley's plan. 'I do not consider', wrote the *Kaid*, 'it a reasonable proposition to launch a mere 1000 soldiers armed with rifles and one or two machine-guns into the mountains of Ethiopia against a European-led army vastly superior in the air, in ground numbers and in armament, on nebulous information with no known local chieftains to rely on for support and insurrection.'

So much for Dick Whalley—a fly crushed by the logic of a sledge-hammer. But General Platt's report was not at all to the taste of the Foreign Office. 'I don't much like the Khartoum attitude of always cold-douching the enthusiastic Captain Whalley,' noted one official. The Foreign Office returned to the attack, asking for the Sudan Defence Force to be doubled in strength. On 3 May Sir Stewart Symes rushed to the defence; there was no money, there were no men, it was all too late. 'There', wrote Sir Miles Lampson to the Foreign Office, 'we at last have Symes's real opinion. It exposes the dangerous inadequacy of our military strength in the Sudan.' Sir Robert Vansittart, Permanent Under-Secretary at the Foreign Office, was more forthright. 'I urged Symes', he noted, 'to increase the SDF in 1936. He said it was adequate. For this lack of prescience I have not forgiven him because it is unpardonable. . . . Will anything be done even now?' Nothing was. Inertia prevailed. General Platt went up to Djibuti with Brigadier Stone in May for staff talks with the French. The conclusions reached were entirely to the taste of all the neighbouring British governors. In the event of war the three British territories bordering on Italian East Africa—the Sudan, British Somaliland, and Kenya—would stand on the defensive while General LeGentilhomme and the fire-eating French boldly attacked down the railway line towards Addis Ababa. Platt seems to have felt no sense of shame at this inglorious role. In mid-June Sir Stewart Symes was summoned to London. Strong with the joint staff plans, he insisted that any aggressive action would have to come from Djibuti, that he had no confidence in Whalley or Erskine, and that the SDF could *not* be increased. He requested Egyptian anti-aircraft gunners—hardly a sign, as the Foreign Office wearily noted, of an offensive spirit. 'It is too late,' minuted a depressed Vansittart, 'our favourite and if I may say so unfailing failing.'

Tension grew again in Europe. In mid-August 1939 a cable came from Rome ordering the Duke of Aosta to mobilize. Ten days later British East Africa mobilized in its turn. Hitler invaded Poland and on 3 September Britain and France declared war on Germany. Churchill and Eden became, once again, Ministers of the Crown. In Addis Ababa restrictions were placed on the use of motor cars and the sale of petrol. No persons of military age were allowed to leave the country.

'I didn't expect', wrote Douglas Newbold in the first circular letter he as Civil Secretary sent out to the nine governors of provinces in the Sudan, 'that the writing of my first monthly letter would be interrupted as it was yesterday by a declaration of war. So far Italy has not come in . . . but the dangers is by no means past. We have had repeated instructions from H.M.G. to avoid any sort of provocation to Italy.'

Nevertheless General Wavell, who had just taken over as Commander-in-Chief Middle East, rescued 'Dan' Sandford from his cathedral close at Guildford and called him out to Cairo to organize Middle East Command's plan for a rising in Ethiopia. There, after various tussles with local officials in the Sudan, Gabre Maskal, a man of many talents[1] who had been Ras Imru's wireless operator and was a devoted supporter of the Emperor, joined him. And though in East Africa the brouhaha quickly died down on both sides of the border as it became apparent that Italy was not going to enter the war, in London a cluster of generals and diplomats gathered to devise a leaflet designed to ferment revolt in its event. It was agreed that it should be printed in Gallinya and Tigrinya as well as in Amharic. The suggested themes were: 'The Suez Canal is closed. The Italians are surrounded and in any case are no fighters. Remember Adowa!'

Inside *Africa Orientale Italiana* the restrictions were lifted as the war-clouds passed, and on 27 September 1939 the dignitaries of the Empire celebrated *Maskal* in great style in the capital. Silver sabres glittered peacefully and ornate umbrellas flowered. Adowa might almost have been forgotten.

Flanked by his new Deputy Governor-General, General Nasi, the Viceroy conferred the style and title of Ras on Dejaz Ayalew Birru who had led the levies of Beghemder and Simien into battle against the Italians and had fought by the side of Ras Imru till the fall of Gondar. Three great Ethiopian lords assisted at this ceremony: Ras Hailu of Gojjam, naturally enough; another Italian-created 'Ras', Haile Selassie Gugsa, the traitor whom both camps despised; and with them a newcomer, Ras Seyum. For Ras Seyum had finally returned from his prolonged 'visit' to Italy.

What they thought as they watched a non-Ethiopian confer the dignities that for hundreds of years had been conferred by the line of Solomon and Sheba can be imagined. There they stood, those great lords who half a decade earlier had led armies and ruled lands and intrigued against each other, conscious now only of their servitude.

But the very fact that the traditional ruling houses of Gojjam, of both parts of Tigre, of Beghemder, and of Wollo were honoured by the Italian Viceroy marked a significant change in the direction of Italian policy. This gathering of Maskal 1939 was

---

[1] Gabre Maskal, who spoke French, Italian, English, Arabic, and Amharic, had crossed the border near Gallabat in the autumn of 1938 and spent 18 months travelling as the Emperor's emissary around Gojjam. In almost Welsh fashion he was known as 'Nifas Silk'—'The Wireless'.

the outward sign of the first steps towards the policy of 'indirect rule' on British lines which was known to be favoured both by the Duke of Aosta and by General Nasi. As the rains ended and a new campaigning season came round, the Viceroy and his military advisers viewed their domain with a mixture of satisfaction and discontent.

They had reason to be satisfied; for their changed policies already appeared to be having a positive effect. The new Abuna Johannes had sent out a pastoral letter ordering all priests and heads of churches not to bless the corpses of those who died as rebels nor to bury them within church precincts. The rebel bands were nowhere on the offensive. To the south of the capital, in the area between Addis Ababa and Jimma the feared Olona Dinkel had been killed, trapped by a woman who added poison to his *kosso*; and to make doubly sure her husband fired on him and killed him. It seems they claimed the 50,000 lire reward and that when the Italians exposed his dead body in public, his long hair ruffled by the wind made it look as if he were still alive so that all fled in horror.

General Nasi seized the opportunity to issue proclamations in May, June, and July asking the local population to advise the remaining rebels to submit, and promising pardon, liberty, the restoration of goods, and, interestingly enough, the opportunity of enrolling in the army. 'The pardon of the government is as generous as the pardon of God. All know this to be so.' The times had certainly changed since Nasi himself had, although unwillingly, executed all eminent Amhara who came in to submit near Harar.

A copy of one of his proclamations reached the Foreign Office. Its peroration read: 'Let then those dreamers (*illuminati*) fade from the scene, those who have been awaiting "tomorrow" aid from abroad even though that "tomorrow" has now lasted four years and will never come, not even when infants who are still in the wombs of their mothers will have seen their beards turn white with age.'

'General Nasi has a fine obstetric style of eloquence', noted a Foreign Office official. Even so Gurassu Duke, the only surviving rebel of importance in these parts, did not come in. But what was worrying Nasi was not the situation to the south of the capital but the situation to the north. In Shoa itself Abebe Aregai was more powerful than ever. His followers had resisted all the

columns sent to eliminate them the year before, and were now
equally impervious to all Nasi's blandishments. Abebe Aregai
was becoming the very symbol of resistance to the Italians.

It was not just Nasi who was bewildered by the phenomenon
of Abebe Aregai. So was Haile Selassie. Shoa was for practical
purposes out of reach of his emissaries, such as Gabre Maskal in
the Sudan, and he must have been intensely mistrustful of Abebe
Aregai. For the episode of the 'Little Negus' proved that Abebe
Aregai had no particular loyalty to the exiled emperor; indeed it
was thought at one stage that the French from Djibuti were
grooming Abebe Aregai himself for the throne. Nor can Haile
Selassie have been unaware that Abebe Aregai's relations with the
Italians were ambivalent.

It was this ambivalence that both infuriated and encouraged the
Italians. Again and again it seemed that Abebe Aregai in return
for money, arms, honours, or power was on the point of
submitting to the Italian regime. It became an obsession with the
Italians and particularly with General Nasi who as Vice Governor-General was *ex-officio* Governor of Shoa; and General Nasi
devoted all his intelligence, all his powers of persuasion, all his
goodwill, to winning over this rebel on the capital's threshold. It
became in the end more than a personal battle of wills, almost a
symbolic contest in which victory for the Italians would have
been a symbol not so much of the final pacification of Ethiopia as
of the final acceptance of their rule by the Ethiopians.

For months Nasi (and finally Teruzzi too on his third and last
visit to *Africa Italiana*) concentrated on winning Abebe Aregai
over. Negotiations only ended on 15 March 1940 when 'some
traitor' (the Ethiopian term) warned General Nasi that Abebe
Aregai, who had promised to take an oath of allegiance that day,
was laying an ambush for him with 20,000 men. Mussolini
appears to have been more relieved than disappointed. He sent a
telegram out to Teruzzi the following afternoon in which he gave
vent to his feelings and called for immediate military action, 'not
excluding the use of gas'. Not a day, Mussolini added, was to be
lost—for many reasons, including the situation in Europe.

And yet the situation in Europe, in mid-March 1940 appeared to
be stabilized. Poland had been conquered by the Germans. There
was calm and quiet on the Western Front. Italy was at peace, a
neutral state, and apparently likely to remain so.

On the lands bordering the Italian Empire this was the general opinion, too. In Kenya, after 'wargames' in January, Barland versus Fowkland (for the uninitiated, a series of mock battles between friendly troops fighting for 'countries' named after their respective commanders—in this case Brigadier Barchard's 1st East African Brigade versus Brigadier Fowkes's 2nd East African Brigade), the six battalions of the King's African Rifles had been sent back to peace stations; and when three Italian deserters and a lorry arrived at Wajir in the Northern Frontier District, the new Governor, Sir Henry Monk-Mason-Moore, prepared to hand them back to the Italian authorities and was only stopped from doing so by the Foreign Office. In the Sudan, Newbold informed his nine governors that it was 'time you had some more news about the Sudan Cultural centre'. Only in Cairo did the British military authorities take some steps. Sandford had Gabre Maskal select eight Ethiopian refugees in Khartoum and bring them up to Cairo to train them as wireless operators. But it was all very hush-hush. Lest the Italian Legation at Cairo, already alarmed by the February visit of the new Dominions Minister ('I have never seen expressions of incredulity, horror and polite enquiry chase themselves so rapidly across the features of a diplomat', wrote Eden of his meeting with the Italian Minister there, Count Mazzolini), should catch wind of the move, Gabre Maskal and his trainees were topped off with tarbooshes—a wily disguise by which to pass them off as members of the Egyptian army, and thus avoid 'provocation' of the Italians, whose continued neutrality was so important.

By mid-April however the war in Europe had begun in earnest. On 9 April the Germans invaded Norway, and a month and a day later they invaded the West. As the German armies poured into France and allied resistance crumbled, Mussolini prepared vulture-like to enter the war on victorious Germany's side.

PART III

THE MILLS OF GOD

MAP 6. The Sudan Frontier on the Outbreak of War

CHAPTER 17

DOMINE DIRIGE NOS

Down at Gallabat on the Sudan–Ethiopian frontier the local garrison, No. 3 Company of the Eastern Arab Corps of the Sudan Defence Force, set up operational headquarters. It was April 1940. They started strengthening the hill-top fort and planning trenches. All this they did, however, without much conviction, gazing over at their friends in the rather larger Italian post at Metemma on the other side of the frontier, marked by the dried river-bed of a khor.

'To be on visiting terms with one's probable enemies of tomorrow must be all too familiar an experience for those garrisoning the land frontiers of Europe,' noted one of the officers, 'but it is fairly rare for the insular British!' He thought back to the 'overwhelming hospitality' of the Italians, to the friendliness of the garrison commander, Colonel Castagnola, 'a small, fat, swarthy, but genial individual, very astute and quite a good game shot'; and to the previous Christmas which Major Saroldi, the second-in-command, had spent with the Eastern Arab Corps officers in their base mess at Gedaref. Saroldi was liked by all, invariably wore 'immaculate breeches and riding boots', and in his turn was 'genuinely fond' of the British he had met in the Eastern Sudan.

As war drew nearer, visiting ceased by mutual consent. But only a week before the declaration of war Major Saroldi sent a letter over to his friend *Bimbashi* Cousens: 'Although things are looking black,' wrote the Major, 'I hope my country will be spared the shame of fighting alongside the barbarians whom I myself was fighting as a boy of eighteen.' No wonder that what was known locally as 'the Gallabat–Metemma Axis' seemed to symbolize the real relationship between the officials who administered the neighbouring Italian and British colonies in Africa.

In Khartoum, however, a month later the British authorities

had lost almost all their earlier hopes of a peaceful settlement. 'Mussolini's antics', Newbold wrote to Margery Perham, 'seem to have brought him near the precipice . . . though I hope the views of the Pope, King and Ciano will prevail.' In his personal diary he was more explicit and less cheery. 'Yesterday May 18', he wrote, 'was the most anxious day of my life.' It seemed from the BBC news of the war that France was on the verge of defeat:

Here in Khartoum we have received warnings from the Foreign Office and the War Office that war with Italy was imminent. The Italians in East Africa have about 250,000 troops and over 200 aircraft. Our forces are under 10,000 and our aircraft one tenth of theirs. We have no AA guns or in fact guns. Kassala is theirs for the asking. Port Sudan probably, Khartoum perhaps. Bang goes 40 years patient work in the Sudan and we abandon the trusting Sudanese to a totalitarian conqueror.
　Yesterday morning I was attacked . . . about lack of defence policy in the Sudan Government, lack of coordination between Army and civil, lack of 'direction' in times of danger. I agreed with much of the criticism but I am not Governor-General or Kaid . . . I never knew till yesterday what real anxiety meant . . . Platt is courageous and works like a hero but is not very approachable. The civil [European] population is amorphous and leaderless and responds to every windy current of rumour. The Sudanese are blissfully unconscious of the danger, are convinced of Allied might, and consider Italy beneath contempt. They may have a ghastly shock . . . I can only say 'Domine dirige nos!'

At about the same time as 'the Gallabat–Metemma Axis' crumbled, the Viceroy of Italian East Africa, the Duke of Aosta, was summoned to Rome. During his stay of three weeks the final Italian contingency plans for war in East Africa were drawn up. But there was no question of marching into the Sudan or Kenya, as Newbold had feared. Quite the contrary. Ciano the Foreign Minister, had a meeting with the Duce shortly after his arrival.

'I saw the Duke of Aosta this morning,' he wrote in his Diary for April 6. 'He tells me that for him it is not only impossible to take the offensive but will also be extremely difficult to hold his actual positions because the Anglo-French are now well-equipped and ready for battle and the population, among whom rebellion is still smouldering, will rise as soon as they have the sensation that we are in trouble.'

The Duke of Aosta was not alone in this unjustified pessimism.[1] The Blackshirt Inspector-General of the Milizia circulated a report prophesying a generalized revolt in the event of war. Badoglio and Graziani, the Chief of the General Staff and Chief of the Army Staff respectively, had no positive proposals. Only one major change was made. General De Biase resigned, and by a royal decree of 27 April General Claudio Trezzani was appointed Chief of Staff in *Africa Orientale Italiana* in his place.

Cold, scholastic, and almost universally disliked by his brother officers, this new military overlord had as his main task to restrain the more impetuous impulses of the Italian generals on the spot and effectively to take over control of the armed forces from the inexperienced Viceroy. He was one of the few Italian senior officers who had never served in a colonial campaign, or indeed in the colonies at all. His career had been that of a professor at the School of War. His interests were in tactics, his approach one of detached calculation. He was Badoglio's man—imbued with scepticism before he ever set foot in Africa. At his first staff meeting in Addis Ababa, which he called on 15 May, he stressed it as a principle that the Empire was on its own, totally disconnected from the general strategic plan, and reduced therefore despite its apparent overwhelming superiority to a defensive role. If the Italians had deliberately decided to choose a general whose prime characteristic was his capacity for lowering the morale of the troops he was to command, their choice could hardly have fallen on a better man.

Trezzani's opposite number, the General Officer Commander-in-chief Middle East, Lieutenant-General Sir Archibald Wavell, had taken up his post in Cairo in August 1939, a month before war broke out in Europe. Wavell was aged fifty-seven. He knew the Middle East very well. In the First World War he had acted as liaison officer to General Allenby, and in 1937 he had succeeded Dill as GOC Palestine.

Wavell never allowed himself to get flustered. He was a man who played golf every day, calm, solid, famous for his silences,

[1] The Italian forces in East Africa, as Newbold had pointed out, but Aosta had not, vastly outnumbered the tiny British and French forces 'encircling' AOI. By August 1940, after mobilization, there were 92,371 Italian soldiers and over a quarter of a million native troops under arms. Armour consisted of 24 medium tanks, 39 light tanks, and 126 Fiat Ansaldo armoured cars. The air force numbered 323 planes, of which 286 were bombers. By contrast the 'allied' forces amounted to less than 40,000 troops, almost all native, with over 100 aircraft in support.

better at expressing himself on paper than in discussion. 'War is a
wasteful, boring, muddled affair,' he had written. He had learnt
about it at Ypres, where he had lost an eye. Practical experience
had made him in his own way almost as cautious as Trezzani.

In the months following his appointment he had spent much of
his time visiting various parts of his far-flung command and
getting to know his commanders. One visit however had taken
him very far afield. Shortly before the Duke of Aosta visited
Rome, Wavell had spent a week in South Africa. In the event of
war on the African continent it was essential to know how far the
South Africans, with their manpower and their resources, would
be prepared to help. The man Wavell had seen was General
Smuts.

Smuts was seventy years old in 1940, and one of the most
distinguished figures on the Continent. In his youth he had led
Boer guerrillas against the British but unlike many Boers he had
accepted whole-heartedly the peace settlement. Indeed he had
fought with the British against Von Lettow-Vorbeck in the
famous campaign in German East Africa in the First World War.
He had been in and out of power in the Union ever since. He was
out of power in September 1939 when the South Africans
debated the question of war: should they, like the Australians and
New Zealanders, follow Britain's lead and declare war on Germany? When the vote was taken, it was found that the pro-
British Smuts had won. By the narrow margin of 80 votes to 67
the Union of South Africa's Assembly voted for war. Smuts
became Prime Minister and Minister of Defence.

Smuts offered Wavell a volunteer force. The Union would
equip and maintain a brigade for war in Africa north of the
Equator. In addition Smuts agreed to send an anti-aircraft brigade and three squadrons of air force pilots—if Britain could
provide the guns for the brigade and the planes for the pilots. On
20 May the 1st South African Brigade was mobilized: The Duke
of Edinburgh's Own Rifles from Capetown, the 1st Transvaal
Scottish from Johannesburg, and the Royal Natal Carbineers.
The Brigade Commander was Dan Pienaar, a Boer whose
favourite topic of conversation with the British was his sojourn as
a prisoner of war in the British concentration camps.

Wavell earmarked the South African forces for the defence of
Kenya; and returned to Cairo satisfied. East Africa Force—
Kenya's defenders—consisted of two brigades of the King's

African Rifles, six battalions, plus, as armour, a squadron of trucks with bren guns on swivels. There were about fifty aircraft. With a South African brigade, and above all, with trained South African pilots, Nairobi and Mombasa should, Wavell felt, be safe from invasion. Most important of all, Wavell had found in Smuts a friend and adviser who was later to help him immensely in his problems and particularly in his main problem, his relations with the new Prime Minister, Churchill.

In mid-May Wavell had his first taste of onslaughts to come. He resisted, successfully, Churchill's plan to arm the Jews in Palestine and thus release for offensive operations the large forces of Empire troops gathering there. Churchill, baulked in one direction, turned elsewhere. On 28 May he fired the following barrage at General Ismay:

Pray bring the following before the Chiefs of Staff Committee. What measures have been taken, in the event of Italy's going to war, to attack Italian forces in Ethiopia, sending rifles and money to the Ethiopian insurgents and generally to disturb the country? I understand General Smuts has sent a Union brigade to East Africa. Is it there yet? When will it be? What other arrangements are made? What is the strength of the Khartoum garrison, including troops in the Blue Nile Province? This is the opportunity for the Ethiopians to liberate themselves, with Allied help.

Churchill knew Africa too well not to interfere. He remembered Smuts, now a personal friend, as a personal enemy. He remembered also his own trip down the Nile nearly half a century earlier and how, outside Khartoum, he had charged against the dervishes of the Mahdi at the battle of Omdurman. He was nostalgic for the great days of the wars of his youth.

He obtained little satisfaction on the Khartoum garrison or the South African brigade, but much more on the question of the 'insurgents'—for the Allies, and in particular Brigadier Sandford, were in fact by now almost ready to help the Ethiopians to liberate themselves. Sandford had drawn up a plan, which was to be the basis of all future plans, for helping the rebels. It involved first the opening of an Intelligence Bureau at Khartoum, secondly a census of Ethiopian refugees in the Sudan with a view to forming them into a refugee battalion, thirdly the establishment of arsenals on the frontier, and fourthly the formation of a Sudanese Frontier Battalion to pass arms and supplies to the rebels.

All this was bitterly opposed in Cairo. It was even more bitterly opposed in Khartoum where both Sir Steward Symes and General Platt disapproved of rebels and refugees both in practice and as a matter of principle. They considered efforts to help the former and to organize the latter a waste of time, money, arms, and British officers. Nevertheless Colonel Elphinstone, the liaison officer between the War Office and Middle East Command, managed to push the plans through—after all opposition meant opposing, in the end, both Wavell and Churchill. Arms were dumped, Ethiopian refugees listed, and an Intelligence Bureau set up in Khartoum under Robert Cheeseman, who years before had been British Consul at Dangila and whose books on Lake Tana had already become classics—a middle-aged gentleman, recalled from his hop gardens in Kent.

The Frontier Battalion was formed. A company was taken from each of the units of the Sudan Defence Force,[1] and the command was given to an officer called in from the Political Service, Hugh Boustead, thus transmogrified into *El Kaim* Boustead *Bey*.

From the other side of the frontier Italian intelligence officers kept a worried eye on what was going on, and spread the news that the new battalion was composed of five different companies of four different races, black Nuba, very light-coloured Baggara, chocolate-coloured Kabalise with—a sinister touch—two upper and two lower teeth missing, and ebony-coloured troops of an unknown tribe wearing ear-rings and a dangerous iron bracelet below the elbow—a nasty collection indeed. The Italian administration made its own rather half-hearted efforts to prepare the ground for a Muhammadan rebellion in the Sudan by inviting a member of the Mirghani clan to tour the Empire—a coup, in the sense that this, in the Muhammadan world, was a personality, indeed the rarest of personalities, a fire-eating lady, Sharifat Alaoui el Mirghani, known as 'the fighting Alaoui'.

The really controversial element in Sandford's plan, however, was his insistence that for the rebellion inside Ethiopia to become dangerous the ex-Emperor would have to be brought back into play. War with Italy was Haile Selassie's opportunity, indeed his only hope of ever recovering his throne. But there was also the

---

[1] In view of the tension, a number of Ford vans were converted into 'armoured cars' by mounting Vickers machine-guns on their roofs. This was the sole 'armour' of the Sudan.

danger that the ex-Emperor might be edged out in favour of leaders already on the spot, either at Khartoum or inside the country; and the further danger that the European 'liberators' of Ethiopia might subsequently take over the 'liberated' Empire. Indeed it was by playing on this second fear, which was shared by all Ethiopians, that Haile Selassie succeeded in avoiding the first danger: he was the symbol in the eyes of the world of Ethiopia's freedom, and the Ethiopians who wished to reconquer that freedom could not afford to jettison the symbol. But before his aim was finally achieved, Haile Selassie still had many difficulties to overcome and many injuries and indeed insults to submit to, more at the hands of his official allies than of his official enemies.

For a start he wrote to remind both the French and the British governments of his existence and to put himself formally at their disposal. It took three weeks for this letter to receive a bare acknowledgement from Lord Halifax, the Foreign Secretary, to whom it had been addressed. But it had not gone unnoted in the Foreign Office. On 20 May a high official minuted as follows:

We have no indications that there is any demand among the rebel natives in Ethiopia for the return of the Emperor. . . . If war breaks out and we proceed actively to assist the rebel leaders in Ethiopia we shall require to be quite certain as to their attitude towards the Emperor before any decision is taken to inject him once more into the troubled arena of Ethiopian politics.

At least the official did not refer to him as the ex-Emperor. But it was not an encouraging attitude.

On 8 June Haile Selassie visited London to attend a christening. He had agreed to be godfather to the newly-born son of George Steer and his wife Esmé. The christening was attended by the proud grandfather, Sir Sidney Barton, and by a friendly Socialist MP, Philip Noel Baker. It took place, in style, at St. Paul's: after the christening the gentlemen retired to the Canon's study where Haile Selassie explained to them how he had written a letter to Halifax but received no reply. What did his friends suggest he should do? They recommended that he should write again to Lord Halifax and told him, cautiously, that he did have many supporters. This was not particularly encouraging, either.

None of the Emperor's advisers, however, were aware that the situation was just about to change drastically. They could not know that a few days earlier, on 29 May, Mussolini had summoned the Italian military leaders to Palazzo Venezia and had announced his final and definitive decision. Italy was going to enter the war, and any day after 5 June would be 'suitable'.

On 8 June Newbold sent out his usual morale-boosting circular from Khartoum.

'Throughout this month', he wrote, 'Mussolini has been crying "Havoc" but has not, (as I write) unloosed the dogs of war. He may do so however at any hour—perhaps before you receive this letter—and our *official* information is that we must assume war with Italy to be imminent and inevitable. . . . We have no information where or how Italy will strike. . . . Here in Khartoum we are enlisting about 200 extra police. . . . I should like to counter talk, which I have heard, that the Sudan is comparatively undefended or does not propose to make any serious attempt at defence. The Sudan of course is not an easy country to defend . . . but the troops in the country and the police are by no means negligible.

'It may be that the more recent minutes of the Sudan Defence Committee with their mention of "evacuation" and implications of Italian "occupation" of places have given the impression that if the Italians come in we are ready to hand them towns and villages on a plate. This, of course, is not so, and especially not so in the case of possible attacks by parachute or airborne troops. Apart from the regular forces, the Sudan Auxiliary Defence Forces and the police will resist any attack to which there is a reasonable chance of resistance. It is the casual franc-tireur or the useless last-ditch defence of an undefended town against overwhelming force which may provoke a massacre and against which we wish to guard . . . but this does not spell "defeatism". Some dismal conclusions have been drawn from the preponderance of Italian air and ground strength in Italian East Africa. It is undeniable that they can strike hard blows and cause damage but their preponderance is more apparent then real. The Italians in Ethiopia are in a large *zeriba* in a hostile continent where Allied forces, though scattered, are consider-able. They may be cut off from Italy, they have to face outwards to French and British Somaliland, Kenya, Sudan and the sea, and inwards to rebels who await the word. Some of their own native troops may be untrustworthy, the economic state of the country is bad, and food scarce. Many of them don't *want* a war . . .

'In case war with Italy breaks out before my next letter, good luck to the Provinces!'

There was a last-minute addendum to this circular:

P.S. 11/6/40. This letter had just been roneo'd when Mussolini decided yesterday evening to take the plunge. . . . All male Italians were interned last night. The scuttling of the Umbria at Port Said yesterday with apparently a large amount of aerial bombs was a good start.

'Popolo Italiano, abbiamo dato la nostra parola . . .'. Mussolini had unloosed the dogs of war, for the second time. This time they were to hound him to the end.

CHAPTER 18

THE FIRST DAYS OF WAR

IN Cairo, Gabre Maskal picked up Mussolini's speech announcing the declaration of war on the Italian radio. That night he went out and spent £18 on celebrating, a fortune.

'Proletarian and Fascist Italy is on her feet, strong, proud and united as never before,' declared the Duce. In England, Churchill casting courtesies aside proclaimed his fellow-heir to Christian civilization 'the jackal of Europe'. Haile Selassie, as delighted as Gabre Maskal, immediately caught a train up to Paddington and installed himself at the Great Western Hotel. After dinner, he met his friends, much more hopeful than they had been two days earlier, at George Steer's house. 'At last', wrote Sylvia Pankhurst, 'the long agonizing vigil is over'.

But in Khartoum—and very nearly everywhere else in Africa —they only learnt that Italy and Britain were at war when they heard the news on the BBC at a quarter past eight that Monday evening. Code cables were immediately sent out to Gedaref and Kassala; but, typically enough, the cable and the phone links with Kassala had broken down. Not that it mattered—the feared Italian 'strike' did not materialize.

Unfortunately, the BBC news came too late for some. At Moyale two British officials had dined the previous evening with the Italian *Residente* on the other side of the Kenya frontier. They strolled over the frontier again at dusk on 10 June, and were promptly, justifiably, but rather unchivalrously, arrested. Thus Assistant Superintendent Carter and Sergeant Bulstrode became the first prisoners of the new war.

At Gambeila Major Praga called on his old friend Major Maurice at lunchtime, informed him of the declaration of war, unofficially, and gave him six hours to get clear and away. The only proviso he made was that the rifles and the powerful transmitter at the British Consulate should be left behind—and intact. So Maurice set off by the only means available, by canoe down the Baro. He was stopped at the frontier two days later at Jokau Post, but eventually let through. He paddled up to Nasir and then went on to Khartoum. So ended—temporarily—the reign of 'the King of Gambeila'.

At Gallabat the cable-system was working; the code message was uncoded to reveal the declaration of war. On hearing it 'the exuberance of Wilf Thesiger expressed itself in a savage war-dance', noted the war diarist of the Eastern Arab Corps which Thesiger had joined a few days earlier, before war was actually declared, as a new recruit. The diarist had noted previously,

Bimbashi W.P. Thesiger, a former Assistant DC, came to No. 3, accompanied by his personal servant who was a reprieved murderer and quite a charming chap if a shade wilful. Thesiger had accounted for over 70 lion during his Sudan career, was a boxing Blue, and altogether a useful man to have about the place.

They had made use of him shortly after his arrival. The first arms had, finally, come for the rebels: a batch of 300 single shot Martini rifles followed by 400 more. On 2 June, 'the Gallabat–Metemma Axis' was formally annulled by the closing of the frontier. Two days later one-eyed Fitaurari Worku arrived from Kwara with 200 men, impatient for rifles. The following day Colonel Castagnola demanded a meeting with his British 'friends'.

They met, formally, at the Sudan Customs shed down by the *Khor*; the round little Colonel Castagnola, with the Prince de Bourbon-Siciles as his interpreter, and, for the British, not Castagnola's old acquaintance *Bimbashi* Wreford-Brown but this extremely tall, rather formidable newcomer, *Bimbashi* Thesiger. Behind them on the fort of Gallabat the Union Jack and the green flag of Egypt floated side by side.

The Colonel complained about rebel activities and British support for them. War, he remarked, had not yet been declared. The *Bimbashi* rejected the complaint. Ending the interview on a more cordial but at the same time more sinister note, he regretted that he was unable to invite the Colonel and the Prince back for lunch owing to 'the manœuvres' planned for that afternoon.

On the rebels themselves Thesiger had had to exercise a very different style of diplomacy: for with the rifles had come very strict instructions not to issue them till war *was* declared. So by 9 June Fitaurari Worku and his men, disgusted, had decided to go

back to their hills again. Fortunately, wheedled by Thesiger they
waited a day. Even then further contradictory cables arrived
saying that no arms or ammunition were to be issued until further
instructions. These were ignored on Nelsonian principles by the
men on the spot; and the Fitaurari acquired both renewed faith in
the British and the long-coveted weapons.

Thesiger's exuberance on that evening of 10 June was,
however, short-lived. Two hours later came further messages
from HQ at Gedaref: according to information received an attack
on Gallabat fort by the Italians was due to be put in an hour before
dawn the following morning. Furthermore, reinforcements of 3
native battalions and 31 tanks had reached Metemma. Four hours
after midnight the two *Bimbashis*, Thesiger and Hanks, charged
with defending the fort, were woken up and had 'a rather solemn
cup of tea', before setting off with their platoons to take up
positions on the Fort and the surrounding ridges. But dawn came
unheralded by gunfire—they gazed out at a 'typical peaceful
African morning' in Metemma: cows being driven to pasture,
and women going down to the *Khor* to collect water. That was
how the war began on the frontier.

At midday the following day the Governor-General Sir Steward
Symes summoned to the Palace in Khartoun the leading
Sudanese, including the three leaders of the three great Muslim
sects; El Shereef Yusuf el Hindi, El Sayed Sir Ali el Mirghani
Pasha, and El Sayed Sir Abdul Rahman el Mahdi.

Sir Steward read out in English a 'Proclamation to the People
of the Sudan'. The Shereef and the Sayeds made short and loyal
speeches expressing faith in the victory of Great Britain. Sir Abdul
recalled the similar meeting called in 1914, at which he, the son of
the Mahdi, had expressed so fervently his loyalty to the British. He
did not mention that the then Governor-General, Sir Reginald
Wingate, had addressed the *Ulema* in Arabic; but perhaps he
recalled Wingate's words: 'God is my witness that we have never
interfered with any man in the exercise of his religion'. This was
still true, and it meant that Italian attempts to stir up Muhammadan opinion in the Sudan were almost bound to fail. The British
could count, up to a point, on the loyalty of the Sudanese.

Three of the Sudan's nine provinces marched with Italian East
Africa: in the north Kassala Province, in the centre the Blue Nile

Province, and in the south the Province of the Upper Nile. The danger lay in the north, in Kassala Province, where the only strategic objective in the Sudan, the railway linking Port Sudan on the Red Sea with the capital passed over the River Atbara. At this point stood the vulnerable Butana bridge—nearly 400 yards long with a span of seven arches. It was along this line that the *Kaid*, General Platt, distributed his best troops. One of his British battalions, the Worcesters, he placed at Port Sudan, the other, the Essex, at Khartoum. At the Butana Bridge itself, he stationed a group of the newly-formed motor machine-gun companies (MMG Coys) of the Sudan Defence Force.

The rest of Kassala Province lying between the railway and the frontier was expendable, and particularly the three places that lay within hailing distance of the Italians across the border. These were the tiny police post of Karora on the Red Sea, the fort and settlement at Gallabat, and between them the town of Kassala. Instructions were issued that in the event of invasion Kassala was to be declared an open town and evacuated. Gedaref and its outpost Gallabat were not to be given up quite so easily. Even though Hussey de Burgh *Bey*, rejoicing in the new title of 'Commander of Troops Gedaref and Gallabat' had told his outlying *Bimbashis* not to hold the fort till the last man and the last round, he had added a more traditional rider: 'But blood must be spilt!'

Titles and forces proliferated. All the District Commissioners —Lea at Port Sudan, Sandison at Kassala, Trevor Blackley at Gedaref, and Hancock,[1] at steamy Roseires—were drafted into the Sudan Auxiliary Defence Force. This was a sort of Home Guard whose job *inter alia* was to deal with 'enemy parachutists or airborne troops'. Anyone with a Sudanese, British, or Egyptian passport was eligible; and even passers-by were enrolled —such as Evans-Pritchard the anthropologist who happened to be working with the Nuer and the Anuak. The DCs in their new military glory set to work forming what they themselves called, stealing the Italian term, their own local *banda*.

Gedaref had been chosen as the centre from which rebel activity would be if not co-ordinated at least encouraged. Cheeseman's Intelligence Bureau swung into action. On 11 June, the day after war was declared, six messengers left Gedaref

---

[1] 'Honcok' to the Italian intelligence officers across the border. They invariably had equal trouble with General 'Wawel'.

to cross the frontier, bearing letters on linen parchment to six rebel chiefs. They were followed a few days later by six more messengers bearing six more letters. These letters, identical, read as follows:

May it reach . . . .
                    Peace be unto you
Now the British and the Italians are at war. In order to crush our mutual enemy we need all the help we can get. If you need rifles, ammunition, food or money, send to us men and pack animals, as many as you can, to the place where the messenger will show you. Whatever you want, we can help you. Also it would be better if you would send us your own representative to speak with us and to consult as to how we can best injure the enemy.

The letters were signed by the *Kaid*. They were sent to most of the major rebel leaders in Gojjam, Armachecho, the Wolkait, the Simien, and Beghemder proper—the only surprising exceptions being Dagnew Tessema and Lij Johannes in Beghemder, and Hailu Belew, in Gojjam.

All was still surprisingly quiet on the frontier. Finally, unable to bear the peaceful pastoral scene any longer, *Bimbashi* Hanks loosed off from Gallabat Fort the opening round of the Ethiopian campaign. It was dusk on the evening of 14 June. His men, sparked by his example, fired with enthusiasm, and managed to expend 8,000 rounds. There was ten minutes' surprised and shocked silence. Then the Italian garrison opened up and fired continuously back for two hours. The only casualty, unfairly, of this noisy exchange, was a Greek merchant in Metemma. Hussey de Burgh *Bey* was furious at the waste of ammunition and cabled from Gedaref forbidding any offensive action whatsoever over the frontier. The following day Colonel Castagnola's men managed to shoot down the Union Jack flying over Gallabat fort. This was considered an outrage. The war on the Sudan–Ethiopian frontier had begun in earnest.

In the air by way of contrast the Italians had taken the initiative. On the day after war was declared they bombed Kassala. One bomb killed the uncle of the Omda. The Omda was extremely annoyed and demanded that the Sudan counter-attack. More important, the infuriated garrison had fired on the offending planes, and therefore it had become impossible to stick to the plan of declaring Kassala an open town in the event of invasion. Emboldened, the *Regia Aeronautica* bombed Khartoum, causing considerable panic among car-drivers. Thereafter Khartoum was blacked out every night and, despite the heat, doors, windows, and shutters had to be closed.

The RAF retaliated. 'In mid-June nine Wellesleys flew majestically abreast over Gedaref on the way to bomb Gondar. From that day on everyone was satisfied that we were winning the war,' wrote the Governor of Kassala Province, Kennedy-Cooke. But the Wellesleys were old-fashioned and out of date, and so were the planes in Kenya piloted by the white Southern Rhodesians of No. 237 Squadron. Wavell hastily accepted Smuts's offer of an anti-aircraft unit, found the guns, and set up the unit at Mombasa, the port which would be used for supply —or for evacuation.

The air war became hottest in the Red Sea area where the RAF, at its Aden base, was strongest. Fortunately a document survives which gives a vivid picture of this war in the air from the Italian side—a diary written by an Italian airman, and eventually captured by the British, translated, and despatched to England to sleep in the War Office files. Or rather the translation was despatched—the original has been lost or discarded and, with it, the name of the diarist. All that we know of him comes from stray remarks in the diary: that he was unmarried, had been at training school at Elmas, had fought in Spain, and was (probably) a sergeant-pilot; that he had a sister called Gina. He may be living still. Just before war broke out he and his squadron were posted to the airfield outside Assab. This was Italy's original trading station on the Red Sea, on the borders of the Danakil country.[1]

---

[1] A little town which he described vividly even lyrically: 'Sometimes we would go into Assab. . . . The houses were white and in Oriental style, and the streets lined with date palms, the sweet fruit of which small boys would offer to the passers-by. Standing apart from the village was the native quarter, stretching down to the sea, with small white houses interspersed with hundreds of *tukuls*. In the narrow streets where one breathed the acreous smell of the native, one came across types of various races and religions: Yemenis from the Asiatic shore, Indians in a thousand different coloured turbans and sarongs, Somalis half naked, and Ethiopians dressed just in rags. There were many Somali women, well-made, backs erect and proud, with round bare shoulders, carrying on their heads bulging water-skins; and their hips covered by ample red and black sarongs. Around their necks, on their wrists and ankles pretty yellow necklaces, bracelets and anklets. The Amhara women in contrast dressed in a simple white flowing robe down to the ankles, tied around the waist with a belt, also white, heads covered in a thick bush of hair, shining, oily with grease, having a vile smell.'

On 12 June three Blenheims from Aden raided Assab, 'destroying sacks of rice, macaroni, and about 20,000 flasks of wine'. The Italian pilots leapt into their Capronis; and 'we follow them out to sea but they have a greater turn of speed and skimming the water are lost to sight in the haze'. The RAF were back that night. 'The moment the plane was heard Colonel Fedeli gave the order to turn off the lights from the main and the man in charge in his agitation instead of turning off the lights illuminated the landing-ground. The plane only waited for this, for him fortunate, incident to start the funfair.' And later in the night the Blenheims were back in force.

The airport had a sinister and desolated appearance [wrote Gina's brother.] 'Firemen gone, our officers gone, the fire, which was burning more fiercely, and the explosion of cartridges which got worse and worse. But the greatest torture of all was to see us running out from the airport with mattresses over our heads. I and a few others, taken by surprise, completely nude, sweating from the exertion of running with the weight of the mattresses, walking and running across the scrub, thorn, tree stumps, and behind us the glare of the fire and the explosions one by one of 3000 cartridges destroyed in a little less than an hour. Midnight was past when with mattresses and sheets on the ground in that hot night full of eruptions we tried to find a little peace and sleep after a day of bombardment, of chasing them in our fighters, of heat and thirst. And tomorrow it will start all over again.

So, demoralized and very, very hot, he and his fellow pilots camped under a solitary pine. The only thing they found working in the morning was, fortunately, the ice-box. The temperature was 104 degrees. This went up the following week, varying between 122 and 130. 'Terrific, indescribable heat,' wrote Gina's brother. 'Brain numbed, the head heavy, limbs aching. If one could only take a refreshing shower of cool water or rest at night!' Luckily they did not stay long—a week later the squadron was posted to Diredawa: 'With our transfer to Diredawa ends our vile life at Assab.' At Diredawa they were given a target of their own: the other enemy, the enemy at Djibuti.

A week after Mussolini had declared war on the Allies Weygand's armies had collapsed, the Germans were in Paris, and Marshal Pétain had taken over the government of France and appealed for an armistice. The following day, 18 June, General de Gaulle broadcast from London to the French people his appeal for resistance. The appeal went largely unheard. On 22 June the French and the Germans signed the armistice outside Paris.

The Italian army, commanded by Crown Prince Umberto, had invaded, or rather attempted to invade an apparently prostrate France. They were held in the mountains and the foothills of the Riviera. Nevertheless, inevitably, an armistice followed. The Franco-Italian armistice was signed two days later at the Villa Incisa in Rome.

These confusing, rapid, and turbulent events totally upset the balance of military advantage, particularly in the Middle East and Africa. With the French armies and navies out of the war, the British were left on their own. They faced in Libya an immensely more powerful Italian army[1] and in the Mediterranean an Italian fleet which was now almost as strong as their own Mediterranean fleet. It was a complete and, from the point of view of the British in Africa, disastrous reversal of fortune—only slightly mitigated by the fact that of the two high colonial officials who responded to De Gaulle's appeal, one was General LeGentilhomme in Djibuti.

LeGentilhomme, though not Governor of Djibuti, was military commander not only of the now 10,000-strong Djibuti garrison, the most formidable force on Italian East Africa's borders, but of the British troops in British Somaliland as well. He was pugnacious and a fire-eater. British officers had always found him pleasant, loyal—and impressively aggressive. The British and French staffs had planned that on the declaration of war LeGentilhomme and his troops would invade AOI and thrust boldly down the railway line for Addis Ababa. It was unthinkable, even at this crisis that a tiger like LeGentilhomme would tamely accept the armistice and thereby expose his comrades in British Somaliland to invasion. Indeed he had been ordered on 11 June to resist 'jusqu'au bout' and to stir up a 'general uprising' within Italian territory. On 18 June the Italians had attacked towards Djibuti

---

[1] The bulk of Italy's vast white army in Libya had been concentrated on Libya's western border, facing the powerful French Army of North Africa, 120,000 strong. The real protectors of the British in Africa had been the overseas armies of France. But with France neutralized, there seemed little to stop the Italians from Libya invading Egypt or the Italians from East Africa invading Kenya; and both linking up in a pincer movement that would easily eliminate the Sudan.

along the main road, only to be bloodily repulsed by LeGentilhomme's troops. Three days later four Savoia bombers had
crashed. The following day Gina's brother took off from
Diredawa, escorting a further group of bombers. 'The anti-
aircraft defence is very poor,' he wrote. 'We make another turn to
see whether any French fighters will have the courage to take off.
Not one!'

But when his squadron had returned to Diredawa, they had an
unpleasant shock. At lunchtime '3 French planes attack us by
surprise—one of our planes is destroyed on the ground'.

Forty-eight hours later the Franco-Italian armistice was signed
in Europe. Djibuti was declared a demilitarized zone under
French control but with port and railway open to the Italians. But
when on 28 June the local Italian Armistice Commission tried to
drive in to Djibuti, General LeGentilhomme halted them on the
frontier. He refused even to receive the emissary sent out from
Vichy as the French member of the Armistice Commission, his
fellow-general, General Germain. The 10,000 troops in Djibuti
were still, apparently, in the war, a great comfort to General
Wavell and a great threat to the Italians.

So the first fortnight of the war in East Africa passed, without any
great events or upheavals, without any changes of frontiers, and
with the death of only two, innocent people—the uncle of the
Omda of Kassala, and the Greek merchant in Metemma. It was a
very half-hearted war. Indeed there was more than apathy, there
was sympathy between the two sides. When the Governor-
General of Libya, Balbo, was shot down apparently accidently by
his own side on 28 June, the 'Sudanese Herald' lined its account of
his death with a heavy black border even though the two nations
were at war. Mussolini on the other hand did not seem 'ecces-
sivamente adolorato'—'excessively saddened'—when one of his
military staff brought the news to him. Balbo's place was taken
by Marshal Graziani. Thus Graziani returned again to the power
and high military command in Africa, of which he had been
deprived thirty months earlier at the end of his disastrous term as
Viceroy in Addis Ababa. Although people in Khartoum referred
with distaste to 'Butcher' Graziani and contrasted him with the
'gentleman' they ignorantly believed Balbo to have been, vast
expanses of almost waterless desert stretched for hundreds of
miles between the inhabited centres of Libya and the Sudan. Even

Graziani's appointment did not seem to threaten Khartoum. It was not enough to stir the apathy of Sudanese officialdom.

Nor was the arrival of Brigadier Sandford commanding the obscurely-entitled 101 Mission and eager to stir up the rebels across the frontier; and even less the appearance at the frontier of three rebel leaders from Armachecho in response to the Kaid's letter, Wubneh Amoraw, Ayane Chekol, and Birre Zagaye. It took the threat of the arrival of a much more distinguished personage to upset the dovecot and provoke a screech of anguished cables. That distinguished personage was the exile from Bath.

For two weeks the ex-Emperor waited restlessly in London while his friends made their various *démarches*. Then with sudden speed, the decision was taken. Precisely a fortnight after Italy's declaration of war a plane took off from the Wiltshire Downs carrying Haile Selassie, his second and favourite son the Duke of Harar, his two secretaries Lorenzo Taezaz and Wolde Giorgis, and George Steer, promoted to Captain and appointed ADC, on the first stage of the long trip back from exile to the throne.

They flew, dangerously, through the night over armisticed and neutral France, touched down at Malta, and took off again in a flying-boat. At tea-time the following day the flying-boat landed in Alexandria harbour, and a launch came out to meet it. Aboard was another old acquaintance, Chapman-Andrews, Oriental Secretary at the Cairo Embassy, who had last seen the Emperor at the dramatic halt at Diredawa where, the capital abandoned, the Imperial train had pulled in. Now, as always, we know nothing of Haile Selassie's inner feelings: we can only imagine the mixed sentiments he must have experienced as, in these days, he saw again so many faces that recalled to him his past, with its glories and its mistakes, but certainly with its importance. We know though that at this stage he was optimistic: with, at last, official British support all seemed possible.

On the spot, though, that support proved to be non-existent. Sir Miles Lampson had been horrified by the cable announcing the flying-boat's imminent arrival. Chapman-Andrews was therefore given the unpleasant task of greeting Haile Selassie with one breath and informing him with the next that he would have to stay incognito in the harbour. Next morning Sir Miles had him flown down to Wadi-Halfa on the Egyptian–Sudanese frontier. It was only, cunningly, after the plane was well on its way that the Embassy at Cairo sent a coded cable to the Palace at Khartoum to inform Sir Stewart Symes and General Platt that Haile Selassie was on his way.

If there had been embarrassment at Cairo, there was consternation at Khartoum. Symes's first reaction was to refuse to have the ex-Emperor in his territory at all. He sent off a cable to Wadi-Halfa giving express orders that the flying boat should on no account be allowed further south. Meanwhile the Governor of Kenya, appealed to by both Symes and Lampson, also refused to receive the unwelcome guest.

The ex-Emperor and his staff were thus suspended in a sort of no man's land on a hot and remote frontier, while governors and proconsuls tried to shuffle off the responsibility between themselves. It was a situation that oviously could not last; and Wavell, finding it quite rightly 'absurd', took a hand. He sent off a sharp cable to the Foreign Office, telling them to sort it out.

The result was that the hapless Chapman-Andrews was sent down to Khartoum for another *mauvais quart d'heure*. There he was faced with Platt who talked angrily about 'provocation' and said that the Emperor's presence would 'invite reprisals' and 'stir up a hornet's nest'. Symes was just as worried about the reaction of the Italians. In the end of course they had to give way. Their position was too untenable; for the Sudan was after all at war, and the Italians were enemies, not allies. But they gave way reluctantly, with pique, and only when Chapman-Andrews had explained what 'a hell of a row' there would be if Haile Selassie was flown back to England.

Chapman-Andrews was sent back to Wadi-Halfa, and this time Brigadier Sandford was sent with him, another old friend of the ex-Emperor. They reached Wadi-Halfa on 28 June and almost immediately went into conference. Chapman-Andrews for a change had good news to announce: that Haile Selassie and his suite would be welcome at Khartoum—and also that a number of prominent exiles had arrived that day from Jerusalem: the Echege Gabre Giorgis, Fitaurari Birru Wolde Gabriel, Dejaz Abebe Damtew, and Dejaz Adafrisau. Sandford however had to explain that there was no expeditionary force waiting; that the British would be able to make no offensive move for months, and certainly not during the rainy season, and that he himself, though head of 101 Mission, had, apart from light weapons, only 4 mortars and 400 shells at his disposal. Haile Selassie sat subdued, making notes, and after dinner commented sadly how distressed he was by the apparent lack of preparation for a revolt inside Ethiopia. Sandford could only reply that the situation might have changed for the better while they were talking: for, a week earlier, he and Boustead *Bey* and Trevor Blackley had motored down from Gedaref to meet the incoming rebels, and with their help the first British offensive had been planned for that very day—an attack on Metemma. Then Sandford took his leave; for he himself was due to fly back early next morning to see how the 'offensive' had gone.

It had, in fact, not gone too well. The plan had been simple enough: a night march by *Bimbashi* Thesiger and his men to a hill on the far side of Metemma, there a rendezvous with the rebels, and the setting up of an ambush—a trap into which the Italians would be provoked to fall by sporadic sniper-shots coming from the hill.

Thesiger took up position successfully enough, and fired off his sniper-shots. But then in the confusion of the night things began to go wrong. The men of Birre Zagaye and Ayane Chekol set up their ambush on the wrong side of the hill. As for Wubneh Amoraw, 'the Eagle', he had refused to take part at all. At dawn Thesiger and his platoon, supported by only about eighty Ethiopians found themselves being attacked by the whole 27th Colonial Battalion of the Beni Amer, the main force of Colonel Castagnola's garrison. They 'withdrew' hastily, Thesiger's personal servant, the reprieved murderer, running down the hill with his rifle on his shoulder, muzzle to the rear, and without turning his head firing the rifle from this position as he ran.[1]

Though casualties were few—five wounded, four missing——this attempt had proved a fiasco. Very clearly much more thought and much more planning were needed before any further combined operations with the rebels were tried out.

---

[1] 'He did not claim any hits.' This was the first encounter in which the British came up against the Italian *bomba-a-manos*, the little red and blue 'money-box' hand-grenades which could be lobbed for about sixty yards. 'They explode on impact', noted the British, 'and make a most impressive noise but rarely cause more than a superficial peppering of the skin with shot-gun pellets and pieces of the metal.' The Mills bombs the British used were more lethal but could be thrown only a short way. Their disadvantage, was, therefore, great: they could be very dangerous to the throwers.

So when Haile Selassie eventually reached Khartoum by train at the beginning of July it was to be greeted with news not of a success but of a discomfiture. He was taken out to be lodged, discreetly and still anonymously, a few miles outside the city, at Jebel Aulia where he found his reconstituted 'court', the exiles from Jerusalem. It must have been another and even more moving reunion; for these, unlike his British friends, were men of his own race, who looked upon him not as an unfortunate exile but as a consecrated Emperor.

CHAPTER 19

AOI ATTACKS

IN the first weeks of July five Wellesleys bombed Metemma. One, peppered, skimmed back over the fort and crashed near the *khor*. Thesiger and his men dashed out to rescue the crew. They found the aircraftsman, Davidson, still alive. They dragged him away and to safety. 'We did a good job, didn't we, sir?' he said to Thesiger. 'I could do with a nice cold pint of beer now. How I'd love to be lying in one of those cool Yorkshire streams.' He died the next morning; he and his pilot, Bush, were the first two British servicemen to be killed in this war.

Next morning just before dawn Italian bombers retaliated. One Sudanese was killed by a splinter; and a few minutes later, sweeping in from both flanks, the Beni Amer of the 27th launched a full-scale attack on Gallabat Fort. It was defended only by one platoon. After a few minutes' brisk exchange of fire the defenders abandoned the fort, as planned, and fell back to the Pass at Khor el Otrub. But though Gallabat had fallen, blood *had* been shed; another Sudanese was killed and four wounded. The defenders claimed, perhaps extravagantly, that they had killed twenty-seven of the Beni Amer in exchange.

Back at the Pass, woken by the bombs and the gunfire, in the half-light of dawn *Bimbashis* Thesiger and Hanks tried to rally their scattered men and contact the rebel leaders—only to find that the rebels had discreetly disappeared. They sent a message off to Khartoum. Expecting an attack any minute, they burnt in approved military style the 'highly-inflammable' code and cipher wires to prevent them falling into the hands of the enemy, and so at the same time were rid of that particular incubus. Khartoum decided that the situation was 'desperate', and sent off a company of the Camel Corps as reinforcements. But by the time the Camel Corps arrived several days later 'fully expecting to march straight into battle', the scare was, much to their disappointment, over. Colonel Castagnola's men had made no further move along the road to Gedaref, not even to attack the miserable two platoons remaining at the Pass.

Simultaneously, further to the north, the Italians attacked Kassala. This was not a one-battalion affair but, comparatively speaking, a massive expedition. Frusci had gathered 12,000 men and 40 guns before launching his attack. But though the town was no longer undefended, its defenders numbered under 600, of whom only six were Englishmen. The issue was never in doubt. The town was bombed, shelled, outflanked by cavalry squadrons, entered by armoured cars, and occupied by bussed infantry and their commander, General Tessitore. The District Commissioner had already moved out to the Gash, the Hadendoa tribal area. The Assistant District Commissioner, Blaikie, blew up the Post Office before leaving and blew it up so effectively that he blew himself out of the door with it. The garrison withdrew; the invaders captured 61 police.

Simultaneously, still further to the north, the Italians attacked Karora—despite the *habub*, the oven-like wind of the plains that made any effort painful. As this post was defended by only nine policemen, they met with even less resistance. So by midday on 4 July General Frusci had successfully captured the three enemy posts that lay on the frontier of his Sector. It looked to the British as if the long-feared invasion of the Sudan had begun in earnest, and as if their postion was indeed desperate.

From Cairo, General Wavell, somewhat shaken, cabled to Eden the same day pointing out his weakness not only in the Sudan but also in Egypt. He appealed for more armour, more anti-tank guns, more artillery. Clearly he feared that the invasion of the Sudan from Italian East Africa was timed to coincide with the invasion of Egypt from Italian North Africa, the vast movement to pinch out 'the wasp waist of the British Empire'. Short of troops though he was, he sent down a third British battalion, the 2nd West Yorks, to replace a 'neutral' Egyptian battalion in Khartoum.

In London there were alarmed recriminations. Churchill deplored the failure to double the Sudan Defence Force in time and told Eden, his new War Minister: 'If you lose Khartoum your name will live in history.'[1] A few days later he set up the Middle East Committee, consisting of the Under-Secretaries of State for

---

[1] Later when reminded of this by Eden he denied it: 'My dear, I would never have said that to you.'

War, India and the Colonies, to co-ordinate the war effort in the Middle East. There was very little else they could do in London. Almost all the British Army's equipment, artillery, tanks, even guns, had been lost at Dunkirk, and with invasion threatening England, they had no reinforcements to send.

Eden cabled back what must have seemed to Wavell a very misplaced message: 'You will share our keen desire to strike out at the Italians, especially if they should attempt to advance from Kassala to Khartoum.' He added, unnecessarily, 'An insurrection in Ethiopia would greatly assist your task.' This could hardly be denied. The question, though, was how to arrange it. For as Wavell was vainly pestering London, so Haile Selassie was pestering, with almost equally fruitless results, Khartoum.

As a first step, with the support of the Mahdi's son, Haile Selassie had installed himself nearer the centre of power, in the 'Pink Palace', a small country house belonging to Shareef Yusuf el Hindi on the outskirts of Khartoum. From there he had set about improving his political position—only to find it almost wrecked at the outset.

Blatta Takele had been away skirmishing and making contacts on the borders of Armachecho, sending word to the chiefs to be very cautious in their dealings with the British; for he knew from his own dealings with them how British officials regarded the Ethiopians, and he feared that Ethiopia's new allies would if successful liberate Italian East Africa only to impose their own rule upon it. His theories, and his fears, were to be much discussed throughout Beghemder. But as soon as he heard that notables from Jerusalem were arriving, he hurried back to Khartoum to try and influence them. There—and he does not seem to have expected it—he found the ex-Emperor, the man who had attempted to have him hanged,[1] also installed. The only figure of influence he managed to win over to his views was the youngest of the exiled leaders, Dejaz Abebe Damtew, Ras Desta's brother and a member of the Menz nobility.

Haile Selassie, confronted, informed the pair of them that the British had promised to reinstate him by force of arms. They demanded to know what sort of a constitution he would impose if and when he was reinstated. Haile Selassie temporized. Mesfin

---

[1] See chapter notes, pages 417–18.

Sileshi, present at the council, defended the *ancien régime* as a loyal
Bodyguard officer should. Blatta Takele, changing his point of
attack, suggested that the loyal Bodyguard officer should, precisely because of his loyalty and rank, advise his Emperor to form
his own army, and not to rely on the imperialist British. The
meeting ended inconclusively. But Haile Selassie, faced with this
open challenge to his authority clearly decided that he must
surreptitiously edge Blatta Takele and the disloyal Abebe Damtew aside. It is equally clear that he, and Mesfin, thought very
hard about Blatta Takele's advice.[1]

For the moment, however, Haile Selassie was totally
dependent on his protectors. So for the Ethiopians inside his
country he set about drafting, with the help of Lorenzo Taezaz,
an *Awaj*, an imperial proclamation. In it he announced his return,
invited those who had submitted, and Eritreans too, to desert and
openly countered Blatta Takele's anti-British warnings. The
Awaj, stamped with the Imperial Seal of the Lion of Judah, was
printed by George Steer who had been placed in charge of a
Propaganda Unit. Soon thousands of copies were being dropped
by plane over military camps and the countryside of Ethiopia,
over occupied Kassala too where Eritreans were seen to kiss the
Seal, press it to their foreheads and weep. The *carabinieri*
instituted (in theory) the death penalty for any askari found
reading it, and paraded whole battalions to search them. From
that time onwards a trickle of deserters began to cross into the
Sudan—living proof of the emotion the Emperor's name could
still, despite years of exile, arouse.

At the same time Haile Selassie turned, at first mildly and semi-
privately, on the British. He addressed a letter to Churchill to put
his queries and his suggestions. First, why were not troops or at
least rifles offered to him from all the reserves in Kenya, the
Sudan, and South Africa? Why could he not be equipped with
mortars and anti-tank guns? He suggested secondly, that the
Ethiopian refugees should be brought to the Sudan from both
Somaliland and Kenya, and the Eritrean deserters as well. There
they should be given military training, formed into battalions,
and put under his command. Thirdly, he wanted his *Awaj*
dropped everywhere. Fourthly, he proposed that Italian outposts
be attacked. It was the sort of letter Churchill himself might have

[1] See below pages 233, 234, 372–7.

written, though more courteous in tone. Though addressed to the Prime Minister, it had of course by etiquette to go to the Governor-General first. And the Governor-General, on 9 July, passed it on to London with his comments.

Sir Stewart Symes, taking up Haile Selassie's four points, confirmed that the first was being acted on, ignored the second and third, but agreed with the fourth in so far as this meant 'minor guerrilla warfare'. He then complained angrily at Haile Selassie's arrival—the Foreign Office comment here was 'We were deluged with destructive telegrams from Khartoum and Cairo.' He ended up by saying that though the Emperor was temperamentally cautious, he appeared to be both dejected and eager for immediate action, and that there was the risk of a sudden, desperate venture.[1]

It seems clear that Haile Selassie must have composed his letter to Churchill in concert with Brigadier Sandford, for it contained all the elements of Sandford's plan, Plan X. It seems equally clear, that both were influenced by Blatta Takele's main point: that the restoration should be seen to be an Ethiopian, not a British achievement. Briefly, the culminating point of the plan was to be the Emperor's triumphant return into Ethiopia leading an Ethiopian army composed of 'Refugee Battalions' trained, equipped, and advised by the British. On crossing the frontier this army would be joined by rebel bands, also equipped and to some extent trained by British infiltrators. Swelling in numbers and size as it moved forward into Amhara, it would finally drive the terror-stricken Italian usurpers from the capital. The long-term basis of the plan was the assumption that all Ethiopians were loyal to the Emperor. The short-term basis was the need to assemble, train, and arm Refugee Battalions; it was this that Haile Selassie's letter was obviously designed to achieve.

Wavell descended on Khartoum and called an urgent conference with the *Kaid*, Chapman-Andrews and the Emperor. Haile Selassie brought in his two secretaries and read out a prepared statement. This was much stronger stuff. Haile Selassie complained that on arrival in the Sudan not only had he found no properly prepared plan of action but he had met with veiled

---

[1] 'Bunk!', annotated one Foreign Office official. This was in fact slightly unfair. 'The kindest thing to do would be to forget about Sir SS' despatch', annotated another. It was probably not forgotten about. Sir SS was moving very quickly towards retirement and sweet oblivion.

hostility from the Khartoum government. He complained also that the Crown Prince had not been sent out. He demanded that his status as Emperor should be recognized in the Sudan—a carefully-calculated limitation here—that arms and ammunition should be supplied, that 600 refugees should be brought to Khartoum from Kenya and another 400 from Somaliland, and that Dejaz Abebe Damtew and Blatta Takele should be sent down to Kenya and given a command there in the remote border zone. He paused only to add a *coup de grâce*: seeing that his suggestions were not being met he had decided to form his own Government and to enter Ethiopia—in a month's time, on 15 August.

This last threat was not perhaps entirely bluff but there was certainly an element of 'bunk' in it. Wavell calmed Haile Selassie down. Wavell explained that with the French surrender upsetting everything it was extremely difficult to make plans. It would be wrong to venture suicidally into Ethiopia but Mission 101 would certainly go in to prepare the ground within the month. The other points would be seen to. The British would do their best.

The two men seem to have got on rather well with one another, with Wavell more amused than annoyed at Haile Selassie's techniques of interview-conducting. For the Emperor had insisted on speaking in Amharic, which an Arabic-speaking interpreter translated into French, which a French-speaking interpreter finally translated into English—which His Imperial Majesty in fact spoke with reasonable fluency.

Shortly afterwards Chapman-Andrews was able to reverse his usual role and tell the Emperor much of what he wanted to hear. The Crown Prince Asfa Wossen had left England and was *en route*. Abebe Damtew and Blatta Takele had been sent down to Kenya, to the Taveta Camp;[1] fifty of the refugees in Somaliland would be brought to Khartoum to form a Bodyguard, and the rest would be sent down to Kenya where two Refugee Battalions destined for the Sudan would be formed. So, by combining a mild letter to the British Prime Minister with an outraged protest to the British Commander-in-Chief, Haile Selassie had won almost all along the diplomatic line. Full satisfaction of his more

---

[1] Probably the British knew quite as much as the Emperor about Blatta Takele's activities and were quite glad, though for different reasons, to have this pretext for getting him out of the way. As regards the Crown Prince, he eventually reached Khartoum on 7 October.

aggressive demands came, however, in only one particular case: Kassala was showered with 15,000 copies of his *Awaj*, mingled with 21 tons of bombs on the Italian *Commissariato*.

By the end of the month the panic was over in the Sudan. It became apparent that the Italians were not going to move forward, not at any rate till the end of the rainy season in the highlands. On both sides of the 'new' Sudan–Ethiopian frontier the 'war' therefore died down, enlivened only by reports such as that announcing the creation of 'Frostyforce' in the Gash,[1] and the 'great jubilation' in the province after the bombing of Kassala.[2]

On the other side what is absolutely clear is that the Italians had no idea of how panicky their moves had made the British. And yet by the use of overwhelming force they had captured three posts, including one province capital, in a matter of minutes rather than hours. They ought to have realized how merely by continuing on the same lines they could have taken the Butana Bridge, Gedaref, Port Sudan, and, eventually, Khartoum. They had the men, and they no longer overestimated the enemy ('enemy forces', noted their intelligence office on the frontier, 'less than we thought'). But all that they did was to set up a Military Administration in Kassala, impose a curfew, release all prisoners, including lunatics, and set about winning over the Khatmia sect. To counter the Emperor's *Awaj*, Italian planes dropped leaflets over the Sudan stressing Italy's mild administration of Libya, Eritrea, and Somalia, Mussolini's love of Muhammadans and keenness on such progressive schemes as cattle-breeding. Italy's war was against the English, not the Sudanese—though all who resisted were warned that they would be severely dealt with.

The British were more worried by these leaflets than they were

---

[1] One hundred and fifty tribesmen of the 'usually taciturn' Hadendoa, named after the Nazir of the Hadendoa, Sheikh Mohammed el Amin Tirih, and raised, to raid around Kassala, mainly among his retainers, by the District Commissioner of the Beja, *Bimbashi* Haseldon. It was he who had bestowed on the Nazir the nickname of 'Frosty'.

[2] But the instructions to the locals on what to do about bombs caused less jubilation. One tribesman walking in the bush came across an unexploded bomb. He had heard instructions to lie down when bombs were about, so he lay down as per instructions near the bomb and, slightly exceeding instructions, hit it with his stick. The bomb exploded and he was blown to bits. His small son lived to tell the tale, having been sent some way away because his father did not think that he could be trusted to lie still.

afterwards to admit. District Commissioners were sent around collecting expressions of obvious loyalty from local Nazirs and Omdas, more to reassure themselves that they were still loved than as proofs of genuine intent. The authorities were both reassured and worried by the news that there had been very little looting and no 'atrocities' in Kassala. Reassured because this indicated that the Italians if they conquered the Sudan would behave well. Worried because this very fact undermined their own will to resist. As Newbold put it, 'people were rather despondent and some falsely aggressive'. The Governor-General, symptomatically, authorized a broadcast on 18 July 'to steady Sudanese opinion'. And General Platt, as a precautionary measure, moved the West Yorks forward to Gedaref.

There had meanwhile been one further incursion on the frontier. But as this took place on a different 'front', south of the Blue Nile, it represented no real threat.

A little war had already been developing on the edge of the Baro Salient. There, with the help of Evans-Pritchard and his Anuak, the District Commissioner at Akobo had boldly seized the initiative, crossed the Gilo and driven in two small outposts of Major Praga's *banda*. The Italians retaliated much further north by attacking Kurmuk. Once again they attacked in overwhelming force, two battalions and bombers against a police post manned by an Assistant DC and seventy police. A visiting missionary had dinner there on Saturday. He woke up on the Sunday morning to find himself wounded by a bomb splinter and to witness a general *sauve qui peut* which included Bell, the Assistant DC, 'a wonderful game-shot'. One policeman was killed; and Mr. Hancock, at Roseires on the Blue Nile, mildly threatened, was mildly reinforced. Bell, burning for revenge, made plans to attack Kurmuk with bows and arrows and flaming javelins. For many of the young men in the Sudan the war was still a light-hearted sport, especially south of the Blue Nile.

This attack on Kurmuk was significant only because it came from the Galla–Sidamo Sector and was therefore taken, rightly, as being the herald of a move south by General Gazzera: the dreaded invasion of Kenya. Moyale straddling the frontier was the first target. On 1 July the Italians tried a probing attack, with air and artillery support, which was driven off. This was clearly only a curtain-raiser. Brigadier 'Fluffy' Fowkes came up to inspect and deploy his forces on 9 July, a day on which 'the enemy was ominously quiet'. He left one company of the 1st KAR in Moyale itself, and placed the rest of the Battalion on the hills around. The 6th KAR was brought up in support.

The next day the Italians attacked Moyale at dawn. The defenders panicked. The counter-attack went wrong. 'Fluffy' brought up his reserve battalion only to have his whole brigade dispersed and almost surrounded. The KAR withdrew, chaotically, under cover of darkness. Orrigo's victorious IX Brigade were rewarded inside Moyale with a great deal of loot—equipment, clothing, stores, and ammunition that had not been destroyed. Moyale was of no importance in itself: a low, red fort-like building, and a *souk* with a few Indian traders, set by a dry brook in thick thorn-bush, patronized by blood-sucking ticks and surrounded by rock, sand, hyenas, and border brigands—on the southern edge of the Ethiopian escarpment. Its loss was no great loss. But what was significant was that for the first time a British brigade and an Italian brigade had clashed on almost equal terms and the British brigade had lost out and been forced, ignominiously, to retreat.

KAR officers analysed the affair despondently. 'Though enemy troops have shown no eagerness to engage in hand-to-hand fighting they have certainly displayed coolness under fire and the ability to creep up to close quarters with their rifles,' observed one. They were 'undoubtedly experienced in bush warfare,' noted a second. And 'they were extremely efficient troops knowing well the value of withholding fire,' according to a third.

All this was an extremely bad omen, a far cry from the war-games of Barland v Fowland the year before. The KAR, who had always had a very high opinion of themselves, even began to wonder whether their training methods were right. 'Judging by these troops and allowing for the fact that they must have had considerable experience in native service, it seems that Italian methods of training, which are probably not so tempered with kindness as our own, are the more effective in producing fighting forces.' In other words the KAR recognized that they were soft and inexperienced. This was self-criticism with a vengeance.

Morale became even lower towards the end of the month when a battalion of newly arrived West African troops—the 1st Nigerians—attacked a group of *banda* at Dobel, 2,000 camels strong, lost two officers and retreated, disorganized, through the almost equally demoralized 6th KAR, whose standard was captured. If even the Hausas of northern Nigeria, well-trained regulars, could be defeated by a group of irregular Somali *dubats*, what hope was there for Kenya and for its defenders?

General Dickinson hastily tried a rather desperate diversionary attack. On the principle of setting a thief to catch a thief, he gave the Ethiopian refugees their head. The '1st Ethiopian Battalion' was hastily formed at Taveta, divided into five companies of a hundred men and issued with old rifles and a hundred rounds per man. It was then launched at the other end of the Galla–Sidamo front beyond Lake Rudolf, towards Maji.

For years the refugees had been languishing in their camps, vainly demanding arms and ammunition and the authorization to attack the Italians. They had after all originally crossed the border in order to ask for British assistance. At long last they had it. Their old chiefs, Dejaz Wolde Mariam, Dejaz Zaudi Ayalew, and Fitaurari Tademme Zelleka took command. They were given three days' rations and escorted to the frontier by two platoons of the KAR. There, just over the frontier, on Ethiopian soil, they raised the Ethiopian flag. The KAR platoons saluted. It was the first time that the Ethiopian flag had been raised over Ethiopia by an invading Ethiopian force since the flight of the Emperor.

It was the best and most romantic moment of this 'invasion'. The little force, 510 strong, set off into the hostile and unknown lands of the Merille aiming to cross to the territory they knew on the far side of the Omo. But the Omo was in flood and impassable, and the land harsh, bare, hostile, and foodless. For thirteen days they straggled along after they had exhausted their rations. A brief skirmish with a *banda* post was enough to halt them and turn them aside. They crawled back along the frontier till they were picked up on 7 August by a KAR patrol and brought back to food and to rest. They had lost only four men but their expedition had been a total failure. They had been launched too hastily at the wrong part of the country. The British authorities in Kenya however blamed not themselves but the refugees. Thereafter they had very little use for Ethiopian fighters whom they usually referred to, deprecatingly, as *shifta*.

The '1st Ethiopians' were reformed at Lodwar, and put under the command of a Kenya settler, Captain Angus Buchanan. At the same time the '2nd Ethiopians' were formed out of the remainder of the refugees at Taveta, also under a British commanding officer, Captain Boyle. There was to be no question in future of allowing the refugees a free rein under their own leaders. Meanwhile the outmanœuvred duo, Blatta Takele and Dejaz Abebe, had reached Taveta. They were officially appointed Staff and Liaison officers, but watched very carefully. Blatta Takele, forbidden to address his countrymen on political matters, spoke much on the texts of Ezekial. It must have been an odd camp at Taveta.

General Dickinson's attempt at creating a diversion had been an absurd fiasco. Yet still General Gazzera made no serious move forward from Moyale; and Nairobi breathed again, and with much relief, when the 1st South African Brigade finally disembarked at Mombasa. They were paraded at Gilgit on 31 July. This meant that there were now in Kenya five brigades where weeks before there had been only two, and many more supporting arms—including soon, three squadrons of the South Africa Air Force equipped with modern Hurricanes by the British. Kenya was no longer naked.

Even so the 'invasion', coming on top of the 'invasion' of the Sudan, had scared London. Ten days after the fall of Moyale Churchill had sent his Chiefs of Staff a scorching note insisting —for the first time—that plans for a concerted *attack* on the Italian position in Ethiopia should be pressed forward.

The Middle East Committee met two days later. After the meeting Eden had to face a violent tirade from Churchill which at times degenerated into 'a heated altercation' about the whole Middle East situation and about Wavell himself. Churchill was becoming irritated with his generals. Even the former Prime Minister, Chamberlain, remarked: 'I'm sorry, Anthony, that all your generals seem to be such bad generals'.

The Middle East Committee issued its recommendations on 25 July: 'no financial considerations should be allowed to stand in the way of fomenting the rebellion in Ethiopia'. In other words the purse strings were to be loosened. Sandford and Haile Selassie would get their equipment, the rebels their arms and money. And incidentally, Sir Stewart Symes was to be transferred. That week Eden went over to Northern Ireland to talk to Symes's appointed successor, a military man, Major General Sir Hubert Hudleston; and was 'much impressed by him'. Hudleston knew the Sudan well. It had indeed been he who had originally raised and organized the Sudan Defence Force—the first *Kaid*. But Wavell was summoned back to London 'for consultations'. Churchill was determined to shake up Middle East Command and avoid any further defeats by the emboldened Italians. But in this he was to be too late.

CHAPTER 20

THE FALL OF BRITISH SOMALILAND

FRUSCI had attacked; Gazzera had attacked; It was now the turn of the commander of the third military Sector, General Nasi, to show what he could do. Large forces assembled at Harar, ready to sweep the enemy into the Red Sea. This was thought to be a comparatively easy matter, for General LeGentilhomme had been ousted from Djibuti by the Vichy emissary. British Somaliland was therefore dramatically alone, facing a far superior force assembled to crush the French hornet, not the British mosquito. No wonder, as the French settled into friendly neutralism, that General Nasi should be exultant and the British demoralized. 'The overrunning of Somaliland seems assured', wrote Newbold in a despondent letter, 'such is the Wops' numerical superiority. Poor Reggie Chater, he deserves a better show but he's a fine soldier and will hold them up for a time. I only hope there isn't a second Dunkirk at Berbera.'

On 3 August the Italians launched their invasion of British Somaliland. The advancing columns numbered no less than forty thousand men; twenty-six regular battalions supported by artillery and planes, and irregulars.

General Nasi had looked at his maps—which, as he was later to discover, left something to be desired—and had made his plans accordingly. His main thrust, as the British had always suspected, was to be directed at Berbera, through the wide pass at Tug Argan; and for this he had formed at Harar a 'Special Division' under the command of General Carlo de Simone, four brigades strong—including the II commanded by the famous Colonel Lorenzini. Somali irregulars were to fan out on the right flank of the main invading force and to probe the narrow pass at Sheikh.

General Nasi probably knew very well that the other two passes, at Jirreh and Dobo, had been allotted to French troops.

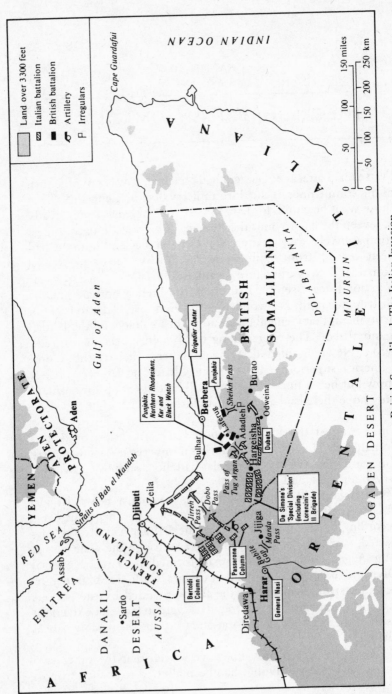

MAP 7. British Somaliland: The Italian Invasion

Now that there were no French troops to defend them they would be defenceless. He planned therefore to push the second prong of his attack swiftly through to Zeila on the Red Sea and along the coast road to Berbera, thus cutting off the British defenders at Tug Argan from the rear and involving them in a catastrophe. To make certain of the success of this left hook, he had indeed not one column but two lined up. In charge of these columns were two generals known to be bitter personal enemies: a Blackshirt general, Passerone (once described by the British Consul as a 'Fascist Firebrand'), and a regular army general, Bertoldi. Thus stirred by emulation—it was Trezzani's original idea and Trezzani's phrase—they would dash forward with winged feet, each eager to pounce on Berbera before the other. General Bertoldi was given the stronger force: two native brigades with two battalions of white troops as well. General Passerone only had a Blackshirt battalion and a native battalion plus artillery—strength for the one, mobility and fire-power for the other.

Italian intelligence officers had, as usual, hugely overestimated the numbers of troops opposing them. They put the total at 11,000 (possibly including the *illaloes*[1] as fighting troops, though in fact the *illaloes* did nothing). There were certainly more than there had been, however. Two Sikh battalions and the 2nd KAR had been sent over from Aden, more than doubling the strength of the 1,600-odd troops already on the spot, and far improving the quality of the defence. For the Indian battalions were highly professional troops—unlike the newly-raised Northern Rhodesians, or the Somali Camel Corps which in its day had been obliterated by the so-called Mad Mullah and whose enthusiasm when engaged against the fellow-Somalis of a pro-Muslim power was dubious. Rather to Italian surprise, the British seemed determined to make a stand. Brigadier Chater gathered his main force around Tug Argan, and sent out a fairly desperate plea for reinforcements.

In fact he had to hand potential reinforcements, keen and quite experienced if highly irregular. These were the Ethiopian refugees—the group already in the camp in British Somaliland, and a further group, 800 strong, who had come across from Djibuti. There was a difference in these two groups, corresponding to a

---

[1] Irregular Somali levies, said to be so-called from their British officers' rallying-cry 'Tally-Ho!'

difference in the attitudes of the two governments towards them. The British had always been disapproving and parsimonious. But General LeGentilhomme and Captain Appert had not only approved of but had armed and retrained *their* refugees. The French had therefore attracted the most warlike of them, including two well-known leaders, Asfau Wolde Giorgis, their own protégé (*Promotion* General Mangin, St. Cyr, 1929–1931), and the notorious Omar Samanthar of Walwal fame, the outlaw on whose head for ten years the Italians had put a price. Well-disciplined, they had been armed with ex-Spanish Civil War rifles. Inevitably, when they left Djibuti and crossed the frontier, they were disarmed and interned by their British 'allies', and their rifles were, with equally inevitable stupidity, destroyed. Just before the invasion, useless and badly treated, they were sent away, shipped off to Aden aboard the *Jehangir*, and from there down to Mombasa and up into Kenya like the others. It was a great waste.

A reinforcement, however, was *en route*. It was Wavell who had decided, against much advice, that British Somaliland if invaded would be seriously defended. So Wavell had sent a battalion of his own regiment, the 2nd Battalion The Black Watch, down to Aden. These Highlanders had an even more warlike reputation than the Sikhs of the Punjab. They were camped uncomfortably in Aden, in a tented camp at Khormahsur when the invading columns crossed the frontier.

There was no resistance. The outlying Camel Corps riders fell back towards Tug Argan without even trying to stop Nasi's 'left hook'. Two days after the invasion, General Bertoldi and his column were in Zeila with the rival General Passerone not far behind, ready to move along the coastal track towards Berbera and cut off the defenders of Tug Argan. It was only the following day that the Black Watch was finally given the order to move, and it is a measure of British ill-preparedness that it took three days to ferry this single battalion over from Aden across the Gulf. There at Berbera the Black Watch took up their position as reserve. During these three days, however, the Italian columns —and this is a measure of Italian inefficiency—did virtually nothing. They moved cautiously forward when they could have dashed, successfully, for their objectives before these were reinforced.

General de Simone was particularly cautious, always moving his unwieldy central column in text-book formation, though scouts were reporting the country ahead virtually clear up to the passes. On 6 August, having captured Hargeisha after a brief exchange of shots with a Northern Rhodesian outpost, the central column paused. On its right the Somali *dubats* halted too. Indeed for two whole days, on the pretext of rain and bad roads, all General Nasi's columns sat down where they were, until they were set moving again by continual prodding from Addis Ababa, from Trezzani, and indeed from the Viceroy.

The British had meanwhile, thanks to the tortoise-like movements of the Italian generals, moved their own reinforcements forward into place. By the evening of 10 August the Black Watch had been lorried up to the little village of Laferug behind Tug Argan. In front of them lay Brigade headquarters on the hill of Barkasan. Three of the other four battalions were strung out, facing the enemy along the sides of the wide gap of the Pass: the 2nd KAR, the 1st/2nd Punjabis and the 1st Northern Rhodesians. The fifth battalion, the 3rd/14th Punjabis had been detached —sent to hold the other pass over to the east at Sheikh. But behind and around and everywhere else was a military void: nothing—nothing except a few roaming troops of Camel Corps and a few Somali police. Berbera lay open almost for the asking if the 'left hook' had hooked in. But the two Italian columns on the coast seemed inexplicably and inextricably delayed.

Meanwhile a set battle loomed at Tug Argan; while from Harar, Gina's brother landed at Hargeisha airstrip, 'which Mr. Englishman had abandoned in his flight the other day. The advanced party which first occupied the place found beefsteaks still hot on the linen-covered tables. Perhaps this was the third or fourth of their five daily meals.' He took off to machine-gun a badly-camouflaged petrol dump down at Berbera: 'The barrels catch fire like matches, sending dense columns of smoke up. What a brutal joy one finds in destruction!'

As Italian light tanks probed forward into the pass at Tug Argan, the Royal Navy offered a saluting gun with thirty shells and three seamen to man it as an anti-tank weapon. The Black Watch thanked the Scottish gods that they had 'borrowed' some bren-guns from their fellow Scots Guards at Cairo, and hastily trained native runners to replace the wirelesses they had never received. GHQ at Cairo—for Wavell was *en route* to London—ordered down a regiment of field artillery by ship which never arrived and a Major-General from Palestine to take command of the defence who did.

Major-General Godwin-Austen, already *en route* to Kenya when diverted, reached Tug Argan on the evening of 11 August to find the usual British Army set-up: a scattering of detached companies positioned on the sides or tops or ridges of a number of newly-baptized hills—Knobbly, Mill, Black, Castle, Observation, and the rest. They had been bombed that day at dawn, and attacked by one enemy brigade, while another, Lorenzini's II, had attempted an outflanking movement round to Laferug. The two Italian brigades were pulled back that evening. Both sides seemed amazed and slightly alarmed at the strength and determination of their antagonists.

General de Simone learnt that over on his right the *dubats* had also been blocked by the Sikhs at Sheikh Pass. He rested a day. Then he attacked and attacked again, and was counter-attacked, and pushed back the counter-attack, and called in the air force and tried, unsuccessfully, more outflanking movements. But he was amazed and distressed to find that the British defence was not just wide and shallow but wide and deep. The native troops, in particular the Shoans and Amhara, dashed wildly forward in their attacks and lost a lot of men. The XIV Brigade had to be taken out of the action, so heavy were its casualties. Furthermore, the terrain was so difficult that Lorenzini's Eritreans, though far better trained and much more experienced, were unable to get round the flanks of the enemy positions however hard they tried.[1] So though the attackers outnumbered the defenders by about four to one, and though two hills were captured, none of the Italian generals were very happy about the way things were going—neither De Simone at the front, nor Nasi co-ordinating from Harar, nor Trezzani back in Addis Ababa.

What they did not realize was that their opponents were even more unhappy, and that the two battalions of African troops, the

---

[1] They were not helped in their endeavours by what the Italian staff still did not realize: that the maps they were using, based on an old 1926 British map, were totally wrong, and had confused the Sheikh-Laferug track with the Hargeisha–Berbera road. This incompetent bit of staff work totally messed up all the attempted Italian turning-movements on the ground and made their commanders unable to believe that the British could possibly have found defensive positions in depth. It is almost impossible to fight successful battles with inaccurate maps, as anyone with the least military experience knows.

2nd KAR and the Northern Rhodesians, were at breaking-point. So was the imported Major-General's nerve. Godwin-Austen had been particularly shattered by an incident on the night of the 13th, when for the first time a company of the Black Watch, till then held in reserve, had been ordered forward. It had been ambushed in the moonlight by Lorenzini's men. In the general confusion Captain Rose, commanding, had eventually escaped, driving back 'like Jehu with a touch of Agag', only to find that the black drivers, even swifter, had preceded him with a laconic but distinctly gloomy report. 'Major killed, captain wounded, all finish, no good.' If even a company of the Black Watch could be dispersed in confusion (and its commanding officer had been replaced on the very dubious official grounds that his 'health had broken down') what hope was there? Though the Major-General had also felt obliged to replace the commanding officer of the 2nd KAR with another Black Watch major, the situation on Tug Argan was worsening. The morale of the Africans was bad, and likely, thought Godwin-Austen (who had been studying reports of the KAR débâcle at Moyale), to become worse.

Major-General Godwin-Austen was not of course to know that the generals on the other side were equally worried. Nasi and Trezzani, meeting in conference, were seriously considering calling the whole operation off—particularly as their machiavellian scheme with the two coastal columns from Zeila had gone very wrong. As Trezzani wrote to Marshal Badoglio afterwards, each of the rival generals concentrated all his energy not on himself advancing, but on stopping the other from doing so. Some of Bertoldi's column had even reached the village of Buchar, three-quarters of the way to Berbera, only to be pulled back. And nothing but complaints about obstructions, lack of water, and non-existence of roads previously reported passable were coming in. So the whole Italian scheme, in theory excellent, had gone awry, because of a still-unrecognized staff error (the map mistake) which had resulted in heavy casualties, and because of the criminal incompetence of two Italian generals and the over-cautiousness of a third. Fortunately for them they were faced with a British general who was not very much better.

For early on 15 August Godwin-Austen threw in his hand. He sent off a cable to Cairo asking for permission to evacuate, saying that he saw no alternative. At midday a cable came back from 'Jumbo' Wilson, that 'rock of strength': 'Permission granted'.

No Thermopylae at Tug Argan—though a Thermopylae would, as those who can be wise after the event are able to judge, have been not only a feat of but a triumph for British arms.

The problem now was 'to avoid a Dunkirk at Berbera'. In this Godwin-Austen, helped it must be admitted by De Simone, was much more successful. Orders were sent out for evacuation. The three forward battalions at Tug Argan were to withdraw through the Black Watch; the four companies of the Black Watch to take up position at Barkusan and hold it till nightfall.

This was easier said than done. The pass at this point was over a mile wide, and the Black Watch companies positioned on either side of it were on the lower slopes. There they could be over-looked and shot down at by any outflanking enemy movement. To stop the Italian tanks they only had one Bofors anti-aircraft gun and one captured Breda anti-tank gun with five rounds. 'Had the enemy used his tanks properly', wrote the regimental intelligence officer afterwards, 'he must have overrun the defence.' But he did not. This was in part very understandable, because one medium and two light tanks were destroyed by Sergeant Major Sandy. The view of such destruction naturally tends to make surviving tank commanders wary.

The Black Watch held on throughout the day. They were attacked in the morning by Lorenzini's Eritreans, who kept in touch with whistles till 'the whole countryside was an elaborate whistle symphony'. The attack looked dangerous. It was pushed forward on the left with great spirit until fifty Highlanders upped and charged wildly yelling, bayonets out, for six hundred yards, a terrifying sight that sent 'the enemy rising and running like hares in their hundreds'. In the afternoon nearly twenty tanks cruised threateningly around in front while a battalion of Lorenzini's, with mules, worked slowly, visibly, and worryingly round to the rear. Just before dusk, having lost only seven men killed, but having successfully covered the withdrawal of the other battalions the Black Watch was given permission to pull back, watchfully, towards Berbera.

Gina's brother was out flying, mightily impressed by his first sight of a battle on the ground beneath him, and ready to believe any tale however tall, of that epic day. 'A bitter battle', he wrote:

On the morning of the 17th our motor transport, lorries, tanks etc. were coming out like huge tortoises and in Indian file setting off down the white road towards Berbera. There was the strongest resistance to the repeated assaults of our white and coloured troops. From above we could see terrific artillery duels . . . Waves of Capronis and Savoias hammered their positions. After days of hopeless fighting our General Staff had outflanked them. Our coloured troops, drunk with spirits and the taste of blood, rushed their strongholds, massacring the Australian and Rhodesian troops in the service of the British Empire.

But those unmassacred—and the total casualties on the British side for the whole Somaliland episode were only 260 as against an Italian total of 2,029—got safely away, totally unharassed by the Italians. For General de Simone apparently never considered a proper harassing pursuit, though the road was open. A few hours after midnight even the rearguard, the Black Watch, had quietly embarked. Italian patrols did not even reach Berbera till forty-eight hours later. As a result they took no more prisoners and found far less booty and equipment than they had a right to expect. What they did find however was a warm welcome, for none of the Somalis were particularly sorry to see the British go. The Camel Corps had more or less dissolved. Just before leaving, the British military authorities had demonstrated their trust in their own appointed officials by tricking the Somali police in Berbera to parade in the square. There they disarmed them under the menacing threat of a Punjabi machine-gun detachment.

So British Somaliland was added, to the general satisfaction of its inhabitants, to the governorate of Harar and annexed by its conquerors to Italian East Africa.

The Italian press was triumphant. The British press, naturally, played the incident down and insisted on the worthlessness of this strip of desolate desert. In public, in the House of Commons, Churchill referred to a 'small but vexatious military episode'. But in Aden the loss came as a shock; and in London too where British public opinion had been led to expect that Ethiopia would fall like a ripe plum into British hands. Public opinion was not consoled by the sudden switch of the nationality of the hands into which the plums appeared to be falling.

The Italian generals involved drew, more quietly, their conclusions. General Nasi considered that they had underestimated the British frontal position, which was true; that the turning movements had been a success, which was not; and that the exercise had in any case been a logistic triumph, which is hardly the kind of pat that a Napoleon would have given himself on the back. General Trezzani, who had pointed out what a splendid attacking spirit the Shoan and Amhara troops, generally considered unreliable, had shown, noted also that white troops—i.e. the Blackshirts—were very inferior in operations of this sort to native troops, too delicate and demanding too many luxuries. He did not claim that the turning movements had been a success. On the contrary the fact that they had been a failure showed that forces even when involved in battle needed not merely prodding but orders from the centre—that is to say, from himself. Marshal Badoglio, more concerned with the general political picture, was happier. While the operation was in progress he had sent a bracing telegram to Nasi to urge him on, implying that peace in Europe was close. All that Italy needed was a clear victory over England to put her in a stronger position at the peace conference.

As for the Duke of Aosta, he had always been against the invasion, perhaps for suspect, almost pro-British, motives. He complained churlishly that valuable reserves of men and materials had been wasted on conquering a useless stretch of sand. This was a criticism that many Italians, particularly military men, were to voice. Their reasoning does not appear justified. Clearly the Sudan or Kenya would have been a greater prize. But either, if only because of the famous 'logistics', would have needed a greater effort; and for that greater effort the experience acquired during this invasion, indeed the mistakes made, would be invaluable. Furthermore, tactically it had removed a possible base for a possible attack. Administratively and ethnically it had rounded off a natural appendage of *AOI*. Strategically it was by no means useless. For the Italians now controlled a continuous stretch of coastline running from the Red Sea down into the Gulf of Aden. This could have been a threat, and indeed the British took it as a threat. One immediate effect—minor but expensive and irritating—was that when the Italians put out the light of the lighthouse on the tip of the horn of Africa, on Cape Guardafui, all British convoys had to go round to the east of Socotra, thus adding 200 miles to their trip and several days to their journey. This delay alone was a worthwhile gain for the Axis war effort.

The real benefit, however, was psychological. The Italian army had taken on, and beaten, the British army—as anyone capable of looking at an atlas could see. This had not been a minor skirmish for an obscure frontier post but a proper invasion in which the British had been hurled back to the sea, and had for the first time in the war lost one of their colonies to the enemy. Italians everywhere were exultant. Their mood was the mood of Gina's brother, as he flew back to the capital. 'Thus I left Hargeisha this flower of the earth, this garden of rich vegetation and springlike climate, which one day will undoubtedly be populated by our peasant families who will cultivate and exploit these immense tracts of land all around, after decades of British domination and injustice.'

As for Churchill, he might publicly play the episode down but in private he was more than vexed, he was furious. His first reaction was to demand that Godwin-Austen should be suspended, nothing less. A 'red-hot cable' went to Cairo. Wavell, in his reply, refused. 'I have no doubt that both General Godwin-Austen's recommendation and General Wilson's decision were correct,' he cabled. Then he added, 'a big butcher's bill is not necessarily evidence of good tactics.' It is said that this last phrase stirred Churchill to greater fury than his staff had ever seen before. But his continuing pressure for at least a military enquiry was in vain.

Wavell was just back in Cairo when these cables were exchanged. He had, while the battle at Tug Argan was being fought, been fighting a defensive battle of his own in London. Summoned by the War Cabinet, he had arrived on 8 August to be taken down the next day to Chequers and confronted for the first time by the man who wanted to judge his calibre, Mr. Churchill. This first meeting had gone only 'reasonably well'. Churchill was warm, exuberant, and a talker. He admired men like himself. Wavell was notorious for his silences, and ill at ease when asked to address civilians. Eden, who was trying to patch over the differences between the two men, became more and more depressed. Wavell was 'not a man to be drawn out or one to make a special effort to please'. There had been 'a very long and exhausting sitting . . . The truth was that Churchill never understood Wavell and Wavell never encouraged him to do so.' And by letter to the Prime Minister—for the meetings were punctuated by the exchange of letters and memoranda—Eden commented: 'Dill and I were very much perturbed at your judgment of Wavell.'

That judgment went from bad to worse. Wavell, in Churchill's opinion on the 12th, lacked mental vigour, lacked the resolve to overcome obstacles, tamely accepted a variety of circumstances in different theatres, and showed a lamentable inability to concentrate upon the decisive point. By the following day Wavell had become a 'good average colonel', who would make a 'good chairman of a Tory association'. Eden pointed out that he had been a scholar at Winchester, had, that is, succeeded in what is probably the most difficult intellectual test that any boy of thirteen in England is ever faced with. Therefore his air of lethargy was merely superficial. But unfortunately Churchill 'did not care much for Winchester or its products, except Sir Edward Grey'. Eden was miserable.

Wavell left London on the night of the 15th to reach Cairo just in time to learn of the loss of Somaliland, and to receive, after the outraged cable, an enormous Directive, prepared before the fall of Somaliland, on the whole conduct of the war in the Middle East. This was 'the first of a long and remarkable series of telegrams', as the Official History with tact puts it, 'from the Prime Minister to one or the other of his Commanders-in-Chief in the Middle East. . . . Some must have been much more welcome than others. They could have left no doubt that there was indeed a central direction of the war, and a vigorous one. There had been nothing like it since the time of the elder Pitt.'

The 'General Directive on the Middle East' resumed and expanded two previous mementoes that Churchill had addressed to Ismay 'for General Wavell' following their initial meeting at Chequers. In the first, Churchill had particularly stressed that large forces were standing useless and idle in Kenya—the South African brigade, 'probably as fine material as exists for warfare in spacious countries', two West African brigades 'brought at much inconvenience from the West Coast', and 'at least two KAR brigades', not to mention the 'East African settlers who should certainly amount to 2000 men.' Churchill proposed therefore that these East African settlers and the KAR should hold Kenya. Meanwhile the other three brigades should be sent by sea to reinforce Egypt and the Sudan where 'the fate of the Middle East, and much else, may be decided.'

In the second memento, two days later, the Prime Minister returned to the attack after what had evidently been a long session during which Wavell had contradicted him. Wavell's line was that the South African brigade was untrained and unready to go into action. Churchill refused to accept this without proof. 'Anyhow', he wrote—it was before the scuttle from Somaliland —'they are certainly good enough to fight Italians.' As for the two West African brigades, they should be sent immediately to Khartoum via Port Sudan. 'I do not know', he complained, 'why these two brigades were taken away from West Africa if the only use to be made of them was to garrison Kenya.' But he reserved his special wrath for the Kenya settlers. He had probably been informed that only a handful had enrolled, and that so far from being eager to fight they were far more interested in following in Nairobi the notorious *cause célèbre* of that summer: the trial of Sir Delves Broughton for the murder of the Earl of Errol. 'Let me have a return of the white settlers of military age in Kenya,' fulminated Churchill. 'Are we to believe that they have not formed local units for the defence of their own province? If so, the sooner they are made to realise their position the better.'

These ideas were expanded and placed in context in the nine points of the formidable General Directive which Wavell received on 22 August and to which he replied in four long cables. It is interesting to see, despite the 'vigorous central direction of the war', how little Churchill achieved. The South Africans were not sent up to Egypt. The Nigerian and the Gold Coast brigades did not move to the Sudan. The Kenya settlers were not conscripted. Despite Churchill's wishes, indeed orders, the situation remained basically unchanged and Wavell's disposition of his forces as scattered as ever.

Indeed the fall of British Somaliland did very little to stir the lethargy of Middle East Command. On 26 August Eden attempted to soothe Churchill with news of comforting reports from Wavell: above all, that there was no immediate danger as regards Egypt, though on the Sudanese border things were 'by no means as reassuring'. Wavell however had decided to reinforce the Sudan—not with the West Africans, though, but with a fresh Indian division, the Fifth. This news must have satisfied Churchill as regards the defence of the Sudan, though not as regards the over-defence of Kenya. Where both Eden and Wavell were totally wrong, though, was in believing that there was no threat to Egypt.

For on 13 September Marshal Graziani invaded Egypt with an enormous force: five divisions invading, two more in reserve, a tank group and 300 aircraft in support. It seems perfectly clear that this invasion was the direct result of the fall of British Somaliland. No doubt it had long been planned. But the plan was only put into execution—and that only after delays, for Mussolini had just as much difficulty in prodding or ordering a most reluctant Graziani into action as Churchill had had with Wavell —when the previous invasion had been successful: when, that is to say, it had been proved that Italians could outfight and out-general the British. This, the fourth invasion by an Italian army of a British territory, was by far the most important both in scale and objective. It should have been decisive. Had it been successful it would have proved Churchill right and condemned Wavell for ever. But Graziani, more tortoiselike even than De Simone, halted at Sidi Barrani and 'consolidated'. Thus he allowed his enemies, now seriously alarmed, the time to build up their strength. Once again, and this time on a decisive scale, an Italian commander failed to take a justified risk. It seems to me that, consciously or subconsciously, the memory of Adowa and of General Baratieri's end must have been preying on the minds of all Italian generals in Africa. Only this can explain their reluctance ever to move forward till they had overwhelming superiority totally assured and lines of communication totally safe. Only this can explain, and perhaps excuse, their inability, even then, to move forward at more than a snail's pace. So many missed opportunities cannot but have been pathological. They were certainly disastrous.

CHAPTER 21

TO FIND A LAWRENCE

IN Khartoum, in this August of 1940, the third month of the war, there was a constant flurry of visitors and of jumpy but rather pointless activity. Major Maurice of canoeing fame was put in charge of all Ethiopian volunteers. A Belgian cyclist lieutenant appeared demanding liaison after King Leopold's surrender, having apparently cycled over from the Congo. A French liaison officer was sent in more conveniently from the nearest French outpost in wavering French Equatorial Africa, Fort Lamy in Chad. The Governor of Darfur Province came with eager plans for forming a *Groupe Nomade* of Zaghawa Scouts to raid up into Libya. Hosts of Air Commodores and Major Generals passed through 'unfortunately omitting to bring their squadrons and divisions,' as Newbold commented in the midst of this 'bloody whirl', where he had to deal with 'incognito Emperors, Richard Dimbleby (who had diphtheria), weeping women of Italian internees, Yemini spies, and the Egyptian Consul at Addis who didn't get out and is now causing us great trouble as we have to arrange a flag of truce in the Gedaref district.'

He had the incognito Emperor to dinner, 'a very mild enlightened courteous person . . . but he didn't wear the famous cloak. He brought his beard though.' He even took his son the Duke of Harar to the movies to see the film of *The Mikado*; he told him he was Nanki-Poo; and the boy replied pertly that there were lots of Katishas in Ethiopia.

But the Emperor was tired and dejected. His initial enthusiasm and vigour had died away as he saw for himself how badly the war was going for the British and realized that even with the best of wills they were not in much of a position to help him. Sir Miles Lampson, down from Cairo, thought he was in need of diversion and suggested a trip to Kenya. But the Governor there, Sir Henry Monk-Mason-Moore, and General Dickinson turned down this suggestion emphatically. It seems they were already having trouble with Blatta Takele at Taveta Camp who at or around this time was put into detention, presumably for expressing anti-British feelings; and in their ignorance they probably felt that all Ethiopians, Emperors or Blattas, were much of a muchness: basically bandits—just *shifta* and trouble-makers. For it will already have become apparent how very ignorant of Ethiopia the Kenya officials were. This was partly for geographical and human reasons. With the wilds of the Northern Frontier District abutting into the almost equally wild southern regions of the Ethiopian Empire Kenya officials had never had any contact with the settled areas of Amhara rule or with the great Amhara nobles. It was partly also because the calibre of Kenya's colonial officials was much lower than that of the élite Sudan Civil Service.

In any case there was no visit for Haile Selassie to Kenya. In his depression the Emperor's thoughts turned more to his family than to his prospects. And he sent a touching telegram to Sir Sidney Barton in London: perhaps the only little document known where human loneliness and affection peeps out from under that calm political mask. 'No letters from the family', read the cable, 'not even Tsahai. Five letters remain unanswered. Very worried. Beg you for information and to give me news. Haile Emperor.'

On the other side of the border Italian intelligence officers gathered reports about the movements of British units and the rebel leaders. They calculated that about 5,000 rifles had been distributed at Gedaref and Gallabat. They knew that one-eyed Fitaurari Worku had received 350 and was planning to attack Major Parodi and his little garrison at the fort of Kwara. They kept a special watch on the man whom they apparently considered the most dangerous, Adane Makonnen: he had told his people they could go on cultivating till 5 September but must rally on 6 September, before Maskal. But what really relieved them was that there were no British officers with the rebels. 'It is amazing', wrote Colonel Talamonti, 'that the British have not yet found a Lawrence to send to Armachecho as the political effect on the populations of other areas such as Beghemder and Gojjam will be considerable.'

But the British were trying to remedy this deficiency.

'I met one of your octogenarian Ethiopian experts tottering around the bar the other day,' remarked a bright young staff officer in Cairo to a friend up from Khartoum. Certainly the British officers who were chosen to lead little groups into the Sudan at this time were, though spry, an odd choice as potential rebel-rousers. There were three of them, Colonel Dan Sandford aged fifty-eight, Major Count Bentinck a year his junior, and Lieutenant Arnold Wienholt aged sixty-three.

They were, all with different ranks—Commanding Officer, GSO I, Intelligence Officer—attached to Mission 101. But their ranks and titles in fact meant very little, since the intention was that they should operate separately. We know why Sandford was there. 'Rocky' Wienholt was an Australian, a volunteer who had five years earlier become transport officer with the Ethiopian Red Cross when the Italians invaded Ethiopia. He therefore 'knew the country'. As for Bentinck, he was a retired Coldstream Guards officer related to a Count Henry Bentinck who had been British Minister at Addis Ababa in the 1920s. Possibly this qualified him as a local expert.

The plan was that these three officers should cross the frontier into Frusci's territory, accompanied by small mule caravans, bearing rifles and money and promises in order to foment more active rebellion among the natives and consternation among the Italians. Bentinck and Wienholt would head separately through Armachecho. But for Sandford there was bigger game afoot.

For word had come from the most reputed of all the rebel leaders, Dejaz Mangasha Jimbirre of Gojjam. He wrote in response to the *Kaid*'s circular letter of 11 June. His own letter was encouraging and, what was rarer, practical. Mangasha Jimbirre announced that the Italians were sitting targets. They were, he claimed, isolated and scattered, controlled no more than a quarter of the country, and had never penetrated into Belaya which was hilly, full of narrow passes, and totally clear of opposition. Since he controlled Belaya, he controlled the gateway into Gojjam—that is to say, the whole long length of the frontier, about 200 miles, between the Italian garrisons at Metemma to the north and Gubba to the south. He stated that to drive the enemy out with—at last—the help of the English Government he needed not only rifles and ammunition but 100 machine-guns and 5 light pieces of artillery. He had therefore, as had been suggested, sent a caravan which was on its way to collect these modest items from the British. And he added a very concrete proposal himself: 'let someone important from the

English Government come to Belaya and choose out an aeroplane landing ground. Once that has been done no other difficulty remains.' He added one warning: to give no one rifles or ammunition without his signature, and to deal therefore only with his right-hand man, Fitaurari Taffere Zelleka of Belaya.

This letter was both encouraging and embarrassing. Encouraging in the general picture it gave of vast stretches of Gojjam totally free of Italians; embarrassing because of the demands it made and because of the implications of these demands. The British had no machine-guns or artillery to spare at all. Furthermore, the 'experts' could deduce that Mangasha Jimbirre wanted cannon as much to bolster up his own power and cow his neighbour and younger rival Negash Bezibeh as to attack the Italians.

As regards the aeroplane landing ground, this too was a most sensible request. Clearly the only practical way of supplying the rebels with arms and supplies would be by air. Yet though in Cairo Air Chief Marshal Longmore had promised air support for the rebellion, Sandford knew that for the foreseeable future there would only sporadically be planes available. At least, though, 'someone important from the English Government' could go to Belaya.

As another letter[1] came in from Fitaurari Taffere Zelleka to announce the approach of his caravan with 160 men, Gedaref hummed. Trevor Blackley organized the administrative side, with the help of the Eastern Arab Corps and under the protection of the garrison on the spot, the West Yorks. The Frontier Battalion was sent down to the other post from which caravans could be passed in and out, to Roseires on the Blue Nile.

Meanwhile there was a burst of activity in the south. Whalley, the enthusiastic but 'cold-douched' Captain Whalley, was at last sent down to the Boma plateau to join his fellow-plotter Cave *Bey* of the Equatorial Corps with orders to raise the South-West. They were to isolate Maji, cut the Gore–Jimma road, and, if possible, also the Jimma–Addis Ababa road. But he was not to be a Lawrence. He was given explicit instructions not to enter the

---

[1] Containing requests for *inter alia* rifles from new stock with numbers on the butt, five fountain-pens and ink, salt, corn and cotton cloth, bags, water-bottles, belts, greatcoats, rifle pull-throughs, oil bottles, and for himself officer-style coat and trousers, tailor-made to fit, good shoes, a goat hat, and a watch.

territory of Italian East Africa in person. It seems that General Platt was prepared to use him but would trust him only as far as he could control him.

On 6 August Sandford and his caravan set out from Gedaref: five Englishmen, five Ethiopians including Gabre Maskal, and fifty mule-men plus servants. A week later they crossed the frontier very cautiously twelve miles south of Metemma, flushing out two hostile Gumz tribesmen, and moved up on to the Kwara plateau, into the comparative safety of one-eyed Fitaurari Worku's territory. Their progress, inevitably, was very slow. Their next 'bound' was to the territory of another minor chieftain, Fitaurari Ayalew Makonnen of Mount Zibist. Half the party left for there with 20 mules, a wireless set, and 2,000 dollars at the end of August.

Meanwhile the other two officers had set out. Bentinck left Gedaref on the 21st, Wienholt passed by Gallabat ten days later. Bentinck had 24 muleteers, 5 Sudanese soldiers, nearly a thousand rifles, and a Sapper officer, Captain Foley; Wienholt, more modestly, half a dozen men and a few donkeys. By the first days of September, Italian military intelligence knew that there were British officers with wireless sets and rifles to distribute in Armachecho. They were much less alarmed, however, after their recent resounding successes. The British, they felt, 'might be thinking of some attempt to raise the morale of their men which must be low after the fall of Kassala and British Somaliland'.

For weeks no news of their progress or adventures was to come back to the Sudan. However, amidst considerable excitement the caravan from Mangasha Jimbirre did finally arrive, despite rumours that it had been attacked and destroyed on the way. A caravan from Negash Bezibeh was approaching too, and Mesfin Sileshi went out to escort it in to Gedaref.

There in the first week of September Haile Selassie had his diversion. He was flown down to Gedaref in Sudan's biggest and most impressive aeroplane, a Vickers Valentia, to meet Mangasha Jimbirre's men. With him came all his reconstituted court including two new and most welcome arrivals from Jerusalem, Dejaz Makonnen Endalkachew, the giant head of the Addisge clan, and his wife, Haile Selassie's beloved niece, Lilt Yashasha Worq. Trevor Blackley did him proud, setting up an embroidered tent on the Polo ground; and the West Yorks officers were introduced to an Emperor shaded in full ceremonial style by the State Umbrella and guarded by Mesfin Sileshi with a hide thong. They were photographed together. George Steer had the photograph copied and printed on leaflets later, adding an interesting caption to the effect that thus the Emperor could be seen in conference with high-ranking officers of the British General Staff.

What of the Italians all this time? Were they content just to sit gathering information about the British and trying to forecast what rebel leaders might do after the rains? The indications are that they were not. There are indications scattered here and there in letters and diaries and reports, that General Frusci was planning a major attack on Port Sudan and the Butana Bridge but was meeting with obstruction from the Duke of Aosta. The Duke put demands to Rome that he must have known to be impossible —for thousands of new tyres for lorries and scores more aircraft to be supplied before invasion could be contemplated. There were, furthermore, internal difficulties in Frusci's Sector due to the abrasive personality of General Tessitore, his Troop Commander. Tessitore was Military Governor of occupied Kassala, the base from which an invasion would have to be launched. 'There will be no peace here', wrote Talamonti in his personal diary, 'till either the Troop Command HQ is abolished or Tessitore "torpedoed".'

So the Italians' final chance of an easy triumph passed as really effective reinforcements reached the Sudan. General Heath's Fifth Indian Division came by train from Cairo to Khartoum. Though it was under strength (numbering only six infantry battalions and one cavalry regiment, Skinner's Horse), these were professional fighting troops: Baluchis and Pathans from the North-West Frontier, Garhwalis from the central hills, Sikhs from the Punjab, Hindi-speaking Mahrattas from the heart of the Mogul Empire, commanded by the experienced campaigning officers of the Indian Army.

To bring the Division up to its full strength the three British battalions already in the Sudan were incorporated. Thus three brigades were formed, each consisting of one British and two Indian battalions. The Sudanese MMG Companies at the Butana Bridge were combined with the motorized Skinner's Horse, formed into 'Gazelle Force' and placed under a dashing Indian Cavalry officer—Colonel Messervy.

But though the Italians were rightly worried about what was being hatched in the Butana Bridge area—which had miraculously survived their repeated bombing attacks—Khartoum was still very much on the defensive. In a private letter Newbold, officially optimistic, gave vent to his genuine feelings.

We are *not* having a purely defensive mentality . . . Platt is as aggressive as they make 'em, a regular little tiger, a fine upright fiery (often testy) capable soldier—but we must prevent them taking Gedaref or Tokar or Atbara and so making *our* advance more difficult when the time comes . . . Few people who urge the Kaid to Attack Now realize the strength and morale of the enemy. Wavell, H.E., Platt and I know too much about his numbers, armament, direction and supplies to do that but people outside our circle and in the Provinces who don't know the facts are inclined to say they are only Dagos and a tribal army of hearty Sudanese with spears and muskets will see them off. However, we *will* see them off and the Sudanese *will* play a large part. I don't know when. It takes time to assemble a sufficient force with transport signals, munitions supply etc. to crush an army of a quarter of a million even though morale is bad and the rebels are lifting their head . . .

In other words the British authorities exactly like the Italian authorities tended to overestimate their enemy's numbers, strategy, co-ordination, and general efficiency and insist on their own 'logistic' difficulties as a pretext for putting off aggressive action. Yet by September the strategic position in the Sudan had dramatically improved.

French Equatorial Africa rallied to De Gaulle; and the Belgian Congo appeared to be following the trend.[1] This meant that a whole wide arc of possibly hostile territories on the Sudan border were now friendly, a great worry removed. It meant furthermore that, logistically, the overland flying route from West Africa via Takoredi was now open for supplies and reinforcements. It meant, strategically, that the Italians in Libya had now to face a serious if minor threat from their south, thereby reducing the danger of their attacking the Sudan. It meant furthermore hopes and promises of future reinforcements of French and Belgian troops for the eventual attack on Ethiopia.

All this however was long-term. In the short term there was

---

[1] Newbold sent a case of champagne to M. Eboué the Governor of Chad and the first to rally to De Gaulle. 'It's fine to see a black man have the courage,' he wrote to his mother.

news from across the border, from the trio of potential 'Lawrences'; some good, some tragic, some almost farcical.

The good news came from Sandford. On 15 September Gabre Maskal set up his wireless high on Mount Zibist to announce that the second 'bound' had been successfully accomplished, that they were with Fitaurari Ayelew Makonnen and had received a letter from the great Dejaz Mangasha Jimbirre fixing a rendezvous. And also that Captain Critchley, Sandford's second-in-command, had been sent aside for a three weeks' excursion to recce Mount Belaya and meet Fitaurari Taffere Zelleka.

The next morning the party had their first brush with the opposition, a very close shave. A plane flew low over Mount Zibist at dawn and spotted them. At 10 o'clock Getahun Tessema out on sentry duty fired a warning round: Italian troops were approaching. In the ensuing panic they ran for shelter in all directions, abandoning their mules and the chests of money on them; slithering down the mountainside to hide in caves hundreds of feet below as the Italian troops tossed hand grenades after them and burnt Ayalew Makonnen's village. But fortunately for Mission 101 the pursuit was called off that afternoon; Sandford and his companions crept back cautiously and were guided to where Ayalew Makonnen was hiding.

Of 'Rocky' Wienholt nothing had been heard since 10 September. Next day armed peasants saw a small caravan with a white man moving thirty miles south of Metemma. They reported it to the nearest *banda* outpost. The *banda* attacked, and the party fled. They believed that the white man was wounded, and they were able to identify him as Wienholt because they captured his correspondence.

In Gedaref, Trevor Blackley waited anxiously for news. Finally one of Wienholt's servants came back, with a confused story. The gist of it, however, was clear. Wienholt was dead. Exactly how and where he died and where, if at all, he was buried neither the British nor the Italians ever learnt. When Bentinck, weeks later, learnt of his death, he wrote indignantly in his diary: 'He was over sixty and was left to scramble after the other columns . . . He could speak neither Amharic nor Arabic. It seems a waste of a good life.'

As for Bentinck, he had been more fortunate, in a sense. The only representative of the enemy he had seen had been Wubneh

Amoraw's captured Italian cook. But to his annoyance no sooner had the Ethiopian with him, Wolde Giorgis, produced Haile Selassie's *Awaj* than both Wubneh Amoraw and Ayane Chekol announced that they were off to Khartoum to visit their Emperor. And in the weeks that followed Bentinck found the same story repeated whenever he met an important chief. 'He also to my horror wanted to go to Khartoum!'—despite his protests that this was absurd; for 'How can I carry out my mission if you're away?' When *Maskal* came, it found Bentinck staying disconsolately with Abba Qirqos the priest and watching disapprovingly the leaderless rebels firing off their new rifles and wasting the ammunition he had brought. He suspected moreover that they had been selling their old, captured rifles back to the Italians.

But at Khartoum there was a large and moderately splendid gathering for *Maskal* when the chiefs from Armachecho had arrived: the first public occasion of happiness that Haile Selassie had had since leaving England. The ceremony was watched by Newbold, who wrote to his mother

I went to attend . . . his first review of his men—a religious service, not just a parade, with his own priests and officers. It was rather a ragged show, poor refugees and some troops of his own, a handful of officers, but they marched past, and he smiled on them and he kissed the Cross which was held by the Ethiopian bishop. I sat next to him, and I wonder what thoughts passed through his mind at the sight of this faithful remnant.

About 30 of us went, representatives of the Council, the Army, the RAF, and as we went out he whispered to me: I am very touched at you all coming on a hot afternoon to support me. It may be that his men will do what Garibaldi's ragged shirted men did. Lots of tyrannies have been overthrown by men like this.

So at long last the Emperor, 'the little man' as the British half-affectionately called him, was publicly, almost emotionally acknowledged by officialdom in Khartoum.

Not so very far away from Bentinck, at Bahr Dar on the shores of Lake Tana where he had just arrived that day, Gina's brother was also watching the *Maskal* celebrations, though with much less sympathy and with a far more critical eye than Newbold.

The country is strewn with *tukuls* where the natives live in a primitive state. It is strange that during 4 years of Italian occupation we have been unable to inculcate in these people some trace of civilization. They live trading cattle, snake skins, crocodile skins and others. Religion is predominantly Coptic with some Muslims. Today 27 September is the Coptic feast of Maskal and from the nearby *tukuls* come their strident and guttural songs accompanied by the beating of tom-toms. Towards dusk they come to the camp around the *tinish robilano* (little planes) doing their dances and fantastic movements, all very strange and primitive. Then a group of stinking natives gets hold of each one of us by surprise and with their arms outstretched throw us high into the air sometimes to a dangerous height, catching us and throwing us again until we promise to give them *falas*. It is their custom and it is better to humour them . . . After dinner we drink to the next victories that we wish ourselves.

Yet Gina's brother, though confident and hopeful, was depressed both by the lack of white women—only one 'represents the female sex among the Italians'—and, more particularly, by his living conditions. The airmen had to live within one square kilometre bounded by wire-netting interspersed with sentry posts and continually patrolled. Why? He gives the answer, disconsolately, in his entry for the same day.

The Gojjam is populated exclusively by rebels, now full of hate and rancour towards the Italians, perhaps more than in 1936 when Starace occupied Gondar, Tana and the surrounding districts. And here, Bahr Dar, is surrounded by *shifta bande* consolidated by Mangasha; they once submitted but are now in open revolt again. Thus our garrison and also the others at Dangila, Burie, Engiabara, Debra Markos, etc. may at any moment be subjected to assaults by the rebels who would be confronted with strongholds supplied with hundreds and hundreds of rifles and machine-guns. No 13 Bomber Squadron stationed here operates continuously and indefatigably on these rebels, smashing up their inhabited centres, markets, herds of cattle, and so on.

No wonder Mangasha and Fitaurari Taffere Zelleka wanted above all else the appearance of British planes in the sky and the bombing of precisely the strongholds mentioned. But no wonder, either, that in these conditions high Italian commanders were following with increasing anxiety the growing power of Mangasha Jimbirre as the caravans wound their way out from the Sudan towards his lands.

With all these supplies and arms *en route*—and the news of real British help at last was known all over western Gojjam—more and more Gojjamis started rallying to Mangasha's power. The news had also come that white men were there, with a wireless.

For Sandford and his party, escorted by Fitaurari Ayalew Makonnen and two hundred men, had at last succeeded in reaching the great leader's territory in the hills around Dangila.

The pro-Italians, the leaders of irregular *bande* such as Dejaz Aberra Imam, were despondent. The Italians had to act. As Sandford and his party moved south to visit Dejaz Negash Bezibeh, Mangasha's rival, near Burie, three battalions were sent up from Burie north to Dangila. When these arrived Torelli launched an attack into the hills.

This action was a brilliant success. Torelli was one of the boldest of the Italian commanders and his brigade, the XXII, were experienced and totally loyal.[1] Not only did he send Mangasha Jimbirre's men running, after killing many of them, and so prove to the wavering that the Italians still had teeth, he also captured the Dejaz's son. The son confirmed the presence of Englishmen with his father, of whom the chief was Mr. Room.

'Mr. Room' meanwhile—the Italians would have been alarmed to know it was Sandford, on whom they had built up a large file—was heading back with his party towards a very shaken Mangasha. The Dejaz's discomfiture had from their point of view a positive aspect: for with his overweening confidence shaken he was ready at long last to patch up his quarrel with his rival Negash. Azaz Kebbede Tessema, of Sandford's party, presided over the negotiations. Though he was slow and too 'old-school' for Sandford's taste, he was the real politician of the party, and he was successful. On 24 October Negash and Mangasha swore a pact to leave all their disputes in abeyance to be settled only when the Emperor returned; from that day onwards to cease interfering in each other's territory; and not to accept any man who deserted the one to join the other. This was considered a great success. When the further good news came that British planes *had* appeared and *had* bombed Engiabara and Bahr Dar there was great rejoicing.

Next day they held a council of war. Gabre Maskal announced that yet another caravan was about to leave from Gedaref, according to radio messages received by him. It would be larger and better, escorted by Mesfin Sileshi and one hundred of his

---

[1] It was said that he never set foot out of camp with less than a thousand men. The British took this, wrongly, as a sign of cowardice. On the contrary it was a habit that gave Torelli great prestige with the population, accustomed to judge all great men by the number of their armed retainers.

men. This too was excellent news. The two Dejaz demanded mortars since there was no hope of any artillery. Sandford agreed with them that with mortars they could capture all but the strongest of the Italian positions, all the forts and outposts outside the garrison towns. Getahun Tessema, also of Sandford's party, reported that he now had agents inside all Italian forts and garrison towns, and had set up a messenger system to cover all western Gojjam. It ended with Sandford despatching envoys far and wide with optimistic instructions to raise the Galla and the Wollo and to contact Ras Abebe Aregai. He himself prepared to move on into eastern Gojjam to contact the leaders there. But first he agreed to send back to Khartoum an urgent request for money. For the two Dejaz argued that only by *paying* their men could they ensure immediate obedience to their orders, and avoid time-wasting discussions of every proposal. It is a difficult business, arranging a revolt. But it looked as if the armed truce in Gojjam was over. It seemed that under the British aegis the rebellion was at last about to turn into a revolt.

The Italians certainly feared this to be so. By the end of September 2,000 single-shot rifles, 2,195 magazine rifles and 676,000 rounds had been distributed from the Sudan to the rebels. The only way to stop the revolt was to liquidate the supply routes and to stop the caravans. But the only really satisfactory way of liquidating the supply routes was to eliminate the bases from which the caravans set out: Gedaref and Roseires.

There seem indeed to have been Italian plans for a move against Gedaref. But Colonel Castagnola at Metemma, the conqueror of Gallabat, had become extremely nervous. He was sending in reports of thousands and thousands of rebels massing to attack him. However the date for the feared attack passed harmlessly, and from Gondar a highly annoyed General Martini called for a confidential report on the nervy Colonel. Meanwhile, the High Command in Addis Ababa, apparently disgusted by the inability shown in Frusci's Sector to arrange an attack on Gedaref, decided to mount their own centrally-controlled operation—against Roseires.

They planned their thrust to go in from the south of the Blue Nile; and having no faith at all in General Gazzera, the Sector Commander, who had displayed almost total inactivity, did not even consult him or his local divisional commander. They sent down from Shoa to Asosa, the base for the attack, two units: Prina's excellent XI Brigade, and one of the most experienced of the *banda* groups, Rolle's 1300 men. The plan was for the *bande* to make a probing attack and spy out the land. Then the regular troops of the Brigade would launch the decisive assault.

From the British point of view it was a sudden, dangerous, and well-prepared move: sudden because they had not been expecting a thrust through the difficult country south of the Blue Nile, well-prepared because it now seemed obvious that three months earlier the Italians had overrun Kurmuk precisely to prepare for this, and dangerous because the path of the invasion lay through the tribal lands of the Watawit who hated the British. It seemed therefore that the Italians might, stealing a leaf out of the British book, be intending to arm the tribesmen and raise a revolt. At the same time Hancock, Roseires's District Commissioner, feared a simultaneous attack from Major Quigini, the Italian commander at Gubba, on the other bank of the Nile.

Hancock was rightly worried. The caravan for Fitaurari Taffere Zelleka had only just moved off and could be intercepted and cut up, with all the unforeseeable consequences that the report of such a disaster would have on the Gojjam rebellion. Moreover, there was only Boustead Bey's Frontier Battallion and a few police to defend Roseires, and it sounded as if the Italians were attacking, as they had always done before, in overwhelming strength. And where were reinforcements to come from when Gedaref was perhaps equally threatened and it would take days to send troops down from Khartoum? It looked as if Roseires, like Kassala and Gallabat before it, was bound to fall. And from Khartoum it looked as if the Italians were at last launching their long-expected post-rains offensive. At Gedaref and Port Sudan and the Butana Bridge the defenders were put on the alert and warned that this time the real invasion was starting.

In the Engessana Hills the Wisko D.C. burnt his papers and abandoned his home as the invaders advanced up the dried riverbed of the Khor Offat. But at Roseires the nonchalant Boustead *Bey* showed a sudden spurt of activity, as he was always to do in times of real crisis. He hired ten broken-down market lorries from Wad Medhani and drove off, ignoring cries of alarm from Khartoum, to meet and attempt to halt the invaders, himself leading his now-mechanized and mobile men in his own little brown box-car.

Rolle and his irregulars were used to fighting in the mountain highlands and living off the land. They crossed the frontier north-east of Kurmuk with only four days' rations, but by the time they reached Wisko the *banda* was nearly starving and its mules were dying of thirst. The invaders could not go on. They turned tail. Ten days after Rolle's force had crossed the frontier, it was back again, having lost fifty-two men and all its animals. But the pursuit by a jubilant Frontier Battalion had ground to a halt. Boustead's box-car broke down first, and one by one the market lorries followed suit. The only casualty on the Sudanese side was a tribesman of the peace-loving Engessana who had seen one of the red and black Italian grenades lying by the roadside and, apparently mistaking it for a money-box, had attempted to chop it in two.

To General Gazzera's quiet satisfaction the XI Brigade and the now-discredited *bande* were pulled back to Shoa. This was the first and last attempt by General Trezzani to put into practice the principle he thought he had learnt from the Somaliland invasion and to direct an operation on the frontier from the distant centre. It was the first failure of the Italians; and therefore it had results out of all proportion to its importance. Khartoum breathed again, realizing that this had been an isolated thrust, not the first forward move in a co-ordinated campaign. The British authorities began seriously to consider going over to the offensive.

It was at this happy moment that the Secretary of State for War, Mr. Eden, flew into Khartoum. He arrived on the evening of 28 October to dine at the Palace—with unnervingly clear ideas, encouraged by the reports of the growing revolt within Ethiopia. He showed himself very anxious that the regular British forces should actually win a battle and so improve morale throughout the whole Middle East. For nowhere as yet had the British successfully got to grips with the Italians. In all the encounters so far they had been defeated. Even Rolle's recent incursion into the Sudan had been turned back not by British troops but by physical difficulties. Furthermore there were odd rumours circulating about the Mahdi's son and his contacts with the Egyptian troops still in the Sudan. The Italians had got wind of these stories and believed that the loyalty of the *Anwar* to the British was not what it had seemed to be, and that old memories of the *jihad* and of the dervishes following behind the Green Crescent were stirring in local breasts.

'Politically the whole situation here,' Eden had cabled to Churchill from Cairo, 'would be immeasurably improved if we were able to gain some military success.' Having no magic powers of foresight, he predictably enough believed that this first success could, would, and should be gained against the Italians in Ethiopia. He mentioned to Churchill the plans that were being prepared by the Sudan Command for the recapture of Kassala.

He had therefore called a full-scale conference in Khartoum. General Wavell had come with him from Cairo. General Platt was there of course but also General Dickinson from Kenya, and a General Cunningham, brother of Admiral Cunningham at Alexandria, who was soon going to replace Dickinson as GOC East Africa. There was General Hudleston too, the new Governor-General and host, and two more Generals, General Smuts and his Chief of Staff General Rynevald. For the South African Prime Minister had flown up specially from Cape Town, just for the meeting.

The *Kaid* set the ball rolling. Platt told the gathering that as he had now 28,000 men plus some artillery and a few tanks, he was confident that he could repel an invasion from Kassala. This was not at all the sort of thing that Eden had hoped for. He had been expecting to hear plans for attacking Kassala, not fears of being attacked from it. He listened therefore all the more eagerly to a suggestion from Smuts for attacking from Kenya into Jubaland and capturing the little port of Kismayu. Smuts too needed a military success in which South African troops would be used to counter the pro-German propaganda of his political rivals at home. Eden knew this, and he believed too that the capture of Kismayu would go some way to satisfying Churchill. It was agreed that Smuts and Cunningham should fly off next day to Kenya to see whether Kismayu could be captured before the rains.

It was very hot that night. They slept on the roof of the Palace. Next morning Smuts and Cunningham flew away; and Hudleston far from well, retired to bed with lumbago. In the early afternoon Eden with Platt inspected the garrison at Khartoum. He was upset by the state of the West Yorks, who were short of officers and under-strength in men, but very much approved of the three MMG Companies of the Sudan Defence

Force with their home-made armoured cars, which were 'ideal for the country'. He noticed, though, 'a surprising reluctance to offend Mussolini and later a difficulty in finding the right type of Arabic-speaking officer'.

In the late afternoon Eden, with Wavell, called on Haile Selassie. It was indeed Haile Selassie who once again had been largely responsible for causing a conference to be called. For, stimulated by the news of Sandford's success and by the *Maskal* celebrations which traditionally marked in Ethiopia the opening of the fighting season, Haile Selassie had suddenly requested an immediate Treaty of Alliance and Friendship and his own recognition as an independent sovereign.

This was a demand which raised the whole question of Ethiopia's future regime. It put, and it was intended to put, the British Government in an awkward spot. The Foreign Office had not yet made up its mind; and there were both in British Africa and in London various schools of thought. At any rate the Emperor would have to be placated.

But Eden, who was already convinced, and Wavell, who was less so, listened to Haile Selassie's complaints with sympathy. Eden was infuriated to learn how little, still, the *Kaid* had done to help and indeed how little interest any high officials in the Sudan had shown in the rebels, and the refugees, or even in Mission 101.

A stormy meeting inevitably followed—though not until after dinner. Both Eden and Wavell, the Secretary of State for War and the General Officer Commander-in-Chief, with the full weight of their combined authority criticized Platt and his staff officers for their lethargy, incompetence, and general lack of aid to the rebels in Ethiopia and to the Ethiopians in the Sudan. 'There are times when it does little good to sit down to a pleasant evening party,' observed Eden; and he, normally so polite, deliberately made himself offensive. The *Kaid*, for once, had to control his testiness and accept criticism in silence. Haile Selassie, had he been there, would have been delighted.

Next day Eden flew off at dawn to visit first the Butana Bridge, then the threatened outpost at Gedaref. There were three sad sights at Gedaref. Firstly the aerodrome, where the charred remains of a number of aircraft—8 Wellesleys and 2 Vincents —shot down by Italian fighters formed a 'doleful framework'. Secondly some of the British gunners, looking very sorry for themselves, all with arms and knees in bandages—'they had been pricked by a poisonous thorn that abounds in these parts'. And thirdly, another and more distinguished victim of an accident, Major-General Heath, commander of the Indian Division 'who, poor man, had lately smashed himself up by driving his car into a camel at night.'

But Eden liked Heath: 'big, pondéré, and, I should think, sound'. He briefly inspected the Essex—'from what I saw I should judge a good battalion' (an unfortunate observation). He then flew back to Khartoum to learn that Smuts and Cunningham in Kenya had approved proposals for an attack on Kismayu and the River Juba early the following year.

Next day Eden was out again, to inspect the Worcesters at Port Sudan, who 'seemed fairly cheerful'. He flew back to Khartoum to work on a full report, which was endorsed by Platt. And the following day, 1 November, he flew out to Wadi-Halfa en route for Cairo after a four-day visit during which misunderstandings had been cleared up, laggards upbraided, and certain precise plans made. Before leaving Gedaref he had met one of Heath's Indian Army brigadiers. 'Well goodbye Brigadier', he had said holding out his hand, 'thanks for your hospitality and for showing me round, and'—with an amused twinkle in his eye—'the best of luck on Wednesday.'

CHAPTER 22

FAILURE AT GALLABAT

EDEN had obtained his wish. There was, after all, to be an immediate military operation. The objective, however, was not the recapture of Kassala but, much more modestly, of Gallabat —the frontier post from which the *Bimbashis* of the Eastern Arab Corps had been ejected.

The brigadier whose hand Eden had shaken at Gedaref and who had been grimly determined not to let even his War Minister know about 'Wednesday' was Brigadier Slim, commanding the 10th Indian Infantry Brigade. Slim was a professional soldier with a sense of humour and humanity, a 'bad-tempered little terrier'. The attack on Gallabat was to be his first active operation as commander of a Brigade. He was determined it should be a success, and it looked as if it would be. It had in fact been prepared by Eden and accepted by the assembled generals at Khartoum. Though they had no idea how nervous Colonel Castagnola was, they knew that there was little to fear from him. He had made no move forward since July, and had not launched the expected attack towards Gedaref. If then Metemma was not attacking towards Gedaref, let Gedaref attack towards Metemma! That was why General Heath had been, despite his camel car collision, down at Gedaref to inspect the ground and lay his plans, and why Slim and his brigade had been quietly moving down to join the highly impressed amateurs, like Thesiger and Hanks, on the spot. But when the decision was finally taken, the keynote was secrecy. For the infantry forces would be fairly evenly balanced: three battalions against three battalions.

Colonel Castagnola whatever his other failings had certainly not been idle as regards defence. He had surrounded the captured fort at Gallabat with a very stout wall and a barbed wire entanglement, six hundred yards long and four hundred yards wide; and he had cleared the scrub and bush all around to give a clear field of fire. Metemma on the Italian side of the frontier was even more formidably defended. Two separate deep wire entanglements encircled the whole area, inside which the buildings were fortified. The road running across the *Khor* linking Metemma to Gallabat was also heavily wired on both sides.

It would have been useless to attack these positions with mere infantry, as the rebels had found out in similar attacks on less well-fortified posts inside Gojjam. Ideally, artillery was needed to break down the fortifications and tanks were needed to break through the barbed wire and the walls. Then and only then could the infantry pour through the gaps that the armour had made. Slim in fact had artillery and tanks—a regiment of artillery and a squadron of tanks, both light and heavy. It was these 'secret weapons' whose presence had to be concealed from the Italians, and it was for this reason that there were such strict security precautions at Gedaref. Without the tanks and the artillery an attack on Gallabat and Metemma could not succeed. With them it seemed certain to.

Slim slowly moved his dumps of artillery shells forward by night to the Khor el Otrub. His tank crews removed their conspicuous black berets lest these should be spotted by an Italian spy and the presence of the tanks guessed at. General Heath approved and added his own suggestion for increasing confusion and alarm among the enemy—that in future everyone should refer not to the Fifth Indian Division but to Five Indian Divisions and so play up to the by-now recognized tendency of Italian military intelligence to exaggerate the numbers of enemy facing them.

Slim planned to seize Gallabat by a surprise attack at dawn, then to push the Essex through for a tank-led assault on the main position at Metemma. This was to be a very different thing from *Bimbashi* Thesiger and a few rebels loosing-off shots from the hills. It was intended to be a highly-organized military operation complete with air support, the first the British had ever attempted against the Italians. Nothing was left unplanned to secure its success. Once that success was achieved, not only would the British have a feat of arms to boast of and the Italians be correspondingly cast down, but the best and by far the most convenient of the caravan routes from the Sudan to Gojjam and Armachecho would be opened up. Caravans to the rebels—or rather to the Patriots as they were now to be called[1]—could then be slipped in and out with speed and safety.

The attack had been planned for the morning of 8 November; but news came that reinforcements for the Italian garrison were on their way from Gondar. It was put forward to the morning of the 6th.

Slim slept at his command post, a small hill in front of the Khor el Otrub, one-and-a-half miles from Gallabat. In the darkness before dawn he was awakened by his Garhwali orderly with the traditional cup of tea.

To the east the hills behind Gallabat, Jebel Negus and Jebel Mariam Waha, began to show up as dark and distant silhouettes against the first pale lemon wash of sunrise. Gently, the lemon deepened to gold and changed to soft luminous blue, but the hill of Gallabat remained invisible, sunk in the blackness of the further hills.

So Slim wrote afterwards. He was an ordinary army officer. But like the best, like Wavell too, he had a streak of poetry in him and appreciated, especially in the setting of this epic land, both the lyric and the tragic—and indeed as was to become clear, the ironic elements of war.

A small group of officers had gathered at the command post. Slatter, the RAF commander, looked at his watch. 'They ought to be over in eight minutes from now,' he said. Colonel Welcher of the artillery, a great telescope hanging from one shoulder, a six-foot spear grasped in his hand, gave orders for the camouflage nets to be thrown off the guns. Sure enough there was a hum from the west and as the bombers and and fighters went in, the guns opened fire for the first time on the Sudanese front. As the planes flew away signalling that a direct hit had been scored on the Metemma wireless station the tanks lumbered towards Gallabat hill and from the ground rose lines of slouch-hatted figures, the Garhwali infantry. As they vanished into the smoke surrounding Gallabat, the artillery ranged further forward on to Metemma. When the din and the clamour had died down, Verey lights rose smokily to burst into green and red over Gallabat fort. This was the success signal. The British had retaken Gallabat.

Slim and his staff drove forward towards the captured fort, to

---

[1] This change of name from 'rebels' to 'patriots' was on Eden's and Wavell's instructions, following Haile Selassie's request. But in Kenya, typically enough, the colonial authorities still went on calling them *Shifta*, unlike the chastened Platt.

be halted by a small but well-laid minefield. At this point firing flared up again all around Gallabat, making them fear that the success signal had been premature. But they finally reached the forward slope of Gallabat hill and roared up through gaps in the wire and the wall obviously torn by a tank, only to come face to face with an Italian officer resplendent in red and gold.

'A Wop general!' cried Welcher.

Highly excited, drawing their revolvers, the Brigadier and the Colonel leapt from the truck. The Italian wisely raised his hands. He was young and fresh-faced. Slim could not help thinking that he looked rather youthful for a general. 'I surrender,' he said in good English. 'I am Capitano in the colonial battalion.' Somewhat crestfallen, Slim asked him where his commanding officer was. 'In Metemma by now,' the Capitano answered bitterly. 'As soon as your bombardment started he rushed out crying, "To the walls, to the walls" and disappeared towards the boundary *khor*. He has not been seen since!'

So the 27th had lost the Fort which they had captured so easily a few months before from *Bimbashis* Thesiger and Hanks; but only, as it were, according to plan. For the Italians had known that an attack was coming. As early as 3 November the airmen at Gondar had been alerted, and in that sense the British attempts at secrecy had failed. But what the Italians had not been expecting were the tanks and the artillery. These had torn through their defences and caused them many casualties. Yet even so the garrison had only been obeying orders when they pulled back to Metemma. For the Italian plan had been to evacuate Gallabat if it was attacked in strength, but then to counter-attack swiftly with the reinforcements concentrated in Metemma—the 25th and the 77th and a company of the Savoy machine-gunners—before the British had had time to reorganize. They had in fact very rapidly put in this counter-attack despite the inevitable confusion caused by the shelling of Metemma. But it had failed, driven back by the efficient Garhwalis, during the minutes when Slim and his staff had been halted by the little minefield.

'I don't think these Wops will try again in a hurry', said the Colonel of the Garhwalis to Brigadier Slim, who had nearly been picked off moments earlier by a Savoy machine-gunner. The two of them were crouching behind an embrasure in the eastern wall of Gallabat, looking out at their next objective, Metemma. Some of the *tukuls* were burning fiercely but Metemma's buildings seemed intact and the formidable wire barriers were unbroken. This was where the tanks would have to break in first.

There had been a lot of trouble in getting these tanks. Tanks after Dunkirk were in the British Army worth almost their weight in gold and were just as carefully hoarded—particularly the heavy 'I' tanks, known as the Matildas, whose armour was so thick that no known Italian anti-tank gun could penetrate it. They were therefore the ultimate weapon—invincible. And Slim had six of them. Or rather, had had. For the squadron leader (of B Squadron, the 6th Royal Tank Regiment) came across with a glum face to report that five of his six Matildas and four of his six light tanks were out of action.

For the Matildas though invincible were not, as Slim now learnt to his enormous dismay, unstoppable. Their caterpillar tracks made out of plates of steel joined by tough rubber had been broken by the glass-sharp, ice-hard volcanic trachyte rocks of Gallabat hill. This was the first disaster. The second had been more tragic. As they went into action, the tank crews had replaced their traditional black berets; when their tanks had broken down, the crews had got out to inspect the damage. Several of them had, because of the berets, been mistaken for Italians and killed or wounded by the Garhwalis. Slim could hardly have been expected to foresee this double disaster but he had to take it into account. He decided, reluctantly, to postpone the second phase of his attack till late afternoon. The Essex were arriving at Gallabat to take up position. But now, in lieu of a sudden tank attack, a prolonged artillery barrage would have to be laid on to break the two belts of wire around Metemma.

Activity died down in the heat of the day. Slim went back to his command post one-and-a-half miles west of Gallabat to prepare for the afternoon's battle. At about three o'clock, as he was talking on the field telephone, he heard the drone of aeroplanes, coming this time from the east. It was a large force, from the bases at Gondar and Bahr Dar, about ten bombers which dropped stick after stick of bombs on Gallabat, escorted by nearly twenty fighters including, inevitably, Gina's brother. 'These are days of real warfare,' he noted in his diary. At long last he had his revenge[1] and his victory. Two lone Gloucester Gladiators came

---

[1] Twice he had been bombed at Bahr Dar. But, as always, his bitterness was tempered by the beauty of the scene, a beauty that he was unable not to appreciate, almost to admire. The first time was at night. 'The RAF, malignant, doesn't wish to

flying out to intercept the raiders, and one of them Gina's brother shot down, his sights fixed on the pilot in the cockpit. The other crashed as he watched.

This was absolutely contrary to Air Commodore Slatter's plan, which had been to attack—if at all—only in strength. Nevertheless more planes in driblets came flying out from the airstrip at Gedaref only to be picked off by the Italian fighters one by one as they appeared. Among the pilots killed was the leader of the newly-arrived South African fighter squadron. It was a great day for General Pinna and his air force. They almost eliminated the few planes still in the Sudan. They also decided the battle.

When the bombing and the dogfights stopped, Slim set off for Gallabat again to see how the Essex and the Garhwali had come through it. He was not unduly alarmed because he imagined his infantry would be at least partially dug in. Not far outside Gallabat, on the track, a traffic control post had been set up. As Slim reached it, he was surprised to see the Baluchi officer in charge running down the hill.

'British soldiers from Gallabat', called out the Baluchi, 'are driving through my post, shouting that the enemy are coming and that the order is to retire. We cannot stop them: they drive fast at anyone who tries!'

'Nonsense,' said Slim, 'they must be just empties coming back to refill. You have misunderstood what they said.'

The *Jemadar* shook his head.

'Look, Sahib.'

Slim looked. Two trucks filled with gesticulating British soldiers were crashing down the hill very fast, refusing to stop,

spare even this corner of Africa; and this morning at 03.45 woke the sleepers with a start and dropped like a cold shower nearly 10 bombs, shining like silver in the moon's reflection.' So was the next. 'We were awakened by sounds of rifle fire which gave the alarm. The moon is accomplice to the plane as it goes buzzing round and round above us. This is truly a real Englishman, the pilot at the controls; he doesn't appear to be in a hurry; calm, calculating, he goes round and round above us poor inert people then he goes off only to return in a few minutes to drop a flare which seems suspended in the air, illuminating the whole target area with the light of day. He makes repeated runs, dropping one bomb at a time, just like at Assab. He is met with string bursts of machine-gun fire, and we could see the tracer bullets crossing each other from different parts of the camp as they missed their target, not quite visible. He drops a few incendiaries which spray us with some choking stuff, and gradually we revive in the black silence which follows.'

despite frantic signals. Then came a third and a fourth, the soldiers yelling as they drove by: 'The enemy are coming!'

Alone, with only a walking stick as a weapon, in a furious temper, Slim marched up the road towards the fort. He met and stopped a straggling group of men walking down, all but one, he noticed, with their rifles. They told a rambling, confused story about how the Italians had retaken the fort with great slaughter. They had resisted desperately and were probably the sole survivors of their battalion. Their colonel had been killed. And, one of them rashly added, 'The Brigadier's killed too!' Slim managed to convince them that this last item was incorrect. He forced them to retrace their steps, picking up *en route* other stragglers including a group with an officer of the Essex, an apparition which reduced him to spluttering fury.

The Essex had panicked. There had been no desperate stands and no great slaughter for the simple reason that the Italians had not only not recaptured the fort, they had not made a move towards it out of Metemma. With splinters bouncing and ricocheting off the hard rock, and the troops unable, obviously, to dig trenches, the bombs had been particularly terrifying. But the casualties had not been high—in the end the Essex lost only 3 killed and 2 wounded. The incident that had touched the panic off had been a direct hit on an ammunition dump near the reserve company. Panic had spread. Men of the Essex had run down the hill, piled into the vehicles at its foot, and fled.

It took until dark to restore order. Obviously the assault on Metemma was off, at least for the moment. For not only were the remainder of the Essex listless and jumpy but it became clear that the tanks could not be repaired. Slim judged the Essex useless for an assault. His third battalion, the Baluchis, up to now held in reserve, would have to be moved forward to replace them. All this meant postponing any possible attack till the following day.

But Gallabat was bombed that evening and again at dawn the following morning, causing many dead among the Garhwali. Furthermore, the Essex—what remained of them—panicked again when the Italians fired smoke shells from Metemma. The cry of 'Gas!' went up. General Heath, coming forward to see what had gone wrong, was in his turn met with a stream of British troops and vehicles heading helter-skelter in the wrong direction.

Reluctantly, and against his better judgment, Slim admitted

defeat. He ordered his brigade to pull out and abandoned the ill-fated Gallabat Fort to the enemy. Italian reinforcements, Polverini's IV Brigade, reached Metemma forty-eight hours later to face in their turn a terrible pounding by British bombers on 20 November that, in Castagnola's words, reduced Gallabat and Metemma to 'a pile of rubble'. The 27th, the Beni Amer, had been, the Italians admitted, 'very badly knocked about'. Polverini's Brigade had to be replaced after only a fortnight, what with the bombing and the continual ground raids by fighting patrols from Khor el Otrub. For Slim kept on harassing the Italians till the end of the month, successfully enough.

But there could be no disguising the fact that the battle had been lost. The easy caravan route from Gallabat had not been opened. Indeed news of the defeat of the British soon spread through Gojjam and, by the end of the month, had dampened many of the Patriots' hopes. Eden had not had his longed-for military success in the Middle East. On the contrary, it had been yet another defeat for British arms, and as much as possible was done to hush it up throughout Egypt and the Sudan. It seemed to prove that, however bad Italian troops might be, English troops were worse. For even Blackshirt battalions had never panicked and fled under a mere bombing.

Furthermore the frightening weakness of British troops had not been compensated for by either the superiority of British technical equipment or the efficiency of their commanders. The Matilda tanks had been torn to shreds in a matter of minutes by a few rocks. Bombers had flown singly and uncoordinated to their destruction. Officers at battalion level had been unable to control their troops, and at brigade level had failed to arrange a successful attack on a weaker enemy force though supported by armour, artillery, and the air. Despondency settled over various levels of Middle East Command and the War Office the more they studied the implications of the action at Gallabat.

The culprits paid. Both the Essex and Brigadier Slim were out of the Sudan before the end of the year. Brigadier Rees, known affectionately as 'the little pocket wonder', took over command of the Brigade; and more warlike Scots, the 2nd Highland Light Infantry, replaced the bucolic levies from East Anglia.

As for the Italians, one sympathizes most with the reactions of Gina's brother: 'It isn't right that after such hard days I am denied a few delicious moments with a lovely native woman.'

CHAPTER 23

A LAWRENCE FOUND

YET the very day that the Essex panicked and the attack on Metemma failed was the day on which an event occurred that marked, though none yet realized it, the turning-point in the fortunes of this war. For on that day, the last and in many ways the greatest of the personages who have appeared in the course of this history made his entrance upon the Ethiopian scene.

On 6 November 1940, Major Orde Wingate arrived in Khartoum, having been sent down from Cairo to work in close liaison with, and as a staff officer to, Haile Selassie. After the Khartoum conference Wavell and Eden, back in Cairo, had decided that such an appointment was overdue. The man chosen ought to be not an Ethiopian expert but a regular army officer, and on the same wavelength therefore as General Platt. He would be able, though technically Platt's subordinate, to press him to put into effect the decisions taken at the conference. Eden and Wavell discussed the various officers available, and they agreed on Wingate. Wavell sent for him; and the three had a long discussion on the aims and extent of the mission with which he was to be charged.

Why Wingate? Why indeed. Eden, with Wingate's dossier before him, would have learnt something about the man before he met him. He would have known, then, that Orde Wingate was aged 37 and had followed an apparently normal enough career as an artillery officer: Charterhouse, Woolwich, and Larkhill; that he came from a military family on both sides; that, interestingly enough, he had already served in the Sudan ten years earlier both at Gallabat and Roseires as a *Bimbashi* attached to the Sudan Defence Force; and, even more significantly—for it meant that his name would be recognized all along the border and in the interior—that his father's cousin had been Sir Reginald Wingate, Governor-General of the Sudan, founder of the Sudan Civil Service, Sirdar of the Egyptian Army, and, twenty-four

years earlier, General Officer Commanding Operations in the
Hejaz, based on Port Sudan. Such a background was no
handicap.

But then Wavell would have had to mention that he knew
Wingate of old. As General Officer Commanding Palestine from
1937 to 1939 he had had quite enough trouble with the man to
remember Wingate very well; and he would have had to draw
Eden's attention to one paper in the file: the report put in by
Wingate's commanding officer at Jerusalem when Wingate was
posted back to England. 'Orde Charles Wingate DSO. Is a good
soldier but as far as Palestine is concerned he is a security risk. He
cannot be trusted. He puts the interests of the Jews before those of
his own country. He should not be allowed in Palestine again.'

Wingate's grandfather had been a Scottish missionary in
Budapest, his father after a lifetime in the Indian Army had
become a Plymouth Brother, and his mother had brought him up
on the Old Testament, the Psalms and Proverbs, and a suitably
harsh and frugal regime. This was the stuff that fanatics were
made of. In Palestine Wingate had become an ardent and active
Zionist, leading the younger members of the kibbutzim in
reprisal raids against the Arabs. For a time the British authorities,
themselves internally divided, turned a blind eye. 'My favourite
madman', Weizmann called him, and Moshe Dayan who followed him on the night raids added that he had never known
Wingate to lose an engagement or to be worried about odds.

But this could not last. Wingate made himself much disliked
throughout the army for his criticism of 'the military ape', the
average British officer, and of the average British soldier—'Don't
imitate the British Tommy,' he advised the young Jews, 'learn
his calmness and discipline but not his stupidity, brutality and
drunkenness.' It was he who was later to describe Slim as 'a bad-
tempered little terrier', and it was typical that Wingate did not
mean it as an insult. 'The only one soldier worthy of the name
East of Suez,' he was to add. Wavell and Eden despite inevitable
misgivings selected him to stir the lethargy at Khartoum. He, for
his part, was eager enough. He had been languishing for nearly
two years in an anti-aircraft unit outside London till a
memorandum he had written on battle conditions in North
Africa was passed up to the Prime Minister. Churchill, impressed, had had him posted out to Cairo. But the military apes had
shunted him aside; and the disconsolate Wingate browsing

among the files at GHQ had been lit by a fresh enthusiasm. He had found a letter there from five weary Australian sergeants stationed in Palestine who had written to volunteer, partly out of boredom, partly out of idealism, to help the revolt in Ethiopia.

Ethiopia was bound to attract a man like Wingate, a land oppressed by white conquerors, heavy with history and inhabited by a people as biblically-minded as the Jews, impregnated —like himself—with the Psalms and the Old Testament. He plunged into the files, studying all he could find relevant to the Ethiopian campaign. His indignation grew as he considered the inefficiency with which it had been conducted—and the wasted enthusiasm of the five Australians and of the many others who must, like them, be kicking their heels in Palestine or Transjordan, eager for action.

He reached Khartoum with a million pounds to spend, and his own ideas clearly formulated. Almost immediately he endeared himself to General Platt by telling him that promises to Haile Selassie had in his, Wingate's, opinion been extraordinarily badly implemented. He added that Brigadier Sandford had been extraordinarily feebly supported. 'I cannot help coming to the conclusion, Sir', went Wingate's peroration, 'that the conduct of the revolt so far shows poverty of invention combined with an intention to limit its scope below what is possible and desirable.' This is not normally the sort of comment that a General accepts from a Major. But when the Major comes armed with moneybags and when behind the Major there is known to be the authority of the Commander-in-Chief and of the War Minister, a wise General grinds his teeth in comparative silence. So the *Kaid* contented himself with observing to his more respectful subordinates that 'The curse of this war is Lawrence in the last.' He felt this sentiment all the more profoundly as other would-be Lawrences such as Major Hamilton of 106 Mission—of whom more later—were simultaneously descending upon Khartoum to plague him. Indeed with the appearance of Major Neville of 107 Mission in Nairobi, missions appeared to be proliferating like rabbits—all under the aegis of a certain Major Quintin Hogg at the War Office.

There is a chapter in *The Prince* in which Machiavelli debates whether it is better for a ruler to be loved or feared, and concludes that on balance it is better to be feared. Wingate may not have read Machiavelli but he acted instinctively on the principle. Within a brief fortnight he had made himself feared by some and detested by many. Even now, over forty years after his death, strong reactions are provoked by the mere mention of his name not only among Englishmen but among the Ethiopians who knew him. What he did not, in any circumstances, inspire was indifference. This was partly because of what he did, but even more because of what he was: his manners, his behaviour, his appearance. Newbold felt such a distaste for him that he apparently could not bring himself even to mention Wingate's name once in his circulars or letters. Major Dodds-Parker, a liaison officer at Khartoum, used to sit at the smallest table in the Grand Hotel to avoid having to share his meals with Wingate. And this is how *Bimbashi* Harris of the Frontier Battalion described him: 'rather an ogre—beady eyes set very close together over a huge nose. His hair was long and far from clean. He wore an incongruous collar and tie. His voice grated like a rasp.' Whatever else he may have been, he was not a typical regular army officer. 'Though he was such a small man,' Moshe Dayan used to say, 'when he was disdainful he could make you feel as tiny as a mouse.' Not a characteristic calculated to put his brother-officers at their ease.

But then it was not his aim to put them at their ease—quite the contrary. One of the first objects of his anger was indeed the Frontier Battalion. It had originally been formed to help the rebels by escorting arms and supplies into their territory. Instead, Wingate complained, it had been sitting garrisoning Roseires, which was not its job.

Before the month was out a caravan was leaving Roseires escorted by one of the five companies of the Frontier Battalion, the bearded *Bimbashi* Acland's, bearing nearly a thousand rifles, ammunition, and 72,000 Maria Theresa dollars, carried on 150 camels, the biggest convoy so far, to Fitaurari Taffere Zelleka's base on Mount Belaya. This was just one example of what Wingate managed to get done. Indeed within three days of his arrival the Armachecho chiefs who had been lingering in Khartoum, Wubneh Amoraw, Birre Zagaye, and Ayane Chekol, had been sent out and back into the fray, accompanied by the Emperor's 'Representative to the North,' Tsehafe Taezaz Haile. Chapman-Andrews (now a Major and Political Liaison Officer to the Emperor) had been sent down with Lorenzo

Taezaz to Kenya to sort out the Refugee battalions there. A military school of sorts under the grandiose name of the Sobat Military Academy had been set up a few miles outside Khartoum to train young Ethiopians as officers.

None of this could have been achieved if Haile Selassie had adopted the same attitude towards Wingate as the other authorities had done. Haile Selassie, however, was only too delighted to find that at long last some dynamism was being injected into the revolt, and indeed into his own future. The first visit Wingate had paid after his row with Platt had been to Haile Selassie. Wingate had immediately taken 'the little man' and his cause to heart—so much so that he had offended some of the Emperor's most loyal supporters, notably George Steer, by criticizing the efforts of the Propaganda Unit.

Yet after the initial success of the *Awaj*, the propaganda unit had been working very effectively and was producing in thousands copies of a news-sheet, *Banderachin*. This was passed out through the caravans to the rebels or dropped over Italian garrisons by the RAF and it had resulted in a considerable number of deserters coming over into the Sudan. What Wingate objected to was not the propaganda itself but the extravagant promises or boasts which were sometimes made. It was a principle of his that all propaganda should be based on truth. 'Lies are for the enemy, the truth is for our friends. Righteousness exalteth a nation,' he said. And in particular he objected to a photograph which showed the Emperor standing on a British tank while reviewing the troops at Gedaref. This went contrary to a principle that Wingate had decided upon even before coming to Khartoum and was never to abandon: Haile Selassie was to be David—not Bethsheba's David but the David of the Psalms. Above all the 'little man' was to be the David who would destroy Goliath. For this the new David needed no large forces nor modern technical weapons as symbolized by the tank, nor indeed foreign support at all, but mobility, the weapons most suitable to mobility, and above all confidence in the justice of his cause and the greatness of his name.

Wingate therefore never approved of 'Plan X'—the original plan by which the Emperor should return to his country at the head of his own large army or at the very least of a reconstituted Bodyguard. Wingate found the idea 'worthy of the Middle Ages'. 'The suggestion that the Emperor should move surrounded by a horde in the manner of Menelik' he considered to be in any case far from sensible for practical reasons. Not only would it destroy mobility and render the expedition cumbersome, it would also present a perfect air target to the enemy. His own idea was that the Emperor should have a personal bodyguard of 100 men—all that was 'necessary or desirable'. Instead of a trailing expeditionary force in one massive column, small groups of highly-trained armed men should spread out all around the Emperor in different directions and at different distances, spreading by their guerrilla tactics alarm among the enemy. It was these guerrilla groups that would provide the Emperor's real protection.

Wingate christened these guerrilla groups Operational Centres —Op Centres for short. In his mind's eye he planned ten of them, each to consist of one British Officer, five British NCOs, and 200 Ethiopians divided into ten squads—206 men in each. Fast moving, lightly but well-equipped, they would open up Gojjam ahead of the Emperor and spread the rebellion—not so much by working in conjunction with the Patriots as by setting them an example.

For Wingate had very strong views on the Patriots too. He believed, tentatively, that they should be allowed to act on their own because their methods would be different from those of trained troops. He held, most definitely, to one negative principle: that the way to foster a revolt was not to issue rifles and ammunition haphazardly to all who demanded them.

This idea struck at the whole root of what Mission 101 and the rest had been doing so far. They had, precisely, been issuing rifles haphazardly to all patriot leaders who had asked for them. And indeed, though this was the obvious method of stimulating a guerrilla revolt, the results had not been good. Many thousands of rifles had been distributed. Theoretically the revolt was under way. But in practice, as Wingate was to point out, very little bar promises had been achieved. Very little damage had been inflicted on the Italians. Though both Sandford and Bentinck had found much talk of raids and attacks, in fact virtually all these projects had vanished into the air when the moment came to carry them out. What attacks there had been had been put in by the Italians. As Wingate stringently said, the presence of the British officers had been 'mildly encouraging' to the patriots but had no effect on the Ethiopians who had adhered to the Italian cause.

One of the reasons, as Wingate pointed out, was that it was useless to hand out antiquated French rifles—'junk'—to a patriot leader who already possessed several hundred modern rifles captured from the Italians. 'The effect was to make him think either that we were laughing at him or that we were deficient in war material.' More than this, however, he was against the very principle of handing out modern rifles except when they were to be used for a very specific purpose. For what was the usual result? The patriot leader's mind—as Wingate described it in a famous passage—tended to work as follows:

This person evidently needs my (very inefficient) help; so much so that he is willing to part with arms he must know I have only the most rudimentary idea how to use . . . I must face facts. Why should I die without hope of victory? . . . I think on the whole the best and kindest way will be to accept the help with gratitude; to hold it on trust in case some day I can use it against the common enemy; and meanwhile to get to learn how to use it by settling once and for all that dispute over the water with the Smiths.

Not long afterwards Bentinck bitterly and empirically came to the same conclusion. 'Does HQ', he noted in his diary, 'realise how dangerous is the wholesale arming of these unruly and turbulent chiefs?'

Wingate's positive ideas on guerrilla warfare and on the ideal role and composition of what he now began to regard as 'his' force echo, consciously or unconsciously, Lawrence, and anticipate Mao Tse Tung—particularly in his major premise, which he laid down in this way: 'While it is the ideal for 100% of the population to be friendly, it is in no way essential. What is essential is that the supposed friends should be trustworthy. These friendly inhabitants are the matrix in which the force has its being.'

Directly contradicting Platt who two years earlier had thought it useless to throw away a thousand men on ill-conceived operations against a vastly superior force, he added: 'Given a population favourable to penetration, a thousand resolute and well-armed men can paralyse, for an indefinite period, the operations of a hundred thousand.'

But to this principle he added various riders. The qualities of both men and commander must be of the highest; they must play an independent role and have unity of command; they must operate in conjunction with a definite propaganda; and they must be given an objective the gaining of which will vitally affect the campaign. These were riders that he was to add later; and in that sense are tinged with the bitterness of disappointment. For he was to complain of divided command, uncertain propaganda, varying objectives and, above all, echoing Wellington's term, of how 'the scum of an army' was selected to do his work.

As regards relations with the local patriot leader, he laid down the correct course of action:

The guerrilla commander, on arrival, will offer nothing; and ask merely for food supplies and information. 'This is curious,' the patriot leader will say to himself. 'The force is very small, but no doubt much larger ones are at hand, or he wouldn't be so confident. I wonder why he didn't ask my help. I had better watch this.' And the next night the guerrilla commander will put in a successful but secret attack on an enemy post. This will bring a worried patriot leader to beg to be allowed to help. 'I am a soldier and I have been fighting the enemy for years. Only tell me what you want me to do, and I will show you that we can do it.'

This is less convincing than Wingate's criticism of the wrong method. Yet it illustrates the two principles in which he always believed and which were always to be the base of his action as a guerrilla leader: personal example founded on self-reliance, and bluff.

Yet Wingate, for all his powers of clear thinking and analysis and despite all his energy, was unable to put his plans for the perfect guerrilla operation into action. This was partly because he was not himself always consistent, and partly because Plan X had already gathered such momentum that it was impossible entirely to change its course. One suspects also that Wingate was influenced, against his own better judgment, by Haile Selassie. At any rate in the end he agreed that for the purposes of prestige the Emperor should cross the frontier not just with a small personal guard but with a comparatively large escort, as befits a descendant of Solomon and Sheba who cannot, as Ras Seyum had said years before, 'skulk in the hills like a *shifta*'. And, inconsistently, he came more to complain of the deficiencies of the Refugee battalions who formed this escort than to criticize their very existence. Indeed he was lit by something of the Emperor's indignation as regards the treatment of the Eritrean deserters in Kenya. This had become a very sore point, for they had been formed not into a fighting unit, though they had all originally been professional soldiers trained by the Italians, but into a Labour Corps and put to work on building roads. Despite the protests of Haile Selassie, of Eden and Wavell, and eventually of Churchill himself, the Colonial Office for months refused to budge. It only gave way and allowed the transformation of the Labour Corps into the '4th Ethiopians' when it was too late for them to take part in the fighting—a waste of fine material and a tribute only to the typical obstinacy of the Colonial Office. It was also a great success for Italian propaganda which had harped on the Eritreans' 'proven unreliability *vis-à-vis* the Ethiopian cause'.

It had been to sort this mess out that Lorenzo Taezaz, himself an Eritrean, and Chapman-Andrews had been sent down to Kenya. But although they were unable to achieve anything with the Eritreans, they reported that a battalion of refugees from Taveta, the '2nd Ethiopians', commanded by Captain Boyle, was almost ready for action; and they arranged for it to be moved up to Khartoum by road, via Uganda and Equatoria Province. Blatta Takele as its Staff Officer was allowed to accompany it only as far as Juba before being turned back. So he and Wingate were never to meet. A pity, for they were alike in their energy and aggressiveness—though meeting Blatta Takele might have shaken Wingate's devotion to the Emperor.

Another battalion, the '3rd Ethiopians', was also being formed, out of the various deserters arriving across the border from Eritrea or Gojjam. It was put under the command of Captain Whinney of the West Yorks, one of the instructors at the Sobat Military Academy where all the bright sparks of the exiled Ethiopian nobility from the Duke of Harar downwards were being, or were later to be, trained.

Yet Wingate, though forced to accept them, disapproved of these Refugee Battalions, partly because a great deal of money was lavished on them, and partly because they had been formed too late. In his opinion they, and the Eritreans above all, should have been assembled at Khartoum within a few weeks of the declaration of war. Most of all, however, he disapproved because they were badly officered. For though an eccentric himself, he was a regular officer and did, sporadically, appear to believe in the values of the regular army. 'To put it briefly', he wrote, 'these Refugee Battalions were an ill-trained, ill-armed, ill-equipped demoralised rabble, led by British officers and NCOs mostly drawn from African colonies, who although of excellent material and full of gallantry were for the most part not qualified to train troops for modern warfare.'

However, there they were. His own Op Centres were not yet in existence, and the Emperor was pressing to be allowed across the border. Haile Selassie could not be held in check much longer, even had Wingate considered this desirable. So, conscious that in the main he would have to accept Plan X, hoping eventually to add his own Op Centres and gradually twist the scheme more towards his own ideas, he flew away from Khartoum. He had been there only two weeks but in those two weeks he had revolutionized the whole atmosphere.

Where did Wingate go? Naturally enough, being Wingate, into the interior, to see for himself how the revolt was going and above all to meet Sandford, his own nominal commander and the god-father of Plan X. He knew that they would at any rate agree about their major aim: the return of Haile Selassie across the border into Ethiopia in the role of past and future Emperor. He knew also that, with a clearer mind than Sandford's he would be bound to disagree with him on many points and particularly on immediate objectives and methods. 'It is a common error', he wrote, 'to think that something has been achieved when forces have been assembled in desolate areas far from points vital to the enemy.' Yet, this, he knew, was what Sandford had done on a small scale and was planning to do on a large. Up to a certain point Wingate would agree with him, and work out the best method of assembling large forces. But the aim was not just to ensure the presence of the Emperor safely inside his Empire; it was to attack, harass, and if possible destroy the Italians.

On 20 November Wingate accompanied by one of the young university-trained exiles, Makonnen Desta, flew across half Goj-jam to land on a specially-prepared landing ground at Sakala. This was in the hills just to the east of Burie in Dejaz Negash's territory. He stayed for only forty-eight hours before taking off again and flying back to Khartoum; but in that time Sandford had explained the situation in Gojjam, Wingate had cross-questioned him on many details, and the two men together had agreed on a plan.

Sandford had just returned from a three-weeks' trip to eastern

Gojjam, Gojjam proper as it was called. There he had found much the same situation as in the west: the Italians confined to their forts and garrison towns and the roads in between, but the rebellion stagnant owing to the rivalry between two great patriot leaders. Strangely enough, he had found the nobleman with the saintly reputation, Lij Hailu Belew, to be a 'rather common-looking man obsessed with grievances against his next-door neighbour,' but the neighbour, the bandit and commoner 'Lij' Belai Zelleka, to be 'a fine-looking fellow with a long thin face and a pointed black beard.' Yet, physical appearances apart, he had got on better with Hailu Belew, whom he believed to be 'a man of his word' and who had promised action at last—to attack two Italian posts. Belai Zelleka had on the contrary appeared gauche, ignorant, unintelligent, and intensely suspicious, sur-rounded by *shum-shum* ('wasters'). He was unable to win over *banda* leaders locally because he had killed too many of their relatives; and though promising to invest Bichenna and even to try and cut off Debra Markos, was unwilling to leave his back exposed to Hailu Belew. Though Sandford had left Azaz Keb-bede to try and repeat his success and work out an agreement, it seemed that at best the two rivals in eastern Gojjam would sign a pact. They refused to meet.

Sandford added that the news of Haile Selassie's presence in the Sudan had filtered through very slowly and meagrely. He was disappointed to hear from Wingate that the Refugee battalions still needed a lot of training before being capable of any action, and very interested in the project for Op Centres.

Wingate, however, thinking ahead, plied Sandford with ques-tions. Was the escarpment up from the Sudan passable for camel transport? Could or would the enemy interfere? Could the camels be met at the top of the escarpment by mules? Was free movement in Gojjam possible? Could ill-protected convoys of mules reach their destination locally without interference from the enemy? Could supplies be purchased locally?

Sandford gave encouraging answers to all these questions. In particular he promised that he would arrange for 5,000 mules to meet the Emperor's force at the top of the escarpment. They made their plan. As soon as possible the Emperor and his force, accompanied by Wingate, should cross the frontier. The rendezvous where they were all to meet, the base for their future moves, should be Mount Belaya, the territory of Fitaurari Taffere Zelleka, Dejaz Mangasha's follower. The news eventually reached the Italians. Their reaction proved it a good choice. As Italian military intelligence had to admit, 'Belaya is an area unknown to us.'

Two further details were settled. Critchley, Sandford's second-in-command, was suffering from serious eye trouble and it was agreed that he should be replaced. Secondly, the name and title of the expedition to accompany the Emperor was chosen, and chosen, evidently, by Wingate: Gideon Force.

Wingate flew back to Khartoum; and a week later, on 1 December, Sandford sent in a report. The caravan with Mesfin Sileshi, and 150 camels, had reached Belaya, alas without mortars or machine-guns. The revolt was going well. *Bande* were deserting after the recent bombing of Dangila. A worried General Nasi was reported to be visiting Burie. The visit of Major Wingate had been most useful, and he was glad to know that Wingate was organizing the Emperor's entry. In fact the whole situation had taken a very favourable turn.

The elder man was accepting with good grace a situation that would clearly lead to his own eventual loss of influence to a younger and more vigorous officer. The Ethiopians with him had recognized in Wingate a natural leader.[1] But Wingate's reaction was less generous. He appears to have considered Sandford's approach woolly-minded, and in particular to have been enraged by Sandford's habit of making promises of arms and airsupport to the rebel leaders which were mere words. Such promises were in Wingate's view counter-productive, though perhaps Wingate here underestimated the Ethiopian capacity for

---

[1] Particularly as he came by plane. Among the more sophisticated, Gabre Maskal in particular was to become devoted to him. 'Wingate was never demoralized,' he told the author. 'I have never seen a man of such courage and so human at the same time'. Gabre Maskal had fallen out with Sandford, not a technician, over the use of his wireless though he admired Critchley, 'an indefatigable man'. As for Wingate he was to become equally devoted to Gabre Maskal and his team, which included Sergeant-Major Grey. In his eventual report he complained of the 'appallingly low standard of the signals provided. A thoroughly incapable officer was put in charge. The one capable man—RSM Grey—was not in charge. The operators were lazy, ill-trained, and sometimes cowardly. The best were Ethiopians who had trained themselves', i.e. Gabre Maskal and his men.

Other comments on Wingate made by recently prominent Ethiopians to the author varied from 'his eyes were impressive' (General Aman Andom) via 'he was a slovenly man' (General Gizau) to 'a very hard man but I liked him very much' (General Abiye Abebe).

not expecting the pledges they received to be any more reliable than the pledges they gave.

At any rate Wingate returned to Khartoum, conscious that the full weight of organizing the Emperor's entry must fall on his own shoulders, and making himself under the nervous strain even more unpopular. At one parade at the Sobat Academy he struck and knocked down an Ethiopian for being badly turned-out. In order to encourage punctuality he ostentatiously wore a small alarm clock strapped to his wrist in place of a watch. His British colleagues he treated with equal abruptness, even accusing two staff officers of cowardice. As for his British subordinates he would summon them to interviews in his bathroom at the Grand Hotel, which he would conduct quite naked, scrubbing himself with toothbrushes. One person he summoned was the officer who had been chosen to replace Captain Critchley, *Bimbashi* Thesiger.

'Are you happy?' asked Wingate.

'Well, yes, I suppose I am, reasonably,' replied Thesiger.

'I am not happy,' said Wingate. 'But then, I have been thinking, no great man ever was really happy.'

Though considered in Khartoum an eccentric, a megalomaniac, almost a lunatic, he was quite clear in his own mind of his powers and of the virtue of his plans. He flew to Cairo at the beginning of December where General Wavell had summoned a military conference to decide on future plans, and there was allowed to harangue the assembled commanders. Some say that he scattered insults, others not. What is certain is that he created a highly favourable impression simply because what he had to say was music to the ears of the Commander-in-Chief and his generals. Wingate claimed that, given support in supplies and in the air, he could raise a revolt that would put an end to the Italian Empire in East Africa and that there was therefore no need to risk regular troops in offensive action. 'Give me a small fighting force of first-class men,' he said, 'and from the core of Ethiopia I will eat into the Italian apple and turn it so rotten that it will drop into our hands.'

Wavell, with his greater sources of information, must have realized that this was a wild claim; and in particular that there were parts of the Italian Empire in which there was no hope of raising any revolt—notably Eritrea and Somalia. Yet Wingate's concept fitted in so well with what he would have liked to be true that thereafter he most stubbornly resisted all attempts from London to force him to invade Italian East Africa in strength. His opinion was that, the rebellion stimulated, Italian East Africa could be left 'to rot by itself'. At the utmost, holding attacks might be launched by regular troops on the borders of Eritrea and Somalia. To this point of view he and his subordinate generals clung with all the obstructive pig-headedness of which they were capable—a fact for which Wingate bears, indirectly, the responsibility.

After this triumph Wingate stayed briefly in Cairo to enrol the nucleus of his first Op Centre, the five Australians whose letter had orginally inspired them. Appeals for further volunteers were sent out through the regiments stationed idly in Palestine and Transjordan. He obtained permission to collect a number of his Jewish friends, somewhere near twenty in all, to be attached to Gideon Force, though only in a semi-civilian role, as secretaries and doctors. Then, followed by this entourage, Wingate flew back to Khartoum to organize Gideon Force and in particular its transport.

For Wavell's conference a report had been called for not only from Sandford but also from the other half of 101 Mission, Bentinck.

Bentinck's report was almost equally optimistic. November had seen (thanks to Wingate's drive) the return of the Armachecho patriot leaders and the Emperor's representative with a caravan of rifles, and the revolt was 'now in full swing'. Furthermore, Captain Foley had been out on his own 'showing great determination and energy', blowing up the road behind Metemma leading to Gondar. At the end of the month he had just arrived at Bentinck's camp 'preceded by men singing and playing a harp and blowing a bugle'. With the help of a handful of patriot volunteers he had managed to blow up twelve lorries and one armoured car. There were reports too that near Debra Tabor Lij Johannes and his men had attacked and destroyed a convoy of 6 lorries, killing 50 troops and capturing 4 machine-guns. As for Bentinck, he had personally received a letter of thanks—in verse—from one of the chiefs, Wanjo of Maraba, 'altogether a most refreshing and unusual epistle'.

But what he needed now in order to exploit the situation was a number of British officers and if possible a company of Gurkhas, plus more rifles. For the Emperor's representative, the Tsehafe Taezaz Haile, whom Bentinck still believed to be 'a kindly old man', had brought only 250 instead of 852 rifles promised, and nineteen chiefs and their followers were at Bentinck's camp (and incidentally having to be fed) waiting for arms and ammunition. There had even been threats from Birre Zagaye to seize the rifles by force.[1]

Bentinck's and Sandford's optimistic reports were both sent in on 1 December. Though they were not to know it, the Italians were equally worried about frontal attacks which they believed to be imminent all along the border and about rebel activity in two other areas. These were the Tseggede where Adane Makonnen, whom they feared more than any of the Armachecho chiefs, had raised his men after *Maskal* and was threatening all the forts and outposts around Adi Remoz and surprisingly even those beyond the Upper Simien inside Tigre. Panicky reports had come through with the news that huge forces—put at 5,000 armed rebels—were gathered in the hills under Negash Workineh. They were not only threatening Makalle but were talking of advancing on Adowa—and this in Tigre, which had always been so peaceful.

The Italians knew that there were British officers in Gojjam and Armachecho (they had by now identified 'Mr. Room' as Sandford). They suspected that British troops had already slipped into those areas; there was even one scary report of seven British battalions in Armachecho. They believed that machine-guns were being distributed, and they had learnt that, though there were no British officers with them, both Adane Makonnen and the highly-threatening Negash Workineh had been in touch with Khartoum. Deeply alarmed by the state of the highlands, fearing how the revolt would spread when Haile Selassie was eventually brought in, the Italians decided on a series of counter-moves. These were to prove most successful.

The brain behind these moves appears to have been that of General Nasi. For a start intrigues and rivalries were to be actively encouraged among all local leaders, and those loyal to the

---

[1] So Bentinck had empirically come to reach one of Wingate's conclusions: the need for a small trained core, an Op Centre or a Gurkha company, as the basis of a successful guerrilla force. He had also recognized (cf. p. 286) the dangers of distributing rifles to rebel leaders.

Italians were to be allowed to form their own *banda* and given increased pay, gifts, and decorations. Certainly Bentinck did not know that Fitaurari Mesfin Redda, whose courtesy and impressiveness he had so much admired, was at the same time having talks with the former Governor of Eritrea, Gasperini, to whom he had said that he was ready to go 'anywhere'. Or that Birre Zagaye had promised to obstruct the British. Or that Adane Makonnen had been befriended by two pro-Italian Dejaz, Abitau Mintuab and Desta Maru, and promised arms and an area to control.[1] But by mid-December Bentinck was growing depressed. He was annoyed at the lack of support his 'sideshow' was getting from Khartoum, disappointed at Tsehafe Taezaz Haile who had shown that he lacked 'personality and energy',[2] and highly disturbed by the stormy atmosphere of his camp where the chiefs spent the whole time plotting and intriguing to obtain each other's rifles and the Tsehafe Taezaz's favour. 'Certainly Foley is the only inspiration to the revolt and his exertions in Chano appear to have set the local chiefs alight,' noted Bentinck. But by the end of the month Foley too was ill and depressed.

As for the threat from the Upper Simien, there the Italians successfully incited Lij Wossene, the heir of the Wagshum, and his mother Woizero Shoanish, against Negash Workineh —though Lij Wossene was ill with malaria and had only 100 men with him and two heavy machine-guns. So successful was Italian intrigue that Lij Wossene and the men of Wag, embittered by Negash Workineh's pretensions, actually attacked the rival leader. There were many dead among the patriots on both sides.

On the borders of Gojjam there was from the Italian point of view one stroke of luck. Fitaurari Worku of Kwara, the One-Eyed, had proclaimed himself Representative of the British Government. The hard-pressed Major Parodi was preparing to

[1] This was not mere treachery and double-dealing. All over Beghemder the patriot leaders had been impressed by Blatta Takele's warnings, and were preparing to fight on two fronts, both against their present overlords the Italians and against those whom they suspected might become their future overlords, the British. They were seriously preparing, from Armachecho to Debra Tabor, to attack the British if the British should show signs of taking permanent root. This inevitably involved them in complicated manœuvring, much of it centred round the imperial personage of Lij Johannes.

[2] Which is not surprising in view of his character. This is the same man who in 1936 abandoned the cadets and their Swedish officers to the lonely defence of Ad Termaber against Badoglio's advance.

abandon his little outpost in Kwara fort when, in the first week of December, Fitaurari Worku was shot and mortally wounded by a Gumz sniper. In the inevitable argument over his successor his followers split. So died the earliest and most reliable of all the British-backed minor chiefs, and one whose territory was the first 'bound' on the route to Belaya. Songs were composed by his brother in memory of his gallant deeds.

Yet all this was a mere foretaste. On 11 December General Nasi made his most masterly move. He brought Ras Hailu back to Gojjam.

Ras Hailu—it was nearly ten years since the son of the Negus Tekle Haimonot had set foot in his father's kingdom. Since then he had been imprisoned by Haile Selassie, released on the Emperor's train to Djibuti, and made Graziani's chief native adviser. Largely because of that, and because of his unfortunate role in the killing of the two sons of Ras Kassa, he had been relegated to the shadows under Graziani's successor as Viceroy, the Duke of Aosta. But even Graziani had been careful not to allow him to set foot in Gojjam. Only the utmost crisis of Italian power permitted Ras Hailu after those long years of absence to achieve his patient wish and return to his people.

That they had not forgotten him became immediately clear. He was welcomed with enormous enthusiasm in his capital of Debra Markos. When he visited the threatened garrison towns of Burie and Dangila he was 'received with great rejoicing by all,' as the British were forced to acknowledge. Sandford sent in a highly alarmed report to say that the local situation appeared critical. Many small patriot leaders submitted again to the Italians. Uneasiness spread among the remainder. General Nasi, who had personally taken in hand the situation in Gojjam, had the entire province detached from General Frusci's Sector and allotted to his own. Striking while the iron was hot, he sent reinforcements to Colonels Natale and Torelli. He formed new *bande*—Dejaz Kassa Mashasha for instance was sent down to reinforce Parodi at Kwara. He announced, not inaccurately, that the British had stopped bombing because they had lost so many planes.

In Khartoum there was alarm; Haile Selassie authorized the opening of negotiations with Ras Hailu. There was reason for alarm, for of the four great rebel chiefs in Gojjam two were related by blood and one by marriage to Ras Hailu. To all of them

Ras Hailu sent letters. The confusion of their spirits and even more of that of their followers can be judged by the reply sent to Ras Hailu by the one low-born leader unrelated to him, 'Lij' Belai Zelleka. In it Belai Zelleka, who signed himself 'Venger of the blood of Ethiopia', rejoices at the return of Ras Hailu. But

Your Highness! The country and I are yours. But inasmuch as we are yours, if, as we have heard has been done already in Shoa and among the Gallas, you have come with the intention of driving us one against the other with deceptions, I shall abandon the country and retire to the desert to resist like a man for the independence and the honour of my country, and I shall so bear myself that my history shall be written in Europe.

Indeed Belai Zelleka had his wish. He did so bear himself; his history has been, and is now again being, written in Europe. But amidst such confusion of loyalties it was clear that no rebellion could flourish.

Three weeks later General Nasi, no mean propagandist, struck his second blow. He issued officially a decree from Debra Markos to celebrate the return of Ras Hailu, expressing the goodwill of Italy, and warning the Gojjamites against the snares of a barbarous and foreign people: 'In your land where milk and honey flow, surrounded by holy Ghion which God has given you as a boundary on every side (the Blue Nile), this people has scarcely ceased from poisoning you with the honey of its words . . .' Unofficially, surreptitiously, and most effectively, he had a forged document circulated bearing, like the *Awaj* of 8 July, the Imperial Seal of the Lion of Judah and Elect of God, Haile Selassie I, and appointing Dejaz Mangasha Jimbirre Negus of Gojjam. This forgery despite shrill denials did its work. All the inhabitants of Gojjam except Mangasha's immediate followers began to despise and detest the name of the usurper. Even more significantly, they remembered how they had been treated by the Negus Negusti in the past and how he had, years before too, appointed over them a Governor, Ras Imru, whom they had never chosen.

Yet though the rebellion came to a standstill, and the garrisons sallied out of Burie and Dangila again, dangerously threatening Sandford who appealed in vain for immediate drastic action, the bulk of the rebels did not go over to the Italians. For the Italians, particularly the Director of Political Affairs at Addis Ababa, Dr.

Frangipani, hesitated to take the really decisive step. They did not give Ras Hailu real autonomy by withdrawing some of their Residents and Commissars. They did not arm him with machine-guns and the four cannon he was 'timidly' requesting. Above all they did not themselves appoint him Negus of Gojjam. This hesitation was their great mistake.

Yet the idea was much in the air. At the same time they had sent back two other great chiefs to their districts, 'Ras' Ayalew Birru to Gondar and 'Ras' Haile Selassie Gugsa to Makalle. In reserve at Addis Ababa they still held Ras Seyum whom they trusted less. Yet even so there was talk of appointing Ras Seyum Negus of Tigre. For with the return of the other great chiefs, even the falsely titled, to their regions, the threat of British-inspired rebellion had been countered—if not ended.

CHAPTER 24

SUCCESS AT EL WAQ

GENERAL CUNNINGHAM had taken over the command in Kenya on 1 November from General Dickinson who was 'tired and in need of rest'. At least the British occasionally managed to get rid of their generals, though by no means of all their 'tired' generals. Under him General Cunningham found no less than three recently arrived generals; first General Wetherall, second a genial South African known as 'Daddy' Brink, and last General Godwin-Austen of Somaliland fame.

These generals had arrived to take command of forces that had, during the summer months, dramatically increased. By November two more brigades of the KAR had been raised and formed, and two more brigades of South Africans had come up to Nairobi. For the overland lorry route to the Cape had now been opened and not only men but materials were streaming up to strengthen East Africa Force. Its power therefore stood, when Cunningham took up his command, at a total of nine brigades.[1] Nine brigades formed three divisions. Hence the need for the three major-generals—one to command each division.

This was a substantial force. In addition there were the supporting arms: Pemberton's local armoured cars, as well as armoured cars and a squadron of light tanks from South Africa; plus about fifty aeroplanes, artillery, a swarm of lorries, and all the other trappings.

There was also a scattering of irregular forces. The Kenya settlers, under command of a Captain Nicholl of the 14th Lancers, had managed to form the Kenya Independent

---

[1] The four KAR brigades were the 21st (Brigadier Ritchie), the 22nd (Brigadier Fowkes), the 25th (Brigadier Owen) and the 26th (Brigadier Dimoline). The three South African Brigades were the 1st (Brigadier Pienaar), the 2nd (Brigadier Buchanan) and the 5th (Brigadier Armstrong). The other two Brigadiers were commanding the West African brigades which had arrived at Mombasa in July. The Nigerian Brigade was commanded by Brigadier Smallwood, the Gold Coast Brigade by Brigadier Richards.

Squadron—eighteen men, with forty-six horses and mules, which had the glory of being the smallest unit in the British Empire. But, more importantly, a number of 'Irregulars' had been raised, first as companies, then, increasing in strength, as Irregular Battalions.

The inspirer of this move was a colonial official from British Somaliland, by the name of Curle, the same Curle who had been attached to the Anglo-Ethiopian Boundary Commission that had been attacked at Walwal. Evacuated, like all the civilian officials, from Somaliland, indignant at the waste of good fighting material in the Ethiopian refugees there, he had got permission to form from them an armed group: the '2nd Irregulars'. He promised to pay, feed, and clothe his men. They in their turn agreed to accept one punishment only: twenty-five lashes. As for the other officers, an equally rough bunch of Kenyan settlers, they included an Austrian who had fought both British and Italians in the First World War, and an Estonian called Nurk who had escaped from prison in Italian East Africa. By the beginning of November, Curle had raised five companies, each of sixty men, and by mid-November he had absorbed the remnants of the '1st Ethiopians', those of the failed 'invasion' north of Lake Rudolf. They had been retrained by another of these curious Kenya adventurers, Angus Buchanan, a man who had once led two exploring expeditions for Lord Rothschild. But Buchanan knew nothing at all of the Ethiopians. His attempt to run his unit like a British battalion was disastrous. Trouble broke out, and both Buchanan and the old Ethiopian leaders—Dejaz Wolde Mariam, Zaudi Ayalew, and Fitaurari Tademme Zelleka, Ras Desta's lieutenant—were removed. Most of the rest were absorbed into the '2nd Irregulars' which rose to a strength of twelve companies. A few were sent up to Khartoum to join Wingate's No. 1 Op Centre.

Meanwhile, two other groups of Irregulars were formed out of Somalis in the no man's land between the Tana and the Juba, one under Captain Dougie Douglas. In the far north-west ten companies of fierce Turkana were raised to form the '5th Irregulars'. And Mr. Bonham, the Intelligence Officer at Marsabit, raised his own group of local tribesmen—'Bonham's shifta'.

General Cunningham underestimated the importance of all native troops, regular as well as irregular. He trusted mainly in the fighting qualities of his three white South African brigades—because they were white. Cunningham was a conventional officer, with no experience of the colonies. He was in fact as typical a regular soldier as it might be possible to find: approachable, unlike General Platt, sociable, unlike General Wavell, and very cautious, unlike his fellow-gunner Major Wingate. He applied to his armies the principles he had learnt to apply to his guns: they would function well provided they were lined up exactly on a well-observed target, equipped before battle with a substantial stock of reserves, and above all used well within their range.

He and Smuts had left Eden's Khartoum Conference in order to fly down and see if an attack on Kismayu was feasible. They had visited most of the front together, and discussed plans. While Cunningham stayed in Nairobi to take up his new post, Smuts flew back to Cape Town. From there on 5 November Smuts sent an enthusiastic cable to Churchill: not only would it be possible to take Kismayu, but from Kismayu Cunningham should be able to attack northwards and threaten Addis Ababa. This was exactly what Churchill wanted to hear. He was even more delighted when Smuts added that with internal unrest inside Ethiopia and a thrust from the North as well, 'the Italians may crack in the summer.' This was very different from the vague plans for attack and the very concrete news of defeats that Churchill had been used to receiving from the Middle East up till then. He was also delighted with his new General in Kenya and with that new General's offensive spirit. For he naturally assumed that Smuts and Cunningham had agreed.

They may have done. But within days Cunningham's innate caution reasserted itself. Not only was there no more talk of threats to Addis Ababa but Cunningham reported to Wavell that he had decided that it would be impossible to attack Kismayu before the spring rains were over; before, that is to say, May. Wavell cabled the news to General Dill. The inevitable outburst followed from Downing Street. Why this delay? All that Dill could rather feebly say was that Wavell had called a meeting in Cairo of all his military leaders and that doubtless the plans would be discussed and decided there. 'None of us were satisfied with this,' noted Churchill grimly, and he dispatched memoranda and cables in various directions in an attempt to influence the result of the military conference.

As usual, this attempt failed in face of Wavell's immense passivity. As a sop to Churchill, Eden promised that Cunningham would make a minor attack towards Kismayu before the February rains. But Churchill, disgusted with the pusillanimity of his British advisers and at the way in which planned operations inevitably appeared to be both postponed and watered down, had turned with enthusiasm to a new proposal put forward by a new figure who appeared briefly but dramatically on the East African scene: General de Gaulle.

The Free French at least appeared to want to fight, unlike the infinitely more powerful British. This, in Churchill's eyes, was their main merit. It compensated both for the never-ending internal intrigues and even for their outward vanity—only too apparent in the boasting and lack of secrecy which had just led to the failure of the expedition against Dakar in West Africa.

De Gaulle had come back from this débâcle chastened but unabashed. He was encouraged by the news that the Belgian Congo had at long last followed the example of his own obscure fief, French Equatorial Africa, and declared itself by the voice of its governor-general, M. Pierre Ryckmans, 'officially and juridically at war with Italy.' In London he found waiting for him the other fiery French general, LeGentilhomme.

LeGentilhomme seemed to bear a charmed life. Not only had he got out of Djibuti safely but he was one of the few survivors of the ship in which he sailed from Aden to England: the *Empress of Britain*, sunk on 26 October. Three days later LeGentilhomme had reached London safely, and three weeks later De Gaulle joined him. Together they formed a plan for a 'Dakar' on a less-ambitious scale: the recapture or rather recovery of Djibuti. Three Free French battalions including the Foreign Legion would be transported by the Royal Navy round the Cape and under General LeGentilhomme's overall command hover outside Djibuti till the Senegalese troops and their officers there rallied to their former commander. To this plan they gave the code-name of 'Operation Marie'.

Then with Djibuti once more in Allied hands (and with, incidentally, the power of the Gaullist forces doubled) the original Franco-British plan for invading Ethiopia down the railway line towards Addis Ababa could immediately be put into effect. It was no doubt this second stage that Churchill most appreciated.

When he and De Gaulle met in London in the last week of November, Churchill approved enthusiastically the plans for 'Operation Marie'. He regretted only that it would be probably two months before the sea-borne force could appear outside Djibuti: not, in other words, until 1 February 1941. De Gaulle and LeGentilhomme looked forward eagerly to combined operations against the despised Italians—once they had rallied the Djibuti garrison back again to the Cross of Lorraine.

General Cunningham probably felt a pang of conscience at postponing his attack on Kismayu when he learnt that in mid-November a cargo boat had docked at this port loaded with supplies: rice, sugar, and more important, petrol and tyres. Kismayu was clearly important to the Italians. Cunningham made haste to put into action the 'minor thrust' towards it which he had promised would take place before the February rains. It was indeed a minor thrust, for its only aim was the water-hole on the artificial frontier between Kenya and Somalia named El Waq.

General Pesenti was Commander of the Juba Sub-Sector, Military Governor of Somalia, and Cunningham's opponent on this front. He had, after the usual alarm felt by all Italian commanders at the outbreak of war, settled down confidently to a quiet existence. There had been no attacks at all on his front, merely sporadic bombing raids which spared, as he noticed to his annoyance, the port of Kismayu—undoubtedly because the British intended to use it eventually for their own ships. One group of his famous white-turbaned Somali *dubats*, a thousand strong, was stationed forward on the frontier at El Waq, and Pesenti had recently reinforced it with a native battalion, the 191st. This threatening force of 2,000 men stood then on the Kenyan frontier, just over a hundred miles from Wajir.

It was this force that Cunningham decided to attack. He took even less chances than the Italian generals had in their attacks on the small Sudan frontier posts. He assembled at Wajir the Gold Coast Brigade and Pienaar's 1st South Africans, added Pemberton's armoured cars and some light artillery, had seventeen aircraft provided for air cover, and numberless lorries for transport. He then put the whole force under the command of General Godwin-Austen.

With a force outnumbering the enemy's by nearly four to one,

Godwin-Austen could hardly go wrong. The unhappy Colonel Garino, a chemist by profession, called up to command the outpost at El Waq, saw his men swept away by these motorized columns. But the *dubats* put up a brave defence, even halting temporarily a line-abreast charge by the armoured cars with their noisy hand-grenades. The defenders lost only fifty men, including prisoners, against, admittedly the attackers' casualties of two. The next day the attackers withdrew, the 1st Transvaal Scottish having captured the colours of the 191st.

But the repercussions of this little skirmish were extraordinarily extended. All the malaise and sense of inferiority from which the troops in Kenya had been suffering disappeared almost overnight (even though General Cunningham had been careful to use neither the Nigerians nor the KAR, the troops which had previously been defeated). At the same time the generals were pleased with themselves. For the first time in East Africa a British operation had gone as planned, without the slightest hitch, and this despite the fact that it was a complicated operation carried out at a temperature of 106 degrees, involving troops of different nationalities and colour, mechanized transport, air support, armour, and considerable distances—the famous 'logistics' problem. It had been almost a text-book exercise.

Correspondingly, the Italians in Somalia were extraordinarily depressed by this proof of British efficiency and immediately decided that they had after all been underestimating the enemy. General Pesenti, a music-lover and a composer in his spare time, was particularly struck by the harmony with which the British commanders had orchestrated their movements. From this moment on he considered the war, which he a non-Fascist had never viewed with favour, as good as lost. So much do small incidents, particularly at the beginning of a campaign, affect the morale and behaviour not only of soldiers but of generals.

The Duke of Aosta first learnt of the skirmish over the BBC News, where it was much boasted about. He immediately called for an inquiry, having received in reply to a cable to Pesenti the astounding news that Pesenti knew nothing of the incident. Upon which he himself flew down with his ADC General Volpini to take charge of the inquiry personally. On his arrival at Mogadishu airport he was greeted by General Pesenti whom he ordered abruptly to present himself at the Palace. There the most extraordinary scene took place. General Pesenti, having given his account of the El Waq affair, drew from it the conclusion that the struggle was hopeless. He suggested that the Viceroy should ask the British for an immediate armistice, as a prelude to a separate peace between *AOI* and Great Britain. Though he was immediately ordered by the Duke to be silent, he insisted on speaking, pointing out the political and psychological repercussions that such an audacious move could have in Italy. He upset Amedeo of Aosta by referring to his ancestor Carlo Emmanuele, and by adding that the King had never wanted the war—so Badoglio had told him, Pesenti.

There is a curious sentence in a long memo sent out by Churchill to the Chiefs of Staff a week or so later. The sentence is this: 'At any time we may receive armistice proposals from the cut-off Italian garrison in Ethiopia.' The section, part of a near-directive on the whole conduct of the war in the Middle East, goes on to explain why an Italian collapse could be near. But the significant point is this precise reference to 'armistice proposals'. It seems almost as though the British Government must have known of General Pesenti's feelings. This implies either that a highly efficient intelligence service informed them of the confrontation at Mogadishu after the event—or more likely, that General Pesenti had in fact, though he claimed to be speaking spontaneously, already been in contact with the opposing commanders. Pesenti himself recounts that only a month before the declaration of war he had been on a business trip to South Africa. It is clear therefore that he could have kept his lines open.

It is equally clear that the Duke of Aosta must have been seriously tempted. His heart was not in the war against his British friends and he had already done much to keep its tempo at a low level. But at the same time Pesenti's anti-fascist arguments and appeals to ancestral example were a two-edged weapon. Pesenti ought to have remembered that the Duke's father, Emmanuele Filiberto, had been indirectly responsible for the success of Mussolini's March on Rome and had been rewarded with honour though not with the throne to which he had aspired. Amedeo of Aosta was no Fascist and never appears to have been eaten by the ambition that devoured his father, yet he owed more to the Duce than to the King. So, perhaps hesitantly, he again halted Pesenti, remarking, according to one account, that Pesenti ought to be shot for making such treasonable remarks and he himself for listening to them.

Pesenti was not shot. He was relieved of his command, and replaced by General de Simone, the sluggish conqueror of British Somaliland, who had at least proved more than a match on that occasion for General Godwin-Austen. But unexplained changes of general, except for clear reasons of military defeat, are bad for morale; and it must be assumed that this was one of the reasons why the morale of the Italian troops standing on the line of the River Juba and awaiting a British attack went into a long decline towards the level at which it was to end: at zero.

CHAPTER 25

THE BALANCE SWINGS

In the second week of December events occurred far from East Africa which had a decisive effect upon the East African campaign. Eden finally obtained his desired military success, though in the place where he had least expected it.

Marshal Graziani and his enormous invading army had been camping for three months inside Egypt without moving forward. On 9 December, six months almost to the day since Italy had declared war, Wavell's Army of the Nile attacked the invaders. 'News of the attack on Sidi Barrani came like a thunderbolt,' noted Ciano in his diary. Two days later he referred to a 'catastrophic telegram' from Graziani. The British had swept through the Italians' position, and had captured 38,300 prisoners, 237 guns and 73 tanks—for the loss of 624 casualties themselves.

For a month the war in general had been going badly for Italy. First their offensive in Greece had collapsed. Then the RAF had bombed the Italian Fleet in Taranto harbour. Thirdly, in a naval action off Cape Sparavento, a number of Italy's best ships had been sunk by Admiral Cunningham. But none of these came as such a shock as the catastrophe in North Africa. At one stroke the threat to Cairo and the hope of linking the two halves of Italy's African Empire were removed; and at one stroke Italian morale dissolved. Within the week Badoglio was dismissed from his post as head of Italy's armed forces to be replaced by another man who had made and lost a reputation in Ethiopia, Cavallero. As for Graziani, 'Here is another man', said the Duce, 'with whom I cannot get angry because I despise him.' Graziani remained in place, only to conduct an even more catastrophic retreat before being recalled in ignominy. Italian military men everywhere were despondent. At Addis Ababa there was, according to Colonel Talamonti, nothing but confusion, with everyone giving orders, and the Viceroy, by insisting on seeing everything, wasting time, and deciding nothing. Italy had entered the war only because it seemed that the war would be over in a matter of weeks rather than months. But in Addis Ababa, after the disaster in Egypt, they gloomily predicted at least another year of war, and even more gloomily considered their own predicament. This was the atmosphere in which a Pesenti could talk of an armistice with no real danger of facing a firing squad. Not that all the Italians were demoralized. Gina's brother spent Christmas with her, attending the same mass on Christmas Day in the Cathedral as His Royal Highness; on 31 December he noted: 'Being the last day of the year, I must admit that it has gone very well indeed (certainly not like last year).' He went out riding and in a fall skinned his knees and grazed his elbow. It is just as well that he did not have the gift of foresight. Worse things than skinned knees and grazed elbows were to befall him, the Duke of Aosta, and all the Italians in East Africa before the next year was out.

Churchill, exultant with victory, just before Christmas, broadcast from London to the Italian people:

Our armies are tearing and will tear your African Empire to shreds and tatters . . . How has all this come about and what is it for? Italians, I will tell you the truth. It is all because of one man . . . That he is a great man I do not deny but that after eighteen years of unbridled power he has led your country to the horrid verge of ruin can be denied by none.

It is unlikely that many Italians listened to Churchill's words. But the sentiments expressed certainly reflected the new mood of the British, who after so many failures had just won their first great victory of the war.

The winning of it had an almost immediate effect on British plans. Churchill had never been resigned to virtual inactivity on the Kenya and Sudan fronts. He was less than ever inclined to accept the mild projects of Middle East Command now that, in his view, the weakness of the enemy had been thoroughly revealed. The battle at Sidi Barrani had been fought and won by only two British divisions: the Seventh Armoured (and on desert ground the unstoppable Matildas had come into their own) and the Fourth Indian. It was therefore with mixed feelings that he learnt that Wavell was pulling out the triumphant Fourth Indian and sending it down to the Sudan. On the one hand this meant a less effective pursuit of the defeated armies of Graziani. On the other hand it was proof that Wavell did intend to launch a more serious offensive in the Sudan and that at any rate the recapture of

Kassala (for which Eden had demanded extra troops) was definitely on.

But it was, naturally, among the Ethiopians that the defeat of Graziani had the greatest effect. He had been their conqueror and, as Viceroy, their tyrant. As the victorious Army of the Nile pressed on and in its turn invaded enemy territory to capture first Bardia and then Tobruk with fresh hordes of prisoners, George Steer issued leaflet after leaflet with photographs of long lines of Italian captives. He prepared a bumper issue of *Banderachin* in which he hammered away at the theme of Graziani's defeat, and at the failure of all the boasts made by the Italians in East Africa. 'After *Maskal*, what did they do? Four months of fighting weather have passed and the Italians have not gone forward.' Nor would they now, for: 'Even as the prophet Isaiah has foretold, "Yet a remnant of the Lord shall return, and come with singing into Zion, and sorrow and sadness shall flee away." '

Wingate, in a state of nervous exhilaration, was all for speeding up the return into Zion and profiting from the enemy's disarray. It was decided that Haile Selassie's entry could not be delayed until the Op Centres or the Refugee Battalions were trained and ready. Sandford, in view of the alarms in Gojjam, agreed.

The plan then was for the Emperor to cross the frontier within weeks rather than months. He would be escorted by his own personal bodyguard of young noblemen, by the 2nd Ethiopians, the only moderately well-trained refugee battalion, by No. 1 Op Centre and by the Sudanese troops of Boustead's Frontier Battalion. For after their initial brush Boustead and Wingate got on surprisingly well. Superficially this was unexpected; for Boustead was an epicurean where Wingate was a stoic, faddy about his personal comfort, insisting for instance on eating off a table covered with a table-cloth and properly laid, whatever the circumstances. In other words Boustead was, in his own more urbane way, also an eccentric. But he was a fighter too. Though he had been for sixteen years in the Sudan, latterly in the Political Service, he had deserted from the Navy in the First World War in order to see active service and had enlisted as a private in the Gordon Highlanders. Winning a Military Cross, he had received at the same moment the King's pardon and the King's decoration. He had been one of the original officers to join the Sudan Defence Force when General Hudleston, clearing out the Egyptians, had founded it.

This long acquaintance with the new Governor-General was extremely useful. Boustead and Wingate now put all their energy into collecting the camels that would be needed to carry the supplies of Gideon Force to the top of the Ethiopian escarpment. The Frontier Battalion had only 900 camels, and no saddles for mules. But thanks to General Hudleston's support and in particular thanks to the Governor of the central camel-raising province of Kordofan, the transport problem was solved. It was not easy. Knowing it useless to conscript unwilling tribesmen, Wingate hired them and their camels as civilians for an arms-running contract, playing off tribe against tribe. Within four weeks he had 25,000 camels and 5,000 camel men converging on the base from which Gideon Force was to set out, Roseires on the Blue Nile.

Meanwhile, however, a difficulty had occurred that put the whole project in peril.

It has already been mentioned that Major Hamilton of 106 Mission had arrived in Khartoum on the same day as Wingate. He was a hearty, boisterous Army officer of a very different kind, six foot four inches tall, a heavyweight boxer, and winner in his day of the Sword of Honour at Sandhurst. He was only passing through Khartoum. His destination was Aden—he had been for seven years a political officer in British Somaliland—and the task of his mission was to sabotage Djibuti and to blow up the railway line leading to Diredawa and the capital. He found at Aden an assembled Mobile Force (known locally as the 'Mobile Farce') featuring *inter alia* a red-bearded British officer l/C Dhows, by name Cardell-Ryan, but Lawrence-style, addicted to Arab clothes and to calling himself Haji Abdullah. Hamilton also found confusion about his own role. The plans for 'Operation Marie' were being co-ordinated, in rather muddled fashion, between London, Cairo, Brazzaville, and Fort Lamy, and it seemed pointless to provoke the French in Djibuti at precisely the moment when a concerted effort to win them back to the good cause was being planned. So Hamilton listened to the suggestions for making better use of his abilities that were put forward by an officer attached to this Mission named Courtenay-Brocklehurst.

Courtenay-Brocklehurst had been a game-warden in the Galla country in the old days. He had known Sandford who had been down in Maji at the time. But he had also known the Galla; and he disagreed with Sandford profoundly.

As another British officer in Aden at the time was later to write on the whole subject of irregular warfare:

Too much reliance was also at first placed on the views of the Local Expert . . . He had probably been in his region for many years and would have been very fond of his particular tribe or race. As a Galla man for instance he would be very pro-Galla and would have nothing to do with the Amharic expert, being infected himself by local animosities . . . The Local Expert was extremely useful as an adviser but not so good as a commanding officer.

These were wise words. Courtenay-Brocklehurst was a Galla man, as Captain Erskine of Gore had been before him. Like all Galla men he detested the Amhara and knew that the Galla in their great majority wished to be free of Amhara rule. So far the Amhara experts had had it all their own way. But from the Galla expert's viewpoint the Amhara experts were involving a naïve and ill-informed British government in a dastardly attempt to reimpose Amhara rule and an Amhara emperor on the Gallas under the guise of 'liberation'.

Courtenay-Brocklehurst and Hamilton flew down to Khartoum to try and halt 101 Mission and in its place to lead 106 Mission into Galla country. They would raise the Gallas with the promise of genuine liberation, both from the Italians and from their previous and more oppressive masters, the Amhara.

Their arrival caused a considerable stir. From the Kaid's point of view, and from Wavell's too, they were merely a nuisance. But the Foreign Office felt differently. They had always questioned the wisdom of restoring Haile Selassie and had been extremely sceptical about reports of his continuing popularity within the country. They had an important file on the Western Galla Federation of 1936 which had vainly appealed for British protection. They knew that the Galla experts were not lying when they claimed that Haile Selassie's restoration would not be viewed as 'liberation' south of the Blue Nile. Moreover, they suspected that the Emperor's value as a rallying-point north of the Blue Nile had been much exaggerated by such biased Local Experts as Sandford.

The debate was of great moment. Willingly or unwillingly, the British held the whole future of Ethiopia in their hands. Their decision to support or not to support the Emperor would be of personal importance to many millions of Ethiopians. Haile

Selassie, with Wingate's support, wrote directly to Churchill, appealing to be allowed to enter his country immediately—an obvious way of forcing the British government's hands. Churchill, who appears to have been badly briefed, and confused by reports that Mission 106 had been prevented from entering the Galla country, sent one of his ACTION THIS DAY memos to Eden, just appointed Foreign Secretary, and to Ismay:

It would seem that every effort should be made to meet the Emperor of Ethiopia's wishes. We have already, I understand, stopped our officers from entering the Galla country. It seems a pity to employ battalions of Ethiopian deserters, who might influence the revolt, on mere roadmaking. We have sixty-four thousand troops in Kenya, where complete passivity reigns, so they could surely spare the roadmakers.

On the first point I am strongly in favour of Haile Selassie entering Ethiopia. Whatever differences there may be between the various Ethiopian tribes, there can be no doubt that the return of the Emperor will be taken as a proof that the revolt has greatly increased, and will be linked up with our victories in Libya.

I should be glad if a favourable reply could be drafted for me to send to the Emperor.

This virtually decided the issue. Eden did retort the following day, 31 December, with a memo warning against being 'stampeded into premature and possible catastrophic action', and suggesting that nothing should be done for several months with the Emperor. Churchill was surprisingly mild in his own reply to this; mild but firm. 'One would think that the Emperor would be the best judge of when to risk his life for his throne.'

The decision was taken. The crisis was over, and 106 Mission and its officers discredited and sent on their way. Once again by diplomatic skill, by playing in this case on the British Prime Minister's desire for and admiration of brave action, Haile Selassie had come safely through a potentially disastrous turmoil. The decision was taken for Gideon Force to cross the frontier in the third week of January.

Ras Kassa arrived from Jerusalem to join the Emperor, the greatest of all the exiled nobles, with his fourth and only surviving son, Asrate. His other sons, Wondossen, Aberra, and Asfawossen, had been treacherously killed on the orders of Graziani. Ras Kassa himself had led the Armies of the North against Badoglio—two enemies now disgraced. On both sides of the frontier the lords and lesser lords of Ethiopia moved into place; in Roseires, Haile Selassie, Ras Kassa, Dejaz Makonnen Endalkatchew, and the Imperial Fitaurari Birru Walde Gabriel; down in Kenya Dejaz Abebe Damtew, whose brother Ras Desta had also died at Graziani's command; and ranged over against them Ras Hailu, long the personal enemy of Haile Selassie, back at last with power in Gojjam; 'Ras' Ayalew Birru, more uneasy, at Gondar; and, in the greatest dilemma of all, Ras Seyum at Addis Ababa, protected by the Italians whom he and Ras Kassa had fought together in the Tembien and with Haile Selassie at the bloody field of Mai Ceu. Perhaps as they wondered on whom fortune would smile and who, if any, would be left alive to claim the imperial throne at the issue of the struggle, they spared a thought for Ras Imru far away in his island prison but freed from their rivalries and the turbulence that now threatened them all.

CHAPTER 26

JOY IN THE MORNING

PORT SUDAN was very, very hot. Even the newly-arrived Indian Army officers complained of the prickly heat and left their baths standing all night. The only wartime landmark was a shot-down Italian fighter on view in the market with a money-box beside it for appreciative contributions (in the first three hours £50 was collected). 'The only trouble the police had', noted Mr. Lea the DC, 'was with a number of people who wished to show their contempt for Mussolini by using it for an improper purpose.'

Outside the town there had been the usual dramas with unexploded bombs which seemed to have an irresistible attraction for the Beja, who took the brass fittings for pure gold until they learnt better. The Beja had largely replaced the Beni Amer in Lea's own *banda*, 'Meadowforce', partly because the Beni Amer had too many kinsmen fighting magnificently for the wrong side and partly because the Beja despite feigned innocence were experienced raiders. Steer watched them being issued with rifles. 'Over-reacting heavily, each man had insisted on being shown how to load and fire.' When targets were put up at 300 yards, 'each man plugged his entire clip of bullets clean through the bull's eye.'

Very different were the Hadendoa of 'Frostyforce' down in the Gash, whose uniform was a red sash and a fuzzy mop of hair and whose idea of training was, according to their own commander, 'to lie on their backs in the sun for 3 days, then turn over and shoot a few rounds and then turn over again for another three days' rest.' Not that it mattered. They had had a surprisingly calm war in the Gash, amusing themselves since the fall of Kassala mainly with the 'Gash Code', based on the striking resemblance of the frontier at that point to the map of London. Gedaref was 'Chelsea', the Gash Delta 'Soho', Atbara 'the Edgware Road', and Kassala itself 'Piccadilly Circus'. This had agitated the Italian wireless interceptors and alarmed their superiors who imagined these code-words to refer in some mysterious way to the massing of British troops on the frontier. Those who used it became adept at improvisation—the friendly Sheikh Othman Ali Keilu became known as 'Eros' not for any heart-piercing exploits but simply because he lived plumb in the centre of 'Piccadilly Circus'.

It was at Butana Bridge that the newly-arrived commander of the Fourth Indian Division, General Beresford-Peirse, established his headquarters with two of his three brigades, the 11th and the 5th. This, with Messervy's Gazelle Force of Sudanese and the other Indian Division, Heath's, made a formidable concentration. It was strengthened by a squadron of tanks (B Squadron, 4th Royal Tank Regiment) and by the first French troops to arrive, theoretically for 'Operation Marie'—a squadron of Spahis who immediately distinguished themselves by attacking and routing an Italian patrol at Om Ager to the south.

The black hump of Jebel Kassala dominated the skyline for miles in all directions. Messervy suggested that the attack should be launched in the third week of January.

On New Year's Day 1941 came the first active bit of excitement for the year on the border—reports that Major Quigini and his men had evacuated Gubba way down to the south.

A week later an RAF plane occupied Gubba, carrying only George Steer and his assistant at the Propaganda Unit, the fat and jovial Mamur, with 500 dollars and the Imperial *Awaj* to distribute. They found Gubba deserted; no replies came to their shouts in Amharic and Arabic. The Hamej had fled from their homes and were watching from the hills. Steer hauled down the blue and yellow flag of the *banda* and raised the lion-banner of Ethiopia; the first raising of the flag over a 'conquered' Italian post on the Sudan frontier. He also found, abandoned but not destroyed, invaluable large-scale maps (1:50,000) of parts of Eritrea.

The evacuation of Gubba proved Wingate wrong. A combination of bombing, propaganda, and circling rebels had been enough to scare the Italians out without a hard core of professional guerrilla troops taking part. It was of course only a small outpost, but at least theoretically it barred the route to Mount Belaya. Therefore with its evacuation the only threat to the

Emperor's safe entry was removed. To the north Kwara, surrounded and distant, was the nearest Italian outpost.

Steer flew back to Roseires to prepare his most dramatic news-
letter for the great day. Three weeks later, the great day had
arrived. As *Banderachin* put it:

On January 20 His Majesty the Emperor Haile Selassie I accompanied by
the Crown Prince and the Duke of Harar, by the Echege, Ras Kassa,
Dejaz Makonnen Endalkatchew, Dejaz Adafrisau, by his delegate to the
League of Nations Ato Lorenzo Taezaz and by his principal secretary
Ato Wolde Giorgis, by the Chief of his Imperial Guard Kenyaz Mokria,
by two powerful Ethiopian and English armies equipped with war
material superior to the Italian, crossed the frontier of the Sudan and
Ethiopia and entered into his own . . . Therefore we rejoice in the tender
mercies of our God and of Jesus Christ and we give thanks before the
Divine Throne.

Or as Newbold wrote: 'The Emperor left here for Ethiopia
today, flying to the frontier and then in by ground. I hope he
doesn't get blotted.'

The Emperor and his cortège had flown from Khartoum to
Roseires on 18 January. Two days later they were flown to the
hamlet of Um Idla near the border, a place Wingate had chosen as
being 'practically incapable of detection or interception by the
enemy.' There was not then, nor was there ever to be, any
question of Haile Selassie leading his troops in person: his person
was too valuable to risk. He and his bodyguard of young
noblemen, with Chapman-Andrews always by his side, followed behind where Wingate and others led.

Wingate had reached Um Idla a few days before the Emperor,
almost simultaneously with one of the 'two powerful armies',
Captain Boyle's 2nd Ethiopians. The other 'army', the 'English'
one, was Boustead's Frontier Battalion of Sudanese which in fact
did not accompany the Emperor. For at this stage of the invasion
of Gojjam there was no danger at all. The sole object was to
assemble the different entities of Gideon Force in the interior at
Mount Belaya where one of Boustead's four companies, the
bearded *Bimbashi* Acland's, was already in position.

It took a fortnight to get the Emperor there. While Haile
Selassie camped for a week thirty miles inside the frontier by the

banks of the River Dinder, Wingate ranged ahead with two trucks trying to find a suitable route for the Imperial convoy. By 3 February Haile Selassie had reached 'Road's End Camp' but only after reducing his personal escort from seventy-strong to twenty, abandoning his lorry and riding in on Boyle's white horse. At Road End's Camp Wingate had, in his turn, abandoned his two trucks and gone on alone by horse. The following day he rode back to camp on a bedraggled steed, with a British sergeant and three exhausted mules, to announce that they were still fifty miles from Belaya. On 4 February 'the powerful army' set out on mules and camels: Wingate, Boyle, Chapman-Andrews, His Imperial Majesty, and two or three Ethiopians. That day they covered six miles. The following day was the grimmest and hardest of all. But on 6 February they finally reached the foot of Mount Belaya, to find a smiling Boustead already there. He had come from Roseires by the easier, southern route, opened up by the evacuation of Gubba. 'You were right, and I was wrong', admitted Wingate. Behind them the 2nd Ethiopians struggled slowly in and the endless columns of slow-moving camels, many dying as they were driven up into the highlands, followed the blazed trail.

Sandford was also at Belaya, having arrived there a week earlier from the interior—but without the 5,000 mules he had promised. Mules were as valued as rifles in the highlands. Promises to supply them or even to sell them were almost invariably broken, as all the British officers attached to the Patriots were to learn to their cost. So with trucks unable to cross the bitter country, and mules as scarce as diamonds, Gideon Force was reduced to relying on camels for transporting its supplies, in a country totally unsuitable for camels. 'I do not recommend this archaic form of transport for campaigns in other theatres', wrote Wingate later. By 12 February, when Haile Selassie presented their colours to the 2nd Ethiopians, hundreds of dead and dying camels were littering the foothills of Mount Belaya. Wingate and Sandford were not there for that ceremony. The landing strip had been completed the day before, and they had flown back to Khartoum, to consult with General Platt. The Emperor and Gideon Force were in position. But what was the next move to be—and who was to decide it? For by then the position had changed dramatically, both in the north and the south.

THE SOUTH

Boustead had detached from the Frontier Battalion his No. 5 company of Nuba tribesmen under *Bimbashi* Campbell for a little rampage of their own. On 20 January Campbell crossed the frontier, bypassed occupied Geissen and made for the Shogali crossing. But it was not till 14 February that he actually seized it. At about the same time the 2/6th KAR, the only KAR battalion to be used in the Sudan, occupied Kurmuk. Its commander, Lt. Colonel Johnson, was given the overall command of all operations in this area. His base was at Malakal.

Here, as all along the Galla-Sidamo frontier, in the hot low-lying jungles, bush country, and desert, the various British advances were opposed mainly by General Gazzera's *Gruppi Bande Frontiere*. By seizing the Shogali crossing, *Bimbashi* Campbell had effectively countered any plans by General Gazzera to send reinforcements into Gojjam and thus threaten the Emperor from the flank.

Further south lay the Baro Salient, held by Major Praga at Gambeila with the 3rd *Gruppo*. Here the local District Commissioners fought their own little raiding war with their Anuak and Nuer levies. 'Romilly Force' captured Jokau Post on the Baro on 23 January. Evans-Pritchard intrigued with the Anuak nobles along the Gilo, where the District Commissioners Renny and Lesslie (later to die in this 'campaign') fought a skirmish on the 28th. A few potential Galla 'rebels' were brought to the province capital at Malakal and given money to spread the rebellion. They spent the money on clothes.

Further south still, Cave *Bey* and Captain Whalley stood on the Boma plateau at Towoth Post with the Equatorial Corps, facing Major Gobatto and the 2nd *Gruppo*, based at Maji. Whalley's string of urgent reports to Khartoum had died down. Groups of would-be rebels had come and, finding no arms or ammunition available, had gone back into the interior. But it seems that permission was at last given for Whalley and his men to cross the frontier. The post of Eribo was attacked on the 25th. But it was very difficult country.

Round the corner, inside Kenya, a newly-raised KAR Brigade, the 25th, was intended also to thrust towards Maji. The brigade was based in Turkana country, north of Lodwar, on the Sudan side of Lake Rudolf. The objectives given in its operation order of 31 January were the little posts of Todenyang, Namuruputh, and Kalam to the west of the Omo.

Brigadier Owen, the commander, had only two KAR battalions; but over a thousand Turkana tribesmen had been raised and armed under the supervision of their District Commissioner, Major Gregory Smith. They were formed into the '5th Irregulars', and split into spear companies and rifle companies, led by Captain Bilborough.

This gave the invaders a strength of somewhere near 3,000 men. Across the frontier lay a few *banda* of the *Maji* group but above all the ferocious Merille tribesmen, who with their allies the Donjiro were blood enemies of the equally ferocious Turkana. Between them the Merille and the Donjiro were 4,000 rifles strong; and they were on the best of terms with the Italians whose *Residente* at Kalam, Lieutenant Modesto Furesi, had been arming and supplying them. 'Any Merille seen are to be attacked,' said the operation order. When captured, Merille tribesmen were to be segregated, six to be selected, given two white arm-bands and a white flag and split sticks with messages for the three great Merille chiefs; the very old half-paralysed Lokweria, the powerful Tappo, and Lomoromoi, leader of the Moran. All were to be invited to come to Kalam for a *Baraka* to discuss stolen cattle, blood payments for past killings, and the question of hostages.

This was tribal warfare in all its traditional glory. Todenyang was occupied, Namuruputh was taken after a skirmish, but the Merille gathered to defend a ford on the road approaching Kalam, and the 2/4th KAR was driven back, though bombing shook the tribesmen. By 12 February 'peace talks' had been opened with the Merille.

THE NORTH

Thus all up and down the 1,200-mile frontier between the Sudan and Italian East Africa the *Kaid* had, in conjunction with General Cunningham in Kenya, planned a series of attacks and raids —some large, some small, some mere feints, some with serious objectives—to coincide with the entry of the Emperor. But the main blow was to be struck from the Butana Bridge. General Platt's most serious objective was the recapture of Kassala —long-discussed, now decided and planned in detail. Immensely meticulous battle-plans had been drawn up for this, the most vital thrust of all. Both the *Kaid*'s Indian divisions circled Kassala, ready to put in their textbook attack. As it turned out, however, all the carefully prepared staff work was wasted effort. On the morning of 19 January Messervy's Gazelle Force reoccupied the town without a shot fired. The Italians had abandoned Kassala two nights earlier. It was, for the military at least, highly frustrating.

But the civilian authorities were delighted. Kennedy-Cooke, the Province Governor, moved back into his house, glad to find that the damage done had been much less than expected. The temporary occupiers had broken a few windows but had kindly dug a number of underground shelters. These latter were a mixed blessing, however. A few months later the lavatory of Kennedy-Cooke's spare bedroom disappeared into one of the shelters during the night. The two Sayids came to pay their respects. They explained somewhat evasively that they had tried to get a message out to announce the Italian evacuation but had failed. With the reoccupation of Kassala, the threat to the Sudan was over. The initiative now lay definitely with the British.

The situation on the early morning of 19 January was this. On the British side the two Major-Generals, Beresford-Peirse and Heath, had the bulk of their two divisions—four brigades— concentrated at Kassala. Two more brigades were out on the flanks. Briggs's 7th stood on the Red Sea coast, assisted by Meadowforce. In the south Mayne's 9th, with the Eastern Arab Corps, faced Slim's uncaptured Metemma.

Less than two hundred miles from Kassala lay Asmara, capital of Eritrea and seat of Frusci's command. Half-way between the two stood the town of Agordat, linked to Kassala by two highways, an upper and a lower. General Frusci strung out five brigades along these two roads. Behind Agordat, where the lowlands ended and the highlands began, on the mountains overlooking the picturesque little town of Keren, he placed a sixth brigade, Lorenzini's famous and never defeated II, fresh from its triumphs in British Somaliland. With six of the eleven Italian brigades in Eritrea facing an invading force of only four British brigades, the odds appeared definitely to favour General Frusci and the defence. But despite their own misgivings, yielding largely to Churchill's insistent pressure, the *Kaid* and his two Major-Generals decided to attack.

The so-called Battle of the Lowlands that followed was more a battle of manœuvre than anything else. Messervy's armoured cars and lorries swung round unmarked tracks to take the Italians in the rear and scare them out of one position after another back into Agordat on the upper, or Barentu on the lower road. This caused much frustration to the Indian Army which never had a chance for a really blood-curdling engagement.

The only resistance to speak of was met at the gorge of Cheru, the scene of one of the most heroic and picturesque incidents of the war. The British had halted outside the gorge and had trundled their guns up into position. As the guns were being sited, just after dawn, the gunners were suddenly aware that they were being charged, literally charged, from the flank by about sixty horsemen led by an Italian officer on a white horse. The horsemen galloped forward in extended line, firing wildly from the saddle and throwing grenades as the gunners hastily swivelled their guns right round and fired point blank, their shells piercing the horses' chests without exploding or slithering across the ground. Even this did not halt the charge. A Brigadier and the Gunner Colonel who, against regulations, were not carrying their personal sidearms, attempted to seize rifles from the soldiers around them. 'No fear, that's mine', cried an indignant private, as small-arms fire opened up.

The last of the horsemen fell within twenty-five yards of the guns. Of the sixty who charged, two-thirds were killed including their brave leader Lieutenant Togni. They were part of the *Gruppo Bande a Cavallo Amhara*, a cavalry unit commanded by Lieutenant Guillet. An hour later he, rashly but not so wildly, attacked again, with all his *bande*, over 500 strong. They overran the 4/11th Sikhs who had moved forward, but sheered off when faced with the artillery behind. In all that morning's work, 179 horsemen were killed and 260 wounded—89 horses were killed, 68 wounded. It must have been the last great European-led cavalry charge in Africa. Churchill, who himself in his youth had charged with the 8th Hussars at Omdurman, would have approved. Togni's charge very nearly succeeded. It had certainly shaken the British, and proved to those who doubted that Italian officers knew how to fight and how to die. Guillet withdrew his surviving horsemen to the heights of Shanfalla that night, patrolling out on the flanks of the British.

But though the advance of the invaders was held up, the retreat of the defenders was chaotic and disorganized. Had it not been for Guillet and his horsemen, almost all the Italians would have fallen into the hands of the blocking column behind Cheru. As it was the Highland Light Infantry took 700 prisoners including a brigade commander, Ugo Fongoli, the first Italian general to be captured.

Six days after the invasion the position was, then, from the Italian point of view serious but not disastrous. They had lost ground, been outmanœuvered and were minus one general. But in recompense their brigades, instead of being strung out, liable to be gobbled up one by one, were concentrating in strength. Their confusion and panicky withdrawals could be attributed mainly to a lack of co-ordination between their own commanders as opposed to the close co-ordination between the two British generals. Strings of contradictory orders had been issued from Addis Ababa, from Asmara, and from the three divisional commanders. The Italian High Command took steps. Even though Addis Ababa proclaimed the invasion to be mere 'tentativi di infiltrazione', the Duke of Aosta ordered the immediate dispatch to the area of half his reserve, the 11th Savoy Grenadiers. And at dawn on 25 January General Trezzani arrived at Asmara and then went out to Agordat with Frusci and the air force commander, General Pinna, to co-ordinate the defence.

An immediate decision was taken, and a wise one. Lorenzini was promoted to General, his II Brigade was called forward from Keren to Agordat, and he was given command of the whole zone. Unfortunately after Trezzani's departure Frusci sent a brace of Generals, including the disastrous Tessitore, back to 'advise' him. This meant that two whole days, vital to the planning of defensive or offensive moves, were wasted. By the evening of the 27th Lorenzini had, by cabling strong protests, rid himself of his 'advisers'. But by then it was almost too late. That evening Lorenzini stood with four brigades at Agordat, Bergonzi with two at Barentu, each facing an attacking force of two brigades. The antagonists on both sides were now concentrated.

The blow fell first on Agordat. The 'I' tanks, the heavy Matildas, lumbered forward along the plain. Mines had not been laid, there were no sharp rocks to cut their tracks as at Gallabat, and eleven of the outgunned Italian tanks sent out to halt them were blown away. Meanwhile, the 11th Indian Infantry Brigade moved north-east to cut the road behind Agordat leading back to Keren. This was the finish. The armoured cars of Gazelle Force led the infantry into Agordat at midday on 31 January. Lieutenant Guillet and his horsemen were again the last to leave, holding out till the end and then escorting the whole garrison down the railway line, avoiding the road and its trap. So, of the 15,000 troops there, less than 1,000 were taken prisoner.

It was bad luck on Bergonzi. He and his two brigades had that very day successfully counter-attacked their besiegers. Certainly the Fifth Indian Division was not up to the standard of the Fourth. They had not enjoyed a triumph in the Western Desert as the Fourth had done. They had not, like Beresford-Peirse's men, gathered in acres of surrendering Italians. Indeed their only taste had been that of defeat, at Gallabat. The two brigades of the Fifth attacked on 1 February, to be met with a stubborn defence. That night, skilfully, Bergonzi pulled out. With Agordat gone he had no choice. Next morning the attackers shelled an empty town before moving in to occupy it.

What the Italians called the Battle of the Lowlands was, therefore, over less than a fortnight after it had begun; and a large section of the ancient colony of Eritrea had fallen into British hands. There was no particular reason why the invaders should have been successful. Indeed if the Italian generals had been as courageous or as active as the Italian cavalry lieutenants, the British advance would not have gone very far. But even the reputed Lorenzini had put up only a poor defence at Agordat. Above all, the Italians never seem seriously to have considered a determined counter-attack. The British circled around them, and cut them off from the rear. But they, though having more troops, never circled around the British. All that can be said in their favour is that they did conduct their retreats—always a difficult military manœuvre—most skilfully. Their brigades fell back to the prepared positions at Keren with very little loss. From outlying Om Ager, Colonel Postiglione and his brigade were also pulled back across country, successfully.

There was, however, nothing inevitable about the invaders' success, as events on the north edge of the Northern Front, on the Red Sea, showed. There, as the attack on Agordat was being planned, Brigadier Briggs and the 7th Indian Infantry Brigade were ordered to recapture Karora. Karora was garrisoned by merely one *Guardie di Finanza* (Customs Police) battalion. The

Royal Sussex set out by lorry from Port Sudan, 180 miles away, to launch the attack at dawn on 24 January, supported by Meadowforce, already patrolling forward. But by evening the lorries, which had been moving at only eight miles an hour, had bogged down in the sand. At dawn the next day they were still ten miles away. Meadowforce, however—three Englishmen and ninety tribesmen—had not received the order to cancel the operation; when they skirmished forward they were attacked and very nearly surrounded. The whole thing was, in the military phrase, a balls-up. Next morning, Italian planes strafed the stranded lorries. Two Italian brigades, the V and the XLIV, were moved up into the area to hold off any repetition of this attack and cover the northern flank of what had now become the key of the whole Italian defensive position: Keren.

It was on Keren that, belatedly, as Agordat fell and Lorenzini's columns retreated, Trezzani and the Duke of Aosta were concentrating their will and their reserves. Two more brigades, the VI and the XI, were sent up from Shoa; and the 11th Regiment of the Savoy Grenadiers were hastily recalled from the line of the Juba and sent up in non-stop convoys to reinforce Keren. To relieve General Frusci of all other responsibilities the governorate of Amhara was detached from his command and a new Sector, the West Sector, was formed out of Shoa and Amhara and allotted to General Nasi. Thus the area of Frusci's command was reduced to the governorate of Eritrea; and both sides concentrated the best of their forces at what General Platt referred to as 'the horrible escarpment', Keren.

On 2 February Gazelle Force leading, as always, the pursuit of withdrawing Italians, halted at the dried bed of the river Baraka, 150 yards wide. The bridge over the river, Ponte Mussolini, had been rather uselessly blown. But the river-bed was mined and the retreating men of Lorenzini thus protected. It took Messervy's men eight hours to clear a path through the minefield; and as the last Italians struggled up and into the gorge ahead engineers blew down massive sections of the cliff-face behind them. At five o'clock that evening the armoured cars of Gazelle Force came up against the first Italian road-block, five miles from Keren. Ahead of them, the road and the railway wound through the Dongalaas Gorge. On both sides of the Gorge, mountains towered—Samanna, Sanchil, Dologorodoc, Falestoh, Zeban.

KENYA

Over on the far side of Lake Rudolf, to its east, General Cunningham in his turn had been preparing a major thrust. Two of his three South African brigades, the 2nd and the 5th, were spread out around the Marsabit area. General Cunningham's plan here was to recapture Moyale and thrust towards Mega, thus opening up the whole southern area of General Gazzera's command. One or two swift military successes would, he was sure, put life into the latent rebellion.

Unfortunately (as Cunningham should have known) there was very little rebellion latent. There were to be even fewer military successes. The South African troops appear to have been very bad. Curle's '2nd Irregulars' (nearly 2,000 strong after the absorption of the '3rd') who operated with them under the overall command of General 'Daddy' Brink, had a very low opinion of the whites. There was a skirmish on 17 January—a preparatory attack on the little outpost of El Yibo. After it the Irregulars judged the South Africans to be 'poor soldiers', 'unwilling to close', and 'had a very poor opinion of them.' The men of the Natal Mounted Rifles sold their boots to the Ethiopians, and the crews of the South African armoured cars mowed down whole herds of oryx with their machine-guns.

At the end of January a more serious attack was launched. But at Moyale the single defending battalion, the 54th Colonial, pushed back the attackers. The two South African brigadiers consoled themselves and their senior generals by each capturing a waterhole: Gorai for Brigadier Buchanan of the 2nd, Hobok for Brigadier Armstrong of the 5th. This was hardly what General Cunningham had been hoping for from troops which he, and Wavell too, persisted in regarding as the 'best' on the southern front.

There was between Platt and Cunningham no open sign of that professional and personal jealousy which six years earlier had animated the previous invaders of Ethiopia, Badoglio, and Graziani. But Cunningham would hardly have been human if he had felt no pique at the thought of all the success and all the kudos going to the credit of the dour Platt: and Cunningham was a very human man. With things going badly on the remote side of Lake Rudolf—which was not important—and worse in the Meg-Moyale area, which was—he decided to have a go on his third 'front'. On 28 January he asked for permission to try for Kismayu on the coast. Permission was granted. On 2 February, Wavell sent the Prime Minister a cable that was honey and balm to Churchill after so much frustration. 'In Kenya', read the cable, 'I have approved the proposal to attempt the capture of Kismayu about the middle of February . . . Generally I have given instructions to both Cunningham and Platt for the maximum effort they can make against Italian East Africa in the next two months.'

It was hardly surprising that in his speech to the House of Commons one week later Churchill was unable to resist a triumphant reference to the campaign in East Africa. Three weeks after the invasion all the British posts in Italian hands had been recaptured. British forces, large and small, stood deep inside Italian territory in half a dozen places and poised to strike in half a dozen more. And the Emperor was safely back inside his Empire.

'Give us the tools and we will finish the job', was the theme of Churchill's speech. After describing the triumphs in Libya, he went on—with broad accuracy—as follows:

Fifteen hundred miles away to the southward a strong British and Indian army, having driven the invaders out of the Sudan, is marching steadily forward through the Italian colony of Eritrea, thus seeking to complete the isolation of all the Italian troops in Ethiopia. Other British forces are entering Ethiopia from the west, while the army gathered in Kenya—in the van of which we may discern the powerful forces of the Union of South Africa organized by General Smuts—is striking northward along the whole enormous front. Lastly, the Ethiopian patriots, whose independence was stolen five years ago, have risen in arms; and their Emperor, so recently an exile in England, is in their midst to fight for their freedom and his throne.

Here, then, we see the beginnings of a process of reparation and of chastisement of wrong-doing which reminds us that though the mills of God grind slowly, they grind exceedingly small.

CHAPTER 27

THE BATTLE OF KEREN

ELEVEN peaks dominated the approaches to Keren. Seven were to the north of the road, ranging from Samanna, the highest of all at 5,922 feet, to Sanchil just above the gorge. Four were to the south—Dologorodoc, Zeban, and Falestoh grouped like a hostile triangle, and slightly on its own, separated by the Acqua Col, the peak of Zelale, known as the Sphinx. Each peak was a fortress, each garrisoned. For 150 miles north and south the Keren escarpment stretched unbroken. Many miles to the south Postiglione and his brigade, pulled back from Om Ager, barred the only possible route that might be used to outflank the position, at Arresa. The northern approach from the Red Sea through Karora would not, in the opinion of the British staff, bear 'the traffic of a large force'. In any case the British seemed to welcome the necessity of a frontal attack, of what both Platt and Newbold were to call, with apparent pleasure, a real 'ding-dong battle'.

Yet at first the British commanders seem to have imagined that they could sweep away the defenders as they had swept away the defenders in the lowlands and at Agordat. On the afternoon of 2 February the armoured cars of Gazelle Force had reached the foot of the wall of hills that shut off the Keren plateau; and only twenty-four hours later Savory's brigade, the 11th, was attacking up to the peak on the north of Dongalaas Gorge to Sanchil. In the next three days as the Cameron Highlanders, the Rajputs, and the Punjabis attacked and won and lost again, Platt and his subordinate commanders came to realize the strength of the defenders' position and the enormous difficulties of the enterprise facing them.

The weather was hot, and the hillsides waterless. Shells for the British guns had to be lugged up by hand; and when a man was wounded, it took twelve men to carry him down the slopes again. Worse still, all the British movements on the road and the gorge were in full view of the enemy on the heights. Very soon

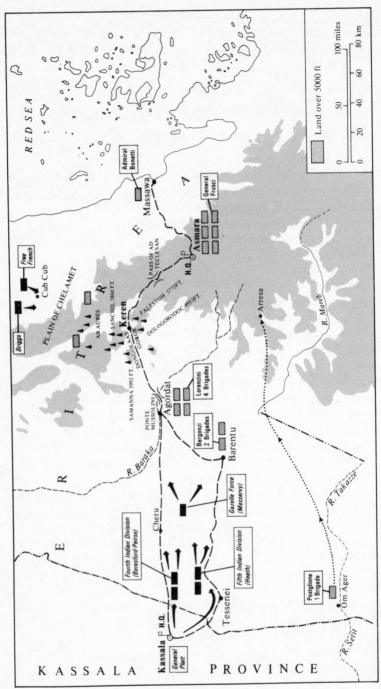

MAP 8. The Keren Campaign

the British learnt wisdom and moved only by night. The 'I' tanks were blocked by the cliff-face which the Italian engineers had blown, a huge tumble of rocks, boulders, and crags.

The actual Italian defences were well-sited and well-prepared. Their forward positions, the only ones that the British artillery (because of the trajectories involved) could reach, were situated on false crests, below the main peaks; protected in front and behind, out of bombing range, by a double apron of loose wire. Machine-gun positions in stone *sangars* swept the approaches and covered each other with supporting fire. And if a false crest were taken despite the hand-grenades which were rolled down on the advancing troops, despite the defence by the bayonet which became habitual, even then mortars hidden behind were ranged on to these crests—mortars that were, as the intelligence reported, 'accurate, well-sited and well-handled'. They quickly made the attackers' position untenable. The Italian counter-attacks were characterized by 'bold and clever infiltration, with sniping, by small parties supported by fire.'

This was a very different enemy from those whom the invaders had grown quickly and unwisely to despise. There was a pause, hesitant, alarmed. Major-General Beresford-Peirse brought forward his other brigade, the 5th, and tried a night attack to the south, against Acqua Col. There was confusion, as there so often is in night attacks. The signals broke down, and the leading companies of the Royal Fusiliers and the Rajputana Rifles suffered heavily. The lesson was clear. Isolated assaults by single brigades were worse than useless. The general prepared a combined assault, a major attack both north and south of the Gorge with both his brigades against the enemy which had been such an easy prey to his Division in the Libyan desert.

The Duke of Aosta himself visited Keren on 7 February. General Frusci was in overall command of the sector, back at Asmara. General Carnimeo had been appointed commander of the Keren area. He skulked in a cave on the right of the little town of Keren that lay down in the valley behind the Dongolaas Gorge, and was never seen. But Lorenzini with his II Brigade was sent south of the gorge to cover the dangerous gap at Acqua Col, with the XI Brigade, sent up from Shoa, in support on the nearby peaks. The VI, formerly at Metemma, covered the railway and the gorge, with behind them on the heights above Keren three brigades pulled back from the lowlands. From the Red Sea area, the V, forward near the frontier was called back.[1] But above all, excellent Italian troops, their best, manned the peaks north of the Dongolaas Gorge, from Samanna to Sanchil. These were the three battalions of the 11th Regiment of Savoy Grenadiers, commanded by Colonel Corso Corsi, reinforced on about 10 February by the *Alpini* 'Worq Amba' Battalion of the 10th Regiment, and by the best of the Blackshirts, the three battalions of the 11th Legion. In all, the defenders numbered some 25,000 men (with 144 guns under the command of Colonel Lamborghini), conscious that the fate of Eritrea and possibly of the whole war depended on their efforts.

On the afternoon of 10 February the Fourth Indian Division launched its two-pronged attack. The fighting swayed, backwards and forwards, for forty hours, almost non-stop. To the north of the Gorge the 11th Indian Infantry Brigade twice captured, twice lost, Sanchil's twin, 'Brig's Peak', while the Camerons backed up on 'Cameron Ridge' down below. To the south Gazelle Force and the 5th Indian Infantry Brigade attacked, fruitlessly, Lorenzini's brigade at Acqua Col. Subadar Richpal Ram of the Rajputana Rifles won in this attack a posthumous V.C. for his bravery in the bitter hand-to-hand fighting. By midday on 12 February Beresford-Peirse decided to cancel further operations. Gazelle Force could not get back that night nor the following day—it was forty-eight hours more before Messervy's men wearily escaped.

The two brigades pulled back to lick their wounds and to rest. Beresford-Peirse left the front to confer with Platt, now promoted to Lieutenant-General, who called off all further attacks. For a month the invaders halted, doing very little. The two brigades of the Fifth Indian Division, the 10th and the 29th, which had taken no part in the fighting, were recalled to Barentu and given intensive mountain training. There they were joined by the division's third brigade, the 9th, called up from the Gallabat–Gondar road where it had been halted. Gazelle Force was dissolved; and Colonel Messervy, its dashing and successful

---

[1] This opened the road to Brigadier Briggs's 7th Indian Infantry Brigade which, reinforced by two French battalions from Equatorial Africa including the famous 13th Demi-Brigade of the Foreign Legion, crossed the frontier and moved swiftly south till it was halted at Cub-Cub.

commander promoted to Brigadier, was given command of the
9th. Meanwhile the air war intensified. RAF bomber squadrons
based on the captured airstrips at Barentu and Agordat raided,
besides Keren itself, Asmara, Massawa, and Makalle. It was by
no means a one-sided affair; the *Regia Aeronautica* destroyed 13
British planes on the ground in a single raid against Agordat. But
by mid-March there were less than 50 serviceable aircraft in the
whole of *AOI*. Gina's brother made curt entries. Three months
had passed since the joyous feast-day of the Madonna of
Loreto—patron of all Italian airmen—a day on which he had,
irreligiously, visited streams in out-of-way places 'where I surprise native girls bathing . . . and manage with a bit of trouble to
catch the nude roundness of some young girl in my view finder
and so augment my collection of black Venuses.' In those three
months the Italian air force had been virtually destroyed. As late
as 8 March, however, a batch of new planes flew in from Libya.

Masters of the skies, the RAF dropped thousands of leaflets
over Keren, bearing replicas of the Ethiopian flag, and messages
in both Tigrinya and Amharic from the British to the soldiers of
Eritrea. Another carrying Haile Selassie's seal was addressed in
particular to the Shoan and Gojjami levies of the XI and VI
Brigades.

Gojjamis! It is in faithful Gojjam that I have set up my flag and won my
first victories. Come back to your homes, Shoans of the XI Brigade! . . .
Come to me through the English. Ras Kassa is with me in Gojjam, and
when all Gojjam is ours you will be our army to cleanse the Italians from
Salale and Debre Brehan.

This propaganda had its effect, particularly on the Shoans of
the XI Brigade, who began to desert in increasing numbers
—though the barbed wire that defended the Italian positions
hampered deserters, and Italian patrols ruthlessly shot any askaris
spotted trying to crawl through the wire. Even so, by early
March almost 600 deserters had, since the invasion of Eritrea,
reached the British lines.

The Italians attempted to react to the Emperor's propaganda
and to the news of the presence of the revered Ras Kassa, who six
years earlier had commanded the Armies of the North against
them, by a major political move. On 26 February the Viceroy
appointed Ras Seyum Negus of Tigre and shortly afterwards sent
him back to his capital of Adowa. To ensure his loyalty, and to

show their trust, the Italians issued the new 'Negus', rapturously welcomed, with 7,000 rifles. Almost simultaneously they sent 'Ras' Ayalew Birru back to Gondar. Both leaders, it should be noted, were closely watched: Ayalew Birru by General Martini and the Gondar garrison; Ras Seyum, who might pose more of a threat if treachery were in his mind, by Colonel Delitala's Brigade, the garrison of western Tigre.

On the ground, on the night of 23 February the Italians followed up their political moves by a fierce counter-attack. It was led by a reputed Eritrean battalion, the 4th Colonial, 'Toselli', famed before the Battle of Adowa for the defence of Amba Alagi. Colonel Persichelli commanded, and with the help of four armoured cars, drove the Indians back from their advanced positions.

Lieutenant-General Platt planned a two-division attack for mid-March. This was timed to coincide with an assault from the Red Sea side by Brigadier Briggs's troops against the mountain range to the north of Keren. But Lorenzini's II Brigade had been moved to meet and counter precisely such a threat. 'The Keren battle is in full swing,' wrote Newbold in a letter on 10 March. 'It is the biggest in the war so far in the Middle East, as the Western Desert ones were rather a walk-over.' He was right about the size and importance of the battle, wrong about it being in full swing. There were still five days to go before the major British attack. 'It is going to be a bloody battle', Platt said, 'against both the enemy and the ground. It will be won by the side which lasts longest.'

Saturday 15 March was a heavy, thundery day. At dawn the bombers flew over—Blenheims, Wellesleys, and Hardys. An hour later the artillery opened up ahead of the Fourth Indian Division as it attacked to the north of Dongolaas Gorge. The guns then switched over to the south as Messervy's brigade, the leading brigade of the Fifth Indian Division, made for Dologorodoc.

For forty-eight hours the noise and mêlée of battle rose on both sides of the Dongolaas Gorge, peaks lost and recaptured, counter-attacks delivered, held or not held, colonels wounded, junior officers killed, battalions decimated. These were the great days of the Indian army, of the Sikhs and Punjabis, the Garhwalis and Mahrattas, the Pathans and Baluchis, and the Rajputs of the lands around Jaipur. Over fifteen battalions of Indian troops were involved in the fighting, supported by only three battalions of

English troops and two of Highlanders. Messervy was the most successful of the British commanders. He captured and held Dologorodoc. But all the other attacks were beaten back by the Italians. As both divisions withdrew, the peaks on the north from Samanna to Sanchil remained inviolate, and of the peaks on the south only Dologorodoc remained in the hands of the attackers. The attack had failed.

It had failed too to the north of Keren, where Lorenzini had held the mountain range of Ab Aubes against the combined Anglo–French attack. By now he was virtually commander of the whole defence of Keren, recognized as such in all but title. He came south, after a day's pause, to direct and lead the first of seven counter-attacks against Messervy on Dologorodoc. And there he was killed. Twenty-four hours later Newbold was writing his nutshell obituary 'General Lorenzini, the "Lion of the Sahara", who was in command at Keren was a capable, energetic chap and his death in action is a blow to them as they have few capable generals.' Persichelli of the 4th Colonial had been seriously wounded. Corsi of the 11th Savoy Grenadiers had been wounded, and one of his battalion commanders, Colonel Barzon, had been killed. Although the defenders had won the battle, they had paid a heavy price—and from 20 March onwards Frusci's reports became hourly more anxious.

But the British were not to know this. Churchill, who had been expecting an early victory, cabled Eden in Cairo to ask whether reinforcements would be needed, as the battle seemed 'rather evenly balanced'. At Dologorodoc the *Alpini* of the 10th Savoy Grenadiers came within 80 yards of Messervy's brigade headquarters. That night the seventh Italian counter-attack (which Messervy's men had no means of recognizing as the last) was supported by three Italian tanks. On their side the British had only a few tanks in reserve, and had used up 1,000 lorryloads of ammunition, and 110,000 shells for their guns. They attempted to make up by stratagem what they lacked in force. Earl Baldwin's son, Lord Corvedale, rigged up a loudspeaker system to broadcast extracts from Italian Opera over the hills; and having stirred nostalgia, followed up heroic Verdi with prosaic announcements of Italian defeats in Libya. Battalion commanders resorted to strange and ingenious devices in their attempts to breach the unbreachable defences. The 4/11th Sikhs attacked up towards Sanchil like medieval warriors, each turbaned soldier carrying in front of him a full-length 'shield' of corrugated iron.[1] As they approached the enemy wire, the artillery fired smoke-shells for five minutes to cover their final charge uphill. Yet even so they were driven back with 71 casualties. Platt, like Frusci, was wavering. The British were envisaging a retreat.

Yet there was one hope for the British. During the attack forward from Dologorodoc sappers had reached and examined the road-block in the gorge, and had reported that, given forty-eight hours, they could clear it. With Messervy on Dologorodoc giving them cover and supporting fire, the Indian sappers worked by night—and, dangerously exposed, even by day—at the task.

On 25 March, under the eyes of two anxious generals, Platt from Khartoum and Wavell from Cairo, two brigades, Messervy's and Rees's, attacked straight up the Dongalaas Gorge on both sides of the railway line. They scrambled on foot to their objectives beyond the tumbled cliff-face of the road-block and held their positions grimly—Mahrattas and Punjabis on the left, Highlanders and Baluchis on the right—in the face of mortar and shellfire, while the sappers came forward with their trucks and explosives and tackled the road-block seriously. Italian troops, massing for a counter-attack in the afternoon, were dispersed and scattered by British shellfire. By evening there were contradictory stories circulating at staff headquarters of white flags having been seen on the peaks, and of counter-attacks threatening that night.

The counter-attacks failed to materialize; the white flags, if any, disappeared. But the road-block gradually shrank and diminished in the day that followed until by late afternoon it was almost cleared. Next morning, 27 March, an hour before dawn, the Worcesters and the Garhwalis attacked forward from Dologorodoc towards Zeban. They found the peak deserted. The 'I' tanks rumbled through the road-block, followed by the Central India Horse 'remounted' in 50 Bren carriers. At 7 a.m. air reconnaissance reported Keren evacuated, and an hour later the tanks thundered down through the Gorge into the pretty little town.

Simultaneously the four battalions under Brigadier Briggs's

---

[1] One of the attackers reported that six grenades bounced off his shield, leaving him with only a headache.

command supported by air and artillery, with a newly-arrived company of French marines in the van, launched a well-co-ordinated attack on the pivots of the Italian position to the north of Keren, Mounts Engiahat and Ab Aubes. 'Rien n'y manquerait', noted a caustic officer of the Legion, '—si l'ennemi n'avait jugé bon de décrocher dans la nuit.'

Frusci had decided that the situation was hopeless. On all sides the Italians had faded away during the night. The advancing British bombed and shelled and fired upon empty rock and air. Only a few white flags fluttered, finally, on Sanchil where a group of isolated defenders had been left behind. Apart from that, it had been a most skilfully conducted retreat. 'I *believe*', wrote Newbold in a postscript to a letter dated that day, 'Keren is falling. The road block is overcome and I hear our tanks are in town. But it's still secret and no details. Great news if it is so.' The battle of Keren was over. It had cost each side over 3,000 casualties.

The French hurried down through the mountains and by the following day had cut the road behind Keren. The Foreign Legion took over a thousand prisoners, including 50 officers and 200 survivors of the Savoy Grenadiers 'qui retraitaient en bon ordre'.[1] But the pursuit was not sustained. Though only just over thirty miles separated Keren and Asmara, another pass lay ahead—another fearsome gorge, Ad Teclesan. General Platt feared that this position might be an even tougher proposition than Keren, for there would be less room for the British artillery to deploy in front of it.

In the two-day pause that followed, General Frusci rearranged his troops and their commanders. General Carnimeo was ordered to lead the defenders of Keren back to Asmara, not to take up position with the 10th Regiment of Savoy Grenadiers under Colonel Borghese at Ad Teclesan. The soldiers were weary and discouraged. For the first time ever Eritreans were deserting—not to the British, though, but to their homes and families. Even the faithful askaris of the II Brigade were thinning out. Colonel Delitala was ordered to move from Enda Selassie into Adowa, with his brigade, and to extract guarantees from Ras

---

[1] 'Le Général Platt', noted Captain St Hillier of the 2nd Company with justified complacency, 'est heureusement surpris de l'arrivée de la brigade française.'

Seyum. Frusci was doing what he could. And, changing his mind, he ordered General Tessitore to transfer four native battalions to Ad Teclesan, to reinforce the fresh but untried Grenadiers.

In the lull before the attack on Ad Teclesan, De Gaulle flew in from Agordat with his chief of staff, Colonel Brosset, to review the *Brigade Français d'Orient* on the plain of Chelamet below Cub-Cub. Next day he flew away again, following Wavell back to Cairo, 'où battait le coeur de la guerre, mais un coeur mal accroché.' There Wavell faced 'toutes sortes d'entraves politiques'. 'Je dois dire,' added De Gaulle—who found him to be 'par bonheur fort bien doué quant au jugement et au sang-froid'—'qu'il les subissait avec une noble serénité. A tel point qu'il mantenait son quartier-general au Caire, où elles l'enser-raient de toutes parts. C'est au coeur de cette ville grouillante, dans le tumulte et la poussière, entre les murs d'un petit bureau surchauffé par le soleil que l'assaillaient continuellement des interventions exterieures à son domaine normal de soldat'—the presence of Eden, 'télégrammes comminatoires' from London, 'et voici que j'arrivais, incommode et pressant.' But De Gaulle was not longer pressing for 'Marie'. Content with the success of his forces, he was resigned to what was to be two more years of 'nefaste obedience' by Djibuti to the government at Vichy. The chapter was closed. Behind him he left, though only for the moment, the two battalions and one company of French troops. They were destined to join LeGentilhomme's division in Egypt for the trial of strength looming ahead in the Middle East, De Gaulle's great chance.[1]

Before dawn on 31 March Messervy and his brigade attacked Ad Teclesan. Two hours after the attack started, 19 officers and 460 men of the 1st Battalion of the 10th Regiment of the Savoy Grenadiers had surrendered. Fighting went on all day and Colonel Borghese was killed, but it was obvious that the defenders were not of the calibre of the 11th Regiment and that the pass would fall. At 10.30 a.m. General Frusci declared Asmara, capital of Eritrea, seat of the governate, and head-

---

[1] At Cairo, as in Khartoum, he spent much time in the Zoo, opposite the Legation of France, from whose window gazed 'visages tendus . . . dont le regard cependant suivait le General de Gaulle.' The author believes he is the first to have noted (though he would not endeavour to explain) the General's predilection for Zoological Gardens.

quarters of his Sector, an open town, and prepared to evacuate. At dusk he sent a message to General Carnimeo at Ad Teclesan to break contact and pull back along a side road towards Metemma, to General Tessitore's command. In Asmara rioters and looters, held in check by the Chief of Police, were joined in the evening by grenade-throwing native troops of the disbanded 50th and 51st Colonial Battalions. At midnight precisely, General Frusci sent a last message to Addis Ababa:

Words cannot describe the gallantry shown by my troops during the superhuman struggle in which they have taken part. Before destroying the radio I send to Your Royal Highness the loyal greetings of my troops and myself. *Viva Italia!*

It was a melodramatic moment for all Italians, this loss of their former colonial capital, the city built out of nothing by themselves, for so many decades the centre of their power in Africa. Yet if the Italians had held on just a little longer at Keren, if they had not in the end cracked under pressure, they might have pulled off the victory. A British retreat would have been disastrous for British morale. The loss of Keren was the turning-point of the war, a very close-run thing. During the night Frusci and his staff left for the town he had chosen as his new headquarters, Adigrat.

Before dawn civil envoys were out on the road, armed with white flags, led by the Bishop. They were met and, regrettably, fired upon in the half-light by the advancing 'Flitforce'—Colonel Fletcher and the Central India Horse in their Bren carriers. The Italians did not hide their eagerness that the British should take over as quickly as possible. In this war there was often an unspoken, sometimes indeed an open complicity, between the opposing white men, especially when there was a risk of native 'anarchy'. By midday the 10th Indian Infantry Brigade had occupied Asmara; and Admiral Bonetti, Commander of Massawa on the coast, had been persuaded to restore the water and the electricity supplies which he controlled and which he had, as an act of war, cut off. On 2 April the British authorities officially took control of the civil and military administration of the capital of Eritrea, Italy's oldest colony—delayed but sweet revenge for the débâcle in Somaliland eight months earlier.

CHAPTER 28

GIDEON FORCE

GIDEON FORCE camped at the foot of Mount Belaya, waiting for Wingate and Sandford to fly back from Khartoum. It was a motley collection of men and beasts. A few hundred Ethiopian refugees, an ex-Emperor plus a bevy of impoverished nobles who had spent the last five years in the Coptic monasteries of Jerusalem, were balanced by a few hundred Sudanese soldiers with their amateurish British officers. A little group of Kenya settlers, five Australians, a handful of Jews, and several eager young cavalry subalterns from the regiments stationed in Palestine added more to its confusion than to its effectiveness. The fighting force was totally outnumbered by the thousands of hired camelmen with their dead and dying camels. There was hardly a professional army officer in the force, Wingate apart.

But if there were a lack of regular soldiers there was a plethora of professional writers[1]—though, curiously, the man who was probably the greatest writer of them all, Thesiger, has never described that period of his life. But Thesiger was described most notably by another *Bimbashi* of the Sudan Defence Force, Harris of the Frontier Battalion, who found him already installed at Belaya as

'one of those hardy men who seem to take a delight in being as uncomfortable as possible . . . I found him naked in the middle of the stream having a vigorous bath in the freezing water. Thesiger had breakfast with me and, after informing me that he had lived on the country for the last two months and could not imagine why people troubled to take rations with them, proceeded to finish my last tin of grapefruit, half my remaining supply of sugar, and most of my one and only remaining pot of marmalade.'

[1] Wingate himself was no Lawrence with the pen, though his reports were concise and, in an abrupt style, well-written. But his Jewish secretary Akavia, the English journalist Leonard Mosley, the American journalist Stevens, and the South African Laurens Van Der Post were all with Gideon Force and wrote accounts of its—or their—exploits.

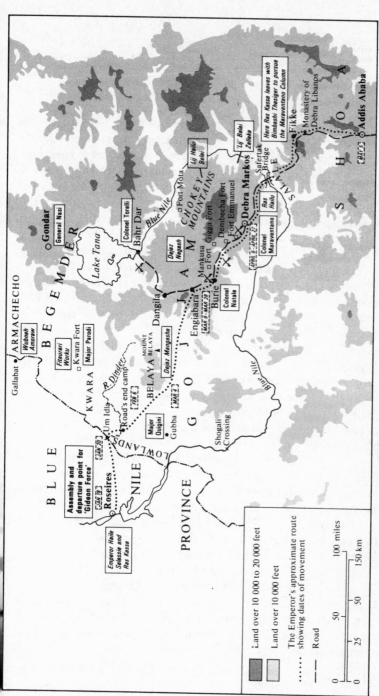

MAP 9. Gojjam: The Campaign of Gideon Force and the Return of the Emperor

A motley collection, indeed, to reconquer an Empire.

Wingate and Sandford spent four days in Khartoum hammering out their plans with General Platt. It was decided that Gideon Force should harass the Italians all over Gojjam and as far north as Gondar. Its objective would be not to drive the Italians out but on the contrary to pin down as many troops as possible within this whole vast area of operations. That had been Lawrence's strategy in the Hejaz. The Arab Revolt of 1917 was designed to harass but not destroy the railway to Medina, thus leaving the vast Turkish garrison there intact but useless, in a state of perpetual tension. The regular officers of the British Army had at the time scoffed at this plan. But by Wingate's day it appeared, encouragingly, that even a Platt, despite his well-publicized views on would-be Lawrences, had learnt this particular lesson from the First World War.

Platt gave his approval. Wingate flew back to Belaya on 15 February. But by then the whole situation had changed, and the planned strategy could no longer be applied. The Italians had, infuriatingly, made a move themselves. A week earlier, on 8 February, General Nasi had flown to Gondar, the city that was to be his future base, to take up his post as commanding officer of the new Western Sector. The following day—he was still Vice Governor-General—he installed Ras Seyum solemnly at Adowa. Having done his best to cover his northern flanks, he turned his attention to the south, to Gojjam.

The road curving down from Gondar to Debra Markos passed through four garrison towns: Bahr Dar on the southern tip of Lake Tana, Dangila, Engiabara, and Burie. The British had always assumed that the Italians would do everything to keep this road open—it was after all the highway linking Gondar to Addis Ababa. This would have meant holding the four garrison towns. But General Nasi confounded British expectations. He ordered all forces to withdraw from Dangila north to Bahr Dar, and all forces to withdraw from Engiabara south to Burie.

Major Simonds and a handful of men from 101 Mission were already up on the highland plateau, near Dangila, urging Dejaz Mangasha Jimbirre on. Dejaz Mangasha had at least 4,000 patriots with him but despite Simonds's urging he failed to attack the Italians as they retreated north from Dangila.[1] The fact of the matter was that the Dejaz had no interest in risking the lives of his

[1] A failure condemned, rather unfairly, by Wingate as 'a classic example of the folly of springing a trap too soon.'

men now that the Italians were voluntarily and, it seemed, permanently retiring from the prize he had coveted for years: the town of Dangila. He entered, installed himself as its ruler and, honour and prestige satisfied, took no further part in the campaign.

'Torelli bolting towards Bahr Dar,' Simonds signalled. 'RAF could annihilate, Sitting Target.' But no planes came. Only orders from Wingate for Simonds to go north, chase Torelli into Bahr Dar 'and, if possible, out of it'. Simonds with his personal escort of 24 riflemen and No. 3 Company of the Frontier Battalion under *Bimbashi* Jarvis, an exiguous force, set off immediately to 'chase' Torelli's 10,000 men.

Meanwhile, the main body of Gideon Force wended its way from the foothills of Belaya up the steep and arduous escarpment of Malakal. At the top lay the long-desired highland plateau which Mark Pilkington, a young subaltern of the Household Cavalry Op centre (who reached that point two weeks later) described as follows:

It was attractive, very fertile, undeveloped meadowland, a bit like the Cotswolds in places, with green belts of trees down all the rivers, and many little ridges of hills, some rocky and like Scotland. It was much cooler in the day and bitterly cold late at night . . . We came through some beautiful arable valleys, most fertile, and carrying a good stock of large-humped cattle, sheep, goats and stock horses. We fed extremely well on this part of the journey, being able to buy bread, milk, eggs, chickens, goats, unripe peaches, *tej* (native beer made from honey) and even a bull.

But not so well as the British officers who went forward with Wingate into deserted Engiabara and there enjoyed their first and most memorable spoils of war—soup, mushrooms, spaghetti, peaches and cream, all washed down with Chianti. Morale rose. Morale needed to rise. The striking column of Gideon Force assembled outside Engiabara on the afternoon of 23 February. It consisted of 700 camels, 200 mules, three companies of Boustead's Frontier Battalion,[1] Boyle's 2nd Ethiopians, No. 1

---

[1] *Bimbashi* Johnson and No. 1 Company, *Bimbashi* Harris and No. 2 Company, *Bimbashi* Acland and No. 4 Company. But even these were not at full strength, for various platoons remained behind to cover the Emperor's ascent. Haile Selassie and his escort did not reach the plateau till 4 March. Sandford, from this point on, remained in the rear with the Emperor.

Op Centre, and a Propaganda Unit—1,500 men in all. This small force proposed to rout an army.

THE BATTLE FOR BURIE: 24 FEBRUARY TO 8 MARCH

The small town of Burie barred the road to Debra Markos, capital of Gojjam. At Burie Colonel Natale had been ordered to stand fast. He had several thousand troops, both regulars and irregulars, plus artillery and air support. A line of fortified posts stretched behind him towards Debra Markos. Natale was an experienced colonial fighter who for years had led columns to and fro across the country, with rebels in front, to the rear, and on all sides. The Brigade he commanded, the III, was one of the most experienced in the Empire.

Gideon Force moved forward slowly by day, harassed by Italian planes whose pilots, seeing the long straggling columns of camels, reported the approach of a large invading force. Natale, misled, stayed behind his defences. Wingate, within striking distance of Burie, decided—as his strategy dictated—not to attack the town but to bypass it and cut it off. He therefore prepared Gideon Force for a night march that would take his men across country to the rear of the enemy by dawn the following day. The white camels were camouflaged with mud[1] and Wingate set out ahead with thirty Ethiopians to light fires as beacons. The plan was to leave two Ethiopians by each fire, who would identify themselves by whistling—long short short, long short short. Just before dusk the huge snakelike column of camels set off. But 'everything', wrote *Bimbashi* Harris, 'seemed to go wrong the moment it grew dark.'

The columns spread out and straggled, halted, were bumped into and bypassed, and lost their way. Then almost inevitably, one of the beacon fires got out of control spreading to illuminate the whole countryside.

'It was a wild scene', wrote an officer of the 2nd Ethiopians, 'that no-one who was present will ever forget. Rolling downs across which whistled a cutting wind, heavy clouds in an inky sky, the glare of the fire roaring in the background, strings of ghostly camels coming from every direction out of the night, men huddled in blankets waiting patiently for the orders to move on, everyone trying to protect themselves from the bitter cold.'

---

[1] 'Wingate was no respecter of men or animals, particularly the latter!' *Bimbashi* Harris.

'Nerves', added the officer, tactfully drawing a veil, 'were so taut with anxiety and fatigue that there were unnecessary recriminations.'

Bimbashi Harris was less tactful. Completely lost with his company, but by good chance heading in the right direction:

I heard a string of English oaths uttered in Boustead's unmistakable voice followed by a torrent of Arabic in which the words 'ma talukhabat'—'don't get muddled up'—frequently occurred. Boustead was almost beside himself with wrath, and Wingate was in a paroxysm of rage.

Two of Boyle's companies had gone astray, and dawn was not very far off. The wretched Boyle, by profession a Nairobi car-dealer, was not spared.

'Wingate when I reached him was seated on a boulder drinking tea out of a thermos,' *Bimbashi* Harris continued. 'On learning that I was present and correct he offered me a cup and proceeded to tell me at length what he thought of Ethiopians in general and of Boyle's Battalion in particular. He was far from polite, and I was sorry for Boyle who was sitting looking rather dejected, well within earshot.'

The fire was now lighting up the whole countryside.

We were within easy striking distance of a large enemy garrison sitting in a sort of floodlit arena at the mercy of any force which chose to come out against us, and we had to sit there for another 3 hours waiting for stray sheep.

But Colonel Natale did not seize this opportunity to attack, rout, scatter, and probably end the career of Gideon Force. He sat behind the fortifications on the cone-shaped hill of Burie, secure in his defences, while Gideon Force reassembled and set out again. Despite another last-minute drama—the markers failed to whistle ('they were Ethiopians and half of them didn't know how')—by 6.45 a.m. the whole force were under cover in a large wood, on the outskirts of Burie. Half an hour later two Caproni bombers flew over; but they saw nothing. Despite the chaos the night-march had been successful. Gideon Force was almost in position.

They lay up in hiding all day. Wingate adapted his plan to the new circumstances. The following night he sent Boyle and the 2nd Ethiopians off on a long detour to cut the road behind Burie leading to Debra Markos. He and Boustead prepared to attack with the Sudanese and, hopefully, to scare the defenders out into the Ethiopians' waiting ambush.

One fort defended Burie to the north. By dawn on 27 February Wingate was round in the rear of this northern fort, with a hundred of Acland's Sudanese, blazing away. Boustead, with the main force, remained hidden in the woods on the other side till the late afternoon. Then he and most of the remaining men broke cover to attack Burie itself.

This was the opportunity for which the defenders had been waiting. Italian mortars opened up and set the wood on fire. As Boustead's men, now out in the open, hesitated, they heard 'the hoofs of galloping horses accompanied by the high-pitched luluing of savage horsemen as they bore down upon us through the smoke'. Fifty strong, the horsemen wheeled up firing from the saddle, and veered away. 'We bolted for our lives back into the wood.'[1] It appeared to be a total stalemate. The attackers were too weak to press their attack, reluctant to use their mortars on a town full of Ethiopians, and without any air support. The defenders sat smugly inside their fortifications. Almost the only encouragement for Gideon Force was the discovery that the *bande*, and indeed regular native troops as well, showed an almost unconquerable reluctance to fire on the Ethiopian Flag. Indeed the display of the flag was bringing deserters over, in dribs and drabs. Natale worriedly reported these desertions. But a message came, from the Duke of Aosta himself, ordering him sternly to hold Burie come what might.

By the morning of 1 March Wingate had taken three measures which, he hoped, would unblock the sitation. First, he had rid himself of the encumbrance of the baggage train by establishing a camel camp in a ravine three miles to the east of Burie. Secondly, he had given up his fruitless attack on the strong northern fort and was concentrating at another, isolated fort, the Fort of Mankusa—six miles down the road defending the rear of Burie to the south and manned only by two companies of Italian native troops. Thirdly, he had summoned to his side Boustead and most of the men-from-the-wood. *Bimbashi* Johnson and his Company crossed in front of Burie, by day but at long range, thus enticing the defenders to waste a great deal of ammunition. Boustead

---

[1] 'Boustead, delighted and much tickled, said he had had a similar experience in the last war in Russia, and agreed it was most awe-inspiring,' noted *Bimbashi* Harris.

followed more cautiously by a moonless night. There at Wingate's camp they had been joined by Zelleka Desta, Dejaz Negash's chief military adviser, and a horde of Patriots, guided in by Thesiger. Wingate's immediate objective, with the help of all these reinforcements, was the capture of Mankusa Fort. He calculated that Natale, like most commanders, would be alarmed at the thought of being cut off, and 'surrounded'—however tiny the force 'surrounding' him might be.

The defenders of Mankusa Fort first realized they were under attack when George Steer's Propaganda Unit blared away through the loudspeakers, announcing the nearby presence of the Emperor and the imminent liberation of all. The Eritrean askaris shouted back scornfully that they knew nothing about *Janhoy*. They were Italian subjects, not slaves! Thesiger had reported that irregular *banda* under Fitaurari Haile Yusus were ready to desert that morning. But the morning passed, and no *banda* came out.

Wingate ordered an attack. The Patriots were to charge, and his men would give covering fire with their machine-guns and mortars. It was the first time Wingate had tried, against his own principles, to direct an attack with his own troops and Patriots combined. It was also the last, for he quickly learnt his lesson. The wild Ethiopians charged with too much abandon, and far too fast. The first mortar shells fired by the Sudanese landed among them. The charge broke up. The attack, dismally, had failed.

But, meanwhile, in reply to Gideon Force's desperate appeals air support had at long last appeared. RAF Wellesleys flew to bomb the Burie forts.

'Patriots,' Wingate wrote, 'and, I fancy, most guerrilla forces attach great importance to air action. Undue importance, as I think this campaign shows . . . At the same time the right bomb in the right place (in cooperation with a Fifth Column) is worth a lot.'

This was the only time the RAF supported Gideon Force, but it was certainly the right bomb in the right place. There was a fifth column of sorts within Burie. The Emperor was nearing the plateau, and Lij Mammo[1] was wavering in his allegiance. That day he and his *banda* took to the hills outside Burie, to await the outcome of events; 1,500 men in all. Colonel Natale knew that the British were in his rear, and believed that the Fort of Mankusa

---

[1] Lij Mammo was Ras Hailu's great-nephew and leader of an experienced *banda* that had long fought at Natale's side.

was likely to fall. Lij Mammo's desertion, coupled with the bombing, shook his already-wavering morale. He radioed a panicky report to Gondar, requesting permission to evacuate Burie before he was totally cut off.

On the morning of 4 March the amazed and delighted 'besiegers' in the hills, *Bimbashi* Harris among them, watched 'file upon file of enemy troops come marching out of the town preceded by four light armoured cars. The road was soon black with troops animals and transport as far as the eye could see and still they came on in increasing numbers.' They watched, and ran. Three Caproni bombers flew overhead, and as the column passed through the village of Mankusa it was joined by the defenders of the Fort. Wingate's plan had, against all expectations, succeeded. But Wingate himself, arriving a little later, was highly annoyed to find that Boustead had missed a 'glorious opportunity' to shoot up the retreating column. Boustead pointed at the aircraft overhead: his Sudanese were in open country, and would have been annihilated by the bombers if they had revealed their postion.

That night, however, the Frontier Battalion did harass Natale's camps; and next morning, as the Italian columns moved forward once again towards Debra Markos, *Bimbashi* Harris with his Sudanese subaltern Hassan attacked them from the rear. Too excited, they came too close, and round the next corner found themselves facing yet another cavalry charge—six little infantry men facing 50 horsemen only 200 yards away. They ran as fast as their legs could carry them, floundering over a stream into the safety of thick bush.

'It had been a very near shave,' wrote *Bimbashi* Harris afterwards, 'and we were completely exhausted. But the reaction to such a situation is often curious and all that we could do at that moment was to lie back and laugh. We laughed until the tears rolled down our cheeks.'

On the other side of the road, Boustead and Acland had also had to run for it, lugging bren-guns with them. Wingate meanwhile was back in Burie, happily inspecting the captured enemy stores and arranging, with Sandford, for the town's occupation by No. 1 Op Centre, the Australians. In fact it was Dejaz Negash and his men who took over much as Dejaz Mangasha had down at Dangila to the north. The Dejaz appointed himself Governor and prepared to welcome the Emperor back to *his* town with *his* men.

That night, the night of 5 March, Boustead's men once again sniped at the encamped Italians; and the following morning took up, though more cautiously, their pursuit. Suddenly, to the amazement of both pursuers and the rearguard of the pursued, there was a violent din away at the head of Natale's column far to the south-east. The explanation came three or four hours later; abandoned camels wandered into view—camels belonging to Boyle's Battalion.

The 2nd Ethiopians had been almost totally out of touch with Wingate and the rest of Gideon Force for five days. Boyle's orders had been to cut the road leading south from Burie towards Debra Markos near the little fort of Dembecha. This, after an unsuccessful but tiring night attack on another little fort, Gigga, he had proceeded to do. Then the 2nd Ethiopians, in Wingate's words, 'sat down in the line of the enemy's retreat . . . in what must have been one of the worst tactical positions for defence in history.' He was generous enough to Boyle to add the two-edged compliment: 'It was to this that the Battalion owed its partial survival.'

Natale's retreating columns, lorries, armoured cars, machine-guns, cavalry squadrons, with the Caproni bombers still overhead, suddenly ran into the 500-odd men of the 2nd Ethiopians, with their seven white officers, in open country on the banks of a dried-out river. The Italian forces, some 8,000 strong including 500 white troops, were—according to Wingate's theory—so surprised to find the enemy in such an exposed position that they simply could not believe their eyes—until, from very close range, Boyle's men opened up. One of his companies even charged forward to the attack. After the first shock the Italian armoured cars opened fire with their machine-guns as the long columns behind them halted. Unabashed, Corporal Wandafresh Falaka with eight rounds of his anti-tank gun scored direct hits on two of the armoured cars at a hundred yards' range. But then the milling mob of Italian troops burst over and through the pitiful opposition. *Banda* spread out to attack and loot Boyle's camel camp, while three columns of infantry charged straight down the road and on both sides of it, overrunning his totally-outnumbered little force. By midday it was all over. A quarter of the battalion lay dead or wounded, the rest were captured or had disappeared. But though the 2nd Ethiopians were barely to function again as an active unit in the Gojjam campaign, this, its one battle, had much impressed the Italians. For Natale's column left 250 dead behind them, plus their two disabled armoured cars. They had even lost a bomber, shot down from the ground.

The advance guard of Boustead's Frontier Battalion arrived at the scene of the carnage an hour after the tail of the enemy had passed through. Much to the indignation of the survivors of the battle, his Sudanese commandeered the Italian flag that Boyle's Ethiopians had captured.

That night the enemy rearguard still held the Fort at Dembecha. As *Bimbashi* Harris, with his men, machine-gunned it from 2,000 yards, he was wounded. This meant the end of the campaign for him. 'Stop making such a bloody row and get on back,' ordered an unsympathetic Boustead. He got on back, and Wingate personally bound up his wound. He was evacuated with the other wounded, by lorry, to be welcomed by 'the genial countenance of Colonel Sandford' at Burie Fort.

It was a fierce little engagement at Dembecha. Wingate went forward, with Gabre Maskal his preferred radio operator at his side, just in time to face a series of bayonet charges by the enemy. 'Retire!', ordered Wingate. Gabre Maskal took no notice. 'Go away!', shouted Wingate. 'How can I leave you alone?' asked Gabre Maskal reproachfully, walking slowly backwards all the same. Wingate had the quality of leadership. He, in Gabre Maskal's words, was 'never demoralized'. 'I never saw a man of such courage, and so human at the same time.' And he looked after the followers he judged efficient—in the thick of the fighting he remembered to send a horseman to guide Gabre Maskal and the others back to the safety of Boustead's base. It was not till forty-eight hours later that its 500-strong garrison evacuated Dembecha, burning down the *tukuls* around the Fort. They pulled back to the last Italian stronghold in Gojjam, the capital of the province: Debra Markos.

THE PAUSE: 8 MARCH–17 MARCH

As the Dembecha garrison pulled back, an infuriated General Nasi flew down from Gondar. His first action was to relieve Natale of his command and to despatch him, ignominiously, to join Admiral Bonetti's sea-girt garrison at Massawa. In the General's view Natale had been bluffed out of Burie and had failed to crush a far inferior enemy. He had furthermore just evacuated two outlying posts, Boma and Fort Emmanuel, and against Nasi's express instructions had not defended the line of the Tamcha river. In his place, as commander of the Debra Markos garrison, General Nasi appointed another and far tougher colonial officer, Colonel Maraventano. Debra Markos was strengthened: by artillery, by aircraft, by 1,000 Blackshirts, and by most of the XIX Brigade, until the total strength of its garrison had risen to 12,000 men with another 3,000 irregular *bande* out in the hills behind. Before flying back to Gondar, General Nasi, with Ras Hailu at his side, assembled the garrison at Fort Dux in Debra Markos and harangued them. There was no point, he said, in retreating out of Gojjam across the Nile, to face even stronger forces of the enemy. It was disgraceful for Gojjamis to be beaten by the Shoan Tafari Makonnen. Let them in their turn counter-attack and drive the invader out of their land!

Wingate, meanwhile, having in his turn addressed a 'Victory Parade' of the 2nd Ethiopians at Dembecha Fort, had gone back to Burie, to find an Emperor angry at being kept so little informed and a brigadier angrier for more weighty reasons. Sandford complained that Gideon Force appeared to be driving the Italians out of Gojjam instead of harassing them inside Gojjam as had been agreed. The more subtle strategy originally decided on had been abandoned, and there was a risk of the Gojjam garrisons reinforcing other sectors of the front contrary to the agreed plan of operations. To this Wingate had no answer—except, presumably, to tell Sandford to concern himself with his political affairs, and to leave the military decisions alone. As Wingate later put it, 'for what appeared to be sufficient reasons, an officer was appointed to command with the rank of Lt-Colonel while a Brigadier was given a roving commission in the same theatre. This could not work and did not work . . . I need hardly add that the confusion created in the Ethiopian mind was considerable.'

Wingate was in a bad mood, in any case. He was dissatisfied with Natale's escape, for he was certain that with air support he could have wiped out the whole Italian force when it was held on the road by the 2nd Ethiopians. He was dissatisfied with himself for having failed, owing to a lack of maps, to cut off Natale's retreating column outside Debra Markos at the Tamcha river. Furthermore he was dissatisfied with the supply base at Belaya, which he considered served no useful purpose.

In conference at Burie on 11 February an agreement on this last point was patched up. Sandford was to take over all the supply problems and set up Gideon Force's base at Burie. There was one piece of good news in this respect. *Bimbashi* Le Blanc and Captain Foley had succeeded in driving a dozen trucks up the escarpment, and the days of camel supply only were over. But there was still no artillery of any sort, no pack-guns even. Wingate sighed for just a couple of light tanks.

Both Wingate and Sandford were preoccupied about the Op Centres. Ten had been formed, but most of the ten were wandering undirected about the highlands and lowlands. In Wingate's view they had in any case been formed too late. They should have been ahead of the main body, not behind it. As it was, two of them were defending Burie in the rear—the Australians with No. 1 Op Centre and the newly-arrived Scots Greys' Op Centre, Bill McLean's. Mark Pilkington of the Household Cavalry Op Centre was coming in, very proud of having acquired 40 good mules. And another Op Centre, No. 2 commanded by Captain McKay, was moving north to join the intrepid Major Simonds outside Bahr Dar.[1]

From Gondar, General Nasi on the other hand now viewed his command with more satisfaction. He ordered traffic across the Takazze into Ras Seyum's country to be suspended as a pre-cautionary measure but reported to Addis Ababa that inside his own sector Ras Hailu's loyalty, unlike Ras Seyum's, could be counted on totally. Before leaving Debra Markos Nasi had sent Ras Hailu to join his *banda* in the hills; and there were satisfactory reports of fierce fighting in the Chokey Mountains to the east between the rival forces of Ras Hailu and of Lij Hailu Belew, his 'rebel' nephew.

Like Nasi, Wingate realized very well that Ras Hailu's attitude would be the key to success or failure in Gojjam. He decided therefore to attempt to win Ras Hailu over to the Emperor's side. His next move was a dangerous gamble. With only three hundred Sudanese as escort, he marched across country past Debra Markos into the foothills of the Chokey Mountains. Ras Hailu

---

[1] With Captain McKay came a genial personage, the Imperial Fitaurari Birru Wolde Gabriel, accompanied by an escort of 500 Patriots. They had been armed with new rifles at Um Idla by the British: '450 of them', noted Simonds bitterly, 'deserted the following day, anxious to sell their rifles'. The Fitaurari had already been appointed governor-general designate of Beghemder by Haile Selassie; but despite this, Simonds after a failed raid reported that beyond the Blue Nile 'the entire countryside was hostile to us.'

came down with 6,000 armed men to confront him. The two forces camped warily, two miles apart, by Abba Mariam. Wingate sent a messenger to Ras Hailu's camp, bidding him to acknowledge Haile Selassie as his liege lord and submit. Ras Hailu sent a messenger back, courteously refusing. He could certainly have attacked and probably have annihilated Wingate's tiny force then and there; but he was either too chivalrous or too cautious. Next day, 15 March, he entered Debra Markos with half his strength, leaving—astutely—3,000 *banda* in the hills to block any further outflanking move by Wingate.

For Wingate, being Wingate, had indeed had an ulterior military purpose behind his move into the eastern hills. He had planned to seize the strategic bridge at Safertak over the Blue Nile. This would have cut the highway and snapped the link between Debra Markos and Addis Ababa, isolating Gojjam from Shoa. There was no other way across the Blue Nile. Colonel Maraventano and his men would have been cut off, and if forced out of Debra Markos, thoroughly and totally trapped.

Wingate, foiled by Ras Hailu's watchful men, did not abandon this plan, though he modified it. He ordered Captain Foley with his demolition squad and *Bimbashi* Thesiger with a small escort of Sudanese to slip forward, make contact with 'Lij' Belai Zelleka and lay an ambush at the Safertak bridge. Thesiger and Foley were experienced officers, and he knew he could rely on them. Having done his best to set the trap, Wingate himself with most of his Sudanese escort turned back. It would now be a question of driving the Italians out of Debra Markos into the waiting trap—or, if things went wrong, of himself being driven back to Burie and beyond. It would be a battle of wills as well as a battle of men.

THE BATTLE FOR DEBRA MARKOS: 18 MARCH–6 APRIL

On the western outskirts of Debra Markos, about two and a half miles from the town, the road from Burie ran through a line of small hills, the Gulit Ridge. Here facing Gideon Force Colonel Maraventano placed two battalions, his first line of defence. Wingate and Boustead took up position in front of the ridge with their men and mortars. The active strength of Gideon Force was by now very low. Platoons of the Frontier Battalion were scattered over a good part of Gojjam garrisoning local strong-points, and the besieging force amounted to merely 400 Sudanese and a dozen Englishmen—'besieging' 16,000 armed men. Behind the 'front', the 2nd Ethiopians were—theoretically—resting, recovering and re-forming at Fort Dembecha. No. 1 Op Centre was due to come forward to reinforce them. Wingate counted on these reinforcements and on Maraventano receiving bad news of enemy activity in his rear, at Safertak bridge, This he hoped would lead to Maraventano being flushed out by bluff, like Natale at Burie. Meanwhile the Sudanese mortared away at the Gulit Ridge by day, and sniped from closer in by night. These tactics were surprisingly effective. The irregular *banda* began to desert in great numbers and come over to join the besiegers. But in another sense all this was very suspicious, for there were no Patriots with Wingate at this stage. All the Patriot chiefs, great and small, were converging on Burie, well to the rear of the battle, to pay their respects to Haile Selassie.

Then things took a turn for the worse. On the 17th, a Greek trader arrived with a string of camels carrying supplies. He should have gone north-west, to Fort Emmanuel, twenty miles away, which (abandoned by Colonel Natale) had been taken over by a platoon of Sudanese; and Wingate sent him angrily on his way. Two days later he was back again, with panicky news: there was much fighting at Fort Emmanuel, and many shiftas[1] were being killed.

What had happend was that for the first time in this whole campaign, the Italians had taken the initiative. Maraventano had sent two battalions out from Debra Markos and recaptured Fort Emmanuel, sweeping away the Sudanese platoon that held it and their local allies. At the same time he had sent another battalion to reoccupy Mota. Then, two days later, the Italian forces on Gulit Ridge actually went on the offensive and attacked 'High Hill Camp', the little base of the besiegers. It was beginning to look as if Maraventano was not to be bluffed as Natale had been. 'Local patriots were adversely affected,' noted Wingate. 'We seemed to them to be in an absurd situation.' This was an under-statement. The garrison at Fort Emmanuel threatened their flanks. The garrison at Gulit threatened their front. To make the situation even more absurd, the little force of besiegers was surrounded by three times its number of 'friendly' deserters—1,200 *banda*, camping all around but keeping their distance. Was the desertion

---

[1] 'Dog of a fool', said Gabre Maskal, 'we call them Patriots, not *shiftas*.'

genuine or a ruse? Makonnen Desta, at Wingate's side, considered that treachery was 'most probable'.

Gideon Force had never been in a more dangerous position. Its allies were demoralized, its units were scattered, and the enemy was concentrating. News came that Ras Hailu had brought in lorry-loads of mules from the hills. This seemed to presage a sortie *en masse* by his men, a final punitive expedition that, combined with a treacherous attack from the deserting *banda*, would put paid to Boustead and the Sudanese and Wingate with them.

As for the hoped for 'reinforcements' from Dembecha, they were in an even worse state. In the rather coy phrase of one of the 2nd Ethiopians' officers: 'It was becoming noticeable at Dembecha that the battalion was beginning to be affected by excessive drinking.' Boyle and the adjutant, Captain Smith, were 'in a nervy condition'. Physically minor wounds and cuts were turning septic. Mentally the officers were under a strain. Drunkenness among the men led to clashes and a state of near mutiny. No. 1 Op Centre had arrived, but was in much the same state. Indeed three of the five Australians (whose enthusiasm for Ethiopia had originally inspired Wingate), Sergeants Howell, Body, and Wood, had to be sent ignominiously back to Khartoum.

Wingate hesitated, and considered pulling back to the Tamcha riverline. But Gideon Force had, up till then, never gone backwards, always, whatever the odds, forwards. A retreat of any sort would be justifiably taken by the enemy as a sign of weakness. Colonel Maraventano and Ras Hailu would certainly debouch from Debra Markos and probably succeed in sweeping the scattered and demoralized elements of Gideon Force back to Burie. There they might even seize the person of the Emperor. It was a nightmare vision. Whether Wingate, Boustead, and the Sudanese withdrew or stayed where they were, disaster loomed.

Wingate made up his mind. When in doubt, whatever the odds, attack. But on the morning of the 24th the Italians attacked first, just before dawn. However, warned by the *bande*, the Sudanese cleared out of High Hill Camp, where they had bivouacked, before the attackers reached it—an encouraging incident that dispelled most of their fears of treachery. That night Boustead's men split into three groups and in their turn attacked the enemy posts on the Gulit Ridge with machine-guns, grenades, and the bayonet. At the command post an Italian machine-gun drove back the attackers; three Sudanese were killed there, and Captain Allen badly wounded. But on the other parts of the Ridge the Sudanese rampaged, led by *Bimbashi* Acland and his men.

This night attack succeeded temporarily in its aim. It put a damper on the dismayed enemy. Neither the Gulit Ridge battalions nor the garrison in Debra Markos made any further move forward. Nevertheless the stalemate persisted. A tiny force of besiegers were besieging an enormous garrison that might be bluffed into staying on the defensive but would not be bamboozled into evacuating. So how to break the stalemate? Wingate, at his best when faced with apparently insoluble problems, devised a new plan: all the Patriots, led by the Emperor in person, should move up from Burie for an all-out attack on Debra Markos. Only the Emperor's presence on the British side could, Wingate calculated, counter-balance the presence of Ras Hailu on the Italian side. Only that would tip the scales favourably.

Wingate enthusiastically hurried back to Burie, leaving Boustead in charge of the siege. Sandford opposed such a dangerous policy. While fierce discussions followed at Burie, Colonel Maraventano, noting the inactivity of the enemy, planned another and more wholehearted attack. Unfortunately, for the whole of this Gojjam campaign, memoirs and documents, official and unofficial, though plentiful on the British side, are totally lacking on the Italian side. But it seems that General Nasi, co-ordinating the operations of his subordinates from Gondar, was preparing a pincer movement: a counter-attack that was to throw the invaders of Gojjam back into the hills. Colonel Torelli was to attack southwards from Bahr Dar and Colonel Maraventano westwards from Debra Markos. The attack was planned for 27 March.

On the evening of 26 March, however, General Frusci had given the order to evacuate Keren: an order that within hours became known to all Italian senior officers in the Empire. From other fronts (most noticeably from the South—from Galla Sidamo and Somalia) that day brought further bad news. Everywhere the situation appeared to Italian commanders to be fluid and liable to change from hour to hour. They looked to their rear, and considered lines of retreat.

So, fortunately for Boustead and his Sudanese, there was no attack from Debra Markos on the 27th. In the north, however, Colonel Torelli did attack, though with two days' delay. Captain McKay of No. 2 Ops Centre had been seriously wounded and evacuated a week earlier, and Major Simonds had been deluged with innumerable orders and counter-orders from Burie and Khartoum.[1] He was now faced with 'a strong well-planned attack on my main position.' With him Simonds had only 250 Sudanese under *Bimbashi* Jarvis, and the Imperial Fitaurari Birru Wolde Gabriel with 75 followers—a force that Torelli (who had estimated it at 3,000) attacked with 5 battalions, pack-artillery and 1,000 *banda*, in three columns.

The 'besiegers', naturally enough, fled into the hills. Why Torelli did not continue with his advance down the road and recapture Dangila is a mystery. Admittedly without a similar movement from Debra Markos, threatening Burie and the person of the Emperor from both sides, the strategic advantage would have been small. Possibly also Torelli had learnt that Lij Mammo and his *banda*, on hearing that Keren had fallen to the British, had finally decided which was the winning side, and had come down from the hills to join the Patriots. Torelli lost 175 men killed or wounded by Simonds's sniping. He withdrew back into Bahr Dar only seven hours after issuing forth.

Stimulated by the good news from the north and the west, Wingate, still at Burie, issued his orders. Bill McLean and his sergeants from the Scots Greys were to go north, with No. 6 Op Centre—180 men—to join Fitaurari Birru and Simonds. This combined force should then break away from Bahr Dar and head boldly into the interior towards Debra Tabor where Colonel Angelini and a strong garrison guarded the road between Gondar and Dessie. There they would link up with the rebels of Lij Johannes and Dagnew Tessema. Thus confusion was to be spread, and the enemy's communications cut, all over General Nasi's command.

Meanwhile, *Bimbashi* Jarvis and the rump of 'Beghemder Force' were to be left to conduct the 'siege' of Bahr Dar. Further north still, to the north of Gondar, word went out to Basil

---

[1] 'As I had received clear and concise orders originally from Colonel Wingate, I continued to obey these.' Wingate's orders to Simonds's 'Beghemder Force' had been to invest Bahr Dar and compel the evacuation of all small enemy forces in its neighbourhood.

Ringrose of the Sherwood Rangers (whose Op Centre had joined up with the priest Abba Qirqos) to cut the road north of Gondar. The whole area north of the Gondar–Gallabat road, in what had been Bentinck's beat,[1] was by now in ferment. Wubneh Amoraw and his followers were planning—but still only planning—to attack the pro-Italian Kemant. Fitaurari Mesfin Redda was active in the Wolkait. The formidable Adane Makonnen after a visit to Bentinck's camp *did* attack the Italians 15 miles north-west of Gondar at Tukul Dingia, and fought a fierce skirmish there. British officers were quartering the hills, and on 29 March Lt. Railton with a company of the 3rd Ethiopians (the 'new' deserters) was sent north from Wahni towards Tukul Dingia to join *Bimbashi* Sheppard. But it was not all one-sided. Adane Makonnen was routed by the Kamant north of Gondar; and a few days later *Bimbashi* Jarvis reported that he was, not surprisingly, in 'difficulties' by Bahr Dar.

Meanwhile, Wingate had turned his attention back to the west. Orders went down to Boyle to recapture Fort Emmanuel; and this time the 2nd Ethiopians, stiffened by some platoons of Sudanese, pulled themselves temporarily together and did the job well. The two native battalions defending the Fort retreated to Debra Markos that evening.

Closer in, Boustead was cock-a-hoop, predicting, rightly, that the Gulit Ridge garrison, 2,000 strong, would probably withdraw the following day, 1 April. He planned a real massacre, herding them backwards with his Sudanese into the arms of the 2nd Ethiopians who would carefully have been posted in ambush in their rear, along the road back to Debra Markos.

It did not work out. The 2nd Ethiopians were not only not in position but had relapsed into a state of total chaos. 'A' Company had mutinied, and a deputation was sent to the Emperor, as he and Wingate moved slowly forward from Burie, to complain that they had been struck and treated like slaves by their white officers. Boyle and his adjutant Smith were called back to explain, and finally relieved of their commands.

Once again the opportunity of annihilating by ambush a mass of retreating enemy troops had been lost. Maraventano and all his forces were now safely inside Debra Markos. Nothing daunted, Wingate set about planning a repeat on a far larger and more

[1] The wearied Bentinck was about to be replaced by *Bimbashi* Sheppard, a youthful Professor of Poetry from Cairo University.

dramatic scale of the whole manœuvre: the masterstroke-to-be of his whole campaign. Now up with Boustead on Gulit Ridge, he was confident that with the Emperor present he could frighten Maraventano out of Debra Markos as he had frightened Natale out of Burie. But this time the enemy should not escape. Twenty-five miles to the east of Debra Markos, at Safertak Bridge, Thesiger and Captain Foley were reported to be in position to cut the Italians off with 'Lij' Belai Zelleka and his bandit Patriots. To join them Wingate sent past Debra Markos over half of Boustead's remaining force.[1] A bold, indeed in the circumstances almost a Napoleonic decision.

Inside Debra Markos, now seriously besieged, there was much toing and froing, with Maraventano receiving and issuing his last-minute orders while Ras Hailu sent out and accepted emissaries and messages from all sides. On 2 April mortar shells struck the *ghebbi* of Ras Hailu's daughter. Uncertainty was spreading. Morale was collapsing. Wingate's plan was working.

On 3 April the watchers, inside and outside the city, saw the sight which they were now half expecting. Lorries, cavalry, and infantry were pouring out of the eastern gates of the city—two Brigades, the III and the XIX, 7,000 native troops, 1,100 Italians, and, with the column, over 2,000 women and children. Wingate smiled when the news was reported. He knew the column was doomed.

But before leaving the city Colonel Maraventano had handed over command of all the irregulars, plus all ammunition, rifles, and stores that he had not taken with him, to Ras Hailu. With over 6,000 well-armed followers Ras Hailu was the master of Debra Markos, and the potential master of all Gojjam. Wingate, Boustead, and the Sudanese, the Emperor, Ras Kassa, and the court, waited tensely outside the city for Ras Hailu's next move. At dusk they saw the Ethiopian Flag raised and flying above the citadel. But no offer of submission came. Makonnen Desta, sent in to Debra Markos, overcome by awe, prostrated himself and kissed Ras Hailu's hands and feet. After so many years Ras Hailu was back as lord of the capital he had once ruled, among his faithful people. After so many humiliations he had, very nearly, his old enemy Tafari Makonnen at his mercy.

---

[1] *Bimbashi* Johnson and No. 1 Company; *Bimbashi* Riley (Harris's replacement) and No. 2 Company; 140 loyal 2nd Ethiopians under Lieutenant Rowe; plus Azaz Kebbede and his followers.

It must have been very tempting for Ras Hailu to use his power. But though immediate success and, possibly, revenge lay within his grasp, in the long term the odds were against him. Against Haile Selassie alone he might have risked a coup. Against Haile Selassie supported by the British he knew he could not. Yet for two more days he enjoyed his brief but total independence, before, gracefully and with dignity, announcing his submission.

These were two vital days. The Maraventano column had halted, and seemed prepared to hold the Forts between Debra Markos and the Blue Nile. But Wingate intercepted an Italian phone-call to what they still believed to be headquarters. Thinking quickly, he called in Stevens the American journalist, who spoke excellent Italian, and had him order the Fort commanders to evacuate. The ruse, of which both were justifiably proud, was successful. Maraventano and his column were forced to move rapidly towards the Blue Nile and the trap at Safertak Bridge waiting to be sprung. Meanwhile, however, a wilier man had played a yet more cunning hand.

Ras Hailu knew he could expect little mercy from either Haile Selassie or Ras Kassa in whose sons' deaths he had been involved. Yet very few Ethiopians then or later condemned him outright. Some said he had always been a Patriot at heart; others that he had mollified the severity of the Italians, particularly of Graziani. The people of Gojjam saw him as their rightful ruler and protector. More generally, it was felt that in the long struggle for Imperial power, from the death of Menelik through the reigns of Lij Yasu and of the Empress Zauditu, he had like all the great lords tried his fortune. At the time he had lost but the coming of the Italians had given him an unhoped-for chance of turning the tables. Was he to be blamed if he had seized it?

In British eyes, however, Ras Hailu was a traitor and a collaborator, nothing more nor less. Possibly if he had at the last minute turned on the Italians, he might have played on British sympathy. But Ras Hailu appears to have been, in his way, genuinely a noble man. Not only did he not turn on the Italians in their distress, he gave his word to Colonel Maraventano that he and his column would pass safely across the Blue Nile.

As soon as Ras Hailu had announced his submission, Boustead and his men drove merrily past Debra Markos to join their advanced companies and to attack the Maraventano column in the rear. They expected to find the retreating Italians confused and panicky, unable to cross the Safertak bridge into the safety of Shoa. Instead they found no Italians, and only a smouldering bridge. Nearby Thesiger and Foley were waiting disconsolately, with dismal, apologetic stories of Belai Zelleka's treachery, of Maraventano's successful crossing of the bridge, and of a sharp rearguard action.

It had been Ras Hailu's last service to his allies and erstwhile protectors. He had sent messengers to 'Lij' Belai Zelleka ordering him to let the Italians through. Thesiger and his handful of Sudanese, in Belai Zelleka's power, had been unable to do anything to prevent this. Captain Foley alone had succeeded in setting off his demolition charges on the road and by doing so had destroyed—which was at least a gesture—a number of Maraventano's lorries. It was rumoured that Ras Hailu had, in return for this favour, promised Belai Zelleka one of his daughters in marriage, and that the thought of such social advancement had turned the ex-bandit's head, and corrupted his loyalties. There was nothing Wingate could do, except fume. His best-prepared and most dramatic trap had failed.

But with their crossing of the Nile Gojjam was finally free of the Italians—except for one isolated battalion, left behind in Mota. On Palm Sunday, 6 April, Haile Selassie drove in triumph into Debra Markos, on the front seat of a truck driven by *Bimbashi* LeBlanc, with his chief officers and courtiers inside the truck or hanging on to its sides. Thanks to Wingate, the Emperor had 'recaptured' 'Holy Gojjam'.

CHAPTER 29

CUNNINGHAM'S COUP

IN Nairobi sat a wretched and forlorn figure. Major Ralph Neville, a gunner, had been sent out by the War Office in its moment of euphoria to head 107 Mission. In theory he was to be to Kenya what Sandford of 101 Mission was to the Sudan. In January he had seen General Cunningham, who had spoken most encouragingly and who had told him to get on into the south of Galla–Sidamo and organize the rebellion. But not till early March was he given an assistant—Captain Bilborough, who had been with the 5th (Turkana) Irregulars—and not till the end of the month was he allotted a clerk. Still less was he given any wireless equipment, any transport, or any heavy arms. He had however a certain amount of money and a dump of rifles and ammunition to distribute. Back at Taveta refugee camp he found the only two Ethiopians who seemed capable of raising followers and using his rifles: Dejaz Abebe Damtew and Blatta Takele Wolde Hawariat.

Major Neville knew nothing of Ethiopian history and politics, even less (if that were possible) than the Kenya authorities. Having found his men, he armed them and sent them in. So Blatta Takele and Abebe Damtew, each with a little group of less than a hundred followers, joined the merry fray in Galla–Sidamo. They headed for the country around Neghelli, where the Borana tribes were already up in arms.

In this jungly, roadless, heavily populated country inhabited by a myriad of primitive tribes, among whom for the past five years isolated groups of Amhara, reduced to the status of bandits and pursued by the local *banda*, had wandered, it was almost impossible, particularly with the spring rains coming on, to conduct 'serious' military operations. Confused and confusing skirmishes took place over a vast area. The Amhara bands, both old and new, plus Curle's 2nd (Ethiopian) Irregulars, spread out and clashed with the *banda* by the Great Lakes and were bombed, once or twice, by their own allies, the South African pilots, as

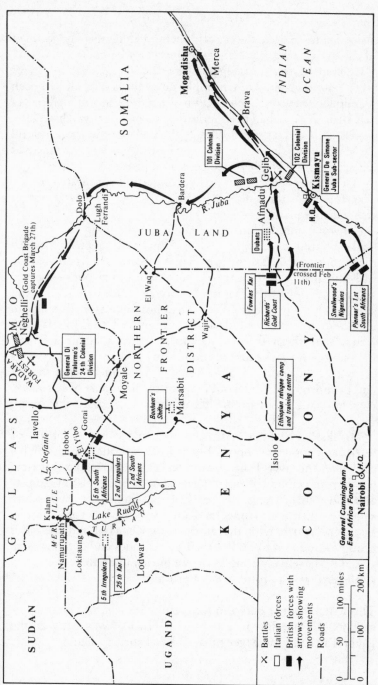

MAP 10. The Kenya Frontier

they tried to encircle the regular enemy battalions. The focus of all this activity was the Italian-held town of Neghelli.

By mid-March messengers were streaming back to Major Neville in Nairobi. They brought news that Neghelli had been abandoned, news that Neghelli had not been abandoned, news that Blatta Takele had been seriously wounded, news that Blatta Takele had been taken prisoner by the Italians. But it was not till 27 March that there was definite news. Yes, the Italians had withdrawn, and Neghelli had been occupied—but occupied from the far side, by a force coming up from a different theatre of war. That force was the Gold Coast Brigade, and the theatre of war was Italian Somalia.

General Cunningham's plan had been to open up the whole of Galla–Sidamo east of the River Omo and to push forward through Neghelli and the great lakes towards Addis Ababa. He had launched two of his three South African Brigades—the 2nd and the 5th—over the frontier at Moyale, with half his KAR in support. But the South Africans had not done as well as he had expected.[1] In fact the whole attempt to move into Ethiopia from Kenya's northern frontier had turned into a bit of a fiasco. Cunningham turned his attention to what was, in his view, his secondary and minor front—Somalia. He remembered that he had promised Eden he would try for the little port of Kismayu, two hundred miles inside Italian territory, before the spring rains.

Thanks to the South Africans, he could count on plenty of lorries and good air support. But he had only four brigades on his start-line, the river Tana. Opposite, on the river Juba that runs north from behind Kismayu, General de Simone, his antagonist, also had four brigades: the 101 Colonial Division inland, 6,200 rifles and 24 guns strong, and on the coast the 102 Colonial Division, which with the garrison of Kismayu and the *dubat* groups amounted to no less than 14,000 rifles and 60 guns. The 102nd was itself as strong as the whole invading force.

Nevertheless a promise was a promise.

The actual frontier between Kenya and Somalia was an imaginary straight line drawn across the desert, half way between the River Tana and the River Juba. On 11 February Cunningham's

[1] cf. page 325.

two leading brigades moved off from their positions behind the River Tana and crossed this invisible frontier, Brigadier Smallwood's Nigerians heading directly for Kismayu along the coast road, Brigadier Fowkes's KAR moving towards Gelib on the Juba line.

At dawn the next day the town of Almadu, reportedly heavily fortified, was rushed by the KAR. One prisoner was captured, plus 18 camels and much saddlery. The Gold Coast Brigade, following close behind the KAR's thrust, moved through to fight a sharp skirmish on the banks of the river Juba. But meanwhile extraordinary news came in from the coast: the Italians were abandoning Kismayu. Sure enough, on the late afternoon of 14 February, Pemberton's armoured cars, leading the Nigerian advance along the coast road, entered Kismayu unopposed. They found it not only undefended but with all its guns intact. There were 25 ships in the harbour, and—so much for the pretence that the Italians were short of fuel—a million litres of petrol, and half a million litres of aircraft fuel were there, undestroyed.

It was almost unbelievable. Within three days of crossing the frontier, with barely a shot fired, with no interference at all from enemy aircraft, General Cunningham had not only kept his promises but had captured, to his own amazement, an immense quantity of booty. He could only imagine that the evacuation of Kismayu was part of the enemy's strategy, mishandled owing to a confusion of orders, and that the real enemy defence was planned behind Kismayu along the line of the Juba.

In its last fourteen miles, the Juba running through flat marshes almost into the sea, was a formidable obstacle: tidal water 580 feet wide. But further north it was by no means an ideal defence line. Both of its banks were covered with thick tropical vegetation and at this period, before the rains had brought torrents down from the highlands, it could in many places be waded. General Cunningham brought his fourth brigade, Pienaar's South Africans, up into the lead. On the night of 17 February an advance guard of the South Africans waded the Juba. The following day Brigadier Richards's three Gold Coast battalions, after a feint attack at Gelib, started to cross too. Behind the infantry bridgeheads pontoon bridges were thrown across, and the lorries and the main body of troops followed, fanning out north and south and east, across the flat, low plains of the Somali country. Fowkes's

KAR came across in their turn. The appearance of three enemy brigades in their rear naturally spread panic among the four Italian brigades strung out in long lines along the riverbanks with the enemy now behind them.

The almost complete collapse of General de Simone's two divisions followed: first little groups, then larger groups surrendered here and there to the exultant Africans and their British officers and even, in a batch several hundred strong, to Pipe-Major Buchanan and five kilted pipers of the Transvaal Scottish. The KAR switched to the coast road and reached Brava by the 24th. Then the Nigerians drove through them and on down the coast road to Merca.

Seventy miles ahead of Merca lay Mogadishu, capital of the Italian colony of Somalia, seat of the governorate and of De Simone's command. That same day the Nigerians, led by Major Wacker in an armoured car, occupied Mogadishu. The Blackshirt commander of the garrison, Consul-General Eugenio Fioretti, had fled. The only resistance was offered by a young Italian naval Lieutenant Luchini, who died at the head of his men.

As for the booty, it was enormous: 1,800 tons of both petrol and aircraft fuel, plus lorries, weapons, ammunition dumps, military supplies of all sorts, enough uniforms to equip a division and enough food and drink to keep ten thousand men well-nourished for seven to eight months. At the aerodrome 21 Italian planes that had taken no part in the defence of the Juba line lay damaged on the ground. In the harbour were more ships, and in the prisons a number of interned merchant seamen, delighted to be released—179 British, 13 French, and 36 Yugoslavs.

General Cunningham, exalted, cabled to Wavell to ask for permission to try for Harar, over 800 miles away. Permission was granted.

It was at this stage that he called away the two South African brigades from the Gallo–Sidamo front. His strategy had been turned topsy-turvy: he had imagined that his main thrust would be up through Galla–Sidamo towards Addis Ababa, and the attack on Kismayu had been in his mind a sop to Churchill. But with the collapse in Somalia (and in addition to the booty, thousands of prisoners were beginning to come in) plus the disappointing showing in Galla–Sidamo, the situation had been reversed. Cunningham therefore decided to bring the two South African brigades in Galla–Sidamo, the 2nd and the 5th, round to join the 1st South African brigade, Pienaar's, and thus reform the South African Division. But not just for military reasons.

I was considering employing the 1st South Africa Division [he later wrote] for the advance from Mogadishu into Ethiopia as not only did I think that their greater firepower and superior equipment would be needed in the Ethiopian highlands where the conditions would be strange and difficult but also because I wished *for political reasons* [Author's italics] to give the South African Division a more prominent part in the campaign.

In fact, however, Cunningham never put into practice his project to prove his white soldiers' superiority to his blacks. Possibly events were moving too fast. Or possibly he realized that, objectively, the two South African brigades in Galla–Sidamo had proved themselves the worst of all his troops. In mid-March they embarked at Mombasa for Egypt, to disappear first into the Western Desert and then, fairly ignominiously, and with little delay, into Rommel's prisoner-of-war camps.

After three days' pause at Mogadishu, the Nigerians—'thanks to the petrol captured from the enemy'—resumed their advance, along the road that led into the Ogaden, the road that Graziani's invading columns had followed five years earlier. General De Simone was by the first week in March back at Dagghabur, where five years earlier Dejaz Nasibu, resisting a similar invasion, had also set up his headquarters.

But unlike the Ethiopians, the Italians did not resist. Seventeen day later the Nigerians were well past Dagghabur on the far side of the Ogaden driving into Jijiga, only half an hour after the Italians had pulled out—an advance of 744 miles, the swiftest advance in the whole war.

The previous day, 16 March, the British had had an even sweeter taste of revenge. A flotilla from Aden, Vice-Admiral Leatham of the East Indies station commanding, had set sail across the Gulf, to effect the first successful landing on enemy-held beaches of the war. It had an imposingly aristocratic vanguard. Lt.-Commander the Marquess of Milford Haven, the King's cousin, was commanding HMS *Kingston*, with on board Lt.-Colonel the Marquess of Graham, heir to the Duke of Montrose, as Forward Observation Officer.

As the cruisers and destroyers hove into sight, General Bertello, military commander of the annexed territory, took to his mule. The advance guard of the two Punjabi battalions landed unopposed. They were met by the colonel commanding Berbera, with his sixty officers and men formally drawn up. 'War can be very embarrassing', one of the British officers present recorded. The Italian Colonel handed over his revolver and promptly burst into tears.

General de Simone would have done better to withdraw all his troops, without even a nominal struggle, from the lowlands and deserts of the Somali plains. In the highlands around his new headquarters at Harar he had now, despite the preceding débâcle, grouped a force still superior to that of the invaders: five brigades in a strong defensive position.

As the Nigerians halted in Jijiga, looking up doubtfully at the high hills above them, and the KAR and the South Africans took their lorries through the Ogaden to join them, the Gold Coast Brigade had been sent off on a tangent, chasing the dispirited 101st Division up the Juba river line into Galla–Sidamo. At Dolo, just below the highlands, they caught one of its brigades, the XX, and the commander, staff, and 3,000 men surrendered. The surviving brigade, the XCII, retreated towards Neghelli. Slowly the Gold Coast Brigade advanced along that difficult road, with rumours of *shifta* and tribesmen ahead, to find Neghelli abandoned and occupied only by *shifta*, on 27 March.

The road from Jijiga wound up through the boulder-strewn hills of the Marda Pass and continued for nearly 100 miles through country ideal for the defenders before debouching into the plateau of Harar. Brigadier Smallwood and his officers christened the peaks above them: Saddle Hill, Observation Hill, Camel Hill, and, with more originality, Marda's Left Breast, Marda's Right Breast and Marda's Behind. They had been ordered to wait for reinforcements before attacking, but they were unused to waiting, and three days in hot and dusty Jijiga were more than enough. Despite orders, they attacked.

This time it was not a walk-over. The 1st Nigerians, leading the assault to the right of Marda's Breasts, had two officers killed—Captain Rogers and 2nd Lieutenant Rogers—and many wounded. At dusk after five hours' shelling by the South African guns, they held the Left Breast, but the XIII Brigade, the defenders, still held the Right, and Marda's Behind.

That night, however, the XIII Brigade withdrew. The

previous night one of its battalions had deserted *en masse*, leaving the Commandant and officers to hold their hill alone. In the morning the last Breast and the Behind were occupied by Smallwood's salacious soldiery. The Nigerians moved up into the highlands and carried forward.

At the next defensive position along the road to Harar, the Babile Gap, the Italian artillery held up the Nigerians for two days and a half. But, wrote an Italian officer:

The days we spent at Babile were really terrible. The lives of the officers were in danger every night, every night more askaris were deserting, and then firing on us in the hope of terrorising us to the point where they would be able to get away with the battalion's arms and equipment.

Booty, not treachery, was the motive.

The withdrawal of the Brigade, once highly reputed, was 'the final disaster.'

When we started the Companies consisted of 30–40 men each, most of whom were Eritrean NCOs whom we thought were still faithful to us, but during the march the askaris were going along firing and throwing grenades constantly. It was impossible to stay on one's mule because bullets were whistling around our ears from every side. The orders and reproofs of the officers were ignored, and it was clear that we were faced with complete and irreparable collapse. When one sees one's authority going by the board in this way, one falls into a feeling of utter despair, having to stand by impotently during the most barbarous and disgraceful scenes without being able to do anything to stop them.

After a last fight at the Bisidimo river ten miles outside Harar, the Nigerians entered the city. They netted an 'embarrassing amount of prisoners'—which brought the total number taken in six weeks' campaigning to nearly 50,000, or roughly three times the strength of the invading force.

Brigadier Smallwood wrote with both justified pride and eulogistic rhythm to 'My dear General':

I think I may be permitted to take this opportunity to tell you how completely the Nigerian soldier has falsified all doubts as regards to his reactions to the conditions of these operations.

It has been said that he could not go short of water; he has done so without a murmur. It has been said he could not fight well out of his native bush; at Marda Pass he fought his way up mountain sides which would be recognized as such even on the Frontier. It has been said he would not stand up well to shelling and machine-gun fire in the open; at

Babile, under such fire, men were trying to cut down enemy wire with their matchets. It has been said that he would be adversely affected by high altitudes and cold; at Bisidimo, after a freezing night on the hill, he advanced over the open plain at dawn with the same quiet, cheerful determination he seems always to carry about with him. He is magnificent.

One might almost believe 'My dear General' had been heard publicly to vaunt the South Africans, and deprecate the blacks.

Pienaar's South Africans were now moved into the lead. At occupied Harar, they were saluted on entry with a banner made from sheets bearing the inscription 'Welcome from the Congregation of the Presbyterian Church'. Their first task, curiously enough, was to rescue their enemies and chastise their allies.

On the night of 28 March the 40th Colonial Battalion stationed at Diredawa on the railway below Harar refused to board the last train for Addis Ababa. They mutinied and seized the arsenal. The mutineers festooned themselves with hand-grenades and, crossing the dry river bed, which separated the 'native' from the 'European' quarter, set about celebrating and looting in the traditional Ethiopian fashion. The head of the Italian police force thereupon telephoned Harar, begging to be 'invaded' and 'occupied'. But by the time the Transvaal Scottish reached Diredawa, four civilians and three Italian policemen had been killed. One of the police officers had defended himself to the death, with rifle, pistol, knife, and bare hands. The mutineers rejoiced at the arrival of their new 'allies', but to their utter disgust, the South Africans, in a day and a night, in the only street-fighting of the war, restored 'order'.

Despite all the rules of logistics, General Cunningham, who had promised only Kismayu, decided to try for the capital of the Empire, for the great prize, Addis Ababa. There the Duke of Aosta and General Trezzani had learnt with discomfiture of the fall of Somalia, with amazement of the fall of Harar, and with alarm and horror of the events at Diredawa. In Addis Ababa there were over 11,000 Italian women and 7,000 Italian children for whose safety they were responsible—as General Wavell tactfully reminded the Viceroy in a message the RAF dropped by air over Addis Ababa on 30 March.

All Italian officials knew very well how the population had behaved in the three-day period of anarchy between the flight of the Emperor and the entry of Marshal Badoglio and his troops, in

May 1936. They remembered too the massacres in Addis Ababa perpetrated by rampaging Blackshirts in the days following the attempted assassination of Graziani. There was reason to fear that the population would, indeed, get out of control.

But though the Duke of Aosta sent an envoy by plane, as Wavell had suggested, behind Cunningham's lines, he was not to be bluffed—as Wavell had intended—into surrendering the capital. He could not believe that the British would indeed allow fellow-whites, women and children too, to be massacred (and the denouement of the Diredawa incident appeared to prove him right). Moreover, what with police forces and the Blackshirt garrison, there were over 10,000 armed Italians inside Addis. Ras Abebe Aregai, who might have posed a major threat to the Italians, was instead waiting, surprisingly inactive, in the Ankober Hills.

Addis Ababa itself, lying in a basin of hills, could hardly be defended from an enemy attack. But the road from Harar was long. Pienaar's Brigade, now in the lead, moved fast along that road (and along the railway that ran side by side with it across the Danakil desert) into the foothills to the south and east of Addis Ababa. But not before General Trezzani had dispatched a company of Savoy Grenadiers machine-gunners, with two battalions of Italian troops, six tanks, and Rolle and his *banda* to hold the last possible line of defence, the Awash river, 'to the last man and the last round'. The river was sixty feet wide. The force holding it was a respectable one. Yet on 3 April, as Fowkes's KAR took over the lead from the South Africans and came up against this barrier, opposition quickly melted away. The only real fight was put up by the machine-gunners, most of whom were killed. But it took the rest of the day and night for eighty men to drag across the six armoured cars which were planned to lead the final thrust towards Addis Ababa.

In Addis Ababa, as bad news came from the Awash crossing, the Viceroy held his last Council at Villa Italia. There could be no question, militarily speaking, of a last stand in the capital. Should he go south to join General Gazzera, in the Galla–Sidamo 'redoubt' at Jimma? North-west to join General Nasi at Gondar? Or north to join General Frusci on the great *Strada Imperiale*, the highway linking lost Asmara with doomed Addis Ababa? North, insisted Trezzani. So at 5 o'clock on the evening of 3 April the Duke of Aosta and his escort with his ADC and old friend

General Volpini, with the commander of his almost non-existent air force General Pinna, and with his chief of staff General Trezzani, left his capital for the great mountain stronghold of Amba Alagi.

Next day, as the RAF bombed and shot up the last of the Italian aircraft on the Addis Ababa aerodrome, advance patrols of the KAR entered Awash town. There they netted most of the defenders, though Rolle and his *banda* had headed away north-west across the desert towards Dessie. The six armoured cars patrolled forward twenty miles while engineers worked to repair the two bridges. The whole of Fowkes's brigade, and the rest of the armoured cars were over by 3 a.m. and moving forward. Shortly after dawn they were met on the road by an enemy car, decorated with a white flag and bearing an emissary from General Mambrini, military governor and chief of police of Addis Ababa. The emissary was Major Fausto de Fabritis, escorted by thirty Blackshirts, and his request was for the 'enemy' to occupy Addis Ababa as quickly as possible. The armoured car squadron, with two lorried companies of the 5th KAR, raced ahead. Just before dark, they reached Akaki on the outskirts of the city. But there a senior police official halted them, courteously passing on a wireless message from their own General, from Cunningham. The entry into the capital was to be a more solemn affair than a mere dash by the Kenyans.

It was not, therefore, till next morning, and till a reasonable after-breakfast hour, that a solemn column[1] set out from Akaki to enter Addis Ababa. General Wetherall, flanked by Brigadier Fowkes and Brigadier Pienaar, escorted by C Squadron of the Kenya Armoured Car Regiment, followed by first the South Africans, then the KAR, drove forward through lines of ululating Ethiopians, held in check by armed Italian police and by armed Blackshirts, to the Little Ghebbi where General Mambrini and his Fascist Guard of Honour solemnly surrendered to the conqueror the capital of *Africa Orientale Italiana*.

Forty-eight hours of what the Official History calls 'delightful tripartite cooperation' followed—the culmination of what was 'not so much a war as a well organized miracle.' In under two months General Cunningham's four brigades had captured Mogadishu, Harar, and Addis Ababa—three of the six capitals of

---

[1] Headed, unsolemnly, by journalists and photographers.

the six governorates of Italian East Africa. They had defeated, dispersed, or captured, without any aid from the rebels, forces many times their size and strength—for the total loss of 135 officers and men killed, 310 wounded, and 52 missing.

CHAPTER 30

THE RETURN OF THE EMPEROR

'THE Emperor', wrote Newbold, 'is all agog to march into Addis Ababa.' And what could have been more natural—or, one might imagine, more simple? The Emperor had entered Debra Markos on the same day that his allies had entered Addis Ababa. Wingate, informed of this good news by General Platt, sent a message of congratulations and added a request for a plane to fly Haile Selassie to his capital.

The request was refused. Why? Newbold in unofficial language gave the official answer. 'We restrained him a bit because there are 100,000 Ethiopians there and 40,000 Italians and we don't want a massacre or incidents as the Ethiopians will all go mad at the triumphal entry.' This was the line: that Haile Selassie's return would create 'a dangerous situation' and that therefore Haile Selassie should not return.

No one in the Emperor's cortège, Wingate least of all, believed in the reasons given. They saw it as a far more sinister affair. Their suspicions increased as stories came through from Addis Ababa of the increasingly arrogant behaviour of white officers, of the banning of Ethiopians from certain hotels and public places, and of General Cunningham's military police regime, which more resembled an occupation than a liberation. The latent Ethiopian fear that the British were planning to take over rather than to hand back their country revived, for after all, as De Gaulle had stylishly put it: 'Quelle situation unique aura désormais l'Angleterre dans tout l'ensemble: Ethiopie, Erythrée, Somalie, Soudan!'

Were these fears justified? Eritrea and Somalia were occupied enemy colonies and therefore would have to be administered, until a peace treaty with Italy was signed, by the British according to the traditional formula of Occupied Enemy Territory Administration—OETA. Once it became clear that the Italians were collapsing, the British set up a skeleton organization which, as more territory was conquered, swiftly expanded. To head the OETA General Wavell chose Sir Philip Mitchell, a man who had already had experience in this field in the First World War, when German East Africa was occupied. A logical but an unfortunate choice, for Sir Philip Mitchell had until the outbreak of war been Governor of Uganda. And to assist him he had two province governors from the Sudan: Kennedy-Cooke of Kassala Province and Lush of Northern Province. It looked very much as if neighbouring British colonial governors were moving in in force to take over as the Italians moved out. This seemed even more to be the case when OETA was extended—without any consultation with Haile Selassie—to the 'liberated' areas of Ethiopia proper. The Ethiopians saw the white men installed in their capital and organizing police forces, law courts, and money. Worst of all, they saw the British Army confiscating, wherever possible, captured Italian stores and equipment and weapons—wealth on which the Ethiopians had been counting and which they thought they deserved.

Hurt and incensed, Haile Selassie even talked of British 'looting' and condemned his allies as plunderers. What had really offended the Emperor, though, was the title OETA. His Empire was no longer 'Occupied Enemy Territory'. It was in his view friendly territory that had been occupied but was now liberated and ought therefore to be restored entirely to his control. The choice of the wording 'Occupied Enemy Territory' was one of the worst mistakes the British made. It resulted in long-lasting suspicion of British intentions.

There was a further dark suspicion in Haile Selassie's mind, as he sat impotent in Debra Markos. Under Sir Philip Mitchell's cold control at Cairo, Lush was Deputy Chief Political Officer for Ethiopia and Kennedy-Cooke DCPO for Eritrea. But 'Eritrea' included under this arrangement not only the Italian colony of Eritrea, but the Ethiopian province of Tigre. Sir Philip Mitchell showed no signs of detaching Tigre from this vastly expanded new 'Eritrea' and restoring it to Ethiopia. Furthermore Haile Selassie had had news of Ras Seyum which was not altogether reassuring.

Keren had fallen; Asmara had fallen; and as Colonel Delitala on Frusci's instructions withdrew his brigade from the Adowa area, Ras Seyum reverted to his old loyalties. He could hardly be accused of betraying the Italians. Though he had submitted, he

had been exiled to Italy and had only been restored to favour and
to power at the very last moment in a fairly desperate attempt by
General Nasi to bolster up a crumbling military position. The
Italians can hardly have expected Ras Seyum to act otherwise
than he did; for he had old scores to settle from the days of the
battles in the Tembien when he had been harried, bombed,
gassed, and driven back to that last battlefield at Mai Ceu.

So the day after the British took over control of Asmara, Ras
Seyum rode into the city and presented himself to General Platt
and the new DCPO for Eritrea and Tigre, Kennedy-Cooke. He
offered his services to fight the Italians and asked, inevitably, for
money and arms. Platt discouraged him on the grounds that there
was a risk of clashes between Ras Seyum's men and his own. Not
that in the event Ras Seyum took the least notice of Platt's formal
or informal wishes, for he had many thousand Italian rifles and
already 7,000 men at his orders. But there was one point that the
British particularly noticed. Ras Seyum stressed the alliance of his
grandfather, then the future Emperor Johannes, with the British
at the time of Lord Napier's expedition against Magdala and the
Emperor Theodore.

This was gloomy news for Haile Selassie. Could it be that the
British would encourage separatism? Could they be planning an
independent state of 'Greater Eritrea'? Could they be hoping to
deny his claims and impose their own administration when 'law
and order' had irretrievably broken down? Might they even be
grooming a rival Emperor?

On 8 April a letter from Ras Seyum in Adowa reached Debra
Markos. It was addressed not to the Emperor but to Ras Kassa.

How have you kept since we separated? Thank God we are well—
apart from our longing for you. Even though we were not separated in
thought, we were unable to speak face to face or to write to each other
and my sorrow at this was boundless. But since by the will of the kind
God the hindering yoke has been taken away, my joy is limitless at my
ability to write you this letter. I have recently returned from a visit to the
British Government authorities in Asmara. You will know that no man
will be more contented than I when the flag of Ethiopia, the sign of our
fathers and grandfathers, has been planted again in its country. Seyum
Mangasha Johannes.

Admirable duplicity. Nothing in this letter could be judged
treasonable or disloyal; on the contrary. *But* there was no

reference to Haile Selassie. *But* . . . the father and grandfather of Ras Seyum had been great men indeed. Ras Mangasha had died at Ankober, imprisoned by Menelik for rebellion. The Emperor Johannes in his day had, like his grandson, been simply the Ras of Tigre, and had reached the Imperial throne thanks to the support of the then British Government. Once again it seemed as if Ras Kassa's attitude and reactions might decide Haile Selassie's fate.

Although, in a more immediate sense, the fate of Haile Selassie lay in Ras Hailu's hands. It was an extremely paradoxical situation at Debra Markos. Ras Hailu had, indeed, submitted, but he was in his capital. His retainers, now 'Patriots' too, retained their arms, retained their forts and far outnumbered their new 'allies' and recent enemies, Gideon Force. Secretly Haile Selassie sent a message to Khartoum asking if the British would intern Ras Hailu in the Sudan. It seems that this request was refused—a refusal which could hardly fail to make the Emperor feel even more isolated. His isolation was only relieved by the arrival from the Sudan of his two sons, the Meredazmatch Asfa Wossen and the Duke of Harar; and by that of Lij Asrate Kassa, Ras Kassa's fourth and only surviving son.

As always, Haile Selassie was patient. Wingate too was forced to be patient, kicking his heels in Debra Markos and following from a distance the movements of his outlying forces,[1] and in particular the very risky move against Debra Tabor.

Debra Tabor stood on the road almost half-way between General Nasi at Gondar and General Frusci at Dessie, linking two of the three remaining Italian 'redoubts'. Colonel Angelini its commander had orders to hold it at all costs. Simonds and Fitaurari Birru had reached the area on 1 April with their personal bodyguards and with two Op Centres, led by the dashing young cavalry subalterns McLean and Pilkington. McLean dashed to great effect. Helped by 200 men of Dagnew Tessema, he ambushed various Italian columns, blowing up lorries and killing 100 *banda*—despite counter-attacks by Farello's *banda* in which several dozen were killed on both sides. 'It is of interest to note', reported Simonds, 'that the Patriots, having found themselves in

---

[1] Maraventano's fleeing column was heading north-east for Dessie, pursued by 'Safforce' consisting of *Bimbashis* Thesiger and Riley, Lt. Naylor and No. 3 Op Centre, and Lt. Rowe and a company of the 2nd Ethiopians. A professional soldier Lt. Colonel Benson of the Royal Ulster Corps had meanwhile arrived in Debra Markos to take command of and re-form the 2nd Ethiopians, replacing Boyle.

a very sticky position, fought with great gallantry and determination. This was the last attempt the enemy made to reach Debra Tabor by motor transport from the north.'

Having cut the road from Gondar, Simonds moved east to the Gaint district intending to cut the road from Dessie too. He surrounded and besieged all the outlying forts in the area: Tarragadam, Ifag, and the fort of Deran towards which the Maraventano column pursued by *Bimbashi* Thesiger and 'Saf-force' was heading.

This was the country of Lij Johannes, but Simonds was Wingate's man, and Wingate the Emperor's. No question of encouraging rival claimants here. 'Lij Johannes', reported Simonds briefly, 'a Pretender to the Throne, who had recently been active on behalf of the Italians and well supplied with money arms and ammunition was persuaded to submit to the Emperor and despatched under guard to Addis.' This was almost totally false. Lij Johannes, like all the rebel leaders, had from time to time had his contacts with the Italians and had, like Ras Abebe Aregai, accepted supplies from them. But he had certainly never been active on their behalf. What had happened was that his follower Essayas, the Oletta cadet, had returned to Burie earlier when news had reached Beghemder of the arrival of Haile Selassie, and had been sent back by the Emperor with a letter for Lij Johannes full of fair words and fine promises. Though distrustful of the son of Ras Makonnen, as any son of Lij Yasu might well be, Lij Johannes set out with a thousand men from Debra Markos, accompanied by Essayas and certainly in no sense under arrest.

The news of his impending arrival at Debra Markos, despite the size of his escort and largely thanks to Essayas's skilful negotiation, was bound to imply submission to Haile Selassie. The Emperor had much to be thankful for. The war was going well. Admiral Bonetti, attacked by the Free French and the Indians, had surrendered at Massawa to Colonel Monclar of the French Foreign Legion. East of the Omo, the Italians, 'rein-forced' by 20,000 men and 20 generals fleeing south from Addis Ababa, were being chased through the hills and jungles by columns of KAR and Nigerians heading down from Addis Ababa, by columns of KAR and the Gold Coast Brigade heading up from Neghelli, and by 'Patriots' rising everywhere. North of Gondar, following Ras Seyum and his own son, Lij Zaudi's, example (and, according to the Italians, influenced by the 'gift' of

300,000 Maria Theresa dollars from the British) Dejaz Ayalew Birru had turned against General Nasi and was moving down to join Simonds. From Debra Markos the boy Duke of Harar was flown by the British to Harar to take up official residence in the Governor's Palace. Best of all a letter dated 18 April arrived from Ras Seyum:

To Haile Selassie, Elect of God, Emperor of Ethiopia, *Janhoy*!
I bow before you in greeting. Thanks be to God, we are well. God working out His work of kindness has fulfilled the word which he spoke by man's mouth that within five years[1] he would show mercy to Ethiopia.
And now may God, the doer of all, satisfy you by enabling you to set up the standard of Ethiopia now that you have returned to your country.

This was equivalent to formal submission. We do not know what reply, if any, Ras Kassa had sent to Ras Seyum's veiled letter; we do not know what pressure, if any, the British had put on Ras Seyum. But we may imagine. With Harar, his father's fief, in the hands of his son, with the danger of Tigrean separatism removed, with a proclaimed rival Emperor and son of Lij Yasu riding in to submit, with Ras Hailu posing less of a threat every day as news of British successes poured in, the Emperor had reason enough to believe that his Allies were going to respect their promises and that he himself would soon set foot once again in his capital. With Wingate's (and possibly Chapman-Andrews's) connivance, he sent Dejaz Makonnen Endalkatchew ahead by plane to Addis Ababa, to prepare for his return, accompanied by three young men, Mulugueta Bulli, Negga Haile Selassie, and Abiye Abebe. Brigadiers Lush and Sandford, brothers-in-law but divided in their allegiance,[1] were already there. And Boustead and his men, who had been sent out to help the attack on Debra Tabor, no sooner reached their objective Fort Mota than, to their disgust, they were recalled. They returned to Debra Markos, cursing Wingate, to find that they were 'to provide adequate protection on the road for His Imperial Majesty.' The final move was near.

---

[1] A reference to a notorious prophecy, word of which had spread throughout Ethiopia, which was almost universally believed and which indeed proved to be true. Its gist was that Italian rule would only last five years.
[2] They were married to sisters. Lush was DCPO—Deputy Chief Political Officer —for Eritrea, and as a former Province Governor in the Sudan frankly in favour of extending British administration. Sandford of course, being like his wife Christine a devoted supporter of Haile Selassie, held quite the opposite view.

Yet there was a final hold-up. On 22 April a telegram arrived from General Cunningham ordering Wingate to halt any move of Haile Selassie's approach to Addis Ababa, by all means 'short of force.' But Cunningham by now was only delaying the inevitable. For on 9 April Churchill had held a meeting of the Defence Committee and instructed that the Emperor should be allowed to return to his capital as soon as possible, and on 19 April a General Telegram had been dispatched to Wavell to the same effect.

So the Emperor took the decision to set out for his capital; and though Wingate had not yet had his orders countermanded, he informed the Emperor that he did not propose to use force to stop him, and indeed would feel obliged to provide an escort. Therefore, on 27 April Haile Selassie, escorted by most of Gideon Force, accompanied by Ras Kassa and indeed by Ras Hailu whose presence he had 'insisted' on, and followed by Lij Johannes who had been promised the governorate of Sidamo, set out from Debra Markos.

It took him a week to achieve his progress; and at every stage good news came in. First, of the surrender of Dessie to Pienaar's South Africans and *Bimbashi* Campbell's patriots; then on the following day of the fall of Socota, seat of the Wagshum, to Ras Seyum and Lij Wossene Hailu Kebbede, heir to the Zagwe dynasty; finally, of the evacuation of Bahr Dar after a battle in which Colonel Torelli, sallying forth, had been seriously wounded. At the monastery of Debra Libanos, where Haile Selassie and Ras Kassa had last prayed when fleeing from the lost field of Mai Ceu, they prayed again together. At his fief of Fikke, Ras Kassa left the Emperor, saw the place of the killing of his two sons, visited their graves, and then with 2,000 men set out to join *Bimbashi* Thesiger in the hunting down of the Maraventano column.

Haile Selassie continued on his way. On 4 May he halted outside his capital. From the hills of Ankober, Ras Abebe Aregai's followers had poured down, and were camped at Entotto on the northern outskirts. Inside the city General Cunningham and his British and South African officers prepared with some trepidation for the morrow.

Next day, five years to the day after Marshal Badoglio and his 'iron-will column' had driven into the city as victorious conquerors, Haile Selassie returned to Addis Ababa. Orde Wingate led the cortège, followed in an open car driven by *Bimbashi* LeBlanc by the Emperor himself. The streets were lined, despite Cunningham's orders, by thousands upon thousands of Ras Abebe Aregai's men. As the Emperor drove to the Great Ghebbi of Menelik where General Cunningham was waiting with a Nigerian Guard of Honour to receive him, Ras Abebe Aregai rode into the city, with his machine-guns and even a few pieces of mountain artillery, with his Italian prisoners in chains, and his fifteen-year-old son Daniel leading his army. It is reported that at the end of the religious ceremony which the priests celebrated at the Great Ghebbi, Abebe Aregai bowed low before Haile Selassie and said: 'I am your loyal subject. I never submitted to the enemy. I never hoped to see you alive again and I am grateful to God for this day, when I have seen the sun shine.'

These must have been the feelings of almost all the population, as smiling, ululating, waving British and Ethiopian flags, they joyously greeted their Emperor on his return. That night, after a day entirely free from unpleasant incidents of any kind, Haile Selassie slept again at his own palace, the Little Ghebbi.

And all around 'the little man' sleeping—if that night he did sleep—others slept. The people of Addis Ababa, happy and drunken; the Italians of Addis Ababa, men, women and children, half prisoners, half free, much relieved; General Cunningham relieved too but disgruntled; Wingate content but disappointed that Gideon Force had not achieved more; Ras Abebe Aregai hopeful; Ras Hailu without hope. Far away, throughout what still was to many *Africa Orientale Italiana*, others slept, or dreamt, or plotted too: General Platt luxuriously at Asmara, planning his attack on Amba Alagi, the enemy's last redoubt; Ras Seyum down in Lasta surrounded by his men, planning *his* attack to anticipate Platt's; Colonel Maraventano near Deraa pursued by Thesiger and Ras Kassa; Colonel Angelini in Debra Tabor besieged by Simonds and Fitaurari Birru; Colonel Torelli back at Gondar, in hospital; General Nasi more comfortably at Gondar in the old castle of Fasildas; General Gazzera down in Jimma comparatively undisturbed by the pinpricks west of the Omo. Over the seas Wavell and Churchill, Mussolini, Badoglio, Graziani and De Bono, Sylvia Pankhurst, and all the other men and women who had played some part large or small in the affairs of Ethiopia retired that night with different sentiments: of joy, pride, disappointment, sorrow, or satisfaction at the news that the Emperor of Ethiopia had completed the wearying odyssey that had led him from the field of Mai Ceu to Addis Ababa, from Addis Ababa to Djibuti, from Djibuti to Jerusalem, from Jerusalem to Gibraltar, from Gibraltar to London, from London to Geneva, from Geneva to cold exile in Bath and holidays at Worthing; and then from Bath to London, from London to Malta, from Malta to Cairo, from Cairo to Wadi-Halfa, from Wadi-Halfa to Khartoum, from Khartoum to Um Idla, from Um Idla to Mount Belaya, from Mount Belaya to Burie, from Burie to Debra Markos, and from Debra Markos back to the Little Ghebbi that he had built and furnished in the English style a decade earlier.

THE END OF THE WAR

THE war in East Africa was not, of course, over. There were still to be heroic, comic, and tragic episodes before the last Italian surrendered, still political intrigue galore before the Emperor's position was totally secured. But there was no longer any chance of an Italian victory or any real doubt of Haile Selassie's eventual success; the tension of the history is gone. So 5 May 1941, the day of the Emperor's return, seems as suitable a moment as any to ring the curtain down.

It is right, however, to draw the curtain briefly aside for a glimpse at the fate of the actors in this great melodrama.

Before the end of May the Duke of Aosta and General Frusci (and Gina's brother with them), besieged at Amba Alagi by Pienaar's South Africans from the south and by the Indians in the north, attacked and harassed and terrorized by Ras Seyum's swollen army, surrendered to the British; and in March of the following year the former Viceroy, POW 1190, died wretchedly of consumption in a Nairobi hospital.

After Amba Alagi, the South Africans and the 5th Indian Division followed the 4th Indian Division up to the Western Desert and into the battle against Rommel; leaving only black colonial troops on the British side to fight the last battles of a purely African war. The Gold Coast Brigade was held in the forests north of Neghelli for many weeks by the valiant defence of General di Pralormo's men. But as the KAR broke through from the south and the Nigerians from the north, the whole Italian position east of the Omo crumbled. West of the Omo Gurassu Duke, with thousands of followers, marched on Jimma; Captain Whalley happily entered Maji (for the Merille successfully blocked their KAR opponents); and Mesfin Sileshi and Azaz Kebbede descended from Lekempti at the head of hordes of 'last-minute' Patriots. General Gazzera and his staff, retreating westwards, preferred to surrender to the Belgians and their Congolese troops moving up into the highlands from the Baro Salient rather than to the rebels; no one, despite their fears, was eaten.

Cut off at Debra Tabor, Colonel Angelini surrendered to McLean and Pilkington and Fitaurari Birru; Pilkington enrolled Farello's Wollo *Banda* (whom General Nasi had described as his 'best troops') under his own command; and McLean did the same with the 79th Colonial Battalion renamed the '79th Foot'. As for Colonel Maraventano, after epic marching and counter-marching his column finally surrendered to Wingate and Ras Kassa —Wingate's last exploit, before Gideon Force was dissolved, and he himself was deprived of command and ordered back to Cairo, where he attempted suicide. From there, as is well known, he went to glory and his death, once more under Wavell's command, in Burma against the Japanese—a death that probably deprived the Israeli army of its first Commander-in-Chief.

General Nasi held out alone at Gondar till the rains were passed. He finally surrendered to the composite forces of 'Fluffy' Fowkes and the Crown Prince Asfa Wossen, and the Patriots of Beghemder, and Pilkington's Wollo *Banda*, and the Estonian Nurk, and the poetic *Bimbashi* Sheppard, and McLean's 79th Foot, and the 'Robber Baron' Dougie Douglas, only after a last fierce battle by Lake Tana. General Cunningham was appointed to high command in the Western Desert, where he failed. General Platt succeeded in 'liberating' Madagascar from the Vichy French. Brigadier Sandford lived for many years outside Addis Ababa, where the author met him, shortly before his death, in his 90th year.

As for the Ethiopians: how Haile Selassie re-established his power and rid himself of his British allies; how Ras Imru was liberated; how a revolt broke out in Tigre and Ras Seyum's position was endangered; how Blatta Takele Wolde Hawariat intrigued and was imprisoned; how the Sultan of the Danakil made his peace; how a false Emperor Theodore arose in the south-west; how Lij Johannes and Haile Selassie Gugsa were arrested and held, till March 1974, in confinement; how 'Lij' Belai Zelleka and others were hanged; how Wolde Giorgis the secretary became the power behind the throne and was then disgraced; how, later, Ras Seyum and Ras Abebe Aregai and many others were killed in the Green Room of the Little Ghebbi; how, still later Blatta Takele died in his old age, machine-gun in hand;

how the Emperor out-lived all of his rivals and most of his own children only to be overthrown by the army he had himself created—all this is another story, part of the continuing history of Ethiopia, and it is not here that it can be told.

BIOGRAPHICAL INDEX

THESE notes are in no sense exhaustive. What follows is neither a full list of all the Ethiopians named in the text nor a full account of the positions, achievements, or lives of those listed. It is simply an aid designed to help the reader trace a path through what may have appeared to be the bewildering maze of Ethiopian names and personages.

Though every effort has been made to be accurate, dates and appointments should be checked where possible. Comments and conclusions are of course the author's own.

Where titles are given, they are *either* the titles most commonly used in the text *or*, in certain cases, the titles by which those concerned were best known in later life.

I. THE GENERATION OF ADOWA

Emperor MENELIK II
Emperor of Ethiopia from 1889 to 1912

Born in 1844. Menelik's father, Haile Melakot, became Negus of Shoa in 1847. When his father died in 1855 Menelik himself was being held at Magdala as the Emperor Theodore's hostage. He escaped, and was proclaimed Negus of Shoa in 1865. He submitted unwillingly to Theodore's successor, the Emperor Johannes IV; but on Johannes's death at the great battle of Metemma in 1889 immediately proclaimed himself Emperor. By 1904 he was ailing. In March 1909 he announced that his heir would be his grandson, Lij Yasu. In October of that year he suffered a stroke and was virtually incapacitated from then till his death on 12 December 1912.

Empress TAITU
The childless wife of Menelik

Daughter of Ras Batul of Simien and Beghemder, she married Menelik, her fifth husband, on 29 April 1883 at the age of 27. Following Menelik's stroke she tried to seize power for herself and her brother Ras Wule Batul but was foiled by the Abuna Matteos, who arranged for a Regency to be proclaimed on 21 March 1910. She died at Entotto on 11 February 1918.

Ras MANGASHA of Tigre
Ruler of Tigre and rival of Menelik

Mangasha, the bastard son of the Emperor Johannes, was legitimated, created a Ras, and declared his father's heir in 1888, the year before Johannes's death in battle. But Menelik of Shoa proclaimed himself Emperor and marched north, securing Mangasha's submission. Nevertheless Mangasha was always in a state of semi-rebellion. He was imprisoned in Menelik's mountain fortress of Ankober from January 1899 till his death in 1906.

Negus TEKLE HAIMONOT of Gojjam
Ruler of Gojjam

Created Negus by the Emperor Johannes in 1881, Tekle Haimonot ruled Gojjam till his death in 1901. In Johannes's reign he attacked Menelik, then Negus of Shoa, but was defeated. On Johannes's death in March 1889 he pledged loyalty to Menelik and so retained both his title and his province.

Ras (later Negus) MIKAEL of Wollo
The power behind the throne from 1912 to 1916

Queen Workitu of Wollo befriended Menelik when he escaped from Theodore's clutches at Magdala. Her stepson Mohammed Ali became Menelik's supporter and close friend; and when in July 1876 Menelik reconquered Wollo for Shoa, Mohammed Ali was appointed its governor. He was promoted to Ras, became a Christian, took the name of Mikael, and married Menelik's eldest daughter, Shoagarad. At Adowa he led the feared Galla cavalry. He founded Dessie, the first town in Wollo and its new capital. Following Menelik's death he was anointed Negus on the instructions of his own son, Menelik's grandson, Lij Yasu. Defeated by the Shoans at the great Battle of Sagalle, he died in captivity on an island in the Great Lakes on 8 September 1918.

Ras MAKONNEN
Menelik's well-loved cousin and right-hand man

Grandson of the Negus Sahle Selassie who ruled Shoa from 1813 to 1847. Menelik's father, the Negus Haile Melakot, and Makonnen's mother, Tenagne Worq, were brother and sister. A diplomat as well as a warrior, he was particularly successful in establishing good relations with the British after the conquest of Harar in 1887. He visited London in 1902 and attended the Coronation of Edward VII. His sudden death in March 1906 almost broke Menelik's heart.

Wagshum GWANGUL of Wag
Ruler of Wag

The Wagshums were descendants of the Zagwe dynasty which had ruled medieval Ethiopia till roughly 1270, from Roha in Lasta (later renamed Lalibela in honour of their most famous Emperor). Wagshum Gwangul's uncle, Wagshum Gobaze, had proclaimed himself Emperor with the throne name of Tekle Giorgis in 1868, following the Emperor Theodore's suicide. He was defeated and deposed by his rival from the North, the Emperor Johannes. But the Wagshums never entirely abandoned their pretensions to the imperial throne.

Ras Bitwoded MANGASHA ATIKIN
Governor of Ifrata at the time of Adowa

Appointed Governor of Gojjam in 1901 on the death of the Negus Tekle Haimonot. Died in 1910.

Liquemaquas ABATE
Menelik's liquemaquas at Adowa

Later, as Ras Abate, he attempted to seize power in Addis Ababa in June 1911, following the death by poisoning of the then Regent Ras Tessema, two months earlier. His attempt was unsuccessful but his punishment light.

Abuna MATTEOS
Head of the Coptic Church in Ethiopia

Loyal to the wishes and memory of Menelik, the Abuna exercised great influence as the most eminent conservative figure in Ethiopia till his death in 1926 at the age of 83.

2. THE SUCCESSORS OF MENELIK

Lij YASU
Menelik's grandson and proclaimed successor

Lij Yasu was virtual ruler of the Empire from the end of the Regency, eighteen months before Menelik's death till his own deposition by the Shoan nobles in October 1916. His mother was Woizero Shoagarad, Menelik's elder daughter; his father Ras Mikael of Wollo. Born in 1896, Lij Yasu died in captivity at Garamulata near Harar in November 1935, on the eve of the Italian invasion.

Empress ZAUDITU
Ethiopia's only reigning Empress

Second daughter of Menelik, she was born in 1875. Reigned from her proclamation on 27 October 1916 till her sudden death on 2 April 1930. Though three times married—the first time at the age of two-and-a-half—she had no children.

Ras GUGSA WULE
Husband of the Empress Zauditu

Ruler of Beghemder, grandson of the immensely powerful Ras Batul, and therefore nephew of the Empress Taitu. Attempted to seize power in 1930 despite Zauditu's apparent disavowal. Killed in battle (or, according to some sources, captured and died in imprisonment shortly afterwards).

Ras TAFARI MAKONNEN
The future Emperor Haile Selassie I

Born in Harar, where his father Ras Makonnen, Menelik's cousin, was governor, on 23 July 1892. Of his mother Woizero Yeshimmabet (reputed to be the daughter of a Gurage war-slave) little is known. Educated first by the Catholic Bishop of Harar. Mgr. Jarosseau, and then at the Menelik II School for Nobles in Addis Ababa. Appointed Dejaz on his father's death in 1906. In 1911 given the governorate of Harar by Lij Yasu.

On 27 September 1916 appointed Ras, Regent and Heir to the Throne by the Shoan nobles in Addis Ababa. On 7 October 1928 after foiling the so-called 'palace conspiracy' anointed Negus of Ethiopia. Ascended the imperial throne on 3 April 1930, taking the throne name of Haile Selassie. Crowned on 2 November 1930. Deposed by the Dergue (the Co-ordinating Committee of the Armed Forces/the Provisional Military Government) on 12 September 1974. Died in captivity of 'circulatory failure' on 27 August 1975 at the age of 83.

3. MAGNATES, NOBLEMEN, GOVERNORS, COURTIERS, AND OFFICERS

Ras ABEBE AREGAI
Most famous of the Patriot leaders in Shoa and a constant thorn in the Italians' flesh

Son of the Nevraid Aregai, the religious ruler of Axum, who was present at the Empress Taitu's side at the battle of Adowa, and grandson of Menelik's Galla general Ras Gobana. Police chief and Balambaras in Addis Ababa at the time of the Italian invasion. Believed to have French support throughout the occupation. Became a most important figure in post-War Ethiopia. Machine-gunned to death by Mengistu Neway and his brother Girmame in the Green Salon of the Little Ghebbi in the failed coup of 1960.

Dejaz ABEBE DAMTEW
Brother of Ras Desta and a Shoan war-leader

At the time of the Italian invasion, governor of the remote southern province of Gemu Gofa. Active on the Kenya border in 1941.

Dejaz ABERRA KASSA
Second son of Ras Kassa and leader of the Resistance in Shoa on the Emperor's flight

Born *circa* 1900; married to a daughter of Ras Seyum; ruled his father's fief of Salale from its capital Fikke. Thought to have imperial longings. Planned the attack on Italian-occupied Addis Ababa in the summer of 1936. Shot, treacherously, by the Italians in Fikke.

Dejaz ABERRA TEDLA
Shoan governor of Mai Ceu; and killed at the battle

Lij (later Lieutenant-General) ABIYE ABEBE
Shoan nobleman, married to the Emperor's second daughter, Princess Tsahai

Born 1918, son of the Liquemaquas Abebe Atnaf Seged who was killed with Ras Lul Seged by the Negus Mikael before the battle of Sagalle. In the early Resistance with Lij Merid Mangasha, he came to England from Khartoum in November 1938. Though his marriage was short-lived, Abiye Abebe became an important figure in post-War Ethiopia. Minister of Defence and Chief of Staff from 28 February to 22 July 1974, he was shot by the Dergue on 23 November, 'Bloody Saturday', together with more than fifty other prominent figures.

Dejaz ADAFRISAU
Menz nobleman, warleader of the older generation

Fought at Adowa as a young man. At Dessie with the Emperor as Commander of the Imperial Guard. Spent Italian occupation at the monastery of Kidhane Meret in Jerusalem. Came back in with Gideon Force and the Emperor. Promoted Ras and died, a Crown Councillor, aged nearly ninety.

Dejaz ADMASSU BIRRU
Brother of the more famous Ayalew Birru; leading member of the Beghemder nobility

Governor of Yeggiu at the time of the Italian invasion.

Dejaz AMDE ALI
Wollo nobleman, son of Ras Ali, the Negus Mikael's general

Dejaz AMDE MIKAEL
Head of the Shoan clan of the Moja

First cousin of the Empress Menen. At the time of the Italian invasion Governor of Arussi in the south-west. Member of the Crown Council in 1943.

Lij (later Ras Bitwoded) ANDARGATCHEW MESSAI
Ethiopian consul at Djibuti during the Italian invasion and conquest

A Shoan from Salale, and originally a follower of Ras Kassa. After the War became the second husband of Princess Tenagne Worq, Governor–General of Beghemder, Chief Representative in Eritrea, and an elder statesman of the Empire.

Dejaz ASFAWOSSEN KASSA
Third son of Ras Kassa

Married to a daughter of Mesfin Sileshi. Overshadowed by his brother Aberra and shot, like him, in Fikke by the Italians in the summer of 1936.

Lij (later Ras) ASRATE KASSA
Fourth son of Ras Kassa

Born 1918. Escaped to the Sudan with his mother after the Italian conquest. Trained with the Crown Prince at Sobat Military Academy in Khartoum 1940/41. After the war became one of the most powerful men in Ethiopia; it was thought he would be the strong man of the regime when the Crown Prince inherited or even make a bid for the throne himself. Shot on 'Bloody Saturday', 23 November 1974, by the Dergue, the fourth son of Ras Kassa to die before a firing squad, the only one to be executed by his own countrymen.

Dejaz AURARIS
Shoan nobleman of the older generation

Governor of Menz at the time of the Italian invasion. Arrested at Dessie with the Wollo leaders on 'conspiracy' charges during the Battles in the North. Subsequently became leader of the Resistance in Menz.

Dejaz AYALEW BIRRU
Ruler of the Simien

Born in 1885 into the ruling house of Beghemder, Ayalew married in 1917 Manalabish the daughter of Ras Kassa. He distinguished himself, as did his brother-in-law Wondossen, at the battle of the plains of Anchim but was bitterly disappointed when Wondossen rather than he was given power in Beghemder. Played a waiting game in the time of the Italians.

Dejaz BALCHA
One of Menelik's most famous—and ferocious—generals

As a young Galla lying, castrated, on the battlefield he was on Menelik's orders saved and brought to Court. Commanded the artillery at Adowa. Thereafter a ferocious provincial governor, particularly in Sidamo, and a conservative diehard. Imprisoned for two years after his failed coup of 1928, then entered a monastery. Died fighting the Italians in 1937.

Dejaz BEIENE MERID
Governor of Bale at the time of the Italian invasion

Born *circa* 1875, son of Dejaz Merid, a former Ligaba of Lij Yasu. He married a daughter of Haile Selassie presumably born before the Emperor's marriage to Menen. She was named Romaneworq. Beiene Merid was killed at Gojetti with Gabremariam on 19 February 1937. His son Samson, Haile Selassie's grandson, is living in exile in London.

Imperial Fitaurari BIRRU WOLDE GABRIEL
Shoan warleader of the older generation; one of Ethiopia's richest landowners

Reputed to be the illegitimate son of Menelik and therefore always treated with suspicion by the Emperor. In disgrace and provincial exile at the time of the Italian invasion but recalled, and fought at Mai Ceu. Spent Italian occupation in Jerusalem. Back with the Emperor and Gideon Force. The Italians at Debra Tabor eventually surrendered to him. Created Ras and post-War governor of Kaffa and Jimma. His sons were hunted down and killed by the Dergue in 1975.

Kenyaz BEZIBEH SILESHI
Shoan nobleman; brother of the more famous Mesfin Sileshi

Ras DESTA DAMTEW
Shoan nobleman; married to Haile Selassie's eldest daughter, Princess Tenagne Worq

Born *circa* 1898, the son of Fitaurari Damtew, famous for having visited Russia. Married Princess Tenagne Worq in 1924 and had four daughters and one son, Lij Iskander. Appointed Governor of Sidamo in 1932 in succession to Birru Wolde Gabriel and founded its two towns, Yirgalem and Wondo. Killed by the Italians on 24 February 1937.

Fitaurari FIKREMARIAM
Commander of the Crown Prince's Guard at Dessie; later a Patriot leader

A Shoan from Menz, of the Moja clan. Distinguished himself at the battle of the plains of Anchim. Mystery surrounds his death. His body was never found but it is thought that he crawled away to a cave to die in or about October 1937.

Ras GABRE HIWOT MIKAEL
Leading member of the ruling house of Wollo; therefore automatically hostile to and suspected by the Shoans

Dejaz GABREMARIAM
Shoan war-leader of the older generation

Famous for his successful attack on the Italians in 1931 when Governor–General of Harar and the Ogaden. Replaced on the outbreak of war by the younger and more progressive Dejaz Nasibu. Killed with Beiene Merid at the last battle of the war, on 19 February 1937.

GABRE MASKAL
Ras Imru's, and later Wingate's, wireless operator

Dejaz GABREMEDHIN
The aged Shum Tembien

Fitaurari GESSESSE BELEW
Member of the Gojjami ruling house

His father was Dejaz Belew, one of the two legitimate sons of the Negus Tekle Haimonot. At the time of the Italian invasion besieged the Shoan garrison in Debra Markos. Died soon after, thought to have been disposed of by the Italians. His brother Hailu Belew became one of Gojjam's four major Patriot leaders.

Ras GETACHEW ABATE
Governor of Kaffa at the time of the invasion

His father was the Liquemaquas Abate (*see* 'The Generation of Adowa') Getachew was created a Ras in 1933. He commanded a column at the battle of Mai Ceu; went into exile in Jerusalem; but then returned and submitted to the Italians. After the War he was arrested. 'I pardon you,' said Haile Selassie, 'but I do not know if God will.' Exiled to a remote province, he is said to have died of drink.

Tsehafe Taezaz HAILE
Haile Selassie's 'Representative in the North' from 1940 to 1941
Had abandoned the defence of Ad Termaber to the cadets in 1936.

Dejaz HAILE KEBBEDE of Wag
War-leader of the Army of Wag

Brought up at the court of his uncle Wagshum Gwangul (*see* 'The Generation of Adowa') who was succeeded by his father Wagshum Kebbede. Fought in the Tembien, at Mai Ceu, and continued the struggle after the fall of Addis Ababa. Killed and beheaded by the Italians.

Emperor HAILE SELASSIE
see RAS TAFARI MAKONNEN in the preceding section, 'The Successors of Menelik'.

Dejaz HAILE SELASSIE GUGSA of Makalle
The traitor—the only magnate openly to side with the Italians during their invasion

Son of Ras Gugsa Araya, ruler of eastern Tigre, and therefore rival of Ras Seyum, the ruler of western Tigre. Married to Haile Selassie's favourite daughter, Princess Zenabe Worq, in 1932. (She, however, died on the eve of the Italian invasion.) After the War he was imprisoned in the Seychelles, Jimma, and Gore, to be released—but only briefly—at the time of the Revolution. It is said that by that time the skin of his wrists had grown over his silver chains.

Ras HAILU
Ruler of Gojjam; and chief collaborator with the Italians after the conquest of Ethiopia

Born *circa* 1868, the illegitimate son of Negus Tekle Haimonot (*see* 'The Generation of Adowa'). Ruled Gojjam from 1907 to 1931. Married many times, most notably to Woizero Assafalach, sister of the Empress Taitu—he in his turn being her fourth but not her last husband. After the War held under house arrest in Addis Ababa where he died in 1951.

Dejaz HAPTE MARIAM GABRE EGZIABHER
Galla potentate; governor of Wollega—Lekempti

Son of King Kumsa of Wollega who submitted to Menelik, was baptized, and thereafter styled Dejaz Gabre Egziabher. Though a loyalist till the Emperor's departure, Hapte Mariam then became the moving spirit behind the attempt to set up a British-protected Western Galla Federation. When that failed he threw in his lot with the Italians; but died soon afterwards, rumoured to have been poisoned by them.

Dejaz HAPTE MIKAEL
Governor of a small southern province

Blattengueta HEROUY WOLDE SELASSIE
Haile Selassie's Foreign Minister

Born *circa* 1879. After 1916 held many important positions as the Regent's liberalizing supporter. 1931 Ambassador Extraordinary to Japan. 1933 Minister of Foreign Affairs. Into exile with Haile Selassie. Died at Fairfield on 19 September 1938. Rumoured by some to have committed suicide on discovery of secret correspondence with Italians. Author of twenty-eight books in Amharic.

Ras IMRU
Member of the ruling house of Shoa

Born *circa* 1894 and therefore younger than his first cousin once removed, Imru was brought up in Harar with Haile Selassie. Both shared early and melodramatic adventures during the struggle against Lij Yasu. On Haile Selassie's accession Imru was appointed Governor of Harar; in 1932 he replaced the deposed Ras Hailu as Governor of Gojjam. In May 1935 he was appointed Regent. In December he surrendered to the Italians and was imprisoned on Ponza till his release by the advancing Allies. After the War he was Ambassador both to India and the United States. In later life he became known for his liberal land-reforming views. His only son, Lij Mikael Imru, was Prime Minister with the Dergue's approval from 22 July to 12 September 1974.

Ras Imru died peacefully in August 1980 and was given a State Funeral by the Dergue.

Ras KASSA
The most respected figure among the Shoan nobility

Born in 1881, the son of Hailu of Lasta and via his mother the grandson of Ras Dargie, brother of the Negus Haile Melakot, Menelik's father. A devout churchman, he ruled the fief of Salale near the great monastery of Debra Libanos in north-western Shoa. Went into exile with Haile Selassie but spent most of the occupation in Jerusalem. Returned with Haile Selassie and Gideon Force. After the War became a Crown Counsellor. Died, full of honours, in 1956.

Dejaz KASSA SEBHAT
Tigrean nobleman

Son of Ras Sebhat, of the House of Sabaudagis.

Ras KEBBEDE MANGASHA ATIKIM
Shoan nobleman

Son of Ras Mangasha Atikim (*see* 'The Generation of Adowa'). Held Amba Alagi with his forces during the Battles of the North. Later submitted to the Italians and became an alcoholic.

Azaz KEBBEDE TESSEMA
Courtier

Fought at Mai Ceu. Spent Italian occupation in Jerusalem. In September 1940 crossed with Brigadier Sandford into Gojjam. Later part of Gideon Force. After the War became an important bureacrat and in 1960 was Chief of Staff of the territorial forces. It is widely rumoured that Mengistu Haile Mariam, the 'Comrade Chairman' of the Dergue and the present military ruler of Ethiopia, is his illegitimate son.

Dejaz LATIBELU GABRE
Courtier and war-leader

A Bajirond in 1935, he subsequently commanded a column at Mai Ceu. Retired to his estates during the occupation, though under constant Italian suspicion. Prominent Senator in post-war Ethiopia. Killed in the Green Salon at the Little Ghebbi in the 1960 coup attempt.

LORENZO TAEZAZ
One of the Emperor's bright young men

Born 1900, an Eritrean. 'Discovered' by Dejaz Nasibu Emmanuel and sent to study in France. Married a daughter of Ras Imru. During the occupation Representative of the Government-in-Exile at the League of Nations—and secretly visited Gojjam and Gondar. In with Gideon

Force. Minister of Foreign Affairs, 1941; President of the Senate 1943. Died 23 June 1946 in Stockholm.

Bitwoded MAKONNEN DEMISSIE
Respected Shoan nobleman

Born 1889, the son of Ras Demissie, who had been Menelik's Afanegus. Married to Lilt Yashashaworq, Haile Selassie's favourite niece. Briefly imprisoned for supporting the Empress Zauditu against the Regent; but thanks to Yashashaworq released. A Governor of Wollega at the time of the Italian invasion. Killed at Amba Aradam supporting Ras Mulugueta, his corpse was cut in two by Major Burgoyne.

MAKONNEN DESTA
Courtier

Born in Gojjam in 1910. Educated Alexandria, Beirut, and Harvard. Associate editor of progressive newspaper in 1930. Spent occupation in Cairo. In with Gideon Force and the Emperor. Minister in various post-War governments. Died 1966.

Dejaz (later Ras Bitwoded) MAKONNEN ENDALKATCHEW
Shoan nobleman, head of the Addisge clan

Tall, highly respected English-style aristocrat, fond of country life, dogs, firearms—and novel-writing. Had eloped with Lilt Yashashaworq, the Emperor's favourite niece at one stage. Governor of Illubabor at the time of the Italian invasion. Spent the occupation in Palestine. Back in with Gideon Force and the Emperor. Minister of the Interior on the Restoration, then Ethiopia's first Prime Minister. Died in 1963. His son, Lij Endalkatchew Makonnen, became in his turn the Emperor's last Prime Minister appointed by Haile Selassie in an attempt to stave off the creeping revolution. He held office from 28 February to 22 July 1974 but was executed by the Dergue on 23 November.

MAKONNEN HAPTEWOLD
Bureaucrat

A small, shabby, crafty man of a Shoan church family brought to the Emperor's notice by Blatta Takele. Director of Commerce at the time of the Italian invasion. Spent the occupation in Paris. In the late Fifties he and his brothers dominated political life in the capital. Killed in the attempted coup of 1960.

Dejaz MAKONNEN WOSSENE
Governor of Wollamo at the time of the Italian invasion

Bitwoded MANGASHA WUBE
Governor of the third Wollega province at the time of the Italian invasion

A Shoan, son of Menelik's general Dejaz Wube Atnaf Seged. His was the

last reserve army, ordered to defend Addis Ababa. His men deserted, he
submitted, but was imprisoned in Italy from 1937 to 1944. President of
the Senate in 1946, he died in 1961.

Dejaz MANGASHA YILMA
Haile Selassie's nephew

Son of Haile Selassie's half-brother Yilma; brother of Yashashaworq.
Director-general in the Ministry of War at the time of the Italian
invasion. Killed at Mai Ceu.

Dejaz MASHASHA WOLDE
Governor of Cambata at the time of the Italian invasion

Lij MERID MANGASHA
Young Shoan nobleman

Born 1912. Married to the daughter of Ras Seyum's sister. In the
Resistance with Lij Abiye Abebe. After the War ADC to the Emperor,
Governor-General of Beghemder, Minister of Defence, etc. Died 1966,
rumoured to have been poisoned.

Shallaka (later Ras) MESFIN SILESHI
Shoan officer and always a loyal supporter of Haile Selassie

Of noble birth, related to the ruling house of Shoa. Commander of the
modernized Guards battalions at the time of the Italian invasion.
Resistance leader in Shoa till he and Blatta Takele took refuge in the
Sudan. In later life Mesfin became the most powerful and detested figure
in Shoa, immensely rich and by repute immensely corrupt. He was shot
by the Dergue on 23 November 1974 in the dungeons below the Great
Ghebbi.

Kenyaz MOKRIA
*Commander of the Imperial Guard in 1934 and again in 1941 with Gideon Force
and the Emperor; a Moja from Menz*

Sultan MOHAMMED YAYO
Ruler of the Danakil; his 'capital' being Sardo

Ras MULUGUETA
Minister of War and Imperial Fitaurari at the time of the Italian invasion

As a young warrior had fought at Adowa. Involved in all the power
struggles that followed Menelik's illness, usually on the reactionary
side. Appointed Imperial Fitaurari to replace the disgraced Birru Wolde
Gabriel. Killed by the Galla while retreating from Amba Aradam.

Dejaz NASIBU EMMANUEL
Haile Selassie's chief collaborator in modernizing Ethiopia

Son of a courtier of Menelik; follower of Ras Mangasha Atikim and of his son Ras Kebbede. Married to the daughter of Fitaurari Babitchev a White Russian emigré. As leader of the Young Ethiopians stage-managed the so-called Palace Revolution of September/October 1928 that strengthened the position of the Regent *vis-à-vis* the Empress and the conservatives. Governor of Harar at the time of the Italian invasion. Died in exile.

OLOL DINKE
Pro-Italian Somali leader of the Ajuran and appointed Sultan of Sciavelli

OMAR SAMANTHAR
Anti-Italian Somali; Mijurtin clansman who passed over to the Ethiopians

RAS SEYUM
Ruler of western Tigre

Born 1887, son of Ras Mangasha (*see* 'The Generation of Adowa') and grandson of the Emperor Johannes. Inevitably as heir to the Tigrean imperial line always a potential rival of any Shoan Emperor. Governor of western Tigre from 1910 to 1935 and Governor of all Tigre, despite his submission to the Italians and complex role in the Liberation, from 1947 till his death in 1960 by machine-gun in the Green Salon of the Little Ghebbi. His son, Ras Mangasha Seyum, who ruled Tigre after his death and was married to Haile Selassie's eldest granddaughter, Aida Desta, was considered a potential Emperor in late 1974; but is now living in exile between the Sudan and Europe. Aida Desta is still in the Dergue's prison.

Fitaurari SHIFFERAW
Governor of the Ogaden at the time of the Italian invasion; Shoan nobleman

Fitaurari SHIFFERAW
Ayalew Birru's advance-guard commander at the time of the Italian invasion. Killed in battle.

TAFERE WORQ KIDANE WOLD
Interpreter at the British Legation at the time of the Italian invasion

Private Secretary to Haile Selassie 1941–55. Then, as Minister of the Pen and subsequently as Minister of the Palace, played a major role in Ethiopian power politics.

Blatta TAKELE WOLDE HAWARIAT
Childhood companion and lifelong bane of the Emperor

Born 1900 in Beghemder; related to the Negus Mikael of Wollo; his grandmother was a Menz Shoan. In the Twenties a progressive and a supporter of the Regent. Resistance leader—and also a Republican. Kantiba of Addis Ababa, 1942; imprisoned 1942 to 1945; Vice Afenegus 1945; imprisoned 1947 to 1954; Afenegus 1957 to 1961; imprisoned 1961 to 1966. Three years after his release Blatta Takele, by then an old man, attempted to blow up the Emperor with a land-mine on the Sabatu road and died, machine-gun in hand, when the plot failed and his ghebbi in Addis Ababa was surrounded.

Dejaz WANDERAT
Shoan nobleman from Marabete

Born *circa* 1854. Fought at Adowa. Died at the battle of Mai Ceu aged nearly eighty.

WODAJO ALI
The Crown Prince's tutor

Virtual governor of Wollo at the time of the Italian invasion. Wounded at Amba Aradam. Deported from Addis Ababa after Yekatit 12 and died in hospital in Sardinia.

WOLDE GIORGIS WOLDE JOHANNES
Bureaucrat

After the War involved in a long-running power struggle with Tafere Worq Kidane Wold by whom he was eventually displaced. Minister of the Pen 1941 to 1955.

Bitwoded WOLDE TSADDIK
President of the Provisional Government in the south-west after the Emperor's flight

Dejaz WONDOSSEN KASSA
Eldest son of Ras Kassa

Distinguished himself as a war-leader at the battle of the plains of Anchim. Fought with his father in the Battles of the North. Led the early Resistance in Lasta where he was killed by the Italians.

Dejaz YIGEZU BEHAPTE
Courtier

Son of Negradas Behapte, a slave in Menelik's mother's household. 1918, Minister of Commerce, Kantiba of Addis Ababa, promoted Dejaz, and married to Lij Yasu's ex-wife Sable Wongel. Rumoured to suffer from leprosy. In Palestine during the Italian occupation. His son Colonel Tamrut Yigezu became governor-general of Beghemder.

YILMA DERESSA
Wollega Galla nobleman

Born 1907, educated partly in England. During the occupation a supporter of Dejaz Hapte Mariam Gabre Egziabher and a moving spirit in the Western Galla federation. After the War a figure of considerable importance, reputedly loyal to the Emperor.

Dejaz ZAUDI ASFAU DARGHIE
Member of the Shoan ruling house

Born 1890. Great-grandson of the Negus Sahle Selassie and grandson of Ras Dargie. Always suspect as a potential rival by Haile Selassie and therefore 'exiled' to a small governorate in the provinces. Became a leader of the Shoan Resistance. Refused to cross into the Sudan with Blatta Takele and Mesfin Sileshi but later forced to submit.

4. HAILE SELASSIE'S FAMILY

Empress MENEN
Wife of Haile Selassie

Granddaughter of the Negus Mikael of Wollo. Born 1891. Her parents were Woizero Sehin, Mikael's eldest daughter, and the Jantirar Asfau of Ambasel. She married her fourth husband, Dejaz Tafari Makonnen as he then was, in July 1912 on Lij Yasu's orders, after eloping from her previous husband, Ras Lul Seged, by whom she had had one child. (Ras Lul Seged was later killed in battle by the Negus Mikael.) The Empress died in 1962.

Princess TENAGNE WORQ
Haile Selassie's eldest child and a notoriously strong character

Born January 1913. Married first to Ras Desta Damtew and then to Ras Andargatchew Messai. She herself was, like many princesses of the imperial house, imprisoned by the Dergue; but she has still not, in early 1984, been released.

Mered Azmatch (Crown Prince) ASFA WOSSEN
Haile Selassie's eldest and only surviving son

Born July 1916. In 1927 appointed Governor of Wollo with the title of Mered Azmatch; and remained governor till the Italian capture of Dessie. Married first to Walata Israel, Ras Seyum's daughter, by whom he had one daughter, Princess Ijjagayehu. (She died in the Dergue's prison.) Married secondly to Dejaz Abebe Damtew's daughter, Madfarish Worq, by whom he had three daughters and one son, Prince Zara Yacob. Never close to his father. Played an ambiguous role in the attempted coup of 1960. Suffered a massive stroke in 1973 and was in London for treatment at the time of his father's deposition. Appointed 'King of Ethiopia' by the Dergue; but, wisely, never returned to take up this (temporary) position. The monarchy was formally abolished by the Dergue on 21 March 1975. Asfa Wossen, still a very ill man, is living with his family in exile in London.

Princess ZENABE WORQ
Haile Selassie's second daughter
Born July 1917. Married to Haile Selassie Gugsa. Died March 1933.

Princess TSAHAI
Haile Selassie's youngest daughter
Born October 1919. Married to Abiye Abebe. Died in childbirth 1942.

Prince MESFIN MAKONNEN
Duke of Harar
Born October 1923. Married to Sara Gizau of Tigre and had four sons.
Died May 1957.

Prince SAHLE SELASSIE
Haile Selassie's third and youngest son
Born February 1931. Married to Mahtsante Habte Mariam of Wollega
and had one son. Died April 1962.

[Of the Emperor's six children, four—the four youngest—predeceased
him.]

5. CLERGY AT THE TIME OF THE ITALIAN INVASION

Abuna CYRILLOS
Successor to the Abuna Matteos. Remained in Addis Ababa

Echege SAUIROS
Went to Jerusalem, into exile

Abba ABRAHAM Bishop of Gojjam
The only Bishop to collaborate with the invaders

Abba ISAAC Bishop of Tigre

Abba MIKAEL Bishop of Gore
Refused to submit. Shot by the Italians at Gore

Abba PETROS Bishop of Dessie
Co-ordinated the early Shoan resistance. Shot by the Italians in Addis Ababa

6. PATRIOT LEADERS AGAINST THE ITALIAN OCCUPATION

Many of those mentioned in section 3 above or section 7 below were also
leaders of the Resistance.

In Shoa

HAILE MARIAM MAMMO
Killed by the Italians

In Wolisso

GURASSU DUKE
Raised an immense following of 'last-minute Patriots' as the Italians crumbled

OLONA DINKEL
Killed by the Italians

In Gojjam

Dejaz MANGASHA JIMBIRRE
Married to Ras Hailu's much-married daughter, Sable Wongel; ruler of Faguta

Dejaz NEGASH BEZIBEH
Of the ruling house of Gojjam; grandson of Ras Bezibeh, legitimate son of the Negus Tekle Haimonot
After the War Negash became President of the Senate and Bitwoded. In 1951 the Bitwoded Negash was involved in a plot to assassinate Haile Selassie. Gurassu Duke, approached for support, informed the court; and the Colonel of the Imperial Guard, Mengistu Neway, arrested the conspirators at bayonet point. Tried and condemned, Negash was pardoned by Haile Selassie but ordered to live under house arrest at Jimma.

Lij (later Ras) HAILU BELEW
Of the ruling house of Gojjam
Son of Dejaz Belew, the second legitimate son of the Negus Tekle Haimonot; and brother of Gessesse Belew. Rival in eastern Gojjam of:

'Lij' BELAI ZELLEKA
Of low birth but a skilled guerrilla fighter
Induced by Ras Hailu to allow the Maraventano column to escape across the Blue Nile. After the War involved in what became known as 'the Gojjam Patriots' Plot' together with Mammo Hailu, the great-nephew of Ras Hailu who had once been an important *banda* commander. He, Mammo, and other co-conspirators were sentenced to death in 1945 and hanged on Janhoy Meda in Addis Ababa. These hangings caused much resentment against the Emperor.

Fitaurari TAFFERE ZELLEKA of Belaya
Dejaz Mangasha Jimbarre's right-hand man

Fitaurari WORKU of Kwara
The 'One-Eyed'. Killed in battle by the Italians

In Armachecho

AYANE CHEKOL
Minor Chieftain

BIRRE ZAGAYE
Very young, ambitious to become Governor-General of Beghemder in place of the dead Wondossen Kassa

WUBNEH AMORAW 'the Hawk'
Impressive leader

Notorious for having tried to hang Blatta Takele in 1939 on the Emperor's apparent orders; and for having shot a group of Italian soldiers from the top of a tree. After the War promoted Ras.

In Beghemder

Dejaz ADANE MAKONNEN of Tseggede
Much feared by the Italians

In February 1940 killed Major Loy, commander of the 14th Colonial Battalion.

Fitaurari MESFIN REDDA of Wolkait
An old man, extremely religious and courteous

Lij WOSSENE of Wag
The son of Dejaz Haile Kebbede

After his father's beheading continued the struggle, raiding from across the Takazze with his mother Woizero Shoanish and his father's lieutenant, Fitaurari Hailu Kibret. Badly wounded in autumn 1939, though first killing Major Tedesco, commander of the 24th Colonial Battalion.

NEGASH WORKINEH of the Upper Simien
Raised over 5,000 men

A highly-ambitious *balabat* he styled himself 'Prince of the Simien'. In December 1940 fought a pitched battle with Lij Wossene's men—which resulted in many casualties on both sides.

Dejaz DAGNEW TESSEMA
Active around Debra Tabor

Born 1908, originally a follower of Ayalew Birru whom his French-educated mother took as her second husband. Fought in the Shire; submitted; joined a *banda* but then rebelled with his brothers in June 1938. Intelligent, courageous, and disciplined. Captured two Italian colonels, then attacked by sixteen battalions.

Lij JOHANNES
The son of Lij Yasu

Tempted to proclaim himself Emperor. Offered the position of Negus of Beghemder at one stage by the Italians. Approached also by Blatta Takele who (Mesfin wrote to Bath) wished to use him as a pawn prior to setting up a Republic. Despite all these intrigues generally active in the Resistance in Beghemder. Involved in a post-war plot in 1942, he was exiled to Jimma. It is uncertain whether he is still alive.

Other Sons of Lij Yasu involved in the Resistance

Lij GIRMA
Held out in Gemu Gofa till, with his followers, he took refuge in Kenya where he died in 1941

Lij MELEKE TSAHAI
The 'Little Negus'.

Crowned Emperor at the Three Ambas by either Abebe Aregai or Haile Mariak Mammo. Died in 1938.

Lij MENELIK
Supported by the French

His mother was probably a Danakil. Last heard of in 1971, farming near Harar.

7. LEADERS OF THE OLETTA CADETS

ABEBE TAFARI
Commander of one machine-gun company

AMAN ANDOM
Later, briefly, the first non-imperial Head of State of Ethiopia

As General commanding the Third Division, Aman Andom, an Eritrean and a Protestant, won great fame in 1963 to 1964 in the brief war against Somalia. He became known as the 'Lion of the Ogaden', but was relegated by the Emperor to the Senate. Minister of Defence and Chief of Staff in the last two Cabinets of Imperial Ethiopia, he became Chairman of the Council of Ministers on 12 September 1974 immediately following the Emperor's deposition. On 15 November he refused to sign an order for summary executions submitted by the Dergue. The Dergue convened on 22 November; and on their orders Aman Andom was shot that afternoon with two members of the Dergue 'resisting arrest'.

ASSEFA ARAYA
Commander of the second machine-gun company of the Cadets

ESSAYAS GABRE SELASSIE
Commander of one of the two Cadet battalions

In contact with Lij Johannes in the Resistance. Later a Lieutenant-General and Senator. Shot by the Dergue on 'Bloody Saturday', the day following Aman Andom's killing, in the wave of summary executions ordered by the Dergue.

KIFLE NASIBU
Brigade commander of the Cadets

Son of Dejaz Nasibu Emmanuel. Later one of the leaders of the 'Black Lion' Resistance movement. Surrendered with Ras Imru to the Italians. Executed by them in the wave of executions following Yekatit 12.

NEGGA HAILE SELASSIE
Chief of Staff of the Cadets

Major-General in 1955, Governor-General of Beghemda in 1962. Now living in exile in England.

MENGISTU NEWAY
Military leader of the 1960 attempted Guards coup

Trained at Khartoum in 1940 to 1941 with Asrate Kassa, Merid Mangasha, Aman Andom, and Mulugueta Bulli. Colonel and then Commander of the Guard as Major-General. Staged the 1960 coup—the moving spirit behind which was his brother Girmame—while Haile Selassie was on a State visit to Brazil. Tried on 10 February 1961, Mengistu was hanged in Addis Ababa on 30 March.

MULUGUETA BULLI
Commander of the second Cadet battalion

A Sidamo Galla and the only Galla cadet. Spent the occupation in Djibuti and Kenya; back in with Gideon Force and the Emperor. Commander of the Imperial Guard and Major-General till replaced by Mengistu Neway in April 1956. Killed in the Green Salon in 1960 by the man who replaced him.

SOURCES AND CHAPTER NOTES

CONSTRAINTS of space have caused almost all of the notes and references to be eliminated. Instead I have attempted to give my general written sources chapter by chapter and to tie these in with the bibliography that follows—itself much curtailed. This method is not totally satisfactory because there is not a source given for every incident or quotation or fact. On the other hand this is a book, not a thesis. The general reader will, I think, prefer some indication of the value of the various sources that can be consulted, and of their quality and contents, to an exhaustive series of factual footnotes. Specialists and researchers on the other hand will have enough indications to point them in the right direction.

All sources given capital letters under the chapter notes that follow are listed in the bibliography. Where the author's name is followed by a figure—e.g. STEER (2)—it refers to the second book listed under Steer's name. Common sense and a process of elimination must guide the reader to the appropriate section of the bibliography. Where there is an English-language edition of an Italian work I have given that as the reference rather than the original. As regards articles and unprinted papers or works, I have listed only those that I have used extensively myself.

In addition to the published or privately-printed sources I have made extensive use of the files in the Public Record Office—particularly War Diaries, Consular Reports and captured Italian documents. It is much more difficult to consult the 'official' Italian archives of this period, many of which still contain very sensitive material; but I was allowed in certain more-or-less strictly military cases to do so. Ethiopian archives do—or did—exist; but permission to see them was not granted to me and (judging by the private papers I had translated from Amharic) I doubt their value as records of fact. St. Antony's College, Oxford, has a large collection of documents and source material on the whole period. The Haile Selassie I University theses listed in the last section of the bibliography are presumably still in Addis Ababa and at the renamed university. Indeed the great difficulty has been not the lack of source or published material but the vast quantity of both.

As regards the notes that in certain cases follow or embroider the chapter sources, these are an eclectic collection indeed. I have chosen to elaborate within the limitations of the space allowed me by the publishers on the points or personages that particularly interested me; and hope that my choice will coincide with that of many, if not most, readers.

PROLOGUE THE BATTLE OF ADOWA 1896

There is a plethora of books, articles, and memoirs in Italian on the Battle of Adowa but very little, naturally enough, in any other language. BERKELEY's book, though published in 1902 and therefore rather too close to the events described, is by far the most useful. Richard Pankhurst's article in the

Ethiopian Observer of 1957 gives, as is always the case with his articles, full and exhaustive references. Most of the direct quotations are taken from LEMMI's *Letters and Diaries* or from MENARINI on Dabormida's brigade.

As for the Ethiopian side, the Amharic chronicles are, as always, more biblical than realistic in tone. MATHEW and WYLDE between them give most of the picturesque detail. For events leading up to Adowa, CONTI ROSSINI is by far the best Italian source. PETRIDES wrote a penegyric on *Le Héros d'Adowa*—his hero being, rather surprisingly, Ras Makonnen, Haile Selassie's father.

Dr. Neruzzini was the Italian peace envoy to the Emperor Menelik. The feared Ethiopian invasion of Eritrea did not take place. A peace treaty was signed in October 1896. The total independence of Ethiopia was acknowledged, Adigrat evacuated and handed over to Ras Makonnen, the prisoners restored, and the boundary between the Empire of Ethiopia and the Colony of Eritrea fixed at the River Mareb. For the next forty years there were surprisingly few attempts by the Italians in Eritrea to interfere in the affairs of the Empire. But Adowa was not forgotten.

CHAPTER I EMPEROR OF ETHIOPIA

There is no decent biography of Haile Selassie. His own Autobiography was published by Oxford University Press for the School of Oriental and African Studies in 1976, perhaps for diplomatic reasons; it yielded little. Unfortunately only Haile Selassie could, had he so wished, have given the real story behind so many events that will now always remain mysterious or confused. Mrs SANDFORD's (2) biography is merely a less-good repeat performance of her previous useful but uncritical work on Ethiopia. MOSLEY's (2) is very uneven, though full of good things. Princess YILMA was the granddaughter of George Bell, a friend of Menelik's, and her biography, published early in 1936, is much more informative than one might expect. Professor Richard GREENFIELD of St. Antony's College, Oxford, is generally informative on the whole period, and excellent on the life and character of Ras Imru, Haile Selassie's cousin. Professor Harold MARCUS of the University of Michigan has written a short biography of Menelik but there is no book specifically devoted to either Zauditu or Lij Yasu that I know of.

The general works that cover the period are of unequal value. Probably the most detailed in tracing Ras Tafari's rise to power and the immensely complex regional and provincial politics is ZOLI's. MOSLEY (2) has apparently had access to sources that give a totally different—and convincing—accounnt of the great Battle of Sagalle from those that appear elsewhere; but, infuriatingly, gives no hint as to what those sources are.

Dr. ZERVOS's immense book is invaluable for its detailed account of provincial affairs, of foreign legations and communities, and of the Ethiopian air force. ZOLI (1) and (2) is also indispensable. DE PROROK for a gossip picture and DUTTON (for Balcha) are helpful. But the best impressionistic picture of the extraordinary cosmopolitan atmosphere of Addis Ababa, which lent itself to vituperative satire, is that given by the French *romancier*, Henri DE MONFRIED, who hated intensely both the capital and the new

Emperor, largely because he and Tafari had fallen out over a profitable arms deal. I have listed most of the series of novels and chronicles in which DE MONFREID describes his own experiences in and around the Red Sea; unreliable as to facts, the atmosphere created is brilliant.

The quotations on pages 5, 13 are taken from Wilfred THESIGER's brilliant and much-admired *Arabian Sands*—which of course only deals very incidentally with Ethiopia. The Thesiger family have had extraordinary connections with the country. Wilfred's grandfather was attached to Lord Napier's expedition to Magdala which led to the eventual suicide of the Emperor Theodore. His father was British Minister in Addis Ababa; and he himself after the various exploits described later in this book went on, briefly, to become a Political Officer in British-administered Ethiopia—a role which he detested.

Waugh in Abyssinia by Evelyn WAUGH was partly reprinted in Chapter Two of *When the Going was Good* under the title 'A Coronation in 1930' from which the quotations in this chapter are taken. Waugh was later as ashamed as such a man could be of his overtly pro-Fascist and anti-Ethiopian stand. 'These books', he stated later, 'have been out of print for some time and will not be reissued.' See Christopher SYKES's friendly biography. Sir Sidney Barton, the British Minister at the time of Haile Selassie's Coronation, is of course the original of the Envoy in Evelyn Waugh's famous novel *Black Mischief*—there known as Sir Samson Courtenay. In the novel his daughter Patience fell for Basil Seal by whom she was, sadly, eaten. In real life Miss Esme Barton (now Mrs. Kenyon-Jones) became the second wife of George Steer; she is one of the few British citizens still to have a house in Addis Ababa.

The description of Ras Seyum is from George STEER (1).

The Belgian Embassy papers were my source for this and all subsequent chapters' information on the Belgian Military Missions, both Official and Unofficial.

HODSON, the eccentric British Consul at Maji, once drove a golf ball all the way from his post to the capital, Addis Ababa. He went on to become Governor of the Falklands—and of the Gold Coast. His widow, Lady Hodson, a personal friend of the author, married her husband *after* his Ethiopian sojourn.

CHAPTER 2 FASCIST ITALY AND ITS COLONIES

For a fascinating portrait of Fascist Italy see MACGREGOR-HASTIE. FINER traces the rise of the Fascist state. The Aosta archives, as far as I know, have never been made available. For the Blackshirts and the militia see VERNI. Italy's role in Libya and her part in the First World War are covered in innumerable books and articles in Italian.

TREVASKIS, though primarily concerned with the British military administration in Eritrea, gives a useful background study of the Italian colony. I know of no general history of Tigre or of the Danakils. LEWIS is excellent on the Somalis, the pet hate of Sir Richard Burton the explorer who described their character in a famous epithet: 'constant in one thing—inconsistency'.

CHAPTER 3 THE 'INCIDENT' AT WALWAL

The best accounts of the 'incident' are given by FARAGO (2) and STEER (1), both more reliable than CIMMARUTA. The author visited Walwal by night—an unforgettable experience.

See DE BONO for Mussolini's plans. Mussolini's relations with Hitler are exhaustively covered in *The Brutal Friendship* by F. W. DEAKIN, Churchill's protégé and the friend of Antonin Besse, the Red Sea trader and arms-dealer who founded—and funded—St. Antony's College, Oxford, of which Deakin was the first Warden.

Besse played a certain part in the resistance to the Italian occupation himself. See the article by WEERTS. It is of course largely because of the interests of their founder that St. Antony's possesses such a diverse collection of documents and archives on the Italians and Ethiopia.

In his *Origins of the Second World War*, A. J. P. TAYLOR writes of the 'events centring on Ethiopia'. 'Their outward course is clear, the background and significance still somewhat of a mystery . . . Revenge for Adowa was implicit in Fascist boasting; but no more urgent in 1935 than at any time since Mussolini came to power in 1922. Conditions in Italy did not demand a war. Fascism was not politically threatened, and economic circumstances in Italy favoured peace, not the inflation of war.'

Part of the answer to the 'mystery' lies hidden in A. J. P. Taylor's own analysis. It was precisely because there was no political or even economic crisis in Italy that Mussolini's thoughts turned to foreign conquest. For many dictators the achievement of power is in itself the ultimate objective; this was distinctly not the case with the Duce. A. J. P. Taylor [cf. his conclusion quoted on page 43] seems to agree.

CHAPTER 4 PREPARATIONS FOR WAR

From this point on the spate of books published in 1936/1937 by professional writers, journalists, and military men who went out either to Eritrea or Addis Ababa and returned to write their 'on the spot' accounts floods the presses both in England and in Italy.

The Belgian Embassy papers have again been invaluable for some aspects of this period of preparation on the Ethiopian side. On the other hand DE BONO is my main source for preparations in Eritrea and GRAZIANI (1) for preparations in Somalia. Of all the rest by far the most valuable, best-written, and informative account is George STEER's *Caesar in Abyssinia*, particularly for the Ogaden and the Emperor. General VIRGIN's memoir gives a useful account of the initial Swedish involvement and of the founding of the Oletta Cadets. ZOLI (3) continues to give full details of Ethiopian appointments and *shum-shir*[1] largely based on Italian Consular reports which were not made available to me. The Walwal negotiations and the reactions in

---

[1] The expressive Ethiopian phrase for the continual reshuffle by which the Emperor tried to prevent any of his subordinates developing a fixed power base.

Europe must be referred to in almost every memoir and history of the period. See KIRKPATRICK for acerbic comments on Drummond in Rome; and of course CIANO.

Sylvia Pankhurst's son, Dr. Richard Pankhurst, was the Director of the Institute of Ethiopian Studies when I was in Addis Ababa. His bibliographical studies and his advice as to sources have been of immense help to me, as to all students of Ethiopia. He has written about his mother in the *Ethiopian Observer* which for many years he and his wife edited till the 1974 Revolution closed it down. The best general account of her life and background that I know of is MITCHELL's.

CHAPTER 5 INVASION

For the Italian invasion the memoirs of the various Italian commanders-in-chief—DE BONO, GRAZIANI, BADOGLIO—are supplemented by the accounts of their own divisional and brigade commanders, namely BASTICO, FRUSCI, PESENTI, etc.

All these and other sources have been carefully correlated and supplemented by DEL BOCA in his comparatively recent (1969) work published both in Italy and in America, which by contrast to that of his predecessors has a rather anti-patriotic slant. Though this invaluable study technically covers the years 1935 to 1941, it concentrates on the invasion and the succeeding battles and is sketchy on the rest.

A fascinating picture of Ethiopia as a whole and of the Red Cross side in particular is given by Major Gerald BURGOYNE's letters and papers. His wife Clarissa went out years after his death and traced, successfully, what happened to her husband: she then proceeded to publish his letters and the results of her own investigation in the *Ethiopian Observer*. Had space permitted I would have liked to have quoted extensively from these in an appendix.

STEER (1) is, as before, by far the best source for the Ogaden. For 'Tamm's Boys' see *Tjanst Hos Negus* by Captain Viking Tamm (Stockholm 1936) whom Christianne Hojer kindly translated for me.

The famous Italian song, still familiar to most Italians, that the invading troops sang as they marched into Ethiopia ran as follows—

Faccetta Nera	Dusky little face
Bell' Abissina	Lovely Abyssinian Damsel
Che gia l'ora s'avvicina	For the hour is near
Quando saremo	When we will be
Vicino a te	At your side
Noi ti Daremo	We will bring you
Un' altra Patria	Another Fatherland
E un altro Re	And another King.

CHAPTER 6 THE ETHIOPIAN COUNTER-ATTACK

After DE BONO's departure BADOGLIO's account naturally takes up the running as the main 'official' Italian source for the campaign in the North. It suffers from the usual defects of such accounts, chief of which is the lack of frankness, but compensates (thanks to the Italian wireless interceptions) with its textual quotations of Haile Selassie's messages. On the Ethiopian side the best authority is KONOVALOFF who was a fascinated observer at the Tembien and, later, at Mai Ceu. Though his facts and figures need to be checked against other sources, his descriptions and atmospherics are totally convincing.

STEER (1) is invaluable—not only for the southern front but also for his general picture of Haile Selassie at Dessie, to which BURGOYNE adds many details.

POLSON NEWMAN, FARAGO and FULLER, all of whom were reporting the war from the Italian side are valuable—unlike the journalists and writers on the Ethiopian side, who were utterly frustrated in their efforts to get anywhere near the fighting. FULLER is the more objective, as befits a military historian; but POLSON NEWMAN, though excessively pro-Italian, gives plenty of useful detail in his accounts of the fighting. MATTHEWS is biased; as is HARMSWORTH. MAKIN's is a useful background account.

Dr. Nystrom was called up to attend Ayalew Birru and I have drawn on the vivid description of the Criniti battle given in his book *Med St Giorgis pa dodsritt* (Stockholm, 1937). DEL BOCA, who interviewed Ras Imru extensively, is most useful here—and on the question of mustard gas.

The use of mustard gas—diclorodietilsulphur—was forbidden by the Geneva protocol of 17 January 1926 which Italy had signed. The decision to use it was not taken lightly by the Italians, and great efforts were made by Italian diplomats in Europe to discredit the reports of journalists and the complaints that Ethiopia laid before the League. These efforts were so successful that even today many Italians quote, perhaps without realizing the source, LESSONA's *Memoirs*, and his claim that only three bombs were used and on only one occasion—to avenge the beheading of the Italian pilot Minniti captured by the Ethiopians on the southern front. It is true that this was the first occasion on which the gas was used, and even then Mussolini did not give permission lightly. A cable came from Graziani requesting permission for 'maximum liberty of action for employ asphyxiating gases'. Mussolini replied: 'Agreed employ gas in cases where Your Excellency considers it necessary for supreme reasons defence.' It was however certainly not the first and last occasion on which gas was used but rather the first of a long series. Leaders and generals in war quickly overcome their humanitarian scruples; though it is only fair to emphasize that mustard gas was not poison gas. It burnt and maimed but it did not kill. Eventually the Ethiopians were to get as used to it as they had become to bombs. It was their mules and cattle who died from grazing on pastures contaminated by the gas, a disaster which was just as serious for their armies.

CHAPTER 7 THE BATTLES IN THE NORTH

Gerald BURGOYNE gives the account of the Bitwoded Makonnen Demissie, and his wife Clarissa tells how he and Ras Mulugueta met their deaths.

See also in addition to the sources previously cited STARACE and TOMASELLINI.

The Bitwoded Makonnen's widow, the Princess Yashasha Worq, had his body returned to Trinity Cathedral in Addis Ababa after the war. The priests would not explain why the tomb is so much smaller than those of the other war-heroes.

CHAPTER 8 MAI CEU

Ras Imru's frantic cable from Gojjam and Haile Selassie's depressed reply are quoted by BADOGLIO. For the Gondar column see STARACE's unintentionally amusing account. The Wollo Plot can only be deduced from scattered references.

The best account of the battle of Mai Ceu from the Ethiopian side is undoubtedly that of the only European observer with the Emperor's forces, KONOVALOFF. On the Italian side BADOGLIO gives a very different account to PESENTI (1).

According to PESENTI who was commanding the First Eritreans, the first Ethiopian column, 15,000–20,000 strong, was led by Ligaba Tasso and Ras Kebbede; the second column, 30,000–35,000 strong, by Dejaz Adefrisau and Ras Getachew; and the third column by Fitaurari Birru Wolde Gabriel. The Emperor had at the Pass of Agumberta 3,000 men and 300 machine-guns with him; behind him at Quoram lay Kenyaz Mokria with 1,200 men and artillery; and to the left, in reserve between Socota and Quoram, Ras Kassa and Ras Seyum and Dejaz Haile Kebbede with 6,000 men.

Again according to PESENTI the Guard did not attack until after midday and was led by Dejaz Aberra Tedla. He puts the first enemy attack by all three columns almost simultaneously at dawn, the second at 10 a.m., followed by a counter-attack put in by the Second Eritreans, and the third after midday. It was at 2.30 p.m. in the afternoon that his own First Eritreans counter-attacked. His book was published in August 1937 and must therefore have been written soon after the events, which probably makes the details more reliable than BADOGLIO's. But battles, and particularly the enemy order of battle, are very confusing, even for generals.

CHAPTER 9 APRIL 1936

See esp. Tamm for an account of the last-ditch defence at Ad Termaber and a general description of feelings in Addis Ababa.

Of the Oletta cadets who survived the Italian occupation many were to play an important part in post-war Ethiopia—particularly Mengistu Neway who as Commander of the Bodyguard troops led the attempted coup in 1960 during the Emperor's absence abroad which is now seen as the precursor of the 1974 Revolution. See Biographical Index, particularly Section 7.

CHAPTER 10 NINE DAYS IN MAY

For the confusion in the capital on Haile Selassie's return and for his own momentous decision to leave, as for his adventures and misadventures en route and the would-be attempt on his life at Akaki, see above all George STEER (1). Steer, *The Times* correspondent, was not expelled till 13 May, a week after the Italian take-over. Also GREENFIELD, MOSLEY, and Salome GABRE EGZIABHER.

The burning and looting of Addis Ababa were of course widely reported by all diplomatic sources.

The story of Negga was told by himself to Dr. Richard Pankhurst, tape-recorded and translated by Tsahai Berhane Selassie.

Sir Edwin Chapman-Andrews gave me a somewhat guarded interview on his role at the time and, later on, in 1941. He died in early 1980.

For the 'column of iron will' see BADOGLIO.

General Essayas Gabre Selassie, an Oletta cadet, described to me his role after the fall of Addis. I had a local account by one of his followers (in the form of an obituary) translated on the career as a 'rebel' of Zaudi Asfau Dargie (and his follower Wolde Johannes).

Mussolini's proclamation of victory was of course reported everywhere in the Italian press and in subsequent triumphant Italian accounts of 'Anno XIV'.

Just before the invasion began, a prominent British politician had made a speech to the City Carlton Club:

To cast an army [he said] of nearly a quarter of a million men, embodying the flower of Italian manhood, upon a barren shore two thousand miles from home against the goodwill of the whole world and without command of the sea, and then in this position embark upon what may well be a series of campaigns against a people and a region which no conqueror in four thousand years ever thought it worthwhile to subdue is to give hostages to fortune unparalleled in all history.

A friendly warning; and typical enough of the general view of Mussolini's mad enterprise. Less than a year later the British politician would have had to recognize (as indeed he was temperamentally inclined to do) that fortune favoured the bold; that he and, like him, all of Europe and most of Italy had been wrong; that the Duce had been right; and that an extraordinary enterprise had been successfully carried through despite the five specified dangers of distance, general ill-will, no command of the sea, difficulties of terrain, and fierceness of the opposing race.

A dozen years later the same British politician wrote as follows:

The Italian Dictator was not actuated solely by desire for territorial gains. His rule, his safety depended upon prestige. The humiliating defeat which Italy had suffered forty years before at Adowa and the mockery of the world when an Italian army had not only been destroyed or captured but shamefully mutilated rankled in the minds of all Italians. They had seen how Britain had after the passage of years avenged both Khartoum and Majuba. To proclaim their manhood by avenging Adowa meant almost as much to Italy as the recovery of Alsace-Lorraine to France. There seemed no way in which Mussolini could more easily or at less risk consolidate his own power, or, as he saw it, raise the authority of Italy in Europe than by wiping out the stain of bygone years and adding Ethiopia to the recently built Italian Empire. All such thoughts were wrong and evil, but since it is always wise to try and understand another country's point of view, they may be recorded.

He concluded however, that Mussolini's designs had been 'obsolete and reprehensible'. Perhaps that is fair enough as a final judgement upon the Italian invasion. But if the conquest of Ethiopia did in the event become obsolete, it was largely because the politician who made the preceding speech and wrote the preceding somewhat contradictory paragraphs, Winston Churchill, stepped onto the centre of the stage determined to play his part in reprehending the conquerors—as the third part of this book will recount.

CHAPTER II *AFRICA ORIENTALE ITALIANA*

At this stage official and semi-official Italian sources (particularly the invaluable GUIDA DELL' AOI, and LESSONA) give the general and often the detailed outline of the story inside Ethiopia as major outside sources dry up.

For Haile Selassie's life in exile the Foreign Office papers are the main source supplemented by newspaper clippings of the time, by MOSLEY, and to a lesser extent by SANDFORD. The same applies to the exiles in Jerusalem about whom a long correspondence between the Colonial Office, the High Commissioners and the Foreign Office built up.

The vivid description of the Ceremony of Submission I have condensed from the report in the now-defunct French magazine ILLUSTRATION. The *Banda* are alluded to in numerous Italian works of the period.

For the Beghemder/Gojjam column see STARACE, TOMASELLINI.

A word about the *Banda*. General CAVALLERO was later to describe them as having four characteristics. Firstly, their members were opposed to long-term service. Secondly they fought for love of adventure and raiding—'which renders their use somewhat delicate'. Thirdly they were unwilling to move far outside their own territory. Fourthly they were unwilling 'to submit to a more rigid discipline, such as that of the native battalions'.

In a less flattering judgement an Italian staff officer wrote as follows: 'The Bande, both the so-called regular and the irregular ones, really are bands and except in the rarest cases have nothing military about them. They serve the interests of the leader who forms them, their commander and their own members, never those of the population and goods whom they should protect.' Physically they were, in this officer's judgment, *a posto*—'as they should be'—but their command was too often given to young officers or inexperienced militia officers and this system ended 'in the moral ruin of their officers too'. Technically a *Gruppo Bande* consisted of 1,200 men, but there were usually 400 relaying each other every few months—though monthly pay was drawn for all 1,200. 'Hence the passion for the formation of *Bande* by Residents and Commissars.'

Nevertheless for all their shortcomings the *Bande* were an indispensable instrument. Not only did they garrison the villages and patrol the highlands at least nominally on Italy's behalf, but they also offered a means of employing the unemployed—but not yet disarmed—levies.

Irregular *bande* were raised and commanded by 'loyal' chiefs, whereas the regular *bande* were commanded by a handful of Italian officers. The first took the name of their leader—for instance the *Banda* Assege in Gojjam. The second took the name of the town or district in which they were raised, and were usually formed into a *Gruppo* of three *Bande* which itself had a more generalized title—the *Wollo Yeggiu Bande* for example. Some of the *Bande* such as the *Banda* Serae or the *Banda* Akele Gazai had long histories going back to Adowa and before; these two were named after two of the three Residencies near Asmara and, since they were formed of Eritreans, were considered more reliable. But others tended to be referred to as the years wore on by the names of the Italian officers commanding them—the Rolle *Bande* was to be the best-known example.

The word *banda* was used to mean both a band and a member of a band. *Bande* is the plural form. Hence *Banda* Debra Tabor, *Gruppo Bande* Lago Tana.

CHAPTER 12 THE ATTACK ON ADDIS ABABA

On the Ethiopian side the main source is the account (complete with contemporary letters) given by Salome GABRE EGZIABHER in the *Ethiopian Observer*. On the Italian side Maria LANDI's letters describe vividly the feelings and sentiments of the surrounded Italians.

Negga (cf. Chapter 10 and notes) has left an extraordinarily vivid account of his part in the attack as a follower of Fikremariam. Bombed and strafed, Fikremariam's men were then attacked by Italian tanks. 'They killed seven of my companions. I felt dizzy. Pulling out the Emperor's sword and at the same time praying the *Melka Edom* (a prayer a priest had told me to say in times of danger) I jumped onto one of the tanks. I saw two men in it. One was short with an ugly red face; the other was fat. I beheaded the short man and hurled him onto the fat man. He shouted three times "Mamma! Mamma! Mamma!"'

It was Negga who persuaded his reluctant commander to call off the attack when the Italian artillery started shelling. 'I the son of Ato Nadew?' Dejaz Fikremariam protested. 'I the son of Ato Nadew? Shall it be said of me that I entered Addis Ababa and then fled? I shall not flee!' 'Where is the glory,' retorted Negga with his usual pithy common sense. 'If one does not escape after killing?'

Fikremariam paid Negga back in his own coin that autumn after *Maskal*, when Negga ambushed a train from Djibuti carrying Lessona on his first visit to *AOI*. 'After defeating the first train another came from the direction of Addis Ababa and shelled us with bullets and bombs. I was shot in twelve places and, being wounded in the stomach, my intestines poured out. I told my servant to put them back in and he did so, using leaves, but my intestines were twisted in the process.' 'I will be sorry,' wrote Fikremariam unsympathetically, 'not for your death but for your loss as a witness to Ethiopia'.

Negga however failed to oblige his chief or the Italians by dying. When Fikremariam's band was finally dispersed, he moved to the far south, to Gemu Gofa where he and many others gathered round the semi-imperial figure of Lij Girma, one of Lij Yasu's sons. In July 1937 they decided (see footnote to page 178) to cross the border into Kenya. 'Take women with you so that you will not be like asses,' was Negga's final proclamation. But 'on finally reaching Kenya,' he himself recorded, 'I became a monk.'

Lack of space prevents the full story of Negga being reproduced here, but these extracts will perhaps give some idea of the extraordinary vitality of the Ethiopian fighting men.

CHAPTER 13 THE HUNTING DOWN OF THE RASES

See LESSONA and—till the evacuation of Gambeila—the British Consular and Foreign Office files. Erskine's are particularly informative, and the whole question of the Western Galla Federation is dealt with at great length. Tadesse Mecha's book on 'The Black Lions' (as the Oletta cadets who joined Ras Imru called themselves), published in Amharic, also deals with the question.

For the surrender of Ras Imru, and for the death of Ras Desta, GREENFIELD is a mine of information; as also on much of the detail of this period. See also the Ethiopian MINISTRY OF JUSTICE's *Documents on Italian War Crimes*. I follow GREENFIELD's version (which he has assured me came from an eyewitness) of the death of Dejaz Balcha.

The death of Ras Kassa's eldest son, Wondossen, is wrapped in mystery. In the case of his brothers Aberra and Asfawossen, Salome GABRE EGZIABHER gives the fullest account; which PESENTI supplements.

A word about Ras Hailu. During the war Italian propaganda spread the rumour that Ras Hailu had been poisoned. On 22 January 1936 foreign journalists in Addis Ababa were invited to visit him and see for themselves. They found him in the apartments of the Crown Prince in good health, with his servants, his regalia and his personal weapon. He recognized an American journalist whom he had met at the Coronation in 1930, and in reply to questions, urbanely stated that he was treated with all the respect due to his rank, was content with his lot, and grateful to His Majesty whom he considered to be, as always, his friend. As the journalists took their leave, he thanked them for their visit and assured them of his prayers to God for themselves and their families. Whatever Ras Hailu's merits or demerits, no one could ever fault his style.

It seems most unlikely that Ras Hailu deliberately betrayed Aberra and Asfawossen Kassa. The killings at Fikke could bring him no possible immediate or long-term advantage. Used as an intermediary and a guarantor, he was almost certainly deceived by the Italians into collaborating in the execution of his own son-in-law. On his return to Addis Ababa he demanded an interview with the Viceroy. In view of Ras Hailu's anxiety Graziani called an audience of notables at the Little Ghebbi and there, and in public, took full responsibility for the killings. General Tracchia was sent back in disgrace to Italy and PESENTI (1) reports the Viceroy as 'pale with disgust' at Tracchia's treachery which he had 'covered'. But according to Ethiopian accounts General Tracchia was heard to say next day: 'What could I have done? Graziani ordered me to do this by cables.'

'I have never succeeded,' wrote LESSONA years later, 'in finding out how and why (given the various mendacious reports that were made to me) the son of Ras Kassa was shot by order of General Tracchia, one of our old colonial hands.' It seems that the brothers had not only been shot but beheaded and their heads exposed to public view next day in the Church of St. George; a sacrilege as well as an insult which could hardly fail to have offended Ras Hailu.

The difficulty about writing of Ras Hailu is that there are no documents (as far as I know) which give his own point of view or 'the case for the defence'. The Italians tended for obvious reasons to play down his importance and the British (as Part III of this book will show) were naturally hostile. As for the Ethiopians, to Haile Selassie and his supporters, Ras Hailu was a most convenient *bête noir*.

CHAPTER 14 YEKATIT 12

The sources for this chapter are above all the Ethiopian MINISTRY OF JUSTICE's collection of Italian cables and directives, the genuineness of which cannot be doubted. Also BEFEKADU WOLDE SELASSIE's personal memoir and Salome GABRE EGZIABHER.

According to the version generally accepted by the Ethiopians the assassination attempt was entirely spontaneous. Eritreans had always been very sensitive to any formal signs of racialism, which had never been the rule in Eritrea—a colony where Italians slept happily with their Eritrean 'madams'. But apartheid-style laws were passed in January 1937, and a spate of articles appeared in the Fascist press on the dangers of mixed and inferior races. This oppressive change in policy was inspired by Lessona. The last straw came when Abraha Deboch and Mogus Asgedom went to the cinema in Addis Ababa and found themselves segregated from the Italian spectators.

Their ends are veiled in mystery. Apparently Abraha Deboch had left the monastery of Debra Libanos on 1 or 2 March and rejoined his companion Mogus Asgedom in the Ankoberino hills with Abebe Aregai. It seems, however, that the two Eritreans were not trusted by the Shoans. They made, it is said, for the Sudanese border but before they reached it were killed by local tribesmen near Metemma.

MITCHELL gives not only a rousing account of Sylvia Pankhurt but also many interesting details on Haile Selassie's poverty-stricken exile. These are supplemented by the Foreign Office Reports. The Emperor had a very gloomy second winter in exile. In December he had a taxi-accident, broke his collar-bone and fell seriously ill. His family was dispersed (his lovely daughter Tsahai training to be a nurse at the Great Ormonde Street Hospital for children was his major comfort); 'his credit with the local tradesmen was none too good'; worst of all, the British Government was moving towards *de jure* as well as *de facto* recognition of the Italian annexation.

In the autumn of 1938 Blattengueta Herouy died at 'Fairfield'; and a month later on 16 November Sir Eric Drummond presented his Letters of Credence as British Ambassador in Rome to 'the King of Italy and the Emperor of Ethiopia'. The next day *The Times* referred to the 'ex-Emperor'. In December Lord Southborough, a Trustee of Wellington College, called at the Foreign Office, informed them of a projected move to send Asfa Wossen to that school, and enquired discreetly whether Lord Halifax considered that the ex-Emperor would be able to pay the fees.

The year 1938 was certainly a dismal one for Haile Selassie. But it must not be thought that even at this low ebb he was totally out of touch with affairs inside Ethiopia. He had strong partisans among the exile groups in the Sudan; and emissaries bearing letters under his seal were constantly crossing, much to the annoyance of the Khartoum authorities, the virtually wide-open border.

CHAPTER 15 THE DUKE OF AOSTA

For an invaluable and beautifully-mapped (though inevitably one-sided) account of the Italian military operations of 1938 see Ugo CAVALLERO. The British Consular Reports from Addis Ababa supplemented by the official reports from the Sudan are vital for the picture of AOI at this time. Mr. Helm of the British Consulate General submitted a much-praised report of 31 pages to the Egyptian Department of the Foreign Office at the end of the year. (The Egyptian Department spread its wings not only over the 'Anglo-Egyptian' Sudan but also, less justifiably, over Ethiopia. Its head during the period leading up to the Second World War was a formidable activist, Cavendish Bentinck).

See also LESSONA; and for the Ethiopian side Salome GABRE EGZIABHER, Richard PANKHURST and the theses written by Ethiopian graduates who under Dr. Pankhurst's spurring went out and interviewed those who had played a part in the Resistance. (These theses were held before the revolution at the Institute of Ethiopian Studies, attached to Haile Selassie I University at Addis Ababa.) But there is much controversy, and many different versions, over actions and events in this confused period. To take a single example: according to one story it was Haile Mariam Mammo, not Abebe Aregai, who crowned the 'Little Negus' on the Three Ambas.

A minor point: I have given inverted commas to the titles the Resistance leaders conferred upon themselves or the Italians conferred upon the collaborators—i.e. 'Lij' Belai Zelleka, 'Ras' Haile Selassie Gugsa. The case of Abebe Aregai was more complicated. Though his title of 'Ras' was in effect self-conferred, the Emperor from his exile, though he at first persisted in writing to 'Balambaras' Abebe Aregai, in the end addressed his letters to 'Ras' Abebe Aregai, thereby giving his implicit consent to Ababe Aregai's self-promotion. Readers will by now, I hope, be well aware that these were not, in the Ethiopia of the time, matters of little importance.

A major point: I have perhaps not sufficiently stressed in the text that over vast stretches of *AOI* there were no rebellions, no resistance at all to Italian rule. The colonies of Eritrea and Somalia were totally at peace. Harar and the

Ogaden were calm once the relics of the Imperial armies had fled or submitted. The whole vast area of the South, united into the single province of Galla–Sidamo was undisturbed except by roving bands of Amhara soldiery and its traditional minor turbulence. The Galla in general, including the Wollo Galla, appear to have welcomed Italian rule—with the notable exception of Olona Dinkel. Most extraordinary of all, Tigre—where revolts on the scale of Gojjam or Beghemder might have been expected—was, almost until the end of Italian rule, generally though not totally peaceful.

CHAPTER 16 EDGING TOWARDS WAR

From this point until the Battle of Keren (Chapter 28) I have made extensive use of Douglas Newbold's letters and circulars in the Sudan, edited by K. D. D. HENDERSON: fascinating material. I would particularly like to acknowledge the generosity of his publishers, Faber and Faber, in allowing me to make such extensive quotations. It is supplemented here not only by the sources named in the last chapter but by, for the first time, War Office files—Intelligence Reports, War Diaries, etc.—which from now on become more relevant than Foreign Office archives as diplomacy is 'continued by other means'. Also JOUIN, CIANO, the Italian archives—and, on Wavell, his excellent biographer CONNELL.

The author can testify from personal experience to the crustiness of General Platt. His predecessor as *Kaid*, General Hudleston, later reappeared as Governor General of the Sudan in succession to Symes (see p. 240). The 'bog barons' was the title generally given to the District Commissioners in the south of the Sudan, who ruled their own little fiefs as benevolent autocrats. It was said that whereas the Indian Civil Service attracted Firsts, the Sudan Civil Service was the natural home for Blues.

Among those also in the Sudan at this period were the two Shoan guerrilla leaders, Blatta Takele Wolde Hawariat and Mesfin Sileshi (see footnote to p. 183). Blatta Takele, despairing—rightly—of British aid, turned to the French not just for aid but for a philosophy. He and his followers—of whom the most notable was Essayas the Oletta cadet—wrote to the French authorities announcing their conversion to the cause of Republicanism and requesting guidance. Mesfin Sileshi, a loyalist, copied these letters—and sent the copies to Bath. There they were greeted with a consternation that became all the greater when it was learnt that early in 1939 Blatta Takele had slipped across the frontier into Armachecho, sending Essayas ahead—for Blatta Takele never believed in having only a single string to his bow—to sound out Lij Johannes, the son of Lij Yasu, a possible rival pretender to the Imperial throne.

The intrigues with Lij Johannes (who was also being wooed by the Italians with the offer of a virtual Protectorate over Beghemder) failed, though Essayas remained at his side. But Blatta Takele succeeded in preparing a Republican-style document for the League of Nations in which were set out the wishes of some 900 Patriot leaders concerning the form of future government in Ethiopia. From Bath, Haile Selassie reacted quickly. He sent out a fairly mild general letter under his seal condemning republicanism as 'an alien concept that would endanger Ethiopia's advance to freedom' but admitting (a cunning concession) that there might be other persons who would better merit the throne. More secretly and drastically he sent orders (probably carried by Lorenzo Taezaz) that Blatta Takele should be arrested and publicly hanged for treason. Arrested he was, by Wubneh Amoraw of Armachecho ('the Hawk'). The hanging was planned for 12 July. But Sime, Blatta Takele's ten-year-old son, escaped and summoned help from a rival local rebel leader Ayane Chekol. Rescued though temporarily cowed, Blatta Takele returned to Khartoum.

The whole story of Blatta Takele, a natural revolutionary and the only contemporary of Haile Selassie who throughout a long life was always prepared to come out in open opposition to him, merits more space than can be given here. But see the entry on him in the Biographical Index, Section 3.

CHAPTER 17 *DOMINE DIRIGE NOS*

Of all the 'old Ethiopian hands' who had been in Addis Ababa before the invasion and who had kept in contact with Haile Selassie during his years of exile, George STEER was probably the most active. He had written an excellent book on the Italian invasion, *Caesar in Abyssinia*, and another, just as brilliant, on the Spanish Civil War which he had also covered for *The Times*. He had visited Djibuti in 1938 and again in 1939 when he published two outstanding articles in *The Spectator*. These were noticeable for their praise of French military preparedness and of the Quai d'Orsay intelligence work. Thereafter, it seems, he played a role as a sort of unofficial spy-master for the exiled Emperor—being instrumental in sending across the Sudan border a shadowy French agent, Paul-Robert Monnier known as 'André'. (This infuriated the Khartoum authorities who reported that General Gamelin had sent in 'very amateurish' spies without even consulting the French government. 'Very jolly' minuted Sir Miles Lampson.)

Steer was not only politically and professionally but emotionally involved with Ethiopia. He had married his first wife, Margherita, a Peruvian journalist, in the grounds of the British Legation in the wild May days of 1936 after the Emperor had fled but before Badoglio's Italians arrived. She died, and he subsequently married in England the former British Minister, Sir Sidney Barton's, daughter, Esme, whom he had no doubt come to know at exactly the same time. It was their son who became in June 1940 the Emperor's godchild.

STEER from this chapter on comes back into the picture with his second book on Ethiopia, *Sealed and Delivered*. It is not as good a book as his first—possibly because it was written in wartime when Steer himself was playing an active role and hence could not be the frank and cynical observer as before. But it is still quite outstanding, particularly for the reporting on Haile Selassie as he moved from London to Khartoum and eventually into Ethiopia.

On the Italian side DE BIASE (who used his father's secret diaries) is excellent for this period of preparation and mutual over-estimation. Mrs SANDFORD (2), obviously, had first-hand information; and CHURCHILL now enters the scene to play a role that continues to the end of this book.

CHAPTER 18 THE FIRST DAYS OF WAR

The campaigns that follow are very clearly described in the OFFICIAL HISTORY (edited by Major General Playfair). The equivalent on the Italian side, for obvious reasons less frank, is the UFFICIO STORICO. For more concise reports from the British side see the STATIONERY OFFICE, the WAR OFFICE, and WAVELL's long (73-page) article in the Supplement to the *London Gazette*.

KENNEDY-COOKE's short work—more of a pamphlet than a book—is full of vivid detail about the Sudan. Newbold is, as always, invaluable, and much used by me for his running commentary on events. MARAVIGNA and MOOREHEAD both describe how reluctantly both sides went to war and how pessimistic each side was about its own chances. STEER (2) gives his vivid account of the Emperor's reappearance on the scene.

The War Office files contain the war diary of the Eastern Arab Corps; and the Foreign Office files a mass of correspondence and reports concerning Djibuti, Haile Selassie, the chances of fomenting revolt—and the necessity, or not, of actually fighting. The UFFICIO STORICO DELLA MARINA MILITARE recounts, but does not explain, the Italians' dismal performance in the Red Sea.

There are some observers, including Leonard Mosley who was in the Sudan at the time, who assert that the Governor-General and many other officials believed the Italian occupation of the Sudan inevitable. 'It is not unfair to add that it was a prospect viewed by Symes and many civil servants in the Sudan with a certain complacency.' Mosley asserts that the Duke of Aosta had privately assured Symes that the Italians would not wreck the British administration in the Sudan. 'Therefore faced by an imminent conquest by the Italians there were many dedicated civil servants in the Sudan who were not cast down by their own weaknesses. Some of them honestly believed that Britain was going to lose the war anyway, and their principal anxiety was to ensure that Italy should assume control of the Sudan with as little unpleasantness as possible.'

All this sounds exaggerated; but it was probably true in substance—if not in June or July, then in August when defeatism was rampant both in East Africa and in a Britain standing alone, blitzed, and threatened with invasion. But Mosley does not reveal his evidence for the private contacts between Sir Stewart Symes and the Duke of Aosta; which is a pity.

CHAPTER 19 *AOI* ATTACKS

CONNELL on Wavell and WAVELL on the campaign complement each other. The Foreign Office files (for Haile Selassie) and the War Office files (in particular the war diary of the 1st Ethiopians) were indispensable. See EVANS-PRITCHARD's article in the *Army Quarterly* for his picture of an anthropologist in action. As regards the South Africans, the SOUTH AFRICAN WAR HISTORIES are the formal source, BIRKBY's eager pair of books the informal source—both corrected by GANDAR DOWER's pro-askari compilations. For the KAR in general see MOYSE-BARTLETT and for the Nigerians HENNESSY.

CHAPTER 20 THE FALL OF SOMALILAND

From the British side I have pieced the story together from the war diaries of the units involved, plus CONNELL, FERGUSSON, LEWIS, CHURCHILL, MOYSE-BARTLETT, and the OFFICIAL HISTORY—which does *not* refer to the 'butcher's bill' cable.

The Italians were naturally less reticent. To say nothing of Gina's brother, the UFFICIO STORICO, CARGNELOTTI, PESENTI, and DE BIASE all tell the story.

Twenty-six Englishmen were taken prisoner in this campaign, including, rather shamefully, 11 officers (6 had been killed). One of the Black Watch 'killed', Corporal Genaudo, was awarded a posthumous VC—only to turn up alive next year, at Asmara. 17 planes from Aden were lost or badly damaged, and over 5,000 rifles and 120 lorries captured.

CHAPTER 21 TO FIND A LAWRENCE

STEER's second book, *Sealed and Delivered*, gives an eyewitness account of Haile Selassie's time in (or outside) Khartoum. How mixed the feelings of Sudan officialdom were towards the 'little man' can be seen from the passages in the letter of NEWBOLD quoted in the text—as self-contradictory as the two passages that follow.

'Tomorrow I'm having dinner with the Emperor again at the Clergy House—the assistant Bishop is giving him a small party as these three days are the great Ethiopian festival of the Holy Cross called Maskal. I have a great admiration for him. Most exiles degenerate but he is still dignified, mild and courteous, even with all this hope deferred and only a shadow court. Some of his followers may be barbaric but so were King Alfred's and the Saxons from Germany, and it was their land and they threatened no-one but Mussolini coveted it and wanted a splash and so he bombed and gassed the poor little man out of his home, which had a history as good as Rome's back to the Queen of Sheba. I hope he gets it back and we'll do our best for him.'

Yet 'I feel less sorry for H.S. than I do for the Duke of Aosta who is a very cultured and kindly man, and a fine administrator, and now finds himself bound to the Nazi machine and sees his colony plunged into war with enemies within as well as outside the gates.' Hardly a tyrant then; and there seems little sympathy here for the black-skinned neo-Garibaldians within the gates.

The Italian intelligence reports of Colonel Talamonti were later captured and can, fortunately, be found in the War Office files—just like Gina's brother's diary. For Eden's visit see his Memoirs (AVON). War Diaries and intelligence reports are the main source for this chapter.

CHAPTER 22 DISASTER AT GALLABAT

I have drawn very largely in this chapter from SLIM's vivid and extremely well-written account of the Gallabat affair in his *Unofficial History*—a delightful book. Naturally enough Slim does not name the Essex as the battalion who ran away; and naturally enough too the Essex War Diary, a pencilled job, is, as it were, hazy and designed to fade. But other unit diaries fill the gap. Gina's brother gives the little we know of the other side of the picture.

This episode, a minor one in Slim's life, is described only briefly in Ronald Lewin's prize-winning biography—which of course goes on to describe Slim's relationship with Wingate in Burma, where the two of them (and Wavell) met again.

CHAPTER 23 A LAWRENCE FOUND

Christopher SYKES's biography of Wingate is good but not excellent: there seems to be an understandable lack of empathy between author and subject. HARRIS has much more fun with him. STEER (2) appreciated his worth but naturally enough disliked being relegated to a secondary role. Mrs. SAND-FORD (2) tries loyally to play down the rivalry between her husband and Wingate—which, however, the War Office files reveal. As for the 'philosophy' of the Op Centres and of instigating a native rebellion via guerrilla warfare, the quotations from Wingate come from his Report in the same section of the WO files that contain Bentinck's and Sandford's more down-to-earth reports.

Wingate, this report reveals, felt particularly hard done by as regards his own Op Centres: 'It was found that Operational Centres as conceived were capable of many and varied uses, but in practice the work was almost always beyond the capacity of the mediocre or inferior officers selected. The standard of the NCOs was so low that they were a nuisance. It is difficult to see justification for sending a thoroughly bad lot of NCOs to the best school of war . . . Experience in the campaign proves that it is better to have one company of a first-class fighting unit than half a dozen battalions of scallywags. This is particularly true of war behind the enemy lines, where bluff plays a very large part, and it is the quality rather than the quantity of blows which demoralises the enemy.' This was written of course *after* the event when the Op Centres (see pp. 350, 353) had proved rather a disappointment.

As for native allies: 'Patriots', Wingate wrote, 'are at their best in fighting on the move. Here they frequently show great courage and desire to come to grips with the enemy. While the offensive spirit should definitely be encouraged in patriots, they do best alone. The conditions of patriot attacks are such as try the nerves of the stoutest of regular officers, and this reacts on the patriots who normally appear unconscious of the appalling hazards they run.' In other words they were simply too brave for the British, and the mere sight of their rashness would send cold shudders down the spine of regular troops. This conclusion was probably the result of the one case in which Wingate attempted a combined attack with the Patriots. See p. 345.

ALLEN, AKAVIA, and MOSLEY (1) were also directly involved in Wingate's preparations and/or operations. His encounter with Thesiger in the bathroom of the Grand Hotel is described in SYKES.

The Italian counter-moves are known from Talamonti's captured diary and notes. For Belai Zelleka's letter to Ras Hailu see Dr. PANKHURST's second article on the Ethiopian Resistance.

CHAPTER 24 SUCCESS AT EL WAQ

General PESENTI (2) gives an extraordinarily frank account of his own débâcle. The British sources are the obvious ones. DE GAULLE and CHURCHILL describe their hopes and plans for 'Operation Marie'—which did not necessarily coincide. For Curle and his Irregulars see the war diaries of the units concerned plus BIRKBY (2) and GANDAR DOWER (1).

CHAPTER 25 THE BALANCE SWINGS

CIANO and CHURCHILL give their opposing views of Graziani's dramatic defeat. (For Graziani's own excuses see CANEVARI). Wingate's difficulties with the abortive 106 Mission are recounted, blow by blow, in the War Office files. The comment on the Local Expert is taken from Gordon WATERFIELD's picturesque account of his time in Aden.

CHAPTER 26 JOY IN THE MORNING

For the Indian Divisions and Cavalry Regiments see (apart from the OFFICIAL HISTORY OF THE INDIAN ARMED FORCES) STEVENS, BRETT-JONES, JACKSON, and above all HINGSTON's massive work. The minor skirmishes on the Galla-Sidamo front are portentously described by General GAZZERA. For the Merille and Turkana my source is the war diaries and intelligence reports of the various units and officers involved. KENNEDY-COOKE vividly describes the recapture of 'his' Kassala. The Battle of the Lowlands is recounted from the official British viewpoint by PLATT and EVANS and from the unofficial Italian viewpoint by CARGNELOTTI who also tells, with understandable pride, the story of Lt. Guillet's cavalry charge (confirmed by British war diaries). CHURCHILL's 'mills of God' speech to the House of Commons indicates that he, at least, had every intention of restoring Haile Selassie to power as soon as possible. (But cf. Chapter 30).

CHAPTER 27 THE BATTLE OF KEREN

All accounts of the campaign give, naturally enough, their version of its one great battle, Keren. In addition to the sources already quoted I should particularly mention BARKER (1) PIGNATELLI and, for the French, ST. HILLIER.

CHAPTER 28 GIDEON FORCE

Mark PILKINGTON's Letters have, unfortunately, only been printed privately. Though quoted here, they really describe the later stages of this campaign when Wingate had left; and give the best account I know of the final capture of Gondar where General Nasi was holding out after the rains, long after all other Italian forces in East Africa had surrendered. W. E. D. ALLEN's minor classic, as Christopher SYKES rightly calls it, unforgivably out of print, gives the feel of the campaign better than any other of the various books.

Mark Pilkington, a subaltern in the Household Cavalry, was a great friend of Bill Allen—'Nobody could want an abler, more amusing or nicer companion. I couldn't like him more. He is a fascinating person—quite a bit older than me in age but not in mind or heart.' ALLEN for his part described Mark Pilkington as 'a quaint dreamy fellow with a slow smile and an interest in the Arabian language and ornithology'.

Both Pilkington and Bill McLean, a subaltern in the Scots Greys, had been with the Cavalry Division that sailed for Palestine in February 1940. There the Division had remained kicking its collective heels, waiting for tanks or armoured cars to replace its horses. News of the 'operations' in Ethiopia brought a spate of volunteers for the planned Op Centres. As the invasion began, a whole group of cavalry officers turned up in Khartoum led by Major Basil Ringrose of the Sherwood Rangers—described by Allen as 'a slight lithe fellow'—to find in the words of Pilkington, that 'the thing that has really brought home the war to us is the appalling shortage of whisky'.

Ringrose led an Op Centre into Beghemder, north of Gondar on 8 February. Pilkington and McLean, each with five sergeants from his own regiment, led their two Op Centres towards Mount Belaya a week later—PILKINGTON with 120 camels carrying arms and ammunition, 'Maria Theresa dollars, very bulky and heavy, grenades, land mines and god knows what else.'

CHAPTER 29 CUNNINGHAM'S COUP

The war diaries of Cunningham's units are, as might be expected, both jubilant and full. On the Italian side all is (apart from a pained DI LAURO) silence—the 'horrors' of the retreat from Harar being described in captured notes, not intended for publication, reprinted by GANDAR DOWER.

The fall of Addis Ababa is recounted by MARAVIGNA; and the Duke of Aosta's subsequent 'stand' at Amba Alagi (which, like General Nasi's far more serious holding-operation at Gondar, falls outside the scope of this book) by VALLETTI-BORGNINI.

CHAPTER 30 THE RETURN OF THE EMPEROR

Ras Seyum's letters are quoted by George STEER (2) who, however, was not sufficiently interested in internal Ethiopian politics to appreciate their significance. Simonds's remarks come from his reports in the War Office files. The fall of Massawa is beautifully and wittily described by ST. HILLIER. A private source, family archives of the Gillows of Waring & Gillow, indicate the style in which the Little Ghebbi was furnished.

For OETA, and the subsequent wartime history of Ethiopia, at least as seen from official British eyes, see Lord RENNELL's massive work (he also describes the actual return of the Emperor) and Sir Philip MITCHELL's memoirs. (THESIGER with a few throw-away remarks points out the uselessness of the whole operation). OETA meant an awkward form of dual control, as Newbold saw very well.

'I have given OETA Eritrea and Ethiopia 15 political officers', Newbold wrote on 30 March, 'and part-time use of another 4 . . . I don't like to see too many good chaps go to Ethiopia. Eritrea is different and needs a very good cadre . . . Ethiopia is a phoney administration. Chaps think it romantic, and so it will be for one or two months, then they will tire of poor staff, diplomatic tangles, an ugly dyarchy of Emperor and OETA, lying chiefs, no money, dirt and an ungrateful rabble of armed peasantry.'

It is clear enough from this letter that at any rate the officials in the Sudan had no desire, still less any design, of taking over Ethiopia permanently. yet the idea of a protectorate was hovering in the air—though Eden in a meeting with Sir Philip Mitchell on 20 March rejected it. It was by no means sure, however, that Cunningham and Kenya and the Colonial Office might not between them try to impose what Wavell and the Sudan and the Foreign Office rejected. Haile Selassie was right to be—as he long continued to be, even after his 'official' restoration—suspicious of Britain's ultimate intentions.

EPILOGUE THE END OF THE WAR

War diaries are the main source for the scattered operations that followed the fall of Addis Ababa, plus (as already mentioned) PILKINGTON for General Nasi's final stand at Gondar and VALLETTI-BORGNINI for Amedeo of Aosta on Amba Alagi.

Troops from the Belgian Congo had reached their 'theatre of operations' —the Baro Salient—in February 1941 (see for the very minor part they played WELLER's bombastic account). Khartoum Intelligence intercepted the Italian report and noted that 'A rumour of the arrival of Congolese soldiers with cannibalistic tendencies has struck fear into the hearts of Italian forces.' Younger members of Cheeseman's Intelligence Staff composed a Joint Ode to mark the occasion. It ran as follows:

> What a heavenly thought
> To sit down to a sort
> Of 'Italiens au Naturel'
> To know that the chops
> Are just slices of Wops—
> Tasty in spite of their smell.
>
> Fricasséed Frusci
> Compôte Granatieri
> Angelini on Horseback of course
> A savoury dinner of General Pinna
> Is a joy to the Congolese Force.

So drink up your Vini
And one wet Martini
Or, if you're teetotal and daft
Acqua Pellegrini
In sensu obsceni
Is rather a nauseous draft.

Aosta, my man,
Make peace while you can
In a normal and usual fashion
It is better by far
To remain as you are
Than to end as a military ration.

Professor GREENFIELD's book gives the most detailed and informative account of the events leading up to the failed Imperial Guard coup of 1960 in which both Ras Seyum and Ras Abebe Aregai were killed.

There is—as yet—no really outstanding study of the 1974 Revolution and its immediate aftermath. What appeared to be at first merely a wave of minor protest movements made only slightly more serious by localized mutinies over pay and conditions in the army culminated on 12 September with the formal dethronement by the Dergue, the Provisional Military Committee, of the Emperor. For a brief period it had seemed that Ethiopia's monarchy might survive with the Mered Azmatch Asfa Wossen becoming a constitutional monarch. Wisely, he remained in exile and is living, a very ill man, in London. Thus he escaped the massacre of 'Bloody Saturday'—23 November 1974—when so many of the old nobility including Ras Asrate Kassa, the only surviving son of Ras Kassa, and Lij Iskander Desta, the eldest son of Ras Desta, were brutally executed. Ras Seyum's eldest son, Ras Mangasha Seyum, was at the time ruler of Tigre; he refused a summons to the capital and at one stage it looked as if he might lead a successful counter-revolution from his provincial power-base. But he too went into exile. Ras Imru was left unharmed. His eldest son Lij Mikael Imru supported the Revolution and even became, briefly, Prime Minister in the months preceding the Emperor's dethronement. Lij Mikael survived both the Red and the White terror that followed; Ras Imru eventually had the doubtful honour of being the only member of the old nobility to be granted a state funeral by the Revolutionary Government.

As for Haile Selassie I, once again the 'ex-Emperor', it was announced on 28 August 1975, eleven months after his dethronement, that he had died the previous day of 'circulatory failure'. The Dergue has not yet, however, dared to reveal where he is buried.

SELECT BIBLIOGRAPHY

(1) BOOKS IN ENGLISH

ALLEN, W. E. D., *Guerrilla War in Abyssinia* (Penguin, 1943).

AVON, Earl of, *The Eden Memoirs: Facing the Dictators.* Vol.III: *The Reckoning* (Cassell, 1962).

BARKER, A. J., (1) *Eritrea 1941* (Faber, 1966).
  (2) *The Italo-Ethiopian War 1935–36* (Cassell, 1968).

BADOGLIO, Marshal, *The War in Abyssinia* [Foreword by the Duce] (Methuen, 1937).

BERKELEY, G., *The Campaign of Adowa and the Rise of Menelik* (Constable, 1902).

BIRKBY, C., (1) *The Saga of the Transvaal Scottish Regiment* (Howard Timmins for Hodder & Stoughton, 1950).
  (2) *It's a Long Way to Addis* (Frederick Muller, 1942).

BRETT-JAMES, A., *Ball of Fire: The Fifth Indian Division in the Second World War* (Aldershot: Gale & Polden, 1951).

CHEESEMAN, Robert, *Lake Tana and the Blue Nile* (London, 1936).

CHURCHILL, Winston, *The Second World War*, Vol.I *The Gathering Storm* (Cassell, 1948). Vol.II *Their Finest Hour* (Cassell, 1949). [Especially Appendices: 'PM's Personal Minutes and Directives']

CIANO, Galeazzo, *Diary 1939–43* (Heinemann, 1947).

CONNELL, John, *Wavell* (Collins, 1964).

DEAKIN, F. W., *The Brutal Friendship* (Weidenfeld & Nicolson, 1962).

DE BONO, Marshal, *Anno XIII: The Conquest of an Empire* [Introduction by the Duce] (Cresset Press, 1937).

DE PROROK, Byron, *Dead Men Do Tell Tales* (Harrap, 1943).

DEL BOCA, Angelo, *The Ethiopian War 1935–1941* (Chicago, 1969).

DIMBLEBY, Richard, *The Frontiers are Green* (London, 1943).

DURAND, Mortimer, *Crazy Campaign* (Routledge & Kegan Paul, 1936).

DUTTON, E., *Lillibulero on the Golden Road* (Zanzibar, 1944).

EDEN, Anthony, *see* AVON, Earl of.

FARAGO, Ladislas, (1) (ed.) *Abyssinian Stop Press* (Robert Hale, 1936).
  (2) *Abyssinia on the Eve* (Putnam, 1935).

FERGUSSON, Bernard, *The Black Watch* (Collins, 1950).

FINER, Herman, *Mussolini's Italy* (Gollancz, 1935).

FULLER, J. F. C., *The First of the League Wars* (Eyre & Spottiswode, 1936).

GANDAR DOWER, Kenneth, (1) *Askaris at War in Abyssinia* (Nairobi, 1941).
  (2) (ed.), *Abyssinian Patchwork: An Anthology* (Frederick Muller, 1949).

GENERAL STAFF (INTELLIGENCE) HQ TROOPS IN THE SUDAN, *Handbook of Western Italian East Africa* (Khartoum, 1941).

GREENFIELD, Richard, *Ethiopia: A New Political History* (Pall Mall, 1965).

HARMSWORTH, Geoffrey, *Abyssinian Adventure* (Hutchinson, 1935).

HENDERSON, K. D. D. (ed), *The Making of the Modern Sudan: The Life and Letters of Sir Douglas Newbold KBE* (Faber, 1953).

HINGSTON, Major W. R., *The Tiger Strikes (The Indian Divisions)* (Thacker's Press and Directories, Calcutta, 1943).

HODSON, Arnold, *Where Lions Reign* (Skeffington, 1925).

KENNEDY-COOKE, B., *Kassala at War* (Khartoum, 1943).

KIRKPATRICK, Sir Ivone, *Memoirs* (Macmillan, 1959).

LEWIS, I. M., *The Modern History of Somaliland* (Weidenfeld & Nicolson, 1975).

LONGRIGG, Stephen, *A Short History of Eritrea* (Oxford University Press, 1945).

MACGREGOR-HASTIE, Roy, *The Day of the Lion: The Life and Death of Fascist Italy* (Macdonald, 1963).

MAKIN, W. J., *War over Ethiopia* (Jarrolds, 1935).

MARCUS, Harold G., *The Life and Times of Menelik II* (Clarendon Press, 1974).

MATHEW, David, *Ethiopia: The Study of a Polity 1540–1935* (Eyre & Spottiswoode, 1947).

MATTHEWS, Herbert, *Eyewitness in Abyssinia* (Secker & Warburg, 1937).

MINISTRY OF INFORMATION, *The First to be Freed: The Record of British Military Administration in Eritrea and Somaliland 1941–1943* (London, 1944).

MINISTRY OF JUSTICE, *Documents on Italian War Crimes*. Vol. I: *Italian Telegrams and Circulars* [submitted to the United Nations War Crimes Commission] (Addis Ababa, 1949–50).

MITCHELL, David, *The Fighting Pankhursts* (Jonathan Cape, 1967).

MITCHELL, Sir Philip, *African Afterthoughts* (London, 1954).

MONELLI, Paolo, *Mussolini: An Intimate Life* (Thames & Hudson, 1953).

MOOREHEAD, Alan, *Mediterranean Front* (Hamish Hamilton, 1941)

MOSLEY, Leonard, (1) *Gideon Goes to War* (A. Barker, 1955).
   (2) *Haile Selassie: The Conquering Lion* (Weidenfeld & Nicolson, 1964).

MOYSE-BARTLETT, Lt.-Col. H., *The King's African Rifles* (Gale and Polder, 1956).

NELSON, Kathleen, & SULLIVAN, Alan, *John Melly of Ethiopia* (Faber, 1936).

OFFICIAL HISTORY OF THE SECOND WORLD WAR—*The Mediterranean and the Middle East* (ed. Major-General I.S.O. Playfair). Vol. 1: *The Early Successes Against Italy*. (London, 1954).

OFFICIAL HISTORY OF THE INDIAN ARMED FORCES IN THE SECOND WORLD WAR (ed. B. Prusad). *East Africa Campaign 1940–41* (Delhi, 1963).

POLSON NEWMAN, E. W., *Italy's Conquest of Abyssinia* (Butterworth, 1937).

RENNELL OF RODD, F. J. R., 1st Baron, *British Military Administration of Occupied Territories in Africa*. War Office: H.M.S.O. 1948.

ROSENTHAL, E., *The Fall of Italian East Africa* (Hutchinson, 1942).

SANDFORD, Christine, (1) *Ethiopia Under Haile Selassie* (Dent, 1946).
   (2) *The Lion of Judah hath Prevailed* (Dent, 1955).

SLIM, Field-Marshal Sir William, *Unofficial History* (Cassell, 1959).

SOUTH AFRICAN WAR HISTORIES: WORLD WAR II (ed. Comdt. N. N. D. Orpen). Vol.I: *East African and Abyssinian Campaigns* (Capetown and Johannesburg, 1968).

STATIONERY OFFICE, H.M., *The Abyssinian Campaign* (London, 1942).

STEER, George, (1) *Caesar in Abyssinia* (Hodder & Stoughton, 1936).
   (2) *Sealed and Delivered* (Hodder & Stoughton, 1942).

STEVENS, Lt.-Col. G. R., *Fourth Indian Division* (Maclaren & Sons, Toronto, 1948).

SYKES, Christopher, *Orde Wingate* (Collins, 1959).

TAYLOR, A. J. P., *The Origins of the Second World War* (Hamish Hamilton, 1961).

THESIGER, Wilfred, *Arabian Sands*. (Longman Green, 1959).

TREVASKIS, G. K. N., *Eritrea. A Colony in Transition: 1941–1952* (Oxford University Press, 1960).

VIRGIN, General, *The Abyssinia I Knew* (Macmillan, 1936).

WAR OFFICE, *The Abyssinian Campaigns: The official story of the Conquest of Italian East Africa* (H.M.S.O., 1942).

WATERFIELD, Gordon, *Morning Will Come* (John Murray, 1944).

WAUGH, Evelyn, (1) *Waugh in Abyssinia* (Longman Green, 1930).
  (2) *When the Going was Good* (The Reprint Society, 1940). [Especially Chapter 2, 'A Coronation in 1930' and Chapter 5, 'A War in 1935'.]

WELLER, George, *The Belgian Campaign in Ethiopia* (Belgian Information Centre, New York (n.d.)).

WIENHOLT, Arnold, *The African's Last Stronghold* (John Long, 1938).

WYLDE, Augustus, *Modern Abyssinia* (London, 1901).

YILMA, Princess Asfa, *Haile Selassie I, Emperor of Ethiopia* (Sampson, Low & Marston, 1936).

MANUSCRIPT AND PRIVATELY PRINTED WORKS IN ENGLISH

ABEBE TAFARI, Gen., *Personal Memoir* (in possession of author).

AKAVIA AVRAM, *With Wingate in Ethiopia* (Tel Aviv).

BEFEKADU WOLDE SELASSIE, *Memoir of the 12 Yekatit* (in possession of author).

HARRIS, Maj. W. A. B., *Guerrilla Warfare in the Goggiam* (War Office Records).

KONOVALOFF, T. E., *History of Ethiopia* (Hoover Institute).

PILKINGTON, Mark, *Letters* (London).

PLATT, Gen. Sir William, *The Campaign against Italian East Africa 1940–41* (Ministry of Defence, 1962).

(2) BOOKS IN ITALIAN

ANNALI DEL AFRICA ITALIANA Rome, Anno XV–Anno XVIII [especially Vol.II: *L'Attività Militare Dopo L'Occupazione*—Anno XVI (1938)].

BASTICO, Gen. Ettore, *Il Ferreo III Corpo in A.O.* (Milan, 1937).

CANEVARI, E., *Graziani Mi Ha Detto* (Rome, 1947).

CARGNELOTTI, Ten.-Col. Federico, *Scacchiere Nord* (Udine, 1962).

CARNIMEO, N., *Cheren, I febbraio—27 marzo 1941* (Naples, 1940).

CAVALLERO, Gen. Ugo, *Gli Avvenimenti Militari nell'Impero dal 12 gennaio 1938—XVI—12 gennaio 1939—XVII* (Addis Ababa, 1939).

CIMMARUTA, R., *Ual-Ual* (Milan, 1936).

CONTI ROSSINI, C., *Italia ed Etiopia dal Trattato d'Uccialli alla Battaglia di Adowa* (Rome Anno XIII (1935)).

DE BIASE, Carlo, *I'Impero della Faccetta Nera* (Rome, n.d.).

Di Lauro, Raffaele, *Come Abbiamo Difeso L'Impero* (Rome, 1949).
Frusci, Col. L., *In Somalia sul fronte meridionale* (Bologna, 1936).
Gazzera, Gen. Pietro, *Guerra Senza Speranza* (Rome, 1952).
Governatore Generale Dell AOI, *Il Primo Anno dell'Impero* (Addis Ababa (n.d.)).
Graziani, Marshal Rodolfo, (1) *Fronte Sud* (Milan, 1938).
 (2) *Ho Difeso la Patria* (Rome, 1947).
Guida Dell' Africa Orientale Italiana (Milan, 1938).
Konovaloff, Theodore Evgenevitch, *Con le Armate del Negus* (Bologna, 1936).
Landi, Maria Giacoma, *Croce Rossina in AOI* (Milan, 1938).
Lemmi, Francesco (ed.), *Lettere e Diari d'Africa* (Rome Anno XIV (1936)).
Lessona, A., *Memorie* (Florence, 1958).
Maravigna, Gen. Pietro, *Come Abbiamo Perduto la Guerra in Africa* (Rome, 1949).
Menarini, G., *La Brigata Dabormida alla Battaglia d'Adua* (Naples, 1898).
Mussolini, Vittorio, *Voli sulle Ambe* (Florence, 1932).
Nasi, Gen., *Relazione sulle operazioni di grande polizia svolte dal 15 guigno 1937 al 31 marzo 1938* (Harar, 1939).
Pesenti, Gen., (1) *La Prima Divisone Eritrea alla battaglia d'Ascianghi* (Milan, 1937).
 (2) *Fronte Kenya—La Guerra in AOI 1940–41* (Milan, 1950).
Pignatelli, Luigi, *La guerra dei sette mesi* (Milan, 1965).
Starace, Achille, *La Marcia su Gondar* (Milan, 1936).
Tomasellini, C., *Con le colonne celere dal Mareb allo Scioa* (Milan, 1936).
Ufficio Storico Della Marina Militare, *La Marina nella Seconda Guerra Mondiale: Le Operazione in Africa Orientale* (Rome, 1961).
Ufficio Storico, Ministero Della Difesa, Stato Maggiore Esercito, *La Guerra in Africa Orientale Giugno— Novembre 1941* (Rome, 1952).
Ufficio Superiore Topografico Del Governo Generale Dell'A.O.I. vol.III: *La Guerra Italo-Etiopica—Fronte Sud* (Addis Ababa, 1937).
Valletti-Borgnini, Gen. Marino, *Amba Alagi* (Rome, 1962).
Verni, V., *MSVN* (Naples, 1932).
Zoli, Corrado, (1) *Cronache Etiopiche* (Rome, 1930).
 (2) *Etiopia d'Oggi* (Rome, 1935).
 (3) *La Conquista dell'Impero* (Bologna, 1937).

(3) BOOKS IN FRENCH

De Gaulle, Charles, *Mémoires de Guerre*, vol.I: (Paris, 1954).
De Monfreid, Henri, (1) *Vers les Terres Hostiles d'Ethipie* (Paris, 1932).
 (2) *Les Guerriers de l'Ogaden* (Paris, 1933).
 (3) *Derniers Jours de l'Arabie Heureuse* (Paris, 1934).
 (4) *Le Drame Ethiopien* (Paris, 1935).
 (5) *L'Avion Noir* (Paris, 1936).
 (6) *Le Masque d'Or ou Le Dernier Negus* (Paris, 1936).
 (7) *Trafic d'Armes en Mer Rouge* (Paris, 1937).
 (8) *Charas* (Paris, 1947).
Gingold Duprey, A., *De l'Invasion à la Liberation de l'Ethiopie* (Paris, 1955).

GUEBRE SELASSIE, *Chronique du Règne de Menelik II*, 2 vols. (Paris, 1930).
PETRIDES, S. P., *Le Héros d'Adowa: Ras Makonnen* (Paris, 1963).
ZERVOS, Adrien, *L'Empire d'Ethiopie* (Alexandria, 1930).

(4) ARTICLES

Note: I list here only a tiny selection of articles, those in English and French that I have personally found most useful for this book. Students and researchers can find much, much more in journals such as *Cahiers d'Etudes Africaines, Politique Etrangère, Présence Africaine, Annales d'Ethiopie,* published in Paris, *Rassegna di Studi Etiopici* (Rome), the *Journal of Semitic Studies* and the *Journal of African History* (London), *African Quarterly* (Delhi) *Foreign Affairs, Africa Today, The Middle East Journal, Africa Report,* (USA) and others. The most useful journal in Addis Ababa, the *Ethiopian Observer,* was published first monthly by Sylvia Parkhurst from 1956 to 1960, and then quarterly by her son Dr. Richard Parkhurst from 1961 till 1974.

BURGOYNE, Clarissa, and Major Gerald, 'Lost Month in Ethiopia', *Ethiopian Observer,* vol. xi, no. 4 (almost the whole issue), 1966.
BAER, G., 'Haile Selassie's Protectorate Appeal to King Edward VIII' *Cahiers d'Etudes Africaines,* vol. ix, no. 34, 1969.
EVANS, Lt.-Gen. Sir G. C., 'The Battle of Keren'. *History Today,* vol. xvi, 1966.
EVANS PRITCHARD, E. E., 'Operations on the Akobo and Gila Rivers 1940–41', *The Army Quarterly,* July 1973.
GIFFORD, G., (1) 'The Sudan at War', *Journal of the Royal African Society,* vol. xliii, 1943.
(2) 'Fighting in Abyssinia: the Part Played by the Composite Battalion of the East Arab Corps', *The Army Quarterly,* August 1942.
GABRE EGZIABHER, Salome, (1) 'The Ethiopian Patriots 1936–1941', *Ethiopian Observer,* vol. xii, no.2 (almost the whole issue), 1969.
(2) 'The Patriotic Works of Dejazmatch Aberra Kassa and Ras Abebe Aregai', *Proceedings of the Third International Conference of Ethiopian Studies,* Addis Ababa, vol. 1, 1969.
GREENFIELD, Richard, 'Remembering the Struggle', *Makerere Journal,* vol. ix, 1964.
HARPER, H. G., 'Irregular Forces in East Africa 1940–41'', *Bulletin of the Military Historical Society.*
HENDERSON, K. D. D., 'The Sudan and the Abyssinian Campaign', *Journal of the Royal African Society,* vol. xlii, 1943.
HENNESSY, MAJOR M. N., 'The Nigerian Advance from Mogadiscio to Harar', *The Army Quarterly,* 1948.
Illustration, 'The Ceremony of Submission', issue of 1 August 1936, Paris.
'INVICTRIX', 'Abyssinia 1940–41', *Cavalry Journal,* March 1942.
JACKSON, Lt.-Col. D., 'Abyssinia 1940–41: The Indian Cavalry Regiments of the Campaign', *Cavalry Journal,* March 1942.
JARDINE, Douglas, 'At the Coronation of the Empress Zauditu', *Blackwoods,* October 1917.

JOUIN, Lt.-Col. Yves, 'La Participation Française à la Résistance Ethiopienne', *Revue Historique de l'Armée*, no. iv, 1963, Paris.

KNOTT, Brig. A. J., 'The Sudan Defence Force Goes to War', *The Royal Engineers Journal*, 1944.

MARCUS, Harold, (1) 'Last Years of the Reign of the Emperor Menelik', *Journal of Semitic Studies*, vol. ix, no. 1, 1964.

(2) 'Ethiopia 1937–1941', in *Challenge and Response in Internal Conflict*, Cordit and Cooper, Washington, 1968.

PANKHURST. Richard. (1) 'The Ethiopian Patriots—The Lone Struggle 1936–40', *Ethiopian Observer*, vol. xiii, no. 1, 1970.

(2) 'The Ethiopian Patriots and the Collapse of Italian Rule in East Africa', *Ethiopian Observer*, vol. xii, no. 2, 1969.

PANKHURST, Sylvia, (1) 'The New Times and Ethiopia News', *passim*.

(2) 'The Ethiopian Patriots as Seen at the Time', *Ethiopian Observer*, vol. iii, nos. 10, 11, and 12, 1959.

PELLENC, Capt. 'Les Italiens en Afrique', *Revue Militaire de l'Etranger*, 1896–1897, Paris.

SANDFORD, Christine, 'Reforms from Within versus Foreign Control', *International Affairs*, March 1936.

SBACCHI, Alberto, (1) 'Italian Casualties in Ethiopia 1935–1940', *Ethiopian Notes*, vol. ii, no. 2, Michigan 1970.

(2) 'The Italians and the Italo-Ethiopian War 1935–1936', *TransAfrican Journal of History*, vol. v, no. 2, 1976.

(3) 'Italy and the Treatment of the Ethiopian Aristocracy 1937–1940', *The International Journal of African Historical Studies*, vol. x, no. 2, 1977.

ST. HILLIER, Bernard, 'Les FFI en Afrique: 1941', *Histoire*, no. 17, Paris 1968.

STEER, George, (1) 'Ethiopia in 1939', *Spectator*, 3 March 1939.

(2) 'Addis Ababa—Civilized', *Spectator*, 10 March 1939.

SURTEES, Major-Gen. G., 'A "Q" War: An Administrative Account of the Eritrean and Abyssinian Campaign 1941', *The Journal of the Royal United Service Institution*, 1963.

THESIGER, Wilfred, 'The Awash River and the Aussa Sultanate', *Geographical Magazine*, vol. lxxv, 1935.

WATT, D. C., 'The Secret Laval-Mussolini Agreement of 1935 on Ethiopia', *Middle East Journal*, vol. xv, 1961.

(5) UNPUBLISHED THESES IN ENGLISH OR FRENCH

Note: Unless otherwise stated, these theses were all written by graduates of Haile Selassie I University in the late 1960s or early 1970s and held at the Institute of Ethiopia Studies where I consulted them. They are of very uneven value.

ABY DEMISSIE, 'Lij Iyasu'.

ADUGNA AMANA, 'The Ethiopian Church becomes Autocephalous'.

AND ALE MULAW, 'Beghemder and Simien 1910–1930'.

ARAYA HABTAI, 'The Role of Eritrean Askaris in the Italo-Ethiopian War and under the Occupation 1935–1941'.

Bekele Wolde Aba Jifar, Anglo-Ethiopian Relations from the Anglo-Ethiopian Crisis of 1944'.

Fittegu Tadesse, 'La Politique Ethiopienne de la France 1933–1936'. Strasbourg.

Getachew Kelemu, 'Internal History of the Aleta Sidanchos'.

Haile Mariam Goshu, 'Jimma and Abba Jiffar II'.

Kifle Mammo, 'British Foreign Policy and Public Opinion during the 1935 Italo-Ethiopian Crisis'.

Laverle Bennet Bray, 'Anglo-Ethiopian Relations 1935–1945'. Georgetown.

Maniezawal Assefa, 'The Resistance in Beghemder, Wollo and Gojjam'.

Tadesse Bishaw, 'Biography of Yigezu Behapte'.

Tasfaye Abebe, 'The Life and Career of Dejazmatch Takele Wolde Hawariat'.

Yohannes Takle Haimonot, 'The Regency in S.W. Ethiopia'.

Yusuf Omar Abbi, 'The Battle of Maichew and its Historical Significance'.

Zerai Boureziou, 'The Legal Settlement of the S.W. Ethiopian Boundary'.

ACKNOWLEDGEMENTS

DURING the months that I spent in Ethiopia visiting former battlefields and doing the research for this book I encountered everywhere courtesy and almost everywhere reserve. That this reserve eventually disappeared was due in particular to the helpfulness of two men: Dr. Richard Pankhurst, the son of Sylvia Pankhurst and at the time Director of the Institute of Ethiopian Studies at the Haile Selassie I University; and General Aman Andom who was then in semi-disgrace as a Senator.

Dr. Pankhurst, who has left Addis Ababa at least temporarily but whose devotion to Ethiopian scholarship has never wavered, has continued to be most helpful in every possible way. General Aman Andom, appointed head of state by the co-ordinating committee of the armed forces, the Dergue, after Haile Selassie's deposition, was surrounded in his villa a month later by the tanks of the Dergue and killed in the early evening of 22 November 1974. In the subsequent executions on 'Bloody Saturday' many more of my informants were killed—including Ras Desta's son, Lij Iskander Desta, by repute the Emperor's favourite grandson, atrociously blown to death by hand-grenades lobbed at him while his hands were tied behind his back. Major-General Abiye Abebe, briefly the Emperor's son-in-law, Dejaz Kassa Wolde Mariam of the Wollega Galla royal house, and General Essayas Gabre Selassie, once an Oletta cadet, to all of whom I am indebted, were executed on that day—Essayas dragged from a hospital bed to face the firing squad. Count Carl Gustav Von Rosen, with whom I had a long interview in Addis Ababa, ended an adventurous and quixotic life in an apparent attempt to rescue by air the imprisoned princesses of the Imperial family. I would particularly like to thank—if, as I believe, they are still alive—Dejaz Gabre Maskal, Dejaz Kebbede Tessema, General Wolde Johannes Tekle, Colonel Tafere Debrawork, Major Getachew Afework, Fitaurari Markos of the Army of Wag, Fitaurari Haile Beiene (who was one of the leaders of the Eritrean deserters in 1936) and Grazmatch Abdullahi Terapi (who saw and described to me Afework's death in the Ogaden) for the information and help that they gave me.

Colonel and Mrs. Sandford were living on their farm outside Addis Ababa when I was there. Though 'Dan' Sandford was by this time very doddery, his wife Christine, one of the Grand Old Ladies of Africa, was most helpful, hospitable, and, where she felt it necessary, scathing. Both have since died, as has Sir Edwin Chapman-Andrews, who was unfortunately more discreet than open about the important part he played. Brigadier Lush, Sandford's brother-in-law—the two were at total odds over the British role in Ethiopia—talked to me very frankly. Of the other prominent British figures involved in this story I corresponded with Professor Evans-Pritchard, General Platt, and General Cunningham—all of whom have since died.

In Italy it was, naturally enough, more difficult to contact those involved. When contacted they tended to be very careful of what they said and in several cases asked for their names not to be mentioned; but I would particularly like to thank Donna Anna Maria Velardi for her continuing hospitality and for information about the Duke of Aosta under whom her late husband served, and Count Senni, Major Maurice's successor and predecessor at Gambeila.

I gratefully acknowledge the help of the librarians and staff of the Public Record Office, then at Chancery Lane, of the Ministry of Defence at Whitehall, of the *Ministro della Difesa* and of the *Ministero degli Affari Esteri* in Rome, of the *Bibliothèque de la Ministère de Guerre* in Paris, of the Imperial War Museum, and of St. Antony's College.

I would also like to thank for assistance or information or both the British Ambassador and the British Information Officer Robert Miller, in Addis Ababa, the Belgian Ambassador, the Israeli Ambassador, the then Prime Minister of France, M. Debré, Lij Mikael Imru in Geneva, Ras Mangasha Seyum and Tsahai Berhane Selassie in England, Professor Richard Greenfield and Professor Michael Howard in Oxford.

Many other people have over the past years been most helpful and it is impossible to list them all. But I cannot fail to mention Tom Stacey and Robin Wright, Patrick Gilkes and Satish Jacob, Dominique Bertin and Dorika Seib, Hope Leresche and Gwendoline Marsh, Christianne Hojer and Angela Raven Roberts, and in particular Alastair Horne, Thomas Pakenham, and Professor Kenneth Kirkwood, all of or associated with St. Antony's College, Oxford, without whose active help this book would never have seen the light of day. To Judy Cottam and Kate Fraser who typed and retyped the manuscript at various stages go my especial thanks.

Finally I would like to pay a warm tribute to Neal Burton and Peter Janson-Smith, formerly of Oxford University Press, whose encouragement and assistance in preparing this book were quite invaluable and whose tact and skill in dealing with their author's difficulties were in my experience of publishers unrivalled. They both left Oxford University Press before the book was completed; and the task they had undertaken eventually passed to Peter Sutcliffe, whose understanding, wise advice, and calm countenance, together with the enthusiasm of his assistant Irene Kurtz, finally brought this work to, I hope, a successful conclusion.

INDEX